D0399322

citizen-SAINTS

citizen-SAINTS

Shakespeare and Political Theology

julia reinhard LUPTON

The University of Chicago Press ✱ Chicago and London

Julia Reinhard Lupton is professor of English and comparative literature at the University of California, Irvine.

The University of Chicago Press, Chicago 60637
The University of Chicago Press, Ltd., London

Printed in the United States of America

14 13 12 11 10 09 08 07 06 05   1 2 3 4 5

ISBN: 0-226-49669-4 (cloth)

Chapter 1 first appeared as "Citizen Paul" in *The European Legacy* 9, no. 1 (2004): 67–77, see http://www.tandf.co.uk/journals. Chapter 2 first appeared as "The Jew of Malta" in *The Cambridge Companion to Christopher Marlowe*, ed. Patrick Cheney (Cambridge: Cambridge University Press, 2004), 144–57. Reprinted with the permission of Cambridge University Press. Chapter 4 first appeared as "*Othello* Circumcised: Shakespeare and the Pauline Discourse of Nations" in *Representations*, no. 57 (Winter 1997): 73–89. © The Regents of the University of California. Reprinted with the permission of the University of California Press. Chapter 6 first appeared as "Creature Caliban" in *Shakespeare Quarterly* 51, no. 1. (Spring 2000): 1–23, published by John Hopkins University Press.

Library of Congress Cataloging-in-Publication Data

Lupton, Julia Reinhard, 1963–
Citizen-saints : Shakespeare and political theology / Julia Reinhard Lupton.
p. cm.
Includes bibliographical references and index.
ISBN 0-226-49669-4 (alk. paper)
1. Shakespeare, William, 1564–1616—Political and social views. 2. Political theology—History of doctrines—16th century. 3. Political theology—History of doctrines—17th century. 4. Political plays, English—History and criticism. 5. Christian drama, English—History and criticism. 6. Shakespeare, William, 1564–1616—Religion. 7. Christian saints in literature. 8. Citizenship in literature. I. Title.

PR3017.L87 2005
822.3′3—dc22   2004018510

⊗ The paper used in this publication meets the minimum requirements of the American National Standard for Information Sciences—Permanence of Paper for Printed Library Materials, ANSI Z39.48-1992.

For my daughters and my son,
Hannah, Isabel, Lucy, and Eliot

May you blaze your own paths, together and separately,
between Athens and Jerusalem.

CONTENTS

ACKNOWLEDGMENTS

It is a tenet of this book that citizenship draws many circles, describing both local allegiances and broader affiliations. At the University of California, Irvine, I have been blessed with many strong friends and colleagues who have contributed in various ways to the genesis of this book, including Etienne Balibar, Robert Folkenflik, Alex Gelley, Andrea Henderson, Steven Mailloux, Jane Newman, Arielle Read, Victoria Silver, Michael Szalaly, and Ann Van Sant. My graduate and undergraduate students have contributed substantially to the refinement of my ideas; I would especially like to thank Craig Carson, Joseph Chaney, Brian Crawford, Viola Kolarova, Anna Kornbluh, Wes Kriesel, Debra Ligorsky, Philip Lorenz, Steven Miller, Tracy McNulty, Brendan Quigley, Jennifer Rust, Bonita Rhoades, Naomi Silver, Jonathan Singer, Catherine Winiarski, and James Zeigler for their insight, audience, and creative example.

Many scholars outside my immediate circle have variously supported, inspired, or sponsored this work, including Giorgio Agamben, Daniel Boyarin, Richard Burt, Patrick Cheney, Lars Engle, Margaret Ferguson, Lowell Gallagher, Robert Gibbs, Kenneth Gross, Richard Halpern, Graham Hammill, G. K. Hunter, Victoria Kahn, Jeffrey Knapp, Lisa Lampert, Brayton Polka, and Nancy Ruttenburg. The editors and readers at the University of Chicago Press, including Alan Thomas and Nicholas Murray, have provided generous yet pointed commentary.

This book was completed under the auspices of a University of California President's Fellowship (2002–2003). The Humanities Center at the University of California, Irvine, has provided research support and a publishing subvention. Portions of the book have been presented in a variety of settings, including UC Irvine, UCLA, UC Berkeley, UC San Diego, the University of Colorado at Boulder, the Modern Language Association, and the Shakespeare Association of America.

I arrived at the topic of citizenship initially through teaching and service, and only belatedly as a subject for more systematic reflection and writing. Lecturing in the Humanities Core Course, a genuinely collaborative enterprise mounted by UC Irvine's School of Humanities, led to my readings of *Othello, The Tempest,* and *Measure for Measure.* I would like to thank my colleagues in the Core Course, especially Vivian Folkenflik, Gail Hart, Liz Losh, Brook Thomas, and Gary Watson, for providing such a stimulating environment for collective thought. My work in Humanities Out There, an educational partnership between UC Irvine's School of Humanities and local schools, has given me the opportunity to experience the paradoxes and promises of citizenship firsthand; I am especially grateful to Michael Clark, Karen Lawrence, and Juan Francisco

Lara for giving me the chance to do this work. Julie Ellison, David Scobey, and Kathleen Woodward continue to teach me how much I still have to learn about civic engagement.

Robert Moeller, a historian of citizenship in modern Europe, a co-teacher in the Humanities Core Course, a mentor in matters professional, and a partner in off-campus educational enterprises, has contributed on many fronts to the conception and completion of this book.

I couldn't have kept all the balls in the air without help from my several social networks, especially the women and men associated with University Hills, Tarbut v'Torah Community Day School, and Congregation B'nai Israel.

I am sorry that I cannot share this book with my teacher Thomas Greene, or with David Kadlec, scholar, citizen, friend, and friend of my Friend.

Citizenship begins at home. My parents and stepparents, Mary Jane Lupton, Bill Lupton, Ken Baldwin, and Shirley Landon Lupton, gave me the unique privilege of witnessing the great social experiments of the 1960s and 70s; at each moment of decision, experiment, and relocation in my own life, they have encouraged my pursuit of happiness. Frank and Rosalind Reinhard have provided love and support at every turning point and the stops in between. My twin sister Ellen Lupton continues to inspire me with her multimedia mission to build a bigger, better, and more beautiful public sphere. Kenneth Reinhard is my helpmeet, housemate, bedmate, and soulmate; he is also my fellow traveler in thinking the social, and his ideas ring everywhere in these pages. I have dedicated this book to our children, Hannah, Isabel, Lucy, and Eliot. Saints in their sweet singularity and citizens in their miraculous multiplicity, they gave me the excuse to slow down and think more deeply about what I wanted to write, for myself and for them.

A NOTE ON TEXTS

Unless otherwise noted, citations from Shakespeare are from *The Complete Works of Shakespeare,* edited by David Bevington; citations from the Hebrew Bible are from the *Soncino Chumash,* edited by A. Cohen; commentary has been drawn extensively from *The JPS Torah Commentary,* edited by Nahum M. Sarna; citations from St. Paul are from *The Writings of St. Paul,* edited by Wayne A. Meeks; and citations from the New Testament (excluding Paul's) are from the *Oxford Annotated Bible,* Revised Standard Edition, edited by Herbert G. May and Bruce M. Metzger. Biblical citations appear parenthetically in the text; the abbreviations KJV and RSE are used as necessary to indicate the King James version and the return to the (Oxford) Revised Standard Edition of the Bible, respectively. Scriptural works are listed together in the bibliography in a separate section at the beginning.

INTRODUCTION

Sovereigns, Citizens, and Saints

The saint and the citizen would seem to face each other across an unbridgeable historical divide. The saint elects to join the City of God at the expense of the City of Men. Her acts of extremity cannot ground ordinary life except as fantasy and nightmare, and she embraces the most confining restraints and restrictions in order to separate from society rather than establish the grounds of social equivalence, interaction, and deliberation. On the other side of the chasm, the modern citizen is defined and sustained by a system of rights that, among other tasks of division and protection, separates church from state, relegating religion to the private world of individual conscience and purely civil (rather than civic) associations. Ornamented with the attributes of martyrdom, the saint has become the nostalgic afterimage of a lost exceptionality forever eclipsed by the normative routines of citizenship, the regular rotation of offices in the political sphere overseeing the circulatory pulse of getting and spending that measures out everyday existence under capital.

Indeed, the abyss separating the saint from the citizen is marked, even created, by the execution of the sovereign, last saint and first citizen, on the stage of history. In *The Origin of the German Tragic Drama,* Walter Benjamin discovers the figure of the tyrant-martyr, at once sovereign and saint, at the heart of Baroque drama. It is not only that beautiful martyrs are persecuted by dangerous tyrants, in the style of Catherine of Alexandria and other legends of the early Church, but that the tyrant himself is ultimately subjected to martyrdom, killed off by those who have suffered his sovereign decisions. Although such acts usually remain within the pale of monarchy on the Baroque stage, the death of the tyrant nonetheless often intimates the birth of some other form of government, some reconstitution of a constitutional possibility. In the case of Shakespeare, the fall of Macbeth leads to a fundamental change in the procedures of Scottish rule, the death of Claudius leads to the "election" of Fortinbras, and the deposition of Richard II signals the rise of the House of Lancaster. In what is more properly a drama of citizenship, the death of Coriolanus announces the end of the epic heroism that this tyrant-killer drove from the new Republic but failed to expunge from himself. Following a Herculean pattern inherited from Greek myths of culture-formation, the monster-killer, himself akin to the monsters he overcomes, clears the ground for a new political era that must sacrifice archaic heroism in order to institute a new order of law and citizenship.[1] Such chances for change, however, are minimal at best, disappearing long before they have begun to open up, and are best disclosed by a conceptual rather than a contextual apparatus—in this book, by the discourse of citizenship as it shuttles between ancient and modern reference points, skirting the penumbra of Shakespeare's world.

The Baroque drama of sovereignty kills its tyrants without burying monarchy itself. Citizens in anything approaching the modern sense remain at the edges of these plays, offering commentary and comic relief from the street, the graveyard, or the battlefield, classic scenes of provisional social equivalence within a hierarchical order. Yet these dramas' evocations of epochal change echo in a half-remembered key the constitutional themes of Greek tragedy. Performed before the assembled citizenry of Athens, Greek tragedies celebrated the survival of the polis in the wake of the fall of the great aristocratic houses and the forms of clan-based affiliation they represented. At the end of *Antigone,* for example, the hubris of both Creon and Antigone yields to the collective voice of the Chorus, the last speakers on a stage emptied of epic excellence *(arête)* and outmoded kinship love *(philôtes)*. Composed of dull old men speaking in platitudes (yet likely played by *ephebes* preparing to enter into adult citizenship), the Chorus and its normative wisdom represent the best chance for the future of the polis.[2] Greek tragedy both honored the new equality of citizens in the polis and registered the costs, losses, and exclusions—of values, of persons, of groups or classes, and of narrative possibilities—upon which that new order is necessarily founded. "The *good citizen,*" writes Aristotle, theorist of polis and tragedy alike, "need not of necessity possess the excellence which makes a *good man*" (*Politics* 1276b; emphasis added);[3] indeed, one could say that these two excellences are mutually exclusive, the pragmatic social intelligence of the citizenry enforcing a mediocrity at odds with the extraordinary, even dangerous, excellence of the philosopher, the hero, or the saint.[4] Again, Aristotle is pertinent: "[H]e who is unable to live in society, or who has no need because he is sufficient for himself, must be either a beast or a god: he is no part of a state" (*Politics* 1253a). The tragic hero is a sacred monster, both beast and god, and as such he or she must be ostracized or sacrificed in order for the polis to flourish.

For citizenship requires sacrifice—whether on the battlefield, like the fallen citizens of Athens commemorated in Pericles' famous funeral oration, a founding document in the literature of citizenship, or through acts of legal "naturalization" that require disaffiliation from parochial, ethnic, or tribal allegiances.[5] In Greek drama, the tragic hero—tyrannical, monstrous, and unique—is sacrificed for the sake of the polis, indeed, for the possibility of the political as such. Modern tragedy, rising under the sign of Christianity, transforms the sacrificial element in classical tragedy, interiorizing the public face of the tragic hero into the *schöne Seele* of the saint. Tragedy's story of the disruptions entailed by the transition from the aristocratic *oikos* to the democratic polis is remapped onto the redemptive movement from law to grace announced by Christ's sacrifice. Whereas the *institution* of law is the endpoint of the classical story, the *suspension* of law is the grace note of the Christian one. In the great revolutions of modernity, harkening back to Greek and Roman models but within a Christian framework itself undergoing epochal transformation, the sovereign becomes a saint on the stage of public execution, put to death by the citizenry, whether assembled in the Long Parliament of 1642, in which the king's body politic condemned the king's body natural, or in the National Convention of 1792, which put Louis XVI on trial.[6] Each of these acts followed judicial form, yielding not criminal assassinations but legal executions or, in Othello's words at the bed of Desdemona, effecting not a murder but a sacrifice. As we shall see in chapter 4, Othello's slaughter of Desdemona in turn necessitates his own sacrifice: killing himself as the circumcised Turk, as a particularized member of a particularized nation, Othello finally dies into the cosmopolitan Venetian citizenship and its public archives that he has spent his baptized life defending. It is no accident that Othello, like Coriolanus, is akin to *Hercules furens,* a centaur and centaur-slayer who cannot enter the civic world he protects except in death.

In his *General Economic History,* Max Weber found the conditions of modern citizenship in the development of monotheism: with the Jewish rejection of magic, the promise of Pentecostal internationalism, and the Pauline mission to the Gentiles, "the magical barriers between clans, tribes, and peoples, which were still known in the ancient *polis* to a considerable degree, were thus set aside and the establishment of the Western city was made possible."[7] In Weber's analysis, the saints of the early Church, like the citizens of classical democracy, had to disaffiliate from traditional kinship networks and the religious rituals (Gentile or Jewish) that sustained them in order to join a new community based on other forms of identification and participation. Weber enunciates a certain mythos of Western citizenship that forms a recurrent object of reflection and concern in this book, namely, the relation between political and religious forms of universalism and the types of exclusion that define their circles of provisional equality. Both the Athenian polis and the Christian Church, for example, promised an arena of freedom and equality to their members, but that membership in turn was necessarily restricted or constrained (to free male Athenians in the one case, and to believers in Christ in the other). Moreover, participation in the new group required the severance or transformation of older forms of association based on caste and clan. To call attention to these exclusions and losses is not, however, to reject universalism as mere ideology, in favor, say, of particularizing forms of cultural and multicultural identification. Returning to tribalism does not resolve the paradoxes of citizenship; rather, it refuses to engage in the expanding conversation that citizenship has and can be, a conversation often initiated by and around those it formally excludes. So too, identifying religion with tribalism—in order to critique it as delusion, in the tradition of the Enlightenment, or to turn it into culture, in the manner of Romanticism—fails to recognize the contributions that religious discourse, especially that of the three monotheisms, has made to universalist programs, including citizenship.

The saint is dead. Long live the citizen. If saint and citizen face each other across historical catastrophe, the term *citizen-saint* implies not only the opposition, but also the yoking of the terms, an incomplete passage from one to the other that marks their once and future union as a site of bridging as well as division and separation. The citizen-saint is another centaur, a hybrid between sacred and secular forms of community and hence at home in neither. The phrase names the fissures in the secular conception of the citizen. In the United States as constituted by the Bill of Rights, religion, separated from the state by the "wall" of a legal fiction, reappears in the socially recombinatory, countercultural, and disintegrative forms of separatism, fundamentalism, and sacralized violence and finds multiple avenues by which to infiltrate official discourse and actions. But the term *citizen-saint* is not merely meant as ideological critique, exposing a perennially imperfect process of secularization to which modern states and their subjects should all aspire. The phrase also designates and indeed calls forth a positive ethical potential in a retooled conception of both citizenship and religious fellowship that would exist beyond the limited fields of national and sectarian belonging that each has been used to defend. For example, how does circumcision operate as both a marker of ethnic membership and a means of conversion and civic naturalization across group lines? What vision of social equality is embedded in the injunction to Sabbath rest? How do antinomian suspensions, states of emergency, criminal acts of sovereign exception, and Messianic anticipations lead to reconfigured forms of and relations to law in its written and unwritten, political and religious forms? What styles of universality—ecological, trans-ethnic, or cross-gendered—are implied by the abject state of the pure creature, at sea in a creation abandoned by its Creator? These are some of the questions that I will attempt to answer under the rubric of the citizen-saint.

The phrase *political theology* is associated with the writings of Carl Schmitt, a conservative Catholic jurist active in the Weimar Republic; most notoriously, he became the legal architect of National Socialism by drafting Article 48 of the Weimar Constitution, concerning the state of emergency. In 1922, Schmitt recovered political theology for modernity by publishing a small volume entitled *Political Theology: Four Chapters on the Concept of Sovereignty*. The phrase, of course, is much older, as witnessed in Spinoza's *Theological-Political Tractatus*.

It can be used to describe more broadly the premodern romance between political and religious discourses, especially in the theory and iconography of the divine right of kings. In Shakespeare studies, Schmitt's concept of political theology has had a deeply structuring impact via the work of Ernst Kantorowicz and Walter Benjamin. In 1957, Kantorowicz published *The King's Two Bodies: A Study in Medieval Political Theology,* a massive study of the doctrine that sovereignty is divided between the real, suffering, and imperfect body of the physical king, and the transhistorical, mystical, and legal body of the king's office. Writing from the left rather than the right, Walter Benjamin's *Origin of the German Tragic Drama,* published in 1927, takes up the tyrant-martyr as the central figure of Baroque drama. Whereas Kantorowicz presents the king's two bodies as the hinge between absolutism and constitutionalism, examining this trope in relation to political events of the seventeenth century, Benjamin uses political theology against its own conservative bias in order to imagine a Messianic materialism to come. Giorgio Agamben, Benjamin's Italian translator and a philosopher in his own right, has provided original reflections on the relation between "mere" or "bare" life *(zoe)* and political or civic life *(bios)* in Greek philosophy, Roman law, Renaissance political theology, and modern forms of political organization.[8] Finally, Michael Walzer's studies of citizen-saints in the English Revolution and of the sacred dimensions of public regicide in England and France are important descriptions of political theology posed from within liberalism.[9]

In recent years, Shakespeare scholars have increasingly turned to the idea of political theology—in both its Schmittian and its pre-Schmittian variants—in order to capture the strange hybridization of political and religious thinking in the Renaissance.[10] This book contributes to this strain of research, but with attention directed to the corpus of citizens implied by political theology rather than its gallery of dead kings. These pages are inhabited by figures who dwell in the suburbs of sovereignty, whether in the repossessed cloisters of Catholicism, the new cells of civil society, the rough-hewn barracks of martial law, or the barely social shores of the state of nature. The hero of this book is not the tyrant-martyr, but the citizen-saint, not the two bodies of the king but the many faces of the multitude. By searching for signs of the citizen in the domain of political theology, I emphasize the always-emergent future implied by its sacred tropes of fellowship rather than the termination of its mythic past on the public stage of deposition and regicide.

Religion, Citizenship, and Civil Society

Schmitt begins his *Political Theology* with the following dictum: "Sovereign is he who decides on the exception."[11] He goes on to link the radicality of the sovereign's decision, executed during a state of emergency, to the theological concepts of the miracle and creation *ex nihilo*. Yet if Shakespeare's plays, especially his tragedies, are sundered by the lightening bolt of the monarch's caprice, his dramas, especially his comedies, are just as much concerned with the genesis, reestablishment, and renovation of social norms.[12] Although some of this predilection can be accounted for generically, it is ultimately dispositional, temperamental, and even aesthetic. Shakespeare's normative orientation ultimately distinguishes him from Marlowe and from Milton, figures who frame either end of the reading of Shakespeare undertaken here. If the exception orients the foundational metaphors of political theology, the norm forms the baseline for civic discourse, pointing to procedure, process, and precedent and to equity, equality, and equivalence—opposites in every way to the sovereign exception—as the horizon of group membership. Robert Ellickson defines norms as "order without law."[13] Norms, that is, are the medium of civil society, taken as those forms of organization and association—economic, religious, educational, confraternal—that exceed domestic life, yet are not subsumed within politics per se. Hegel was one of the first thinkers to distinguish civil society, *bürgerliche Gesellschaft*, systematically from politics proper. In civil society, located between family and state, individuals pursue their own interests, but in doing so they create systems of relationship that provide a provisional universal significance—a norm—to their atomized actions. In the course of a day, a person might participate physically or virtually, actively or passively, in a workplace, a neighborhood, a trade union, a parent group, a faith community, a bar or café, a set of social services, an organization or activity organized around a racial or ethnic identity, as well as any number of economic transactions. Civil society consists of points of collective identification and agreement that emerge sporadically and unevenly across the open fabric formed by the interaction, both collaborative and competitive, among independent associations. For Hegel, however, whatever universalism emerges in these collective moments remains sundered, unconscious, and unevenly distributed, requiring the higher synthesis provided by the state, whose ideal citizen (his dual being reflected in the mirror of the traditional sovereign) embodies and embraces the subsumption of individual social life within the framework of national institutions.

In the early 1840s, both in his commentary on Hegel's *Philosophy of Right* and in his essay "On the Jewish Question," Marx took up the Hegelian conceptualization of civil society. Rather than seeing the state as the consummation of civil associations, he read the state as the purely imaginary resolution of the contradictions that characterize the economic life of modernity. According to Marx, the state is the secular equivalent of the City of God, a fantasmatic projection and false harmonization of social conflict on a plane of illusory communality.

Rather than transcending or synthesizing the extreme instrumentalization of human existence in bourgeois society, the state instead reinforces and supports the social divisions created and maintained by the exchanges of capital. For Marx, *bürgerliche Gesellschaft*—its instrumental reduction of every aspect of human interaction to a means—is the truth belied by a state designed not to heal but to maintain the economization of existence. At the same time, civil society, insofar as its atomized individuals come together in social instances for specific ends, is also the arena in which new forms of human interaction and emancipation can be fashioned. Marx defines emancipation as those moments when the individual is brought back into contact with the universality promised by social interaction, within the arena of civil society itself: "*Every* emancipation is a *restoration* of the human world and of human relationships to *man himself*. . . Human emancipation will only be complete when the real, individual man has absorbed into himself the abstract citizen."[14] In political theory after Hegel and Marx, the location of civil society between family and the polis—its informal, recombinatory, and associative nature, its infinite capacity for reshuffling, expansion, and contraction, its link to desire and drive, and, perhaps most important, its identification with labor, with the creative and industrious capacities of human life—has made it both the factory in which capital reproduces itself and the workshop in which social and political norms can be rethought, contested, or renewed.[15]

As the title of Marx's famous essay indicates, religion has played no insignificant role in the formulation of theories of civil society. If civil society has functioned in modern life as the historic cancellation of divinely sanctioned forms of sovereignty, it has also provided the breeding ground for heterodox styles of religious association and expression. In the desert, as Spinoza himself insists, there is no state; what is formed at Sinai is a congregation *(edah)* of the children of Israel: an assembly, a gathering, a company, a multitude, a swarm. *Edah,* linked to another Hebrew word meaning "witness" and "testimony," implies a social and linguistic moment of responsiveness to and responsibility for others, juridical without necessarily requiring the mediation of a judge.[16] Israel becomes a *nation,* an emergent *political* entity (no longer a mere multitude or swarm, with its creaturely connotations), insofar as it witnesses the contract as a *congregation,* an itinerant *civil society.* Following a long line of cultural associations between the Jew and civil society that includes Marlowe's Jew of Malta and Shakespeare's Shylock, Marx nominates the Jew as the exemplar of the particularizing strain of civil society.[17] If the Jews of Germany epitomize the structural complicity between Judaism and civil society in Marx's thinking, the United States is the locale where religion's purely civil status has been most profitably pursued, thanks to the legal separation of church and state guaranteed by the

First Amendment: "The infinite fragmentation of religion in North America, for example, already gives it the *external* form of a strictly private affair. It has been relegated among the numerous private interests and exiled from the life of the community as such." Far from withering away, however, religion thrives in its new context, reinforcing the privatizing tendencies of the bourgeois City of Man under a secular state that has taken over religion's universalizing and spiritual functions: "If we find in the country that has attained full political emancipation [*sic*], that religion not only continues to *exist* but is *fresh* and *vigorous*, this is proof that the existence of religion is not at all opposed to the perfection of the state."[18]

In the last decade and a half, both citizenship and civil society, especially in relation to the challenges posed by racial, ethnic, and religious diversity in contemporary democracies, have received increased attention from political philosophers working in the liberal tradition. Michael Walzer, for example, turning his eye from the passion of the *ancien regime* to the conditions of contemporary democracy, has argued for civil society as a field of multiple memberships that both supports particular identities and maps a common ground formed by the junctions of different instances of affiliation: "Multiple and overlapping memberships help to tie all the groups (or, perhaps better, all their individual members) together, creating something larger and more encompassing than any of them."[19] Taken separately and in their totality, these associations offer both a "school for civility," for negotiating social conflict and multiple identities, and a "school for citizenship," an arena for learning the skills and creating the intellectual and social resources necessary for political participation.[20] Complementing Walzer's emphasis on "associational pluralism" with his own focus on the importance of public policy in shaping liberal societies, Canadian political philosopher Will Kymlicka has developed a theory of "multicultural citizenship." This liberal model of the state recognizes and integrates minority rights into a "civic" or "societal" culture that eschews any single ethnic group or religious affiliation as definitive of citizenship, recognizes the relative autonomy of particular ethnic groups, but builds a public culture based on a shared national history and a common public language. Kymlicka's view is more statist, and Walzer's is more civil, but they share a commitment to thinking about liberalism as both an antidote to ethnic fragmentation (by creating an evolving common discourse through civil and civic institutions and values) and a shelter for minority political organization and expression (by encouraging associational pluralism).[21]

For Michael Walzer, the civilian and the citizen are dialectical sides of the same liberal individual: "Though citizenship is the more general role, there is no hierarchy here, for the citizen, outside of his or her associations, is a lonely and insubstantial figure, without political influence."[22] If for Walzer, the pure citizen, conceived apart from her or his associations is an empty shell, a formal placeholder, for Shakespeare, the mere civilian—the participant in civil society who is excluded from civic life—finds intense vitality in the life forms available to him or her but must finally be integrated into a larger political order, though generally at the expense of minoritarian religious associations (the ghetto for Shylock, Islam or paganism for Othello, the convent for Isabella). Take for a moment the case of Shylock: excluded from civic life—political participation as a Venetian citizen—Shylock makes his home in civil society, giving a face to the anonymous operation of capital. Yet even for Shylock, civil society is more than economics and more than secularization as well: thus Shakespeare strives to recreate patterns of exegesis and congregation that would have been peculiar to the incorporated Jewish community of Venice. At the end of the trial scene, Shylock, like his daughter Jessica, has begun to cross over from the ghetto to the larger civic stage of the Republic of Venice through his anticipated conversion to Christianity. Unlike Jessica, however, Shylock remains only in the most limited formal sense "content" with this naturalization; caught between competing circles of citizenship, he, more than his daughter, emerges as the exemplar of modern citizenship and its discontents at the play's end. In his Venetian and Viennese plays, and in *The Tempest,* Shakespeare stages the tension between civil, civic, and sovereign modes of relationship, and the role of religious metaphors and membership protocols in defining the scope and purpose of each. My readings of these plays draw on the resources of contemporary liberalism (with its dual commitment to minority rights and civic culture) to understand Shakespeare's reckonings of citizenship, while also looking at Shakespeare's plays as part of the variegated, even illiberal, prehistory of liberal discourses and institutions.

Marx placed the privatization and proliferation of religion in the American culture of rights purely on the negative side of civil society, under the Judaizing sign of economic instrumentalization. I would insist, however, that religious particularizations, and the laws that protect such diversity, can also offer sites for reconceiving the universal being of humanity from within civil society, outside of or in response to the abstract mediations of the state—sites, that is, for the social emancipation imagined by Marx in the same essay. The question of religious affiliation in the eighteenth century formed part of what Ernesto Laclau has analyzed as the central dialectic of democratic politics, in which "a succession of finite and particular identities . . . attempt to assume universal tasks surpassing them."[23] In the U.S. context, the efflorescence of religious sects and schisms, with their challenges to civic inclusion and redefinition, formed the crystallizing element in a line of further flashpoints in the history of citizenship, including race, class, gender, and sexuality. To reclaim the history and debates about religious tolerance within this liberal line is to probe not only the formal terms of citizenship (who's in, who's out, and why), but also the exegetical genealogy of key texts and concepts in the literature of citizenship. Who is my neighbor? Who is a citizen? What is a creature? What is a person? These fundamental questions about group membership and social formation have been posed repeatedly in the West within and between political and religious discourses, and in the literary works that struggle to relinquish the ideologies of both in order to bear witness to their costs and their dreams. The literature of citizenship documents and dramatizes the imaginative and political contest between local ecologies of cult, culture, and community, and more universal and impersonal economies of law and historical belonging, tensions that define the covenantal consciousness of the West in both its evident failures and its surviving potential.

From within the field of literary studies, this book makes the case for taking citizenship seriously, which means testing the limits of its promises without exiting from the discussion it initiates. I follow Brook Thomas here in his book *American Literary Realism and the Failed Promise of Contract.* As his title indicates, Thomas refuses to either celebrate or debunk contract; rather, he aims to "help contract's advocates avoid the causes of its past failures, and help contract's detractors better address the aspirations of the many in our culture who still sense its promise."[24] Citizenship's attempt to rezone the complex landscape of religious, ethnic, sexual, and economic differences in terms of formal equality and due process is, at every step of its articulation, historically and conceptually compromised by collusion with privilege. Yet precisely because the history of citizenship is nothing more nor less than a sustained address to and self-critique around questions of access and equity, the concept of citizenship remains in a special position, insufficiently remarked in the current culturalist discourses of the humanities, to enable us to think about minority rights in a universal framework. Etienne Balibar distinguishes two notions of the people that confront each other in the history of politics: "*ethnos,* the 'people' as an imagined community of membership and filiation, and *dēmos,* the 'people' as the collective subject of representation, decision making, and rights."[25] Citizenship finds itself at the embattled interface of these two conceptions; insofar as it struggles to distinguish *dēmos* from *ethnos,* it invites us to approach questions of community, sovereignty, and difference from a vantage point *other than culture,* even and especially when "culture" itself emerges as a concept inhering within but not identical with that of citizenship and the public norms it assembles.

This book also takes religion seriously, as a foundational contributor to and other voice in the citizenship debates, beginning with the cultic and ritual origins of Greek democracy itself, which long preceded its philosophical formulations.[26] Christianity defines the principal religious context for Shakespearean drama and hence is a constant reference point in these analyses, above all in the figure of St. Paul, whose Roman citizenship guaranteed him legal immunities and philosophical exit papers in the court of Jewish law. Yet I am also concerned to isolate the Jewish strain in modern thinking about citizenship. Scholars working in legal theory, political philosophy, and Jewish texts have looked to the rights and rites of the *ger* (stranger, resident alien, or proselyte) in ancient Israel as a model for citizenship, pluralism, and naturalization relevant to the civic crisis of modern Israel.[27] In 2000, Michael Walzer and a team of leading scholars of Jewish thought published the first volume of *The Jewish Political Tradition*, a major work of selection and synthesis that places traditional Jewish writings into dialogue with the main stream of Western political philosophy. It is no accident that volume 1, on authority, takes "Covenant" as its opening concept, since the constitution of a people as equal partners in a national community through an act of contractual consent not only describes one version of what happened at Sinai, but also forms one of citizenship's central myths.

The shifting status of contract between religious and political discourses, especially as it takes shape around the archetypal example of marriage, is a recurrent theme in this book. To what extent do the contracts that bring communities into being operate laterally, as an equalizing force among persons now conceived as citizens, and to what extent do these contracts embody a heteronomous element of sheer jurisdiction, coming from above in a stroke of exceptional violence? And why does the marriage contract operate again and again as the legal instrument that serves precisely to mediate or "marry" these horizontal and vertical dimensions of covenant, instituting a civil association based on consent while almost immediately subjecting it to hierarchical regulation? Although the brother has been the central emblem of citizenship since the French Revolution, with his claims to be the representative of representation going back to the classical tradition, a recurrent but less-remarked image of the citizen is surely that of the bride. What else are the virgin queens of civic pageantry than the bridal function of citizenship pranked up and on parade? The bride's consent to marriage both inserts a contractual element into sovereign relations and, in most traditional formulations, institutes a hierarchy between partners; indeed, the rites of marriage wed the contrary principles of contract and coercion, equality and difference, civility and sovereignty in a union whose sublime symbolism of domestic tranquility is matched only by its vulnerability to dissension, adultery, and divorce.

If marriage binds sovereignty and civility in a sacred-secular dance of rights and obligations, the rejection of marriage, embodied by the radical celibacy of the saint, interrupts the romance between horizontal and vertical forms of relation anointed by marriage. Beginning with *Antigone,* the order of celibacy represented by the saint exists at cross-purposes with this fundamental metaphor and organizing bond of citizenship, and is thus part of the socio-sexual unconscious of modern political forms. The marriage of the saint, and with it her consensual binding to a civil order that takes the marriage contract itself as a central emblem of its legitimacy, forms a dramatic turning point in the crossing of sanctity and citizenship from Sophocles to Shakespeare. The problems posed by divorce and remarriage play a role in the political theology of Milton's *Samson Agonistes,* where divorce becomes a figure of God's executive decision *ex nihilo*—all exception, and no norm. Moreover, intermarriage as a means of naturalizing foreigners, as a matrix for multiple memberships, and as an embodied challenge to any citizenship protocol founded on national, ethnic, or religious purity, plays a role in all the dramas examined here, from Sophocles and Marlowe to Shakespeare and Milton.

The Book

Although alighting on several paths in the course of its civic divinations, this book turns around the case of Shakespeare. Shakespeare's plays, I argue, stage the sacramental marriage, civil divorce, and dangerous liaisons between politics and religion in the West, probing the intersection between the founding metaphors of divine sovereignty and modern forms of social organization based on the economic contracts of individuals. Shakespeare's plays, I suggest, are preoccupied by the strange cohabitation of the saint and the citizen, especially in situations of political emergency, when exceptions become the norm. At the heart of Shakespeare's dramas of state and society is the dramatic force of the exception as it veers from the sovereign to the civil domain. Four central chapters identify the crossing of sainthood and citizenship in Shakespearean drama, beginning with the interplay between the particular and the universal in Shakespeare's Venetian plays, moving to the Vienna of *Measure for Measure,* a city at once avowedly Catholic and restlessly secular, and ending in the state of nature explored in *The Tempest* under the theological sign of Creation. My interest is not, as in previous work, in the narratological legacy of medieval hagiography per se,[28] but in theological conceptions of national and ethnic belonging and their imperfect translations into modern forms of civil society, racial theory, and national membership. The word *saint* functions more as a placeholder for a shifting set of linked topics and problems—the sacred, the sacrifice, the exception—than as a character type with a specific literary history. Moreover, far from being restricted to traditionally Christian or Catholic characters, the place of the citizen-saint will be filled by the likes of Antigone, Barabas, Shylock, Othello, Isabella, Caliban, and Samson, each representing a heterodox limit point in their respective social scenes. All of these characters embody features and aspects of the mixed political body that I am dubbing the citizen-saint: figures caught between competing, mutually exclusive, social, political, and religious structures; figures who dwell in the frontier between the secular and the profane; figures who, by virtue of embracing or embodying superceded historical and religious positions, become unlikely portents of social formations to come. In the final analysis, Shakespeare himself is a citizen-saint, an author who, by staging the exception in its political, theological, ethnographic, and socio-sexual variants, instituted a new set of mimetic norms. Ever the civilian, Shakespeare's biographical, affective, and narratological ties to a Catholicism superceded by the Reformation, along with the rather different exegetical attraction of his writings to the cancelled world of the Jews, tie Shakespeare's life and works to a landscape of potent remnants and historical anomalies whose force could be emancipatory as well as regressive.

A key figure throughout this analysis is Paul, the prototype of the citizen-saint, a foundational cross-link between Judaism and Christianity, and the subject of chapter 1. Paul is the defendant who claimed his rights as a Roman citizen at the moment of incipient martyrdom; the writer who developed the universalist strands of Judaism within the framework of an imperial juridical order; the man who both bore the definitive mark of Jewish national membership on his body and carried citizenship papers that would get his letters and his person to Rome, capital of the Western world. Paul's sublation and internalization of circumcision is a guiding motif in Shakespeare's two Venetian plays, where circumcision operates as the sign of an ethno-political form of religious association that excludes its bearers—Jewish and Muslim men—from participation in the Christian commonwealth. The Pauline universalism explored in these Venetian plays is a universalism minus one: minus the circumcised, whose submission to physical subtraction on the real body invites their excision from the body politic. If the theological source of Shakespeare's thinking in these plays is Pauline, his dramatic precursor is Marlowe in *The Jew of Malta;* my journey to Shakespeare's Venice in chapters 3 and 4 follows a visit to Marlowe's Malta in chapter 2, which examines Marlowe's definitive staging of the relation between the Jews and civil society in the early 1590s.

Paul's thoughts on marriage, which he presents as both a symbol of cosmic hierarchy and a promise of social equality, are key to the civil and civic dynamics of *Measure for Measure.* Is the head of a woman her husband (1 Cor 11:2), or are male and female one in Christ (Gal 3:28)? This question, at once theological, political, and socio-sexual, is subjected to public deliberation by the many marriages of *Measure for Measure,* calculating both Isabella's passage from sanctity to citizenship and Vienna's passage from sovereignty to civility in the course of the play. Finally, *The Tempest,* modeled on Paul's shipwreck on Malta on his way to Rome at the end of the Acts of the Apostles, is in some ways an answer to the entailments placed on the Pauline legacy by the Marlovian consciousness of *The Merchant of Venice* and *Othello.* By resolutely locating its drama of political process "Before Circumcision," within the scene of an originary creation, Shakespeare explores the possibility of a creaturely humanism that would exist beyond the division of humanity into the stems of the nations.

Shakespeare was neither Greek nor Jew, neither Republican nor Democrat. He wrote his play under regimes of absolutism, often with a sovereign audience in mind. "Citizen" in Shakespeare's English refers primarily to a city-dweller of independent means, either a merchant or a member of a guild. "The true citizen, (whereof London hath plenty)," wrote George Whetstone, "liveth upon his trade."[29] Citizenship was by and large a category of municipal, not national life, naming a limited moment of urban self-governance and emergent capitalism within an overarching monarchic order. One could be citizen of London and subject of the Crown. Citizenship in Shakespeare's world involves civil society more than civic life, the play of economic association among traditional corporate entities rather than formal political participation by equal persons. What, then, does it mean to place Shakespeare's dramas in dialogue with citizenship understood as an incipiently political category, and how can such a project be other than Whiggish, an early chapter in the *Bildungsroman* of liberalism?

The theological framing of Shakespeare's relation to the citizenship debates is a distinguishing feature of the work pursued here. To look at the nexus of theological and political definitions of membership, within the exegetical scene opened up by Paul's life and work, is to derail any simple model of secularization and liberalization by insisting on the ongoing impact of religious modes of social and political thought on modernity. The result is to place citizenship itself in dialogue with earlier conceptions and variations on the theme of public life, in part in order to recover a broader account of the possibilities of civic experience and experiment in the present moment. To look at what counts as citizenship in the world of Shakespeare's plays is to approach citizenship as a series of open letters, formulated out of a loose yet exacting set of promises—some broken, some kept, and some yet to be thought—posed at determinate points of time but to indeterminate audiences.[30]

For better or for worse, for richer or for poorer, my concerns here are not historical in the current sense of contextualization; although the century of revolution forms one horizon of my readings of Shakespeare, I do not try to resolve Shakespeare's relation to the religious and political controversies of his day;

rather, I aim to weave some of the key metaphors, narrative patterns, and civic settings of his dramas into the larger dynamics of what I delimit here as the literature of citizenship. I have chosen texture over context, the larger tapestry over the mise-en-scène. Heidegger writes that "the essence of technology is nothing technological." I submit that *the essence of history is nothing historical;* rephrasing Heidegger, this book proposes that "essential reflection upon [history] and decisive confrontation with it must happen in a realm that is, on the one hand, akin to the essence of [history] and, on the other, fundamentally different from it."[31] My approach could be called neo-exegetical, building on some of the central insights of such biblically informed masters of Shakespearean criticism as Barbara Lewalski, Nevill Coghill, and G. K. Hunter, and taking broader critical sustenance from the examples of Eric Auerbach and Northrop Frye,[32] but restaging the typological concerns of these thinkers within a stage framed by the destinies of Judaism on the one hand and of liberal political philosophy on the other. Not only do I use rabbinic sources to illuminate key moments of civic engagement in *The Merchant of Venice, Othello,* and *The Tempest,* but I also read Shakespearean drama as an extended midrash on citizenship, that is, as a poetic, exegetical, and narrative exploration of the dilemmas of community-formation that take their orientation from biblical topoi and mythoi. Western literature itself emerges out of Judaism's internal rhythms of letter and spirit, prescription and prophesy, and their reelaboration in Christianity and Islam; the literature we call secular remains intimately linked to the sublime opacity of revelation even as it bravely casts its fortunes with the quotidian exchanges of civil life. Literary study would do well to attend to its own exegetical foundations, not in order to reinstitute a reactionary criticism that would take religion as either content or context, dogma or history, but in order to draw on the considerable resources of exegetical iconography and technique so as to place literature in the broadest possible scene—that of social thought itself.

Moreover, for this critic at least, there could be no neo-exegesis without psychoanalysis, a discourse that translated the taxonomies and typologies of traditional hermeneutics into the cityscape of modern interpretation. Freud's Jewish science and Lacan's Catholic one have mapped the relations among symbolic orders of law and socialization, subject positions within these orders, and unique instances of enjoyment that articulate and exceed these roles via the synapses of fantasy. In his seminar on *The Four Fundamental Concepts of Psychoanalysis,* Lacan insists that

> *with regard to the agency of sexuality, all subjects are equal, from the child to the adult—that they deal only with that part of sexuality that passes into the*

> *networks of the constitution of the subject, into the networks of the signifier—that sexuality is realized only through the operation of the drives in so far as they are partial drives, partial with regard to the biological finality of sexuality.*[33]

Against all odds, Lacan's declaration of equality links the Freudian field to the domain of citizenship. By claiming that all subjects—child and adult, but also male and female—only engage with those parts of sexuality that are taken up into the signifying chain, Lacan introduces the rule of equivalence, the chain of substitutions, as a key feature of sexual life. To enter into sexuality is to *submit to equation,* to subject oneself to the possibility of substitution, to become equal with others on the basis of one's alienating access to sexuality and language. But subjectivity is not pure subjection, and Lacan clearly also means to evoke here a more ethical form of equality, pertaining to the subject itself as separating from the alienating chain in order to capture a new freedom in relation to it. The child, of course, enters here as a form of exception, as the *unmündig,* the minor, the incomplete citizen or citizen *in potentia,* and thus she embodies a form of unequal equality, an equality that is always anticipated and hence never fully calculable.[34] In this book, the position of the child as the unequal bearer of sexuality and citizenship is held among others by the *pais* or girl Antigone, her Shakespearean sister Isabella, and the creature Caliban. That equality should be staked out in relation to the exception is part of the dynamic intrinsic to the debate called citizenship, which has been repeatedly called to examine its paradoxes and extend its privileges in relation to voices and positions that stand just outside its formal bounds. Finally, Lacan refers equality to sexuality—a sexuality programmatically disengaged from reproduction and hence from biological ends. Citizenship, like sexuality in the psychoanalytic sense, always exists at the expense of or in tension with nature. The subjective equality incarnated by the citizen-saint is always linked to the partial drives, their fundamental non-integration into genital sexuality, and their uneven vicissitudes in the field of social equivalence.

Although this book takes Shakespeare as its central focus, my interests are clearly broader. Chapter 7 extends my examination of the creature before the law in *The Tempest* to the creature under the law in Milton's *Samson Agonistes.* The epilogue, "The Literature of Citizenship," argues for citizenship as a category that can organize political reflection on literature in a conceptual and pragmatic framework other than that of culture. Indeed, one goal of this project is to distinguish both religion and citizenship from the field of culture and hence to indicate the critical paths out of the current impasses in literary study dominated by culturalist models. As Jürgen Habermas has argued, citizenship instantiates that set of collective norms and procedures that allows members of distinct and competing subgroups in pluralistic democracies to communicate and adjudicate their interests. So too, religious discourses, far from simply representing tribal or ethnic identities, have historically drawn together disparate groups in collective projects. One need only point here to the bewildering diversity of world Jewry, Christianity, Islam, and Buddhism, as well as the unlikely heterogeneity of panhellenic and Roman paganisms, to see some of the ways in which religious membership can exist across and in tension with cultural specificity or national identity. This is not to say that citizenship and religion have not served to authorize the most egregious forms of legalized and sacralized violence in the service of particular national communities, but it is to insist on the universal language animating both the creative and the destructive tendencies of civic and religious membership drives. If what confronts us at the current moment, both in the academy and globally, is not so much a clash of civilizations (of particularized cultures), but rather a clash of universalisms, of competing yet genetically linked visions of cosmic order, perhaps there is hope that civic and civil norms can be found among them in order that a more viable, if always incomplete, universalism might begin to unfold.

ONE
Citizen Paul

Why should a study of Paul stand in the forecourt of a book on Shakespeare and citizenship? I argue here that Paul's assertion of Roman citizenship rights, first at Philippi and later in Jerusalem, binds Western citizenship to the Pauline corpus in ways that resonate in and beyond Shakespearean drama, linking monotheism and its discontents to a classical juridical frame. Paul's acceptance of Jesus as the Messiah would have monumental consequences for the future of his religion(s), Judaism and/as Christianity, each in a volatile state of redefinition before, during, and because of Paul's life and work.[1] Paul's archetypal conversion from Judaism to a Christianity constituted in part by that conversion makes him a critical figure for thinking through the troubled legacy of Judaism to the imaginative world created by Shakespeare. And the Shakespearean reference point is crucial here, even when it is invisible: I write not as a theologian or a scholar of the New Testament, but rather as a reader of Shakespeare concerned to map a particular conceptual convergence—that between the saint and the citizen, or more broadly, between a theology of exceptionalism and a politics of the norm—as it manifests in Shakespeare's plays. Such tragic and tragicomic characters as Shylock, Othello, Caliban, and Isabella undergo a passage, real or imagined, voluntary or forced, from a situation before or under a particular legal order to a point beyond it, a passage that can take the form of conversion, naturalization, manumission, marriage, or some mix of these modes of radical status change. In each case, moreover, this point beyond is not otherworldly but this-worldly, associated with the social, sexual, economic, and political functioning of a *politea*—a constitution, a commonweal, a citizenry. Each of these characters must in effect *die into citizenship*, into an equalizing form of civic membership and social interchange that requires the renunciation of claims to distinction that had imbued their previous lives with an intensity of purpose verging on the charismatic.

Paul, in his life and work, offers a paradigmatic, even foundational, moment of this death into citizenship. Such a sacrificial passage is part of the classical mythos of citizenship, as developed, for example, in the genre of the public funeral oration, which in collectively burying the citizen-soldiers of the democratic polis also symbolically put to rest epic *arête* founded on the distinctiveness of the great aristocratic families and their master-leaders.[2] The otherwise quite different stories of Antigone and Hercules dramatize a similar itinerary; both of them become icons for political orders they can join only in death.[3] Paul's death into citizenship differs from the classical paradigm because he sets off on the road to Rome—to the imperial trial guaranteed to him as a Roman citizen—as a consequence of his conversion on the road to Damascus. When he crosses from the jurisdiction of the Jewish to that of the Roman court, Paul in effect completes his definitive mapping of Jewish law as a local affair whose peculiar practices must be subsumed and refigured by the universal order promised by the Messiah to all nations. In transferring his case from Jerusalem to Rome, Paul's epic legal journey symbolically legislates a translation and transvaluation of Jewish law that marks it as particular in relation to the universal, reserving for Judaism a quotient of historical significance as a point of original covenant but restricting the continued authority and validity of its codes.

This chapter draws on recent scholarship concerning Paul's relationship to Judaism. Running counter to both patristic and Lutheran insistences on the deep differences between Paul's early life as a Jew under the law and his later life as a Christian through faith, a strand of largely postwar Pauline studies has striven to recover the Jewish grounds and *halakhic* precedents for Paul's thinking about the law.[4] These studies lie behind my Shakespearean appropriations of Paul, whose ongoing debts and loyalties to Judaism drew into Christendom a significant burden of Jewish tropes, ideas, and commitments, even when functioning under the sign of disavowal. However, in narrowing the gap between Paul and Judaism—in showing just how Jewish Paul remained (and, conversely, just how "Christian" Judaism could be)—the revolutionary and epochal, as well as destructive, character of Paul's work threatens to slip out of sight. One must always confront the bedrock truth that Christianity is not Judaism, that Paul represents a crucial moment in their break, and that laws associated with the creation and preservation of a covenantal community—especially circumcision and the dietary laws—are the frequent focus, if not indeed object of attack, of Paul's discourse on Jewish-Gentile relations.[5] Daniel Boyarin, a leader in the field of Jewish cultural studies, has devoted a book to the cultural politics of Paul's letters and their reception and concludes that, although Paul's project "is not anti-Semitic (or even anti-Judaic) in intent, it nevertheless has the effect of depriving continued Jewish existence of any reality or significance in the Christian economies of history."[6]

This chapter uses the category of citizenship, in dialogue with recent work on Paul, to mount an assessment of Paul's legacy that both links Shakespeare to Judaism via Paul and accounts for the tropes of obdurance and legalism that confine the spirit of Judaism to the prison-house of the particular in the Gentile imagination. In this analysis, "citizenship" ultimately provides a more fruitful category than "culture" because it acknowledges local practice (Aristotle points out that there are as many definitions of citizen as there are cities [*Politics* 1275a]), while outlining a template of universal equivalences and civic participation for those who are entered into its set. Moreover, precisely because of its mediation of universal and particular categories, citizenship is not a concept that belongs to any one group as its rightful inheritance, even if (and as) it passes through many hands in the course of its articulation and expansion. Saul/Paul of Tarsus, as we shall see, shared in at least three distinct citizenship traditions: the Hellenistic city-state, the nation of Israel, and the Roman Empire. These multiple memberships, as they play out in his life and work, offer one explanatory ground for Paul's efforts at community-building in different cities and among different citizen-groups in the ancient world.

Paul's real and epistolary journeys to Rome effect a symbolic *translatio* westward of Jewish civic themes, linking the destiny of the Jews to that of the classical and European political tradition. Yet Paul does so by evacuating the central mark of membership in Israel, namely the covenant of circumcision, of its continued validity. Once circumcision has been raised to the level of a symbol, the rite itself suffers degradation into the material reminder of a legal primitivism. In Shakespeare's era, the ranks of the circumcised would include not only the Jews of Paul's Epistles but also the Muslims, who in their Arab and Ottoman waves represented the greatest imperial threat to Western territory and values in the later Middle Ages and Renaissance. The knowledge of the law epitomized by the Jewish and Muslim adherence to circumcision meant that these groups had both more affinity with and more resistance to Christianity than the Gentile barbarians encountered in New World travels. As we will see in subsequent chapters, the difficult dialectic among those before, under, and beyond the law will demarcate the several civil spaces of Shakespeare's plays, giving them a local habitation and a name in relation to ever-expanding and resituating universal frames. My goal is not to relocalize or delegitimate those frames in the name of individual cultures (be they Hebrew, Moorish, Irish, or Caribbean) but rather to recall the integral dream of universalism to its dialogue with diverse citizenship rites and routines, and the calculus of sacrifice they regulate. The following reading of Paul, neither an apology nor a critique, aims instead to provide a founding instance of such a civic recollection, isolating in order to gather in the particular strands of legal, social, and religious thought that feed into the norms and dreams of citizenship.

Paul on the Road to Rome

In his *General Economic History,* Max Weber derived the conditions of Western citizenship from a three-act drama of Judeo-Christian innovation that culminated in Paul's Gentile mission:

> *For the later period in the West three great facts were crucial. The first was prophecy among the Jews, which destroyed magic within the confines of Judaism; magical procedure remained real but was devilish instead of divine. The second was the Pentecostal miracle, the ceremonial adoption into the spirit of*

> *Christ that was a decisive factor in the extraordinary spread of the early Christian enthusiasm. The final factor was the day in Antioch when Paul, in opposition to Peter, espoused fellowship with the uncircumcised. The magical barriers between clans, tribes, and peoples, which were still known in the ancient* polis *to a considerable degree, were thus set aside and the establishment of the Western city was made possible.*[7]

Weber associates Pauline universalism with the possibility of modern citizenship as a measure of formal equality before the law. At stake in Paul's decision to pursue "fellowship with the uncircumcised"—that is, to break bread with Gentile Christians—were dietary laws and circumcision, two bulwarks of Jewish law *(halakhah)* concerning the formation and maintenance of a distinct and distinctive community in covenant with God.[8] Paul's letter to the Galatians records his conflict with Peter at Antioch and applies it to Judaizing counterforces in Galatia (Gal 2). Chapter 3 of Galatians ends with Paul's famous suspension of the law in favor of unrestricted membership in Christ: "There is neither Jew nor Greek, there is neither slave nor free, there is neither male nor female; for you are all one in Christ Jesus" (Gal 3:28). In annulling ethnic, caste, and gender differences around the table laid by the Church, Paul sketched a blueprint for radical equality that runs through the subsequent history of the Christian West as a model of political fellowship, an excuse for coercive conversion, and a continued call for social change.

Linking Paul's universalism to the foundation of postclassical citizenship, Weber does not note that Roman citizenship played a key role in Paul's life. In the Acts of the Apostles, Paul twice evokes his rights as a Roman citizen when he is arrested for subversive activities, rejecting the authority of local laws in order to claim a broader set of immunities. These legal acts of the apostle in turn have implications for Paul's theological and missionary articulations of Jewish-Gentile relations in his letters. Citizenship as a category is mobilized in Paul's life when he crosses from a local to a general jurisdiction or inhabits several jurisdictions at once. For Paul, citizenship is always multiple, indicating a split among allegiances and laws.[9] J. G. A. Pocock, one of the great theorists of the republican tradition in the last century, takes the case of Paul as an example of the transformations that citizenship had undergone since the Athenian ideal of the citizen as a political animal:

> *A famous narrative case is that of Saint Paul announcing himself as a Roman citizen. . . . An Aristotelian citizen, ruling and being ruled, took part in the making or determining of the laws by which he was governed. There had been a time when* civis Romanus *had similarly denoted one who participated in the*

> *self-governing assemblies of republican Rome. But Paul—who is not a Roman, has never seen Rome, and will find no assembly of the citizens if he ever gets there—means something quite different. By claiming to be a Roman citizen, he means that of the various patterns of legally defined rights and immunities available to subjects of a complex empire made up of many communities, he enjoys access to the most uniform and highly privileged there is.*[10]

Citizenship under the Empire was largely passive, a collection of specific rights and protections rather than a mode of civic engagement. Citizenship was by no means a universal category, but rather "a precise expression of one particular set of rights and duties" in a world of multiple municipalities and complex status relations.[11] Built on the Greek model of city-states, yet awkwardly applied to an increasingly larger territory, Roman citizenship remained attached to the city of Rome—*cives,* like *polites* before it and *burgher* after it, means city-dweller, and always retains an urban referent. Neighboring Latin communities enjoyed an intermediary status between full Roman citizenship and *peregrini,* or free foreigners, who were usually citizens of their own municipalities but not of Rome.[12] Foreign soldiers became citizens upon discharge (a model relevant to my reading of Othello's death into citizenship), and the emperor could also grant citizenship to whole communities of foreigners *(peregrini)* or to outstanding individuals.[13] Manumitted slaves, however, were automatically granted citizenship; they lept over the category of *peregrine* directly into that of citizen, and this condition was then passed on to their children.[14]

Paul was either the son of manumitted slaves, according to traditions that date from Jerome, or the son or grandson of a solider awarded citizenship on the basis of outstanding service to Rome.[15] When Paul claims immunities as a Roman in Acts 22:29, the Geneva commentary of 1599 notes that this designation is "Not by nation, but by the law of his city of birth [Tarsus]," acknowledging the provincial mediations and naturalization processes which preceded Paul's inheritance of Roman citizenship. In Paul's peregrinations through various Roman provinces and municipalities (Jerusalem, Antioch, Corinth, Ephesus), he is subject to local law, but as a citizen of Rome, he is also entitled to certain privileges and legal protections, including "*provocatio* (the right to appeal after trial) . . . and the right of an accused citizen to choose either a local or a Roman trial"—rights that Paul will call upon in Jerusalem, sending him on the road to Rome.[16] In the provinces, moreover, citizens were usually exempt from flogging, an immunity that Paul would assert in Philippi, though only after undergoing this punishment (Acts 16:22–23).[17]

Although Roman citizenship was an exclusive category, its coexistence with the citizenship laws of the provinces was key to the Empire's relative stability. The imperial law of Rome maintained its wide reach by recognizing and tolerating local practices that were indifferent to or did not touch upon matters of essential order. Judaism was recognized as a *religio licta* or legal religion.[18] In times of relative peace, two jurisdictions could coexist simultaneously, above all in religious affairs: while early on Rome had tried to suppress the bewildering diversity of foreign cults, it soon learned that the best means of control was toleration.[19] Boaz Cohen summarizes the jurisdictional situation in Roman Judea: "[A]fter the subjugation of Palestine, Jewish and Pagan tribunals had concurrent jurisdiction in civil matters. The rabbis censured those Jews who carried their disputes before pagan judges for settlement. However, if one of the litigants was a Roman citizen, it was necessary to have the issue referred to a Roman judiciary."[20] Records show that diasporic Jewish communities in Alexandria and Sardis were recognized as *politeuma,* that is, organized bodies of citizens within a Hellenistic city; the synagogue was the site where political matters concerning these communities were conducted, and to which issues deemed of internal significance were referred.[21] Yet Roman civil courts were operative in the same civic sphere as Jewish ones, as evidenced in the words of one rabbi, "'In all places where you find *agoriot*—non-Jewish courts in the marketplace—even if they have the same laws as Jewish law, you are not permitted to use them.'"[22] Moreover, unlike the Greeks and the Jews, the Romans distinguished the authority and origins of civil law from those of divine law; the principle "*Fas lex divina ius lex humana est*" (Religious prescriptions *[fas]* are divine, while civil law is human) aided the acceptance of Roman law by European groups in the Middle Ages.[23]

In Acts, the classic statement of this practice of legal toleration occurs in Corinth. Luke reports that L. Junius Gallio, the proconsul of Achaea, declines to judge on the Jews' case against Paul: "If it were a matter of crime or serious villainy, I would be justified in accepting the complaint of you Jews; but since it is a matter of questions about words and names and your own law, see to it yourselves; I do not wish to be a judge in these matters" (Acts 18:14–17). *Words, names, and your own law:* Gallio marks out a realm of local discourse and practices—what we would call "culture"—best left to communal adjudication. In the face of such matters, Roman law prefers to withhold its judgment. The episode provides both a biographical and a juridical ground for Paul's doctrine of matters *adiaphora,* the indifferent, merely cultural, or customary status of rituals such as circumcision. As we will see in the next section, the theory and practice of imperial law provides one model for Paul to relativize the validity of Jewish law, ultimately neutralizing circumcision itself as the physical signature of covenantal citizenship. It is perhaps no accident that L. Junius Gallio was the brother of the philosopher Seneca, as if Luke were building into his narrative a set of analogies between imperial law, Stoic apathy or indifference, and the universalism of Paul's mission.[24]

Roman citizenship constituted the highest set of rights in a variegated landscape of status types and forms of local rule; as an exclusive and limited status, the principle of Roman citizenship allowed Roman law to withdraw from the fields of other municipalities, allowing diversity of social and religious practice and civic membership to hold ground when they did not challenge Rome's economic and territorial interests. In its very nonuniversality—its exclusivity and its foundations in a system of status—Roman citizenship could promote a certain kind of universal thinking about particular things, helping to posit a world in which general laws might coexist with and even shelter local ones. In the words of the Latin jurist Gaius, "The rules established by a given state for its own members are peculiar to itself, and are called *jus civile;* the rules constituted by natural reason for all, are observed by all nations alike, and are called *jus gentium.* So the laws of Rome are partly peculiar to itself, partly common to all nations."[25] Civil law seems to have had two senses: On the one hand, it applies to conflicts among civilians concerning property, damages, and other kinds of private disputes; on the other hand, it was seen as local law—the law of the city as an organized body of citizens. The very concept of citizenship in the Roman imperial period, then, is stretched between the overarching case of Roman citizenship, which takes precedence over other forms of membership, yet remains limited by its historic and juridical links to the city of Rome, retaining as it were a "particular" core, and the many municipalities that coexisted within the imperial framework, largely preserving their procedural, linguistic, and cultic specificities despite their general subordination to Roman law.

Paul is a case in point. When he is arrested in Jerusalem by a representative of the Roman law at the end of Acts, he identifies himself first as a Jew and a Tarsian: "I am a man which am a Jew of Tarsus, a city in Cilicia, a citizen [*polites*] of no mean city" (KJV, Acts 21:39). A few verses later, he will assert his Roman citizenship: "Is it lawful for you to scourge a man who is a Roman citizen [*Rhomaios*], and uncondemned?" (RSE, Acts 22:25). Paul was a citizen of Tarsus, which had a substantial property qualification (meaning, of course, that not all residents of Tarsus were citizens). His family likely gained its wealth from tentmaking, a fitting occupation for one who would travel from city to city creating new communities within existing civic orders. Paul also identifies himself as an active participant in the Jewish community, a largely self-regulating body with its own courts; in Jerusalem we see the young Saul working on behalf of the Sanhedrin. Finally, he was, in his own declaration before the law, a Roman citizen,[26] the last but not the least of his civil affiliations.

Saul/Paul: rather than indicating a covenantal transformation, in the tradition of Abram/Abraham or Jacob/Israel, the two names of the apostle may more accurately be said to signify his membership in more than one community.[27] The Jewish name Saul recognizes his participation in Judaism, the added phrase "of Tarsus" locates his birthplace in the Hellenistic city-state (Acts 9:11), and his Roman name Paul "was part of his triple name as a Roman citizen: it is the Roman cognomen Paulus."[28] These multiple identifications with specific legal orders cannot simply be conceived as concentric circles, with Rome defining the outer limit. Rather, Rome, Tarsus, and Jerusalem define fields of overlapping membership for Paul. Of these, Tarsus follows most closely the outlines of a classical city-state, understood as a qualified citizen group inhabiting a specific urban locale under an established set of laws and institutions.[29] When Paul addresses his open letters to inhabitants of specific cities—Corinthians, Philippians, Colossians, Thessalonians—he evokes this classical tie between *politiea* as citizenship and *politea* as commonwealth. Paul also conceives of Israel as a "commonwealth" *(politeia)* defined by "covenants of promise" (Eph 2:12); the Jewish *politeuma* in Tarsus would have answered to Jerusalem in some matters while remaining subject to Tarsus and Rome in others. Finally, if Rome describes an imperial horizon around these provincial centers, it does so as a kind of inflated polis, a republican city-state blown into an empire and stretched to its conceptual limits: even under the Empire, "the notion of citizenship of small municipalities . . . remained . . . basic to the structure of Rome's dominions."[30] The classical city-state, the diasporic nation, and the inflated *res publica:* these intersecting and often incommensurate circles of jurisdictional identity define the peculiar visa of Paul, citizen-saint, as we see him ticking off each type of membership in his confrontations with the laws of different cities, provinces, and groups.

In the early passions of the Church, starting with that of Christ himself, the local Jewish officials have their own courts, but they are secondary to the Roman court. Jesus, who was not a Roman citizen, was tried by Pilate, the Roman governor of Judea, on charges brought against him by the Jews. In the case of Stephen's death in Acts (he will be called Stephen Protomartyr because he is the first martyr of the early Church), the juridical process is carried out entirely within the jurisdiction of the highest Jewish court, the Sanhedrin: Stephen is accused, tried, and then stoned. In Luke's narration, the form of execution is a collective act verging on riot, but its legality is guaranteed by the presence of Saul: "But they cried out with a loud voice and stopped their ears and rushed together upon him. Then they cast him out of the city and stoned him; and the witnesses laid down their garments at the feet of a young man named Saul" (Acts 7:57).

Saul witnesses the execution as a representative of the Jewish court. When he suffers conversion on the road to Damascus, he will on a symbolic level take the place that his own actions had helped to vacate, repeatedly coming before the Jewish law as a subverter of the laws and a defiler of the Temple, ultimately appearing before the Sanhedrin itself (Acts 23:1–10).[31]

But Paul, unlike Stephen, was a Roman citizen. In Acts, Paul's citizenship first emerges as a positive factor in Philippi, a Roman colony rather than a province, meaning that its citizens were also citizens of Rome, ruled by the *ius italicum,* or law of Italy. Philippi was populated by veterans of war who had lost their lands in Italy when they fought on the losing side of Mark Antony.[32] Philippi had, fittingly, been the site of Augustus and Antony's victorious alliance against the assassins of Caesar in 42 BCE; it thus represents an epochal moment in the transition from the Republic to the Empire, and hence in the historical passion of citizenship itself. In both the Acts of the Apostles and Paul's Epistle to the Philippians, the city is identified with a heightened sense of citizenship. G. F. Hawthorne notes that Paul's exhortation to the Philippians that they "conduct [*politeusthe*]" themselves "in a manner worthy of the Gospel of Christ" (Phil 1:27) literally means "'to live as a citizen, to live as freepersons,' even 'to take part in government.'"[33] The church at Philippi, the first on the mainland of Europe proper, was made up primarily of Greeks. When Paul and Silas are arrested, it is not, as in so many other cases in Acts, because they are disturbing the *Jewish* community, but because they pose a threat to the *Roman* character of the colony: "These men are Jews and they are disturbing our city. They advocate customs which it is not lawful for us Romans to accept or practice (Acts 16:20–21). Paul and Silas are presumably arrested as *peregrini,* foreigners—a word that would under Christianity come to mean "pilgrim," but in the imperial context referred to free foreigners.[34] Only after they have been attacked and imprisoned, and the jailer comes to release them secretly, by command of the magistrates, does Paul assert his rights as a citizen: "They have beaten us publicly, uncondemned, men who are Roman citizens [*Rhomaioi*], and have thrown us into prison; and do they now cast us out in secret? No! Let them come themselves and take us out" (Acts 16:37). Paul demands due process, a public release, and he does so on the basis of citizenship rights that have been violated.

So too at Jerusalem. A riot breaks out in Jerusalem, instigated, Luke tells us, by "the Jews from Asia" (Acts 21:27). The Roman tribune appears in order to restore order and arrests Paul, who initially identifies himself as a Jew and a citizen [*polites*] of Tarsus, but not yet as a Roman (Acts 21:39). Having persecuted Stephen at the beginning of his career, it appears Paul will follow Stephen's path of martyrdom before the Sanhedrin in Jerusalem—until, that is, he asserts his

Roman citizenship, effectively removing him from the jurisdiction of the Jewish court as well as the labile violence of the crowd. He and the tribune exchange the following words: "So the tribune came and said to him, 'Tell me, are you a Roman citizen?' And he said, 'Yes.' The tribune answered, 'I bought this citizenship *[politeia]* for a large sum.' 'But I was born a citizen,' said Paul" (Acts 22:27–28).[35] Paul takes special pride in being born a Roman citizen: he is, in effect, more Roman than the tribune who arrests him, a Roman born of Romans as much as a Hebrew born of Hebrews (Phil 3:5). Yet, as Arthur A. Rupprecht notes, "Paul did not mention that he was a Roman citizen until they began to stretch him out on a rack. It seems to have been a strategy of his that he did not reveal his status as a Roman citizen until he had been unlawfully treated."[36] It is as if Paul will only bring forward his Roman citizenship when his rights have been breached: it is a martyred citizenship, an abrogated or violated citizenship, that is active for him.

In the sequence of hearings that follow from his declaration of Roman citizenship in Jerusalem, Paul ultimately will "appeal to Caesar," that is, request a trial in Rome in order to avoid appearing before the Sanhedrin (Acts 25:12).[37] By claiming this privilege as a Roman citizen, Paul will set course for Rome, a city he has addressed by epistle but never visited in person. Traditions differ as to his fate upon arrival: Was he found guilty and executed, becoming a martyr of the early Church, as Eusebius and Jerome presume, or was he acquitted and hence enabled to pursue his mission in the west, in Spain, as Clement of Rome believed?[38] In any case, at the end of Paul's life his Roman citizenship is, as it were, *brought home,* drawn into alignment with the physical reality, urban locale, and imperial court of the city itself. The saint is a citizen: He has rights, and he will exercise these rights in order to live and die under Roman law, not under Jewish law. Perhaps this was the best way to close the book on Jewish law, to assert its merely local, *adiaphora* character. In dying as a Roman citizen, Paul dies into citizenship itself, insuring that citizenship in modernity will be forever marked by this passage from the particular to the universal, from a Judaism suddenly mapped as local (disavowing its universalist traditions, of which Paul was himself a spokesman) to a juridical instance whose imperial framework promises to universalize it. This at least is one way to link the biographical traditions recorded in Acts with the words of Paul himself in his epistles, and above all in his letter to the Romans. Read in view of Paul's passion of citizenship in Acts, Paul's letter *to* the Romans, to a mixed congregation of Jewish and Gentile Christians, is also a letter *from* the Romans, its open address prescripted by the capaciousness of the imperial vision in tension with the Greek and republican traditions of citizenship it has displaced and the diverse communities it has subsumed.

Of Circumcision and Citizenship, First Cut: Genesis

Paul's Epistle to the Romans, likely composed in 57 CE, stands at the head of the Pauline canon in both the Catholic and the Protestant Bibles, as his longest and most articulated theological statement.[39] Yet it should also be understood as a political and rhetorical document concerned with mediating conflict in a fractured and diverse congregation at Rome, split between Jewish and Gentile Christians. In the first chapter, Paul establishes the parameters of the letter's audience along with its basic theme, the equality of the nations *(ethne)* in Christ: "I am under obligation both to Greeks and to barbarians, both to the wise and to the foolish; so I am eager to preach the gospel to you also who are in Rome. For I am not ashamed of the Gospel: it is the power of God for salvation to every man who has faith, to the Jew first and also to the Greek" (Rom 1:14–16). Paul's address to the Romans presents a double mapping of world populations. Paul first expresses his obligation "to Greeks and to barbarians," taking up the Hellenistic division of peoples between civilized Greek-speakers and inarticulate non-Greeks. Paul then extends his message to the Christian community in Rome, understood as the modern repository of Greek culture. The next verse moves from the Hellenistic opposition between Greeks and barbarians to the Hebraic division of peoples between Jews and Gentiles, the Chosen People and "the nations" *(ethne)* at large. Paul's careful phrasing of the order of God's salvation, "to the Jew first and also to the Greek," recognizes the historical priority of the Jews in the reception of Revelation, yet insists as well on the necessary dissemination of that message to the second, larger group of Greeks. Finally, these lines, like the epistle in general, acknowledge and reconcile the claims of both groups in the new church by presenting faith as the common sign of righteousness for all Christians. Rome represents for Paul not simply another locale for Christian proselytism, but the juridical envelope that can send the Christian message worldwide. It is the only letter in which Paul is not addressing a church that he himself founded; although he writes to a specific community, he also in a sense addresses Rome itself, as a symbol of the future of a Church that would unite Jews and Gentiles in a new corporate body whose physical scope and demographic reach would be identical with that of the Empire itself.

The legacy of Romans to the Western discourse of national membership is split between Paul's urge to discount the legal observances of contemporary Judaism on the one hand and to grant historical significance to the Jews as a people on the other, positions that equally stem from Paul's sense of the Jews as a civil body governed by its own laws. By localizing that jurisdiction, seeing it as one instance of social functioning within a larger historical arena defined by the Gentiles, including the juridical rule of Rome, Paul was able both to acknowledge the continued relevance of Jewish law to the Jews and to discount its application to the Gentiles. The major sign of the Jews' civil status in Paul's writings is the rite of circumcision, a recurrent concern in Paul's conflicted fashioning of a Gentile mission out of his own training in the proto-rabbinic Judaism of the Pharisees. Physical yet not physiological, genealogical yet not genetic, circumcision marks the Jews off as a distinct people without becoming a "racial" indicator in the modern sense of a biologically inherited trait. Put otherwise, circumcision is civic and covenantal rather than natural or native (the latter words being derived from the verb *nascor,* "to be born"). The theological debate about circumcision as it unfolds not only in Paul's epistles and their historic commentaries (Augustine, Luther), but also in later literary and philosophical sublations of the Pauline problematic (Shakespeare, Hegel, Freud, Lacan) demarcates a crucial yet largely unexamined structuration of the contested fields of citizenship, nationhood, and race. Writing as a member of at least three distinct citizen groups (Tarsus, Rome, and Israel), Paul performed an epochal "ethno-graphy," a foundational graphing of the *ethne,* of nations taken together and nations standing apart, of overlapping, expanding, and exclusive memberships and membership protocols. By conceiving of Jewish law as having local jurisdiction, Paul could conceptualize Israel as a discrete historical phase in the past and a regional set of civil and cultural practices in the present. In European Christendom, increasingly distanced from the Jewish grounds of Paul's own life and thought, circumcision would increasingly come to denote a preserve of atavistic, dangerously materialist rites whose persistence continues to challenge the narrative of Western history. Yet even through its racializations and radical otherings, circumcision remains a signature of covenant and hence a founding instance of the literature of citizenship; one strain of this book is dedicated to reading for the civic promise of that covenantal signature beneath its fantasmatic refunctionalizations.

In Genesis God establishes his covenant with Abraham by commanding the rite of circumcision:

> *This is My covenant, which ye shall keep, between Me and you and thy seed after thee: every male among you shall be circumcised. And ye shall be circumcised in the flesh of your foreskin; and it shall be a token of a covenant betwixt Me and you. And he that is eight days old shall be circumcised among you, every male throughout your generations, he that is born in the house, or bought with money of any foreigner, that is not of thy seed. . . . And the uncircumcised male who is not circumcised in the flesh of his foreskin, that soul shall be cut off from his people; he hath broken My covenant.* (Gen 17:10–14)

The commandment of circumcision proceeds by first stating the basic requirement ("every male among you shall be circumcised"), and then progressively clarifying it, insisting on the physical specificity and the full reach of the commandment. The Jewish tradition insists on the genital physicality of the act; the commentaries raise the possibility of other corporeal sites (the lips) or other modes of circumcision (the internal or spiritual operation implied by the uncircumcised heart) only to discount them, often at great length.[40] The genital location sometimes receives moral rationalization; thus Ramban writes that God "has thereby placed a reminder in the organ of lust, which is the source of much trouble and sin."[41] Yet such moralizations feel secondary and apologetic; in the tradition, the real emphasis falls on the fact of genealogical propagation, the marking of that organ through which Abraham will become "the father of a multitude of nations" (Gen 17:4). In the argument of Sforno, "Since the token is connected with the organ whereby the species is perpetuated, it symbolized the eternity of the covenant."[42] Circumcision presents a kind of alleopathic inversion of the promise itself: by removing something from the organ of generation, generation itself will be enabled. The commandment is a nation-marking sign that links generations across time and space without, however, being a physically inherited trait; hence the rabbis agree that even someone who is "born circumcised" (without a foreskin) must still have blood drawn.[43] Unlike a birthmark, which would signify a "natural" or "blood" relationship, the scar left by ritual imposition manifests the maintenance of laws not themselves natural or even moral as the necessary foundation of the nation.

This nation-building emphasis continues to guide the question of the commandment's scope: Who exactly needs to be circumcised? If it were simply the ritual instantiation of a family connection, then the commandment would apply only to Abraham and the offspring promised to Sarah and himself. Yet the passage specifies a larger circle: Abraham's children by other women (Ishmael, born of the handmaid Hagar), and also any sons born to slaves who have no genealogical ties to Abraham; to this group, commentators add converts to Judaism (*gerim,* or proselytes).[44] David Novak, following the lead of the neo-Kantian, German-Jewish philosopher Hermann Cohen, notes that the evolving rules surrounding resident-aliens and converts *(gerim),* which involved both religious obligations and various forms of secular positive rights, form a precedent for "modern notions of citizenship."[45] Circumcision functions as the sign and mechanism of *naturalized citizenship,* since membership in the nation, whether incurred through birth or through other means, is equally ratified by circumcision.[46] During the rite of circumcision, the male person receives a Hebrew name, removing him from the realm of nature or from prior forms of identification and situating him a network of social, linguistic, and legal relations. Circumcision is both denaturing and naturalizing, an initiatory act of separation (from biology) and socialization (in a legally constituted membership set).[47]

So too, the consequences that stem from failure to circumcise do not entail eternal damnation or moral atrophy but rather excision from the group: "[T]hat soul shall be cut off from his people." In Rashi's gloss, "[H]e shall depart hence childless and shall suffer an untimely death"; the uncircumcised male is childless because no one will marry him, and his untimely death may be as much a consequence of social isolation as of divine intervention.[48] The emphasis falls once more on circumcision as a badge of membership in a national group constituted both temporally and spatially—across generations and (by the time of Paul and the rabbis) in Diaspora. It is also constituted legally, as part of a covenant or contract. The institution of *brit milah* falls far short of the nation-founding constitution of Israel at Sinai; it remains an affair of the *oikos,* the patriarchal household, an act of loose affiliation rather than formal political association. Nonetheless, this minimal contract represents an important initial moment of agreement to law and an ongoing commitment to participate in realizing the promises of law in its later evolutions and institutions.

The commandment of circumcision flows from God's earlier promise to Abraham: "My covenant is with thee, and thou shalt be the father of a multitude of nations" (Gen 17:4).[49] There are two sides of the covenant: God promises children to Abraham and Sarah, and Abraham agrees to mark his existing household and himself, and to commit his future progeny to do the same. The future is "under contract": both promised to Abraham, and committed by Abraham to uphold the human side of the agreement. As such, *brit milah,* the "covenant of circumcision," has a performative, contractual function: It operates as a kind of signature, an official imprimatur that validates and authenticates the agreement drawn up between Abraham and God. If Abraham doesn't "sign" the contract, the goods won't be delivered. Circumcision makes the contract effective, bringing it into being as a positive relation. It is an expression not so much of blind faith as of good faith, a willingness to execute one's part of the bargain in order to get the deal going. If Abraham doesn't sign, God won't provide the generations who will carry out the future signing; forfeiture of the agreement abrogates the very ground or "paper"—the bodies of future children—on which the repeated ratification of the agreement is to take place.

If it is contractual, and involves the foundation of a social group, *brit milah* by no means signifies a "social contract" in the modern liberal sense. Abraham consents to be commanded, but he does not command himself; he is not *auto-nomos,* a law to himself. And the male children who submit to circumcision on the eighth day will not do so of their own will; they will be entered into a contract whose meaning and significance must escape them. The element of heteronomy, of an arbitrary law coming from outside, underwrites the scene of agreement. Indeed, circumcision along with a host of *hukkim*, or ritual laws, including those involving diet, the Sabbath, and the mixing of various substances, cannot be derived from human reason and do not submit easily to utilitarian readings. Though it inscribes the subject in a larger legal and linguistic order, the cut of circumcision is not itself a letter or a symbol, not an instrument or sign of reason. As such, it introduces a unique point of traumatic non-signification into the symbolic scene of group enrollment. In this sense, circumcision is fundamentally disengaged from later readings of contract founded on rationality and self-interest. Yet it remains part of the larger story, as an initial binding of command and consent that writes into the later tradition a repeated moment of contained violence, of managed trauma, that accompanies entry into the community formally constituted by its mark.[50] In the terms we have developed here, we could say that circumcision institutes a kind of *little death-into-citizenship*, measuring the passage into social relation through the letting of blood, the loss of flesh, and the severing of previous ties. To symbolize, to own, to take responsibility for that moment of excision is not to reject the rational order of citizenship but rather to render it accountable for the losses that membership exacts.

Does God's promise of "a multitude of nations [*goyim*]" apply only to Israel (as Ramban argues), or also to the other progeny of Abraham, the descendants of Ishmael and Esau (as Rashi suggests)?[51] Although the dominant tradition favors a restrictive reading of the passage, the plurality of "nations" grouped within the entity called Israel guarantees that the promised "nations" will not be defined only along blood lines. Circumcision, even while circum-scribing the boundaries of the national group through a physical sign, also allows for adoption, conversion, and naturalization. If the promise is indeed made to Israel alone, that single nation nonetheless contains "nations" within it, the half-brothers, neighbors, strangers, proselytes, and slaves who enter the community (or are entered into it) through the rite of circumcision. In the Jewish tradition, circumcision is in essence *not universal*, since its main function is to describe the parameters of a group in relation to God. At the same time, the nation signed into being by *brit milah* is a set whose boundaries can be crossed—how? Precisely by this rite.

Circumcision, of course, applies only to men. The means of Jewish naturalization for Gentile women was usually marriage (as in the case of Ruth), though there was a larger household or tribal dimension as well; when a male Gentile converted to Judaism by submitting to circumcision, he "brought into the fold the females, without further ado."[52] An especially interesting case for our purposes is that of the female prisoner of war in Deuteronomy 21: "Then thou shalt bring her home to thy house; and she shall shave her head, and pare her nails; and she shall put off the raiment of her captivity from her, and shall remain in thy house, and bewail her father and mother a full month; and after that thou mayest go in unto her, and be her husband, and she shall be thy wife" (Deut 21:12–13). Heightening the archetypal conflation of wedding and funeral rites, the female prisoner of war on her road to conversion and naturalization performs rites of mourning for her past life.[53] As in circumcision, the prisoner-of-war's forced entry into the Jewish *oikos* involves a death into citizenship brought into symbolization by these prescripted rituals. (The role of marriage ceremonies in effecting radical status change in relation to the *politeia* is explored in chapter 5 on *Antigone* and *Measure for Measure*.)

In exchange for submitting himself and his household to circumcision, Abraham is promised not only land and progeny, but also the more ambiguous offer to become a blessing to the nations, tribes, or families of the world (e.g., Gen 18:18, 22:18). This promise, which will occupy Paul in Galatians (3:8–10) as an invitation to open Israel to the Gentiles, has a mixed history in Jewish interpretation. Does it mean that the nations of the world will be ruled by Israel? that they will envy Israel? that Gentile communities will benefit from the righteous example, good deeds, and prosperity of their Jewish neighbors? These variations all share the assumption that the covenant itself, with its explicit community-defining prescriptions, will be maintained by the Jews, not, as Luther averred, because they thought that following the law would save them, but because obeying the covenant was their means of maintaining both their relation to God and their integrity as a group.[54] Jubilees, a text from the second century BCE, makes the point with almost comic insistence, as if warding off the Pauline reading in advance: "And all the nations of the earth will bless themselves by your seed because your father obeyed me *and* observed my restrictions *and* my commandments *and* my laws *and* my ordinances *and* my covenant" (emphasis added).[55]

The covenant of circumcision plays out the characteristically Jewish tension between the unique election and identity of Israel as a nation apart and the potential universality of its historical example, ethical code, and single God. From the Jewish perspective, the significance of Israel to the nations of the world can be attained only through the careful maintenance and regulation of its own borders. It is not a question of choosing the world or the nation, but rather of opening up to the world—as "light" or example to those outside, as participants in a host community, or as a political force in relation to other groups—precisely by obeying those laws that keep the nation separate (above all, the laws of circumcision, of diet, and of Sabbath rest). Only through its unique identity, a position sustained not by blood but by its special laws, can Israel assume a larger historical function. Circumcision constitutes the subject in a legal framework, denaturing the body in order to produce a *naturalized*, that is purely legal, covenantal identity. In Judaism, circumcision is not opposed to Israel's world significance as a "light unto the nations," but rather lies at the very center of it, articulated by the cut of covenant that determines the boundaries—at once absolutely exclusive and absolutely permeable—of the Chosen People.

Of Circumcision and Citizenship, Second Cut: Paul

Paul's Epistle to the Romans includes an extended analysis of Genesis 17. The scene of Abraham's covenant with God, with its comprehensive commandment to circumcise, had already occupied Paul in his letter to the Galatians (c. 54 CE), a Gentile congregation recently visited by Judaizing Christian missionaries. In Galatians, Paul had declared unequivocally that "if you receive circumcision, Christ will be of no advantage to you" (Gal 5:2). He countered the Genesis prooftext by pointing out that a verse attesting that Abraham "'believed God, and it was reckoned to him as righteousness'" appears two chapters before Abraham receives directions for *brit milah* (Gal 3:6; Gen 15:6). From this, Paul deduced that faith precedes law, which is simply "added to faith because of transgressions" (Gal 3:19), a supplement and crutch to support the Israelites until the coming of Christ.

In Romans, Paul faced a more demanding rhetorical situation, since he likely addressed a mixed congregation of Gentile and Jewish converts, the first group having no immediate relation to the Hebrew Scriptures, and the second circle still invested in the national traditions of Judaism.[56] Paul's concern in Romans both to accommodate and to discount the legal and national claims of Judaism probably reflects the division of the Roman congregation between "Greek and Jew" as well as Paul's own conflicted position as an educated and observant Pharisee who had nonetheless accepted Jesus as the Messiah and hence as the "end of the law" (Rom 10:4). In addition, there is the overarching "Roman" vector of address, not only to the Roman Christians as a distinct congregation, but to the Roman juridical and political framework as a map, model, and shelter for Paul's universalism.

In Romans, Paul returns to the passages in Genesis 17 first broached in Galatians. Once again Paul points out that the Hebrew Scriptures record Abraham's faith (Gen 15:6) before introducing the covenant of circumcision (Gen 17). From this he concludes as follows:

> *We say that faith was reckoned to Abraham as righteousness. How then was it reckoned to him? Was it before or after he had been circumcised? It was not after, but before he was circumcised. He received circumcision as a sign or seal*

of the righteousness which he had by faith while he was still uncircumcised. The purpose was to make him the father of all who believe without being circumcised and who thus have righteousness reckoned to them, and likewise the father of the circumcised who are not merely circumcised but also follow the example of the faith which our father Abraham had before he was circumcised. . . . [Justification] depends on faith, in order that the promise may rest on grace and be guaranteed to all his descendants—not only to the adherents of the law but also to those who share the faith of Abraham, for he is the father of us all, as it is written, "I have made you the father of many nations." (Rom 4:9–17)

Unlike his parallel discussion in Galatians, Paul's discussion here is careful to include the Jews as well as the Gentiles as true children of Abraham; both are encompassed in the "nations [*ethne*]" promised to the first patriarch. As we have seen, an inclusive definition of the nations was also elaborated in one strand of the prophetic and rabbinic tradition, which had debated the extent to which the *goyim* in this passage applied to the other children of Abraham. Moreover, even the exclusive formulation (nations = Israel alone) favored in Jewish exegesis contains within it a mixed group constituted by circumcision as a rite of national initiation shared by slave, proselyte, and native son alike.

Paul, by identifying the *goyim* promised to Abraham with the Gentile nations, resolves this Jewish tension in the most inclusive direction.[57] In doing so, however, he changes forever the status of circumcision as the ritual mark that founds Israel as a nation elected by God. For now it is faith, with or without circumcision, that establishes true inclusion among God's elect, which is no longer conceived as a national unit at all. Indeed, the new Church is more like an empire than a nation, and here our prologue on citizenship becomes relevant. The imperial analogy can be taken in two directions. In one framework, membership in Israel in the messianic era parallels Roman citizenship in the Empire: In each case, membership is exclusive, limited, and linked to a specific city or locale, yet in its very exclusivity acknowledges and even equalizes other domains or jurisdictions. Paul preaches to "the Jew first and also to the Greek" (Rom 1:16); further in Romans he asks, "Then what advantage has the Jew? Or what is the value of circumcision? Much in every way" (3:1–2). In these passages, Paul grants to membership in Israel legal, logical, and historical priority in the vast landscape of multiple citizenries. Like Roman citizenship, participation in Israel represents the highest status available; like Roman citizenship, however, its ranks are also limited, alleviating Gentiles of the need to enter into its ritual of civil initiation. There is a kind of rapprochement here between the Jewish conviction that adherence to the law is what can make Israel into a light for the nations on the one hand, and the republican core, the continued tie to a city and its laws, at the heart of imperial Rome on the other.

Identifying himself as a Jew to the Jews in his Roman audience, Paul writes, "They are Israelites, and to them belong the sonship, the glory, the covenants, the giving of the law, the worship, and the promises; to them belong the patriarchs, and of their race [*sarx:* flesh] . . . is the Christ" (Rom 9:4–5). Paul does not completely dissolve the national difference between Jew and Greek within the new covenant of Christ, but rather translates and preserves membership in Israel into the operative core of a *philosophy of history* that is in turn founded on a *literary hermeneutics.* Israel *is* special, Paul asserts in this passage, and its privilege rests in its historical function, its role in laying the genealogical and prophetic lines that have just now been realized in Christ's death and resurrection. Echoing the Roman framework of citizenship, Paul uses the priority of the Jews in a table of status types to salvage what Hans Hübner calls "the theological relevance [of] the history of Israel" by granting the Jews a unique place as first citizens in a brilliant tableau of peoples participating in God's unfolding plan.[58] To think of Roman and Jewish citizenship protocols as covalent would not have been impossible for a man in possession of both affiliations.

But the Roman analogy works in another (if not opposite) direction as well. In this second scheme, Israel functions as a local jurisdiction whose rules have limited legitimacy in their own sphere, within a larger order that withdraws from passing judgment on regional matters of custom and culture. In this framing of the situation, the Gentiles become the bearers of a natural law—what Gaius in his *Institutes* calls the *ius gentium,* the law of the nations, that transcends the written *hukkim* of the Jews. In Paul's words to the Roman Romans, "When Gentiles who have not the law do by nature what the law requires, they are a law to themselves [*he-auto . . . nomos*]" (2:14). Paul writes further that "those who are physically uncircumcised but keep the law will condemn you who have the written code [*gramma*] and circumcision but break the law" (2:27).[59] In these passages, Paul distinguishes between an unwritten ethical law that is natural or rational in basis and the "written code" of the Jews, signed by the physical act of circumcision. The first is rational and universal, while the second is local and limited.[60] Here we might recall the moments in Philippi and Jerusalem when Paul crosses from the jurisdiction of the Sanhedrin to the court of Roman law by virtue of his citizenship status, in effect localizing Jewish law, calling attention to its regional character. This act "civil-izes" Jewish law—that is, it insists on its character as a local code, mandating a set of customs and practices that cohere into a particular civilization or culture. This civil-ization of Judaism derives from important aspects of Judaism's own juridical-historical consciousness, but, by identifying Israel with the particular, the merely local, as such, it has the effect of undercutting not only the continued authority of Jewish law, but also Judaism's contributions to universal thinking.[61]

This civil-izing instinct is perhaps most visible in Paul's hermeneutics, which historicize Judaism into a particular phase of God's larger plan. It is thanks to Paul's insistent linkage of historiography and hermeneutics that the Hebrew Bible, reconceived as the so-called Old Testament, has been so securely woven into the scriptural canon, exegetical consciousness, and historical impulses of Gentile Christianity, which (very unlike Paul) so often has known nothing or worse than nothing of Judaism itself.[62] Paul's historicization of Judaism into a prior epoch and an "Old" Testament, however, was also designed to relativize the legal foundations that would legislate Israel's ongoing viability as a distinctive nation or people. In Paul's dynamic understanding, Israel's *history* subsumes, explains, and qualifies Israel's *law,* which becomes one moment in a progressive epochal scheme rather than a constitutional body united and constantly renewed by the observance of scriptural commandments. Paul's reading of circumcision in Genesis 17 is a prime example of his programmatic subsumption of Jewish law within an historical hermeneutics. In the Torah, circumcision had functioned as the "token of a covenant [*l'aot brit*]" between God and Abraham, the word "token" recalling the use of official seals to secure documents and mark them as authentic, "equivalent to the modern use of signatures."[63] The performative, contractual language does indeed remain in Paul's gloss, where circumcision appears as a "sign [*semeion*] or seal [*sphragis*]" of faith. Yet the performative emphasis has subtly shifted into a semiotic one, a move enunciated in the placement of "sign" before "seal," *semeion* before *sphragis,* in Paul's introduction of the imagery of tokens. For circumcision no longer "seals" the covenant as a contractual relationship that needs to be brought into effect by a positive act; rather, it has become the external sign of *faith,* an intrinsically internal state or condition. Rather than bringing a relationship into being through ritual performance, circumcision manifests a state that preexists it, instituting a hermeneutic relationship between surface and depth in place of the performative and constitutive function that had earlier defined it.

The *hermeneutic* division between sign and meaning also institutes a *historical* distinction between an initial prefiguration and its later fulfillment. In the case of circumcision, what had once been binding law is now a powerful but limited metaphor of a new, era-defining event, and our access to this resignification of circumcision is the changing meaning of Scripture as it moves from one epochal reading community to another. Thus the Epistle to the Colossians (likely from the school of Paul rather than the apostle himself) states that in Christ "you were circumcised with a circumcision without hands, by putting off the body of the flesh in the circumcision of Christ" (Col 2:11). Here, circumcision has once more become a fully positive rather than a negative or qualified image, the act that unites Jew and Gentile in the Christian community of Colossae. The rite can only carry this affirmative signification, however, because *it is no longer circumcision.* Instead, the passage refers to a new circumcision, namely baptism, figured as the historical and symbolic sublation of *brit milah*—a physical act executed on the flesh of the body—into a spiritual sacrament made "without hands."

In Romans, Paul spells out the historicizing metaphorization of circumcision in the context of the mixed mission to the Romans: "Circumcision indeed is of value if you obey the law, but if you break the law, your circumcision becomes uncircumcision. . . . For he is not a real Jew who is one outwardly, nor is true circumcision something external and physical. He is a Jew who is one inwardly, and real circumcision is a matter of the heart, spiritual and not literal" (Rom. 2:25–29).

In Romans circumcision does not, as in the harsher judgment of Galatians, sever man from Christ (Gal 5:4). Perhaps more devastating from a Jewish point of view, however, circumcision in Romans *simply doesn't matter,* since "real circumcision," and with it "real" Judaism, is now an internal state and not a national mark at all. In Romans, circumcision is *adiaphora,* or indifferent—not counting toward justification, a ruling that grants circumcision a merely local, we could even say "cultural," status, as the sign of one *ethnos* among others but no longer as a legally binding statute that links a single nation to God. In this letter to the Romans, one version of the imperial model—which casts Judaism as a local jurisdiction in relation to the general jurisdiction of the universal Church—takes precedence over its variant, in which membership in Israel would be primary but limited, open to non-Jews only through precisely regulated processes of naturalization.

Paul says in his first letter to the Corinthians, "To the Jews I became as a Jew, in order to win the Jews. . . . To those outside the law, I became as one outside the law . . . that I might win those outside the law" (1 Cor 9:20–21). Here, the religious practices of the Jews become a rhetorically manipulable regional vocabulary used by the master-builder of the new church polity in his task of persuasion rather than a set of divinely prescribed laws. Indeed, Stephen Barton has read the entire letter as an act of "deliberative rhetoric" aimed at building a single eschatological community on the boundary of "two social worlds, two communities," an act that requires Paul to develop the classical political skills of rhetorical accommodation.[64] In a mixed community such as that at Corinth or Rome, the question of law is not simply theological or soteriological, but practical and political, "concerned with laws and the law in so far as they build up or break down a people's common life."[65] At Corinth as at Rome, Jewish law has become civil, in the sense of Gaius's *Institutes:* "[T]he rules established by a given state for its own members are peculiar to itself." But because Jewish Christians have entered into a mixed community with Gentiles, the continued relevance and effectiveness—the civility, the social viability—of these laws is now at issue.

This civil-ization of Jewish law corresponds on the synchronic axis to Paul's epochal definition of the Jewish contribution on the diachronic axis: Whereas in the historical register, Judaism embodies a crucial but superceded moment in the story of God's grace, in the spatial dimension, Judaism represents a set of local practices that have their own limited value and appeal, as long as they do not stand in conflict with the peaceful operation of the new open community that they are invited to join. If the general move of Paul's epistles is to dissolve Israel's covenantal bonds in the universal ideal of Christianity, in Romans, those bonds nonetheless find a new—we could say characteristically modern—place in this universe, as that which gives both an historical period and an existing linguistic and social group its limited, relative coherence within a larger scheme. In this expanding universe, the prophetic references to uncircumcised hearts become a scriptural prooftext for Paul's internalizing revision of the covenantal sign. Once spiritualized, it can also be infinitely extended: No longer the singular badge of Jewish men, this new circumcision of the heart joins both sexes, all peoples, and all classes into common fellowship with Christ. As for physical circumcision, it is a matter of local custom and family tradition—a perfectly permissible "ethnic," civil, or cultural matter, but no longer of fundamental religious interest, since nationality itself is no longer of theological significance except from the historical point of view.

Jump Cut: The Case of Spenser

At stake in the Pauline legacy is not only the Jews themselves as an historic people and specific demography, but also the general economy of historical consciousness, literary imagination, and the creation of political communities in later Christendom. Take, for example, the following passages from the *Faerie Queene,* where Spenser maps a tripartite topography of divine revelation in order to fashion the scene of literary inspiration for the emerging English canon. In the House of Holiness, Red Crosse is led from Sinai to the Mount Olive to Parnassus:

> *That done, he leads him to the highest Mount,*
> *Such one, as that same mighty man of God,*
> *That bloud-red billowes like a walled front*

On either side disparted with his rod,
Till that his army dry-foot through them yod,
Dwelt fortie dayes upon; where writ in stone
With bloudy letters by the hand of God,
The bitter doome of death and balefull mone
He did receive, whiles flashing fire about him shone.

Or like that sacred hill, whose head full hie,
Adornd with fruitfull Olives all arownd,
Is, as it were for endlesse memory
Of that deare Lord, who oft thereon was fownd,
For ever with a flowring girlond crownd;
Or like that pleasaunt Mount, that is for ay
Through famous Poets verse each where renownd,
On which the thrise three learned Ladies play
Their heavenly notes, and make full many a louely lay. (1.x.53–54)

Each mountain is a site of revelation—that is, a place where divine language is concretized as historical act, inaugurating a cultural program recorded, codified, and passed on as inspired poetry. Sinai institutes the epoch of Jewish revelation, inscribed in a Book whose ethical and ritual laws set apart and distinguish—render *kadosh*, "holy" or "separate"—one nation from all the rest. Mount Olive, condensing the sites of Christ's famous sermon, his transfiguration, his untimely meditations, and his ascension, commemorates the replacement of the stony writing of the Old Covenant with the incarnated *logos* of the New, inaugurating a new historico-theological poetics based on preaching the Word to the Gentile nations. Finally, Parnassus houses the Nine Muses of classical mythology, who inspire the secular ideal of heroic and poetic fame that legislates the *translatio* of classical learning. These three moments of revelation—classical, Jewish, and Christian—are not simply mythic archetypes in an ahistorical syncretic vision, since each founds a distinct epoch constellated by its own set of meaningful coordinates, its own habits of religious, poetic, and national imagination—in brief, its own culture or civilization.

In this range of momentous mountains, of summational summits, Spenser sets Sinai off in its own stanza, while the Christian and classical mountains make up two mirroring halves of a single prosodic room. Although each mountain institutes or "reveals" its own historical program, their topographies tend to fall into two rather than three distinct types: three mountains, but in two ranges of meaningful form. On the one side, we have Sinai, which instantiates the topography of the sublime. Sinai glosses "the highest mount"; as first and foremost a simile of size, a visualization of the peak's majestic height, the first line announces the function of constitutive contrast that governs the stanza. As the bearer of a "rod" that "disparted" the Red Sea, Moses, like the God of Genesis, is the agent of a primal division, the at once creative and destructive separation of water from land that allows the Israelites to traverse the Red Sea "dry-foot." This act of creationist separation, the operation of a primal cut or rift, is repeated in the "flashing fire" that accompanies the revelation of the Law at Sinai; according to rabbinic commentaries, only the sublimely unintelligible sound of thunder, and not the content of the law itself, was heard by the Israelites assembled at the base of the mountain. In this reading, the law, and with it the nation, was instituted in and as a flash, a pure punctual cut in the unfolding experience of the people that was only subsequently interpreted and organized into a legal code and a historical narrative.

If Spenser's Sinai is shaped like lightening, its color is red. The "bloud-red billows" of the disparted sea give way to the "bloudy letters" "writ in stone" on the summit of Sinai; in the associative waves of the stanza, the displaced waters of the Red Sea lap against the jagged ridges of Sinai, staining the locus of revelation with the errant memory of desert exile. In the stanza, Sinai represents both an antidote to the wandering of Exodus and a heightened emblem of it, the spaces of the mountain and the desert linked by the shared attribute of blood. As A. C. Hamilton points out, the "bloudy letters" refer to "the blood of the covenant" (Ex 24:8)—not only the blood of animal sacrifice with which Moses signs his announcement of God's ordinances,[66] but also, I would add, the blood of circumcision, another inscriptive stroke that sets apart through its initiatory mark. The circumcision of the name onto the body repeats God's forceful engraving of words in stone; both are acts of violent inscription that mark the legal bonds and boundaries of the national community.

Spenser's picture of the Old Testament is, of course, already colored by the New; Spenser envisions Sinai from the epochal divide traversed by Paul, whose identification of the law with death bloodies the scene of Jewish revelation and lays the groundwork for the transition from Sinai to Olive in Spenser's succession of stanzas and periods. Whereas Spenser's Sinai is governed by the blood-red topography of the sublime cut, the twin peaks of Mount Olive and Parnassus ring with the verdant harmonies of the beautiful circle. In these perfectly paired green worlds, the "flowring girlond" of olive trees that commemoratively crowns Christ's "sacred hill" is mirrored in the music of the "thrice three learned Ladies," whose "louely lay" is an art of circling refrains, of harmonious echoes. At the same time, the two are kept distinct as complementary yet historically distinctive cultural programs; in Carol Kaske's assessment, the stanza's "schematic juxtaposition but not fusion of Christian with pagan elements contributes to the effect of iridescence rather than steady translucence of the divine in the human."[67] Olive and Parnassus, mirroring each other, programmatically oppose the picture of Sinai, which they nonetheless subsume through the at once inclusive/inframing and sublime/contrastive operation of epic simile. Rolling hills rather than jagged peaks, the pastoral mounts of Olive and Parnassus counter and cancel the reddened desert of the previous stanza. Rather than locating the Judeo-Christian worldview on one side of a historical divide and pagan antiquity on the other, Spenser joins Christendom and classicism in a mirroring diptych of complementary epochs that negates the harsher aesthetic of Sinai. It is as if the sublime cut of the law instituted at Sinai established the very possibility of coordinating classical and Christian aesthetics across its traumatic "disparting."[68]

The nation-founding scene at Sinai takes on a specifically English life in the stanzas following the triple simile, in which Contemplation reveals to Redcrosse his genealogy "from English race" (1.x.60.1) and announces his destiny to become "thine own nations frend / And Patrone," "Saint *George* of mery England" (1.x.61.7–9). The celebration of Britain as a nation elected by God depends on the series of symbolizing separations commemorated in the Sinai passage. Canto 10 moves from the bloody cut of Sinai to the "chosen people" of the "new *Hierusalem*" (1.x.57) to the "nation" of "mery England" (1.x.61), a movement from the singular historical nation of the Jews, to its supercession in the cosmopolitan city of elected Gentiles, to its typological re-instantiation as the divinely mandated modern nation of England. Finally, the negative actuality of the Jews in their mode of survival past supercession finds its destiny in an affiliated passage, the Arlo Hill of the "Mutabilitie Cantos." Arlo Hill, a landmark of Spenser's estate in Ireland, provides the occasion for a digressive Ovidian etiology of the "wasting" of Ireland, the fall of the island from pastoral resort to dangerous desert. Like the mountain simile of book 1, Arlo Hill juxtaposes the green world of the garden—associated with both Christian and classical topoi—with the red world of the desert. Reading these mountain sequences next to each other invites identification of the *inveterate Irish* with the *inveterate Jews*, symptomatic signs of a historical process that they themselves have set into motion.

The Pauline discourse of nations allows us to recover specific forms of national consciousness informing Spenser's local, national, and poetic vision, not as an external ground or context, but as a generative element in the very fabric of poetic production. My larger claim is that the vicissitudes of *ethnos* after Paul animate the literary tradition neither as a sociological datum nor as a purely ideological construct, but as one of the crucial mythemes of Western thought, a charged article that constellates biblical exegesis, Renaissance texts, and modern methods in relation to each other.

Ephesian Conclusions

The letter to the Ephesians, likely written by a disciple of Paul to the congregation at Ephesus, pulls together key themes concerning circumcision, citizenship, and the fortunes of typology:

> *Therefore remember that at one time you Gentiles in the flesh, called the uncircumcision by what is called the circumcision . . . were at that time separated from Christ, alienated from the commonwealth* [politea] *of Israel, and strangers to the covenants of promise. . . . But now in Christ Jesus you who were once far off have been brought near in the blood of Christ. For he is our peace, who has made us both one, and has broken down the dividing wall of hostility, by abolishing in his flesh the law of commandments and ordinances, that he might create in himself one new man in place of the two. . . . So then you are no longer strangers* [xenoi] *and sojourners* [paroikoi]*, but you are fellow citizens* [sumpolites] *with the saints* [hagios] *and members of the household* [oikeios] *of God, built upon the foundations of the apostles and prophets, Christ Jesus himself being the cornerstone. (Eph 2:11–20)*

Prior to the messianic moment, the Gentiles had not by and large been included in the *politea*—the commonwealth and citizenry—of Israel, since entry into Judaism had been carefully monitored by the rite of circumcision. Now, however, Jews and Gentiles are drawn together as fellow citizens, *sumpolites,* in a single community built on Jewish and apostolic foundations. Those who had been *paroikoi*—neighbors but not citizens—can now join the *oikos,* the household economy, of the Church. In order to erect this big tent, however, the "law of commandments and ordinances" needed to be abolished, since its *hukkim* were designed to police rather than to open the borders of the Jewish *politea.*

Fellow citizens with the saints: in this phrase from Ephesians, the two key terms of this project are yoked together. The Church builds a community of citizen-saints, of persons from diverse backgrounds, likely with continuing multiple memberships, to come together as equals in a politico-religious body. Moreover, they come together *in this world.* If Pauline citizenship entails the risk of martyrdom and the death of local identifications, it is not simply because a heavenly citizenship is at stake. The standard line on Pauline citizenship translates it to the world above. So rules *The Dictionary of Paul and His Letters:* "The sense that Christians are headed for a citizenship in the next life is a powerful force in Paul's theology."[69] Citizenship can be redeemed as a model of engagement and equality in community, but only when it is projected into the other world, as a *sacra conversazione,* a heavenly civility. Yet is such a translation true for either the

Paul of Acts or the Paul of the Epistles? By pinning Christian action into a legal scene that forever captures it in this world, in the *saeculum,* the playing out of citizenship in the public sphere of Acts leaves in place (though not untouched) the institutions of the imperial *res publica.* By claiming his rights as Roman citizen, Paul refuses to suffer the martyrdom of Stephen or repeat the passion of Jesus. When time is short, public speech is more important than an early death. Paul's declaration of rights materializes a juridical and civic dimension that calls the Church to a certain immanence, a being in the world. Giorgio Agamben has argued that Paul's political theology is messianic rather than other-worldly. Messianic time is, in Agamben's felicitous phrase, *the time that remains,* a contracted time, fraught with possibility and responsibility, a time which is, potently and poignantly, now ("*ho nyn kairos,* 'le temps de maintenant'").[70] The public sphere of Pauline citizenship revolves in the time of the here and now. The deliberative, occasional, and crisis-oriented quality of the Epistles—their political and pragmatic character, and their resulting inconsistencies when read from a purely theological point of view—indicate the civic dimension and urgency of the apostle's interventions.

The new citizenship in Christ may take the geographical limits of the Roman Empire as its horizon and Jewish covenantal thinking as its formula, but it dissolves the status framework of the first and the national exclusivity of the second in favor of a kind of universal suffrage, with "suffrage" indicating not only a set of rights, but also a *suffering,* a bearing, an undergoing, a passion. In order for equality to be born, old forms of local identification must be either renounced or forever transvalued. Citizenship requires sacrifice; destruction precedes construction. In Paul's case, what is abolished—in the Hegelian sense of an *Aufhebung* that lifts what it destroys—is the continued validity of Jewish law as something more than custom, as a covenant that remains binding. The little death-into-citizenship signed by circumcision must now itself die so that it can be reborn as an interior principle capable of equalizing a community fractured by ethnic differences.

But what if certain forms of law and life refuse to die? In the Pauline discourse of citizenship, Judaism represents not only the historic origin of Christendom, but also the troubling beliement of its event, insofar as Israel exists beyond its historical abrogation. In Romans, Paul produced an historico-cultural definition of Judaism within the split registers of space and time, presenting Israel with a forced choice: either be theologically significant, but a thing of the past, or be a present phenomenon, but theologically irrelevant. The problem, of course, was that Judaism continued as a set of religious and social practices into the Christian era. Although not yet an urgent problem in the imminent eschatology of the early Church, the tenacity of Judaism would increasingly embarrass Christian historiography as it normalized into a set of quasi-permanent institutions. The modern Jew became the sign of a historical contradiction, a mote in the dialectical pattern of the Pauline vision. In the period of later Christendom, disengaged from Paul's own passionate and personal contact with Judaism, the historically economized and religiously tolerated *politeuma* of the Jews marked out by Paul could become the space of a negative ethnicity, no longer benignly indifferent but dangerously different and hence increasingly unbearable.

TWO

Deformations of Fellowship in Marlowe's *Jew of Malta*

The Acts of the Apostles ends with Paul's journey to Rome as a citizen under arrest. En route to his imperial trial in the capital, the Roman ship encounters a tempest and is driven off the coast of Malta, where the men swim ashore and are kindly treated by the "barbarian" inhabitants (Acts 27–28). This romance episode approaches the Virgilian in its motifs of storm, shipwreck, and survival and of hospitality and cultural contact within an overarching westward movement leading from the eastern Mediterranean to Rome. Lying between North Africa and Sicily, Malta represents one of several layered topoi in the allusive geography of Shakespeare's *Tempest.* By the time Shakespeare visits Malta, however, it has already been dramatically explored and appropriated by Christopher Marlowe in *The Jew of Malta.* What has happened to Paul's Jews by the time we meet them in Marlowe's Malta? In what kinds of social and political spaces do they congregate, and to what ends? And how does Marlowe's tour of Malta lay the groundwork for Shakespeare's Mediterranean meditations, especially *Merchant, Othello,* and *The Tempest,* each of which revisits Marlowe's Malta in search of civic and theological paradigms that would mediate between universal and particular memberships?

This chapter presents a reading of Marlowe's play in order to map the potentialities of Pauline motifs in the public sphere imagined by public theater in the decade when Shakespeare will find his voice. Barabas, like Shylock after him, resides at the border between the *civil* and the *civic.* Though both words pertain to citizenship, and often function interchangeably, the *civic* refers more precisely to the political participation of citizens in the official life of the polis, whereas the *civil* refers to those social, economic, and domestic associations, *civilian* rather than properly *civic,* that exist outside the operation of the political per se. Excluded from the *civic* order—the political world of rotating offices and legal privileges—Barabas has succeeded in *civil* society (the market), whose prepolitical forms of circulation and interest remain his fluid habitat to the very end. It is within this purely civil space that Barabas engineers, manipulates, and destroys different forms of fellowship, of private association, among Jews, Muslims, and Christians. In the post-Morality architecture of Marlowe's play, circumcision, sublime signature of covenant in the Torah, has been demoted to the material sign of the willful self-exclusion of Jews and Muslims from Christian forms of government. Moreover, the separation of the circumcised from the community of Christians becomes a model for the generalized separation of each from each, within the modern city and on the stage of international relations. At the same time, Paul's difficult conciliation of multiple memberships for himself and for the mixed congregations he struggled to build functions on a deeper level as a template of cross-group affiliation for those who find themselves outside the Christian circle in the play.

In this chapter, I call these civil associations "fellowships," not only because it is the word that Barabas himself uses, but also because of its origins in New Testament language. The Greek word *koinônia* (communion, community, association, partnership, fellowship) has as its core the idea of "having *something* in common with *someone*." In Paul's time, the word covered many types of human enterprise, from economic association to friendship and marriage.[1] Paul used *koinônia* to indicate the new circle of commonality formed by those who participated in belief in Christ and in the common meal or communion that commemorated his sacrifice. In Marlowe's play I argue that a bastardized version of Pauline fellowship—of prepolitical alliances among members of distinct religious groups—emerges as a blueprint for civil society, conceived in largely negative and farcical terms. By drowning his Jew in the hell's mouth of the old theater, Marlowe ultimately betrays the civil paradigms and civic possibilities activated by his antihero, choosing medievalism over modernism both aesthetically and historically.

Paul, the Jews, and Civil Society

In a legal document dating between 7 and 4 BCE, one Helenos, son of Tryphon, a Jewish resident of Alexandria, petitions for the reinstatement of his citizenship, a status inherited from his father that has somehow been rescinded or downgraded. As a consequence, Helenos is now subject to a poll tax, levied on noncitizens for the good of the commonwealth. The document includes a scribal correction replacing one designation—Alexandrian—with another—"a Jew of Alexandria"—to reflect his change in citizenship:

> *To Gaiois Tyrannios [Roman governor of Egypt], from Helenos, son of Tryphon, an ~~Alexandrian~~ a Jew of Alexandria. Most mighty governor, although my father was an Alexandrian citizen and I myself have always lived here and received, as far as my father's means allowed, the appropriate education* [padeia]*, I am in danger of not only being deprived of my native country [i.e., my Alexandrian citizenship], but also . . . [text defective here].*[2]

This fragmentary glimpse into a civic process concerns a Jew who was presumably raised as a legal member of both the Alexandrian *polis* and the Alexandrian *politeuma,* the legally recognized, semi-autonomous community of largely noncitizen Jews. This man's status and being as a citizen involved not only legal rights and immunities, but also an education, or *padeia,* that would have exposed him to the political, literary, and philosophical culture of the Greeks, as we see in the life and work of his famous compatriot, Philo of Alexandria, as well as in the Greek name of the litigant in question, Helenos.

Marlowe's Barabas is a "Jew of Malta" in the same sense that our petitioner is a "Jew of Alexandria": they are resident aliens, permitted to live and work in the city, but excluded from the privileges of citizenship, and subject to special taxation.[3] Excluded from the official life of the city, they nonetheless pursue their own forms of social and religious congregation, organized in and around a synagogue, the Greek term that came to indicate for the Jews in the Hellenistic and Latin Diaspora the act of assembly, the place of assembly, and the community so assembled.[4] In Malta, the Jewish community, in evidence since Roman times, bore the name *Universitas Judeorum*, a recurrent term in laws governing relations with the Jews in late antiquity and Christendom.[5] Malta's *universitas* (literally, "the whole," a number of persons associated in one body) was officially dissolved in 1492 with the expulsion of the Jews from Spain and its dominions, of which Malta was then a part.[6] In Marlowe's Malta, the Jews have not yet been expelled. Instead, they engage in trade and money-lending, and we also see them consulting among themselves concerning matters financial and political. A community apart, bound by their own peculiar rites and hermeneutic habits, they are also capable of interchange with Christians on matters exegetical as well as economic, as seen in Barabas's offer of commentaries on Maccabees to young Mathias, Christian suitor to his daughter.

Excluded from the *civic* life of the city, the Jews of Malta find their vitality in its *civil* operations: in its mercantile economy certainly, but also in the forms of prepolitical association and exchange that make up what has been called since Hegel "civil society" *(bürgerliche Gesellschaft)*—the realm of informal affiliation and negotiation that shapes the give and take of both the stock market and the coffee house, the university and the brothel. Stephen Greenblatt, in one of the strongest general readings of *The Jew of Malta*, has identified with great precision Marlowe's Jew with civil society, by way of Marx's essay "On the Jewish Question":

> *A victim at the level of religion and political power, [Barabas] is, in effect, emancipated at the level of civil society, emancipated in Marx's contemptuous sense of the word in his essay* On the Jewish Question: *'The Jew has emancipated himself in a Jewish manner, not only by acquiring the power of money, but also because* money *has become, through him and also apart from him, a world power, while the practical Jewish spirit has become the practical spirit of the Christian nations. The Jews have emancipated themselves in so far as the Christians have become Jews.'*[7]

Marx's essay took the Jewish question as the topical starting point for his reflections on the nature of civil society, a concept first delimited by Hegel in *The Philosophy of Right,* on which Marx was writing a commentary during the same decade. Hegel staked out civil society as an intermediate term between the family and the state: in civil society, individuals pursue their own interests in activities that coalesce in temporary alliances, whereas in the state, political citizenship systematically reconciles the particular and the universal. Marx took up the Hegelian distinction between the state and civil society, but reversed their order of priority; for Marx, the far-reaching instrumentalizations of *bürgerliche Gesellschaft* constitute the truth belied by a state designed not to heal but rather to maintain the economization of existence. And the Jew is the sign and symptom of life under capital; pursuing his private interests outside of the formal protocols of citizenship and the national identifications they underwrite, the Jew represents the purely civil (rather than civic) impulse that gives the economic associations of modernity their fragmentary and atomistic character.

Marx's movement from the "particular" question of the Jews to the general problem of civil society takes up the Jews as the constitutive example of the particular as such. The Jews are an affront to the main line of Western historiography and consciousness because, despite their foundational contribution to the evolving structures of modernity, they nonetheless have refused to assimilate easily (or, in the term of Marx's day, to be "emancipated" into) the normative functioning of Protestant-secular life. The Jews' residual and resistant religious particularism in the face of a universalism they helped to define in turn becomes the engine and symbol of a profane self-interest dangerously separated from the common good, and yet distributed to every corner of modern life—a universalized particularism, as it were. In Greenblatt's definitive reading of Marx with Marlowe, "Barabas's avarice, egotism, duplicity, and murderous cunning do not signal his exclusion from the world of Malta but his central place within it. His 'Judaism' is, again in Marx's words, 'a universal *antisocial* element of the *present time.*'" (204).

Marx's reading of the Jew as a figure of capital represents a late turn in the movement I named in Paul as the "civil-ization of Judaism," the ascription to Israel of a cultural and historical coherence in an unfolding logic, at the expense of Judaism's ongoing independent legal and scriptural authority. Paul resolved his own Jewish question by conceiving of Israel as a local jurisdiction subsumed within a larger Christian fellowship. The limited *politea* of Israel, founded on an initial covenant with God, has now given way to universal membership in Christ, in which both Jewish and Gentile Christians are *sumpolites,* fellow citizens (Eph 2:20). For these members in the new social body headed by Christ, any remaining elements of Jewish identification are retained as either generalized figure or localized custom, but not as binding law. Paul, of course, was writing in and for a Messianic community for whom the conversion of the Gentiles signaled the realization of Judaism's universal potential at the end of time.[8] The problem for later European Christendom was not the failure of the Gentiles to convert—the Church of the Middle Ages and Renaissance was overwhelmingly Gentile—but the survival of the Jews in spite of the fulfillment of the law brought about by Christ's sacrifice. Declining to become *sumpolites* in Christ, the Jews were in turn denied citizenship in Christian states such as Malta and Venice, yet allowed and even encouraged to pursue certain forms of economic activity that benefited both themselves and the larger commonwealth as well as to maintain significant institutions of self-regulation for their communities. Herein lies the further equation of the Jews with the "civil"—now identified not so much with a particular culture, civilization, or local jurisdiction, but rather with civil society as the realm of economic activity and informal association that takes place apart from the official operation of the state. The Jews, unconverted to the Christian political economy of history, became figures of the uncivil core of civil society. Driving this antisocial sociality is the dynamic yet disintegrative movement of the pursuit of individual interests outside an overarching identification with a common good. Moreover, *self-interests* can aggregate into *special interests,* subversive cells or organs of internal affiliation dangerously separated from the integrated functioning of the body politic by their singular agendas.

Barabas, as Greenblatt first noted, is the consummate figure of such uncivil civility. Early in the play, he disengages his ambitions from anything political, declaring of himself and his fellow Jews that "we come not to be kings" (1.1.128).[9] Proclaiming himself his own neighbor, he firmly separates his destiny from that of Malta: "*Ego mihimet sum semper proximus,* / Why, let 'em enter, let 'em take the town" (1.1.189–90). When Barabas is finally made Governor of Malta by the Turks at the end of the play, he reflects uncomfortably on the acquisition of political power: "I now am Governor of Malta; true—/ But Malta hates me, and, in hating me, / My life's in danger" (5.2.29–30). When he negotiates the former governor's return to office, it is as if he wants to pass on the unfamiliar burden of political responsibility as quickly as possible, in favor of the clearer and more comfortable good of financial gain. Moreover, even within the limited borders of the Jewish community itself, he refuses to cast his lot with a common good. As he tells his fellow Jews and the witnessing audience on their way to the senate house, "If anything shall there concern our state, / Assure yourselves I'll look unto [*Aside*] myself" (1.1.171–72). In Marlowe's Malta, the Jewish *politeuma* is dysfunctional at best; separated from the larger body politic, the purely civil body residing within it is in turn subject to internal dissension, fragmentation, and instrumental exploitation. (The same conditions do not hold for the ghetto of Shakespeare's Venice, as we shall see in the next chapter.) Like the secular Jews of Marx's essay, Barabas's gift for manipulation, applied to his own group as well as to his contacts in Malta at large, signifies a *particular trait*—the perceived self-interestedness of the Jew in and as civil society—that surges up at every turn of social life, relentlessly the same, yet experienced in its insistent reference to the individual as unique. This universalized particularism is no universal at all, if by that word we mean the collective projects, common goods, and shared grounds that orient social action and interaction in the public sphere.

Barabas's renunciation of political ambition in favor of economic gain reflects the actual position of the Jews in the state, dramatized in the trial scene in Act 1 that sets the play's cycle of disintegrative associations into motion. When the Jews are called before the "senate house," an at least nominally representative body, they find no representation in it, no formal political place. When Ferneze first asks the Jews for aid, Barabas responds, "Alas, my lord, we are no soldiers" (1.2.50); the Jews, he says, are permanently and professionally *civilians,* exempt from military and political obligations by their status as resident aliens. The further interchange alternates among civil, civic, and theological definitions of membership and obligation:

> BARABAS: *Are strangers with your tribute to be taxed?*
>
> 2 KNIGHT: *Have strangers leave with us to get their wealth?*
> *Then let them with us contribute.*
>
> BARABAS: *How! equally?*
>
> FERNEZE: *No, Jew, like infidels.*
> *For through our sufferance of your hateful lives,*
> *Who stand accursèd in the sight of heaven,*
> *These taxes and afflictions are befall'n.* (1.2.58–67)

Barabas links taxation to representation—why should noncitizens be taxed? The Second Knight counters that although the Jews are denied civic participation, they are nonetheless allowed to pursue their economic interests in the civil realm and thus owe some of their wealth to the state. Barabas protests against equal contributions—"How! equally?"—a response that posits a certain equality among citizens and resident aliens with respect to taxation. Yet equality is the definitive attribute of citizenship, and Barabas will soon learn that the Jews, residing outside its circle, will be taxed quite a bit more than equally. The grounds then shift from civil law to political theology. Because the Jews are "accursèd in the sight of heaven," Ferneze argues, they must be taxed above and beyond the

Christian citizens by the political body that suffers their existence. The scandal of the Jew's survival into the Christian epoch requires their political exclusion, while their consequent exile into and identification with the purely economic domain of social life justifies their exorbitant taxation. Anyone who refuses to pay "shall straight become a Christian" (1.2.75)—following Paul, though in a coercive spirit, the Jews can become *sumpolites,* fellow citizens, only by converting to Christianity.

In this scenario, which remains hypothetical in Marlowe's play but will be realized in Shakespeare's response, conversion implies naturalization and vice versa. To convert to Christianity meant not simply leaving one confession for another, but also departing from the semi-autonomous Jewish community of resident aliens and becoming to one degree or another a part of the larger civic order. This larger order in turn was itself composed of corporate bodies—the guilds, confraternities, and mysteries, the hereditary classes and estates, and the offices of the Church. In the polities of Christian Europe, naturalization required conversion because Jews were by definition noncitizens—resident aliens who belonged to a separate community. If naturalization required conversion, the inverse was also true; conversion implied some form of naturalization, of entry into the body politic. To convert without undergoing some form of naturalization would have meant becoming in effect stateless (or, more accurately, estate-less, disidentified with any class or corporate body). The shift in religious identification would entail a change in legal status, an entry into full or fuller citizenship, at the expense, however, of continued association as Jews—the "death into citizenship," the mortification of local allegiances, calculated into the citizenship deal from antiquity on.[10]

The offer of conversion comes early in the play and carries the farcical force of a cruel joke played by theology in collusion with politics. It is entertained seriously by no one, and the chance for civic integration, cynical at best in Marlowe's Malta, closes even before it opens. The Jews choose to live (as a dispersed network of noncitizen communities) rather than die (into a citizenship that would cancel their religious affiliation). In this scene and throughout the play, the "life" of the Jews is a code word for the doubled particularism, theological and economic, that they instantiate in negative response to the citizenship deal. Against the Pauline logic of typological supercession and civic naturalization, the Jews have persisted as a religious group living both apart from and within the polity. Insofar as the Jews have survived past their date ("survival" naming the surplus, surfeit, or excess of a half-life or afterlife), there is an uncanny, even undead, quality to the vitality they embody in the Christian imagination. In addition, the feat of survival is associated more with compromise and pragmatism, a less-than-strict adherence to heroic or moral codes, than with fidelity to a signifier or a principle.[11] The survivor fuses the disturbing faces of the ghost and the collaborationist.[12]

The name of Marlowe's Jew offers an exegetical genealogy of the strange, non-substitutable quality presented by the spectre of Jewish survival, and it does so, moreover, within a legal scene of multiple jurisdictions. Barabas derives his name, of course, from Barabbas, the Jewish prisoner who was released by the Roman authorities in place of Jesus at the behest of his Jewish accusers: "Now at the feast the governor was accustomed to release for the crowd any one prisoner whom they wanted. And they had then a notorious prisoner, called Barabbas. So when they had gathered, Pilate said to them, 'Whom do you want me to release for you, Barabbas or Jesus who is called Christ?'" (Matt 27:15–17; cf. Mark 15, Luke 23, John 18). Jesus had earlier been tried in the Sanhedrin, the highest Jewish court in Jerusalem, which then had brought him before Pilate because their own jurisdiction was largely civil and religious, and was limited with respect to the death penalty (*Eerdmans* 912; Cohen 23). In the scene before Pilate, the Jews choose to emancipate Barabbas, not Jesus, forever marking the former as the one-who-did-not-die-in-the-place-of-Christ, the one who was not substituted for Jesus. To this surplus is attached a debt: when Pilate washes his hands, the Jews reply, "'His blood be on us and on our children'" (Matt 27: 25). Represented as having taken this guilt freely upon themselves in the narrative of the Gospels, the Jews will henceforth owe the Christians the price of their own existence as a singular *ethnos* in the unfolding economy of history. This ambiguous quantity of surplus-debt takes shape, moreover, at the intersection of two jurisdictions, the universal authority of Roman imperial law and the local authority of Jewish civil law. Released by Pilate on behalf of the Jews—returned as it were to their jurisdiction—the survival of Barabbas at the expense of Jesus will be irrevocably linked to the civil-ization of the Jews in the several senses I have unfolded here: the neutralization of the authority of the Torah vis-à-vis the New Testament, the formal exclusion of the Jews from political life based on their nonconversion, the identification of the Jews with fiscal dealings and misdealings, and their pursuit of alternative forms of social organization and self-regulation within the commonwealths that host them.

In the trial scene of *The Jew of Malta,* Ferneze, washing his own hands of responsibility for the Jews, explicitly evokes the originary debt accrued by the Jews in the court of Pilate:[13]

> *If your first curse fall heavy on thy head,*
> *And make thee poor and scorned of all the world,*
> *'Tis not our fault, but thy inherent sin.* (1.2.109–11)

When the Jews of Malta are asked to give up their wealth for the greater good of the state, Barabas refuses. Combining the scriptural Barabbas with shades of Melville's Barnaby, Marlowe's Jew of Malta is the one whose peculiar life is defined by preferring not to: declining to contribute financially to a common good that excludes him as a Jew and refusing to die into the new citizenship that would be conferred by Christian conversion. As he declares to Abigail in the development of the scene, "No, I will live; nor loathe I this my life" (1.2.268). *This my life:* the phrase delimits the particularized field of religious survival and economic livelihood that places the Jew both in and out of Malta as a persistent element that resists substitution and sublation within Christian theological and political economies.

As Greenblatt and others have noted, Barabas loses rather than gains in individuality as the play progresses, indeed at the same rate that his survival instinct becomes more and more exorbitant, culminating in his exultant claim just before his fall, "For so I live, perish may all the world" (5.5.10). As an allegory of economic and religious particularism, Barabas is progressively divested of character or personality in favor of type, the means and motor of his survival in popular memory and imagination. What Barabas typifies is particularization itself—the vice of the Vice—as a religious and social scandal.[14] His infamous autobiography of crimes ("As for myself, I walk abroad a'nights . . ." [2.3.179–205]) gathers together a poisonous bouquet of anti-Jewish stereotypes, interwoven with pseudo-Machiavellian motifs of policy and self-interest that display the theological crimes of medieval anti-Judaism in a resolutely profane frame. The speech ends with Barabas's triumphant self-accounting: "But mark how I am blessed for plaguing them; / I have as much coin as will buy the town" (2.3.204–5). At the end of what is in effect a litany of materialized curses, Barabas insistently transfers the concept of blessing from the theological and covenantal register to that of social power through economic success. In Genesis, God promises Abraham, "I will make of thee a great nation, and I will bless thee, and make thy name great; and thou shalt be a blessing: And I will bless them that bless thee, and curse him that curseth thee: and in thee shall all families of the earth be blessed" (KJV, Gen 12:2–3). Whereas Paul had read the blessing of the families of the earth as a prooftext for his Gentile mission, Barabas restricts blessing to himself alone and reads it in material terms, as the "coin that buys the town," the wealth that controls the political order.[15] If covenant remains here at all, its infinite riches have been contracted to the little room of self-interest, which in turn becomes an echo-chamber that traps, redoubles, and caricatures the voices of Isaac's heirs in a transhistorical portrait of Jewish survival in and as the spirit of civil society. Fueled by the initial debt accrued by the scriptural

Barabbas, paid off without hope of amortization by his spiritually bankrupted heirs, and vocalized by the increasingly spectral figure of the Maltese Barabas, Marlowe's Jew becomes the very ghost of the unholy bond between religious and economic particularisms, between the civil-ization of Judaism as a culture apart and the consequent derogation of the Jews to civil rather than civic forms of economic and communal activity.

The New Jews: From Israel to Islam

Barabas delivers his mythic autobiography in neither the Christian churchyard nor the Jewish synagogue, but rather in the profane setting of the slave-market. In the transaction that culminates in his purchase of Ithamore as his sidekick, the speech functions as a kind of down payment in the relationship between the Jew and the Turk, who responds in kind with his own briefer but no less vivid accounting of Muslim crimes. Barabas signs and seals his new bond with Ithamore in lines that constitute the play's most pointed and explicit reference to circumcision: "make account of me / As of thy fellow; we are villains both: / Both circumcisèd, we hate Christians both" (2.3.218–20). Whereas circumcision seems to have failed to create cohesive bonds among the Jews of Malta, it now becomes a sign of commonality linking the Jew to the Muslim, significantly expanding the kinds of prepolitical fellowship possible in Malta to include an alliance between members of two distinct, non-Christian groups.

In Judaism, circumcision had functioned as a rite of civic naturalization linking the members of the Abrahamic covenant to each other and to God. Paul, in his efforts to build mixed congregations, transmuted the covenantal signature of *brit milah* into an interior symbol to be shared by all and a local custom to be practiced by a few. In the post-Pauline world of official Christianities, circumcision became a mark of Jewish obduracy, of the resistant and residual particularism of those who declined entry into the open tent of Paul's church. Moreover, by the time that Marlowe writes his play, the ranks of the circumcised have grown to include the Muslims, bearers of the worldview most immediately at odds with Christian moral and territorial claims. Represented primarily by the Arabs during the medieval period and the Turks during the rise of the Ottoman Empire in the Renaissance, Islam dangerously combined the circumcised legal separatism of the Jews with the universal mission of the Christians. Islam, like Judaism, was a religion living not far away but close at hand, which, far from worshipping many gods, subscribed to monotheisms at least as strict as Christianity's own. Moreover, Judaism and Islam stem from the same Abrahamic lineage as Christianity; the three groups are, in the Muslim phrase, "People of the Book," neighboring religions organized around revealed Scriptures that share many of the same prophets and patriarchs. During the Reformation, Jews and Muslims were linked along with Catholics as practitioners of a deadening law, a pseudo-confederacy often emblematized, following St. Paul, by the observance of circumcision as well as dietary laws.[16] Too wise rather than too foolish, the knowledge of the law epitomized by Jewish and Muslim monotheism meant that these groups had both more affinity with and more resistance to genuine Christian conversion than the Gentile barbarians. Unlike pagan barbarians, the Muslims live not *ante legem*—before or outside the revealed law that singled out the Jews from the nations of the world—but *sub lege*, submitted to the rule of a stringent monotheism untempered by the love incarnated by Christ.[17]

The author of an anonymous tract, *The Policy of the Turkish Empire*, published in 1597, lays out the status of the law in the three religions:

> *For as the Iews had a particular lawe given unto them and published by God himselfe in mount Sinai, . . . so have the Turkes (in imitation of the same) certaine lawes and precepts or Commandements laide downe in their Alcoran; . . . whosoever shal transgressse or violate any of them, is held by their law to be a most sinfull and wicked person. . . . Contrariwise, they do believe that who so doth observe and keepe those commandments, . . . he shall be sure to be saved: be he either Turke or Christian. Which argueth that their confidence and hope of salvation consisteth chiefely in the pietie and merite of their vertuous life, and good deedes: And that they doe not much differ in that point from the opinion of some Christians, who do attribute their salvation unto their merites.* (15)

The passage carefully sets up Islamic law as a belated version of the Torah ("in imitation of the same") and an alienating mirror of the Catholic Church, whose adherents also "attribute their salvation unto their merites." The author of the *Policy* singles out circumcision as a law that, within the epoch preceding the birth of Christ, was "a most holy and sacred sacrament," but "is nowe converted . . . to a most idle and vaine ceremony" among Jews and Muslims who maintain its observance (22). Circumcision links Islam to Judaism as a neighboring preserve of misunderstood and outdated laws, a parodic pastiche "patched up . . . out of the olde and new Testament" (2). In the words of John Pory, in his "Summarie discourse of the manifold Religions professed in Africa" appended to his 1600 translation of the Muslim convert Leo Africanus's *History and Description of Africa*, "*Mahumet* his law . . . embraceth circumcision, & maketh a difference between meats pure, & unpure, partly to allure the Iewes";[18] here, circumcision becomes an act of missionary seduction by which Islam strengthens its historic links to Judaism while expanding the circle of its adherents.[19]

Islam, the youngest of the three Abrahamic religions, came to represent to Christianity a kind of Judaism after the fact, a redoubling of Jewish intransigence to the Christian revelation. As such, Islam executes a second, even crueler blow to Christianity's historical vision of epochal succession, since modern Judaism (from the Christian perspective) is merely a residual phenomenon, a stubborn carry-over from an earlier moment, but Islam from its very inception administered its proselytizing mission in full knowledge of Christian teachings. The rapid expansion of Islam throughout the Mediterranean, the Levant, North Africa, the Far East, and the Balkans, however, presented the inverse of Judaism's dispersed, sequestered, and inward-looking communities. The third Revelation announced by Islam rejected Jewish particularism in favor of Christian universalism; like the rulers of European Christendom, the Arab and then Turkish powers used the theme of spiritual equality among the nations to support their missionary, imperial, and commercial projects.[20] In the Pauline schemes of the Renaissance, Islam represents a double scandal, the catastrophic bastardization of both Christian universalism—through the seductive danger of the Islamic world mission—and Jewish particularism, represented by Muslim allegiance to ritual laws and to an Abrahamic monotheism without Christ.

In Christian exegesis, the Jew and the Muslim were linked through the figure of Ishmael. For Paul, Ishmael had been the type of the carnal Israel, representing the recalcitrance of present-day Jerusalem in maintaining the law despite its abrogation:

> *For it is written that Abraham had two sons, one by a slave and one by a free woman. But the son of the slave was born according to the flesh, the son of the free woman through promise. Now this is an allegory: these women are two covenants. One is from Mount Sinai, bearing children for slavery; she is Hagar. Now Hagar is Mount Sinai in Arabia; she corresponds to the present Jerusalem, for she is in slavery with her children. (Gal 4:22–25)*

With the rise of Islam, the figure of Ishmael as a negative type of the Jew could be shifted onto Mohammad, a translation already authorized by the Arab and later Islamic appropriation of Ishmael for its own prophetic genealogy, and reinforced by Paul's location of the hallowed site of Jewish revelation in Arabia ("Now Hagar is Mount Sinai *in Arabia*"). Although Ishmael and Hagar are the most frequently exploited examples of this displacement of negative types from Judaism to Islam, other figures, such as Esau, Pharaoh, and Herod, could also be brought into this train of thought, promoting the figural coupling of Jew and Muslim as the carnal children of Abraham facing each other across the world-historic break effected by the Incarnation.[21]

In *The Jew of Malta,* Marlowe happily exploits the typological linkages between Judaism and Islam available to him in post-Pauline iconographies of *ethnos*. The name "Ithamore," for example, is a variant of the biblical "Ithamar," the youngest son of Aaron and hence part of the priestly line of the Levites, professional upholders of Jewish ritual law. Islamicizing "-mar" into "-more" (which sounds like "Moor"), Marlowe elaborates the fellowship between Jewish and Islamic legalisms signed by circumcision. Ithamore's legal status as a slave also picks up a theme long associated with the Jews, the motif of enslavement to the law. According to Paul, the Jews under the law were like a child-heir, "no better than a slave, though he is the owner of all the estate; but he is under guardians and trustees until the date set by the father" (Gal 4:1–3).[22] In Paul's Greek, the law is a *paidagogos,* "a slave charged with the general custody, and especially the discipline, of children in a Greek or Roman family."[23] In Paul's analogy of the enslaving and enslaved schoolmaster, the law is a necessary but transitional stage in both the history of world religion and the spiritual development of each individual. Moreover, we should recall here that legal manumission was one of the ways in which foreigners automatically became Roman citizens.[24] For Paul, the image of emancipation from Jewish law was intimately linked to laws concerning citizenship. To be freed from enslavement under the law was to become *sumpolites* in Christ; by implication, in the post-Pauline tradition, to choose to remain under the law—as the Jews and the Muslims do—manifested one's slavish nature.

Ithamore is a slave who will be manumitted at the time set by his adoptive father, Barabas—he will be emancipated, however, not into Christian freedom but into further fellowship in villainy with the unconverted Jew. When Barabas disinherits his daughter Abigail on the occasion of her conversion to Christianity, he adopts Ithamore as his heir and proceeds to poison not only his daughter, but all the nuns with whom she now resides. It is a complex moment of crossings and double-crossings among confessional groups. Abigail passes into Christianity by joining a nunnery that formerly had housed her father and herself. Indeed, she converts twice: first as an act of filial obedience to her father, who will use her as an insider to regain the jewels hidden in the house; and second as an act of filial defiance, of radical disaffiliation, when she learns that her father is responsible for the deaths of her two Gentile suitors. Moving from Judaism to Christianity, Abigail is an instance of the citizen-saint, who mortifies her previous tribal and local ties, her native particularism, in favor of naturalization and conversion to a general economy. Yet the doubling of conversions, like the doubling of boyfriends, sours the sentimental seriousness of Abigail's turn to Christianity. Her initial choice, a pure stratagem orchestrated by her father, presents in debased form the survivalist pragmatism of the *conversos,* the

Jews of the Spanish Empire, including those of Malta, who chose to convert to Christianity rather than submit to expulsion in 1492. So too, her embrace of a markedly Catholic form of life, the object of satire in this pointedly Protestant play, further ironizes her Christian turn. Nonetheless, Abigail's civic ventures lay out the key legal exit strategies from Judaism—marriage and conversion—that demarcate the limited forms of openness that Christian commonwealths, and Christian narratives, entertained in relation to their Jewish populations.[25]

For Barabas, in keeping with Jewish law on this matter, a Christian daughter is no longer a daughter; or, in Barabas's words, "False and unkind; what, hast thou lost thy father?" (3.4.1–2). In her place, he adopts Ithamore: "O trusty Ithamore, no servant, but my friend: / I here adopt thee for mine only heir, / All that I have is thine when I am dead, / And whilst I live use half; spend as myself" (3.4.41–45). Within the new legal framework of manumission and adoption, they proceed to poison the nunnery with a pot of rice, using the occasion of a Catholic holiday, Saint Jacques' Even, to deposit their charitable contribution on the doorstep of Barabas's former home. The adoption of Ithamore, a legal transfer of affect and property conducted in relation to a pot of soup, parodies the biblical story of Esau and Jacob and its typological vicissitudes. In Genesis, Esau is older brother to the younger Jacob, who will inherit the blessing of their father Isaac through a trick arranged by their mother Rebecca, who sends the younger twin to their blind father with a pot of soup and a hairy disguise. In Jewish exegesis, the story narrates the founding line of the twelve tribes of Israel (the name that Jacob will later receive); Esau becomes a type of various neighboring groups hostile to Israel, especially the Edomites. Paul, on the other hand, takes this and other stories about younger brothers ascending over older brothers as an allegory of the supercession of Christianity over Judaism.[26] In post-Pauline anti-Jewish typology, Esau, like Ishmael, will become a type not of Israel's enemies but to the contrary, of carnal Israel itself in its resistance to conversion and its affinity with Islam.

Although one should avoid playing out the typological resonances too rigorously, it is clear enough that Marlowe forcefully if comically links the Muslim slave to the genealogy of Israel at an ethically vexed and hermeneutically contested moment of its devolution. In Marlowe's replay of the story from Genesis, Ithamore delivers the soup that will kill Abigail. He in effect assumes the role of Jacob, receiving the blessing of Barabas/Isaac (two very different Biblical characters who share the feature of not-being-sacrificed) in the place of the more legitimate sibling. As a consequence, the Muslim becomes a formal part of the household of the Jew, once again "displacing" Abigail. In this allegory, the Muslims are the new Jews, inheriting in the place of the legitimate child (who has sensibly converted to Christianity.) In the play's management of biblical motifs, the Pauline figure of Jacob as type of the younger faith inheriting in the place of the older can be "returned" to a Jewish context in order to transfer it to Islam, which functions as a second-order Judaism in the play. If Abigail has made the proper Pauline progress forward in time, from Judaism to Christianity, Ithamore travels in the reverse direction, from the second-order Judaism of Islam to the inveterate Judaism of a legalism that persists beyond supercession. The fellowship of Jew and Muslim represents the double negation of the positive conversion effected by Abigail, who becomes their sorry sacrifice.

Barabas's formal allegiance with Ithamore around the trait of circumcision recalls key aspects of the deutero-Pauline Epistle to the Ephesians:

> *Therefore remember that at one time you Gentiles in the flesh, called the uncircumcision by what is called the circumcision . . . were at that time separated from Christ, alienated from the commonwealth* [politea] *of Israel, and strangers to the covenants of promise. . . . But now in Christ Jesus you who were once far off have been brought near in the blood of Christ. . . . So then you are no longer strangers and sojourners, but you are fellow citizens* [sumpolites] *with the saints* [hagios] *and members of the household* [oikeios] *of God, built upon the foundations of the apostles and prophets, Christ Jesus himself being the cornerstone. (Eph 2:11–20; see discussion in chapter 1, "Ephesian Conclusions")*

At stake in both Ephesus and Malta is the viability of forging a league between members of unlike, even hostile groups: for Paul, congregational unity among Jewish and Gentile Christians; for Barabas, an alliance between the Jewish master and the Muslim slave. In both cases, circumcision, understood as the particularizing mark par excellence, begins to take on a universal function as it institutes relations across groups. Both passages use the word "fellow" to name affiliations that are civil rather than civic, involving voluntary associations across group lines, within a host city or state: Paul's reference to the *oikos*, or household, establishes the prepolitical nature of religious congregation, whereas the Maltese setting of the slave-market places civil association in a specifically economic matrix.

But, whereas Paul's church is built on love and the indifference of circumcision, the alliance between Barabas and Ithamore is founded on their shared enmity for Christians, a hatred signed into being by their joint circumcisions, which are physical marks rather than symbols of interiority. As he puts it elsewhere, the Christian commonwealth is peopled by an "unchosen nation, never circumcised" (2.3.7–8). Barabas's proposed fellowship, contra Paul, reasserts both the ancient priority and the modern exclusion of the circumcised from the Christian polity, and uses both as the grounds of a new form of specifically civil affiliation across confessional groups. Here and elsewhere, Marlowe creates a "Jewish" exegetical voice for Barabas by de-Paulinizing the Old Testament tropes appropriated by the apostle for his Gentile mission. At the same time, Paul's experiments in cross-group affiliation function as a template for new forms of allegiance among distinct religious groups who are not included in the larger civic circle. In his readings of Paul, Marlowe in effect turns off the typological clock and resets it to the time of civil society. Rather than simply "secularizing" the religious iconography inherited from sacred drama, Marlowe finds within religious discourse new patterns for social interaction. Finding *koinônia,* or commonality, in opposition to Christianity, the "fellowship" between Barabas and Ithamore suggests the possibility of affiliations across confessional groups within the realm of civil society, and in opposition to the dominant civic and religious order.

Yet this possibility is never realized in the play itself. Like all of Barabas's alliances, the fellowship between Jew and Muslim is subject to the same instrumentalizing manipulation as that between Jew and Jew. Marlowe's ironizing drive emphasizes the fragmentary quality of civil society over its associational potential, for both the Jew and the Malta that he inhabits and symbolizes. The legal formalism of Barabas's adoption of Ithamore indicates that their relationship remains one of voluntary fellowship, of civil association, and will never attain the pathos of a genuine blood tie. Yet it is the voluntary, formalist quality of the fellowship between Barabas and Ithamore that makes it of interest to the literature of citizenship, since it implies a *universitas circumcisorum* that would link disparate groups in common projects, provisional universals, without dissolving their unique jurisdictions—a pragmatic, material revision of Pauline fellowship.

Within the world of the play, however, it is another story. Barabas is a leader in the Jewish community, the bond among its members signed by the rite of circumcision, yet early in the play he separates his interests from those of his fellow Jews. Via his relationship with the slave Ithamore and then later with the Turkish leader Calymath, Barabas enters into league with the Muslims, circumcised like himself yet distinguished from the Jews as a powerful and unified external political force with its own scripture, history, and destiny. For a time, this new cross-group bond displaces Barabas's familial and national ties to his daughter Abigail, in a rearrangement of loyalties that echoes typological readings of Esau and Jacob. Yet the fellowship rapidly dissolves. If circumcision is the initial signature of fellowship for Ithamore and Barabas, it is soon devalued in Ithamore's dismissive remarks once he has fallen under the spell of the courtesan Bellamira. He mocks the Jew's dietary laws ("he lives upon pickled grasshoppers and sauced mushrooms" [4.4.70]), and then links Barabas' poor hygiene to his circumcision: ""He never put on clean shirt since he was circumcised" (4.4.72). What before had bound the two together in mutual enmity against Christians has now been absorbed into a battery of anti-Jewish images that Ithamore glibly deploys in his bid for inclusion in the brothel culture—another corner of uncivil society—represented by Bellamira and Pilia-Borza. Ithamore closes the scene (and the door on Jewish fellowship) with the evocatively typological gnomism, "The meaning has a meaning. Come, let's in; / To undo a Jew is charity, not sin" (4.4.91–92). Ithamore has learned to speak the metalanguage of the Maltese Christians, who cynically use the Pauline tradition of typological transvaluation to oil the new economy while keeping their hands clean.

Rezoning

All of this takes place not in the margins of Talmudic and biblical commentaries, but in the space of the new public theater. The stage would have consisted of the main platform, an inner stage at the back, and a gallery above, regions easily refigured throughout the drama to represent different locales in Malta (the residences of Barabas, the senate house, the marketplace, the brothel). These rapid scenic remappings, the staple of Elizabethan theater, are symbolic as well as pragmatic, since they involve the rezoning of Malta's civil and religious sectors in relation to the conditions of possibility for public theater itself. The conversion of the Jew's house to a nunnery mobilizes a Pauline architecture of typology, while also alluding to the more contemporary dissolution of the monasteries and the construction of new civil spaces on their evacuated grounds.

Act 1, scene 1 opens with Barabas "in his counting house"—perhaps positioned toward the back of the main stage, more likely discovered in its inner stage, counting infinite riches in a little room. Whether presented within or in front of the inner stage, the enclosure effectively frames Barabas as a type of Avarice, identifying the Jew with the mercantile economy, the uncivil core of civil society, but within an iconographically delimited, blocked off zone.[27] Yet this narrow space soon opens outwards; Patrick Cheney imagines Barabas gesturing expansively to encompass the whole stage "as he speaks the 'infinite' line, thereby identifying the room of the counting-house with the room of the theatre."[28] With this gesture, the emblematic iconography of the morality tradition opens onto the plateau of the public stage, visualizing Marlowe's transitional position between medieval forms of drama and the new theater he was helping to bring into being as well as Barabas's typological location at the crossroads of sacred and civil orders of representation and forms of fellowship.

At the end of the trial scene, Abigail informs her father that he has lost his house:

> *For there I left the Governor placing nuns,*
> *Displacing me; and of thy house they mean*
> *To make a nunnery, where none but their own sect*
> *Must enter in; men generally barred. (1.2.255–59)*

In the "placing" of nuns and the "displacing" of Abigail, the appropriation of Barabas's house by the state for the Church stages in debased form the typological conversion of the synagogue into the church, a theme that appears with some frequency in medieval and Renaissance visual arts. For example, in Annunciation scenes, Mary is often depicted in front of a building in ruins, alluding to the decline of the synagogue and its renovation as the Church, of which Mary herself would become a favorite symbol.[29] Like Mary, Abigail passes from the Old to the New Dispensation, a consummate figure of Judeo-Christian womanhood; and, like Mary's ruins, her calling takes place in relation to the architecture of epochal conversion. Soon Abigail will appear on the balcony of the new nunnery, habited as a nun, while her father frets below like a ghost of pesachs past, calling the God of Exodus to lead Abigail to his hidden wealth: "O thou, that with a fiery pillar led'st / The sons of Israel through the dismal shades, / Light Abraham's offspring; and direct the hand / Of Abigail this night" (2.1.13–15). With the daughter above and the father below—his figure framed perhaps by the doorway of the inner stage?—the mise-en-scène visually schematizes the positioning of superstructure over foundation, Church over synagogue, New Testament over Old Testament, a floor plan drafted in part by Paul, the master builder (*architekton*) of the new temple (1 Cor 3:10; cf. Eph 2:20).

Barabas's reference to Exodus codes the hidden jewels as the gold stolen by the Israelites from their Egyptian households on their way out of Egypt, a favorite metaphor in Christian humanism for the translation and conversion of pagan cultural resources for monotheism.[30] (Shakespeare will return to this motif when he shows Jessica eloping with her father's wealth.) Yet whereas the jewelry of the Egyptians is a typological symbol of successful cultural translation, the wealth reappropriated by Barabas allows him to sidestep conversion, maintaining his life and his livelihood, his confession and his profession. (In Exodus, the Egyptian gold is likely used to make the Golden Calf, a sign that there too, the conversion of foreign goods is only partial.) Hidden "close underneath the plank / That runs along the upper-chamber floor" (1.2.297–98), the stash of wealth is an insurance plan for himself and Abigail, a pocket of moveable property, of liquid assets, that will protect his household against the political decisions of the state and the Jews' uncertain claims to real estate, depositing the chance of Jewish survival in the crawl space of Christian history. Barabas will use the wealth, as Garrett Sullivan observes, to "buy *another* house"—to cultivate another place, another synagogue, in which the identification of Jewish survival with civil society can continue to unfold.[31] The *conversa* Abigail is no Mary; Barabas remains true to his namesake Barabbas, refusing substitution; and the theological rezoning of Malta remains incomplete.

The play's architecture of conversion and its discontents takes place in and as the scaffolding of the stage itself. Mobilizing the iconography of the Judeo-Christian turn, the expropriation has a more contemporary reference as well, namely to Henry VIII's dissolution of the monasteries, including the urban and suburban monastic holdings (liberties) on which some of London's public theaters, such as Blackfriars, now stood. The monastic holdings had always carried the special legal status of "liberties," not subject to royal and municipal jurisdictions and governed by their own ecclesiastical courts that answered to Rome. When the Church's lands passed to the Crown, the tie with Rome was of course broken, but the lands remained "liberties"; exempted from municipal law, the liberties could be leased for various forms of unregulated economic and social activity, including brothels, taverns and theaters, as well as the hospitals and leprosariums traditionally linked to religious institutions.[32] Blackfriars and Whitefriars, theaters built on liberties within the city of London, retained in their names a reference to their monastic origins.

Like the *universitas judeorum* of Malta, the liberties of London isolate civil society as a set of phenomena separate from official civic life—a jurisdiction onto themselves, dynamized by the flow of capital, where various forms of fellowship take root in a volatile microclimate potentially at odds with that of the commonwealth that houses it. Moreover, the evacuation of this space for use by the theater is linked to a complex juridical, political, and theological operation, that of the dissolution of the monasteries. The public theater is given a Protestant frame—the same frame that allows Marlowe to recuperate his corrosive representation of Christian hypocrisy under the neutralizing rubric of anti-Catholic satire. These Christians may be nasty, but after all, they are Spanish Catholics, not English Protestants; moreover, the theatrical space we are currently occupying exists thanks to the break with Rome. But the public theater is not a church; in fact, it may even be an anti-church, a place of sexual, criminal, and economic congregation. In this, it shares something with the community of the Jews.

In *The Jew of Malta*, the architecture of the stage discovers within itself a series of real and symbolic transformations—of synagogue into nunnery, of Catholic monastery holdings into Protestant royal property, and of the old monastic liberties into new theatrical ones—infinite riches in a little room. The flexible stage will accommodate the bawdy house of Bellamira in the space that had been the nunnery—another shift from church holdings to the deregulated fraternization of the liberties.[33] If the Jew is a figure of uncivil society, so too is the actor: each "congregates," setting up and instigating forms of affiliation and transaction, of dangerous fellowship, that exist with some degree of liberty in relation to the political jurisdictions of city and crown. Patrick Cheney has noted the growing equation between Barabas and theater, culminating in his appearance as an actor-poet-musician in the house of Bellamira in Act 4 and his building of the final stage set in Act 5 (154–56). Designing and installing a trap for Calymath, Barabas meanwhile plans a bloody end for the Turkish troops in a "monastery / Which standeth as an outhouse to the town" (5.4.36). Barabas's urban theater of cruelty finds its suburban counterpart in the liberty of the suburb. Here is the final perversion of his fellowship with the circumcised Ithamore: he sequesters and "consumes . . . with fire" the Muslim forces in a traditional space of sanctuary (5.2.82).

While the Turkish soldiers are being cooked alive at their own banquet, Barabas hosts their leader Calymath along with Ferneze, Del Bosco, and the Knights of St. John in his "homely citadel." The setting is presumably the governor's palace that he now occupies as head of state, though Barabas's emphasis on its "homely" quality rezones it for residential use, housing a scene of hospitality rather than formal diplomacy (5.3.19; 5.5.58). Indeed , this final feast is Barabas's literalization of the commensality supported in Paul's Epistles, where table fellowship among Jewish and Gentile Christians is a key feature of the new community in Christ (e.g., Gal 2:11–13). Barabas sets a table where Jews, Christians, and Muslims will eat together, abrogating the dietary laws that have kept both Jews and Muslims from the common table of the nations—but his plan, of course, is to drown the Turkish Selim in the soup pot in order to serve him to the Christian governor in exchange for a monetary reward. The reverse will in fact occur: the bustling stage-engineer, "*very busy*" on his "dainty gallery," will be cooked in his own pot of soup, cursed by his own blessing, as he falls from the balcony into the inner stage below. Cursing the "Damned Christian dogs and Turkish infidels," his dying cries isolate him once more from the triple fellowship among the People of the Book that he had (falsely) promised.

This is the play's final rezoning. In a classic set of reversals, the bearer of bad soup is now stewed in his own cauldron; the scheming host is sacrificed in his own kitchen; the uncivil civilian is submitted to the ultimate "civilizing process," that of being cooked; and the inner stage, once the Jew's counting house, is now his grave. The inner stage is the quintessential space of Barabas, the intimate box that frames our first and last visions of the Jew. From the inner stage he issues, and to the inner stage he shall return. Between these two tableaux, a series of typological remappings has occurred that reflect on the congregational space of the theater itself. Several critics have identified the persona of Barabas with the creative force and directorial energy of Marlowe (Greenblatt; Cheney). My analysis of Malta's urban planning makes a similar point at a more structural level, in relation to the play's civic, civil, and religious spaces as they regroup in and as the place of the stage itself. Marlowe has used the figure of the Jew to begin to disclose a political theology of the peculiar public space where the new theater resides. The Jew of Marlowe operates among different models of the "civil"—as the space of exile or exclusion from politics proper, as the realm of a relentlessly divisive self-interest, as the object of epochal dissolutions and redeployments, and as the site of new, potentially creative forms of association. Insofar as Marlowe connects the libertine grounds of the theater to the civil society of the Jews, the playwright begins to imagine a universe, or at least a *universitas,* a restricted space of incorporated autonomy, in which religious, social, and artistic associations, within and across groups, might begin to take place, both separate from and sheltered by the polity in which they unfold. By drowning his Jew in the hell's mouth of the old theater—driving him back into the abyss of typological transformations—however, Marlowe ultimately betrays the public potential of his antihero. Marlowe chooses to destroy his character in the machinery of the morality play that had helped generate his stereotypical profile, leaving the medieval apparatus largely untouched by the modern ghost it has spawned. Barabas, the archetype of Jewish survival in its pragmatic and spectral aspects, does not survive the play, or rather, he survives it only by heightening, and not by fundamentally transforming, its traditional features.

Early in the play, civic integration had been momentarily imagined, in the inherently vexed form of the Jews' coerced conversion to Christianity. Marlowe places the citizenship deal near the beginning of his play; its brutal terms are never taken seriously by anyone present on stage, and Barabas quickly scoffs it off—he shall be no "convertite" (1.2.85). In a sense, the remainder of the play is a flight from citizenship—a flight on the part of Barabas, but also on the part of Marlowe, whose interests, as Graham Hammill has argued, lie in the extremes of sovereignty unbound rather than in the reconstituted norms of civic life.[34] Except for his momentary rule over Malta under the Turks, Barabas remains a part of civil society, apart from civic life, until the play's end, when he finally plunges into the cauldron and out of the city's representative space entirely.

Shakespeare, rewriting Marlowe's play, will take a different tack. He places the citizenship deal not at the beginning of the play, but at the end. And Shylock, unlike Barabas, consents to conversion; in his words, he is "content." Yet there is no happiness in Shylock's contentment, and he cannot bear to remain in the public space into which he has just been in effect invited. In the next chapter, I suggest that Shylock undergoes not so much a forced conversion as a procedural one, pointing to forms of naturalization that might be nominal rather than national, driving a wedge between *dēmos* and *ethnos,* between political and cultural forms of belonging. Sickened at the prospect of conversion, Shylock figuratively *dies into citizenship,* pressured to leave his religion at the gates of the ghetto in exchange for a limited place in the Venetian polity. Barabas, on the other hand, *dies out of citizenship,* cursing both the "Christian dogs" and the "Turkish infidels" as he goes. It is as if the sheer energy of his dynamic self-interest has created a vortex that sucks him out of the space of modernity he had come to signify and back into the welter of stereotypes from which he had risen. Having thrown his lot with the divisive strain of civil society, becoming its living emblem and demonic stereotype, he has abandoned the possibility of fellowship not only within and across confessions, but also between confessions and the polity. We moderns may find his choice the more heroic one, since, unlike Shylock, Barabas has managed to remain faithful to something, be it nothing more than his own desire. (Like his biblical namesake, he resists substitution and conversion till the end.) Yet Shylock's civic compromise, in all its legal and affective complexity, may finally have more to teach us about the promises and paradoxes of liberalism.

THREE

Merchants of Venice, Circles of Citizenship

Shylock is "of Venice" in the same limited sense that Marlowe's Jew is "of Malta": residing in, yet not fully a part of the city; denizens rather than citizens; members of civil but not civic life.[1] Shylock's money-lending, like Barabas's exorbitant trade practices, places him at the heart of the Venetian economy, but as a barely suffered foreign element. Yet, more vigorously than Marlowe, Shakespeare indicates Shylock's simultaneous habitation in a community apart, defined by its own hermeneutic patterns and forms of social congregation. In sum, Shakespeare attributes to Shylock *a world,* in keeping with his more normative casting of the Jew. Whereas Barabas is identified with *policy,* with the fluid pragmatics of the Machiavel and hence with a hypertrophied exceptionalism, Shylock is wedded to *contract,* the legal instrument that regularizes transactions in a social scene whose increasing complexity, mobility, and diversity preclude reliance on traditional forms of trust. In both plays, the Jewish circle of citizenship is drawn by the rite of circumcision, but with a different thrust for each playwright. For Barabas, a creature of shape-changing shiftiness, circumcision functions as a temporary tool in the crafting of a convenient alliance with the Muslim Ithamore; it is simply one sign among others available for tactical handling. For Shylock, to the contrary, a figure of fixation rather than fluidity, circumcision is the signature of signatures, the sign and symbol of contract and covenant par excellence. The Venetians share Shylock's covenantal understanding of circumcision, but transposed into a post-Pauline key that would replace particular membership in Judaism with universal membership in Christ. The exegetical and dramatic struggle over the meaning and dramatic function of circumcision in *The Merchant of Venice,* and between that play and *The Jew of Malta,* is thus a contest over the aims, limits, and costs of citizenship itself—both of membership in the larger body politic and participation in its incorporated foreign bodies.

It should come as no surprise that Paul's meditations on membership leave their mark not only on the themes and symbols of Shakespeare's play, but also on its mimetic innovations. Paul's coupling of historiography and hermeneutics around the rite of circumcision organizes the competition between Jewish and Christian readings of the Old Testament in the play, a struggle that underwrites the subtexts and subplots as well as the civil interchanges—economic, intellectual, and romantic—that cross the play's several circles of citizenship. Shakespeare exploits the philosophy of history encrypted in Pauline motifs in order to create a coherent order of representation, a Christian mercantile modernity clearly marked off from both ancient and medieval worldviews. The play's primary typological opposition between Jew and Christian is not opposed to Shakespeare's mimetic successes (as the vestige of an older allegorical mode) but provides the vehicle for Shakespeare's epochal synthesis of religious and profane narratives. Although Shakespeare's borrowings from Marlowe's experiments in the modern morality play are most explicit in *The Merchant of Venice,* they are also most fully and programmatically assimilated here into a new, normatively "Shakespearean" representational order. In the line of Erich Auerbach, but tempered by the antisymbolic reservations of Walter Benjamin,[2] I suggest that the play's ability to present historically coherent characters from distinctive citizenship groups constitutes a modern mimesis maintained by Shakespeare's inventive engagement with the legacy of Paul.

To focus on citizenship in the play is not to drop the Jewish question that has (rightly) occupied most recent readings of *The Merchant of Venice,* but to repose it in relation to citizenship.[3] "The Jewish question" itself emerged as a phrase in the nineteenth century in relation to the protocols of modern citizenship: if the Jews were emancipated from their limited corporate identities and given full citizenship rights in the emerging democratic orders of the modern nation-states, would they be capable of leaving behind the distinctive practices, beliefs, and laws that they had maintained with such rigor in the ghettos of Europe?[4] Could the Jews, in other words, *stop being Jews?* Naturalization (as a new citizen) was thus bound up with conversion (out of Judaism and into either Christianity or a secular equivalent). By the end of act 4, Shylock has undergone not only *conversion,* much remarked as an ambivalent feature of the play's denouement, but also *naturalization.* No longer a Jew, the converted Shylock is presumably free to practice trade in Venice, if not participate as a citizen in the forms of public life open to Venetian *cittadini.*[5] In receipt of both his money and his life, Shylock nonetheless must give up his Judaism, dramatizing the fact that *naturalization always occurs at a cost.* From their earliest formulations, citizenship rites come into being by exacting some cancellation, sacrifice, or mortification of prior familial, regional, or cultic allegiances. In *The Merchant of Venice,* Jessica and Shylock represent two different calculations of the citizenship deal. By choosing to marry a Christian nobleman, Jessica effects a fuller passage into the Venetian civic order, but the cost is the total eclipse of her prior religious and domestic affiliations—so total that she appears to have lost the capacity even to measure what she has given up. Shylock, on the other hand, is, in his words, "content" with the terms of the bargain, yet fundamentally "not well," unable to remain in the public space of the court at the close of the judgment; the curtain falls on the prospects of a converted Jew fully at home in neither his prior nor his new circles of citizenship, singularly at sea in the denaturalization that precedes naturalization. Unlike his daughter, Shylock holds onto the habit of calculation that determines not only the stereotype of Judaism in the play, but also the very essence of citizenship itself, as a form of *limited universalism* that equalizes its members in a new public sphere at the expense of their particularized identities.

As such, it is Shylock rather than Jessica who best incarnates the position of the citizen-saint at the end of play, manifesting in his very being the equivocal sign of circumcision as the seal that signifies the tension and passage between particular identities and universal memberships in Judaism, Christianity, and the Western polis founded on their mixed legacies.

Circles of Citizenship

A city on a lagoon, Renaissance Venice was at once an open port in east-west and north-south trade routes, a quasi-island that maintained a distinct identity from cities on the mainland and an internally bifurcated set of neighborhoods that were worlds onto themselves.[6] Alive with foreign merchants, visitors, traders, and slaves, the city nonetheless provided an astoundingly stable set of political institutions for its limited set of enfranchised inhabitants and for its recognized populations of resident aliens. Both an international city and a system of enclosures, Venice is equally emblematized by the imperial argosy and the local gondola. Whereas modern models of citizenship tend to imagine citizenship as one large circle containing a capacious set of inhabitants within it, the Venetian polity is more accurately envisioned as a set of intersecting circles delimiting several distinct forms of membership, or what one historian calls "a network of networks."[7] The *cittadini* (themselves headed by an honorary group of *cittadini originari*) formed the middle estate of the city's mixed constitution: they pursued commerce, could hold honorific and civil posts in city government, and "played a dignified role in the great charitable confraternities of the city."[8] The ranks of the *cittadini* were open to immigrants who met a residency requirement, paid taxes, or married Venetian women, but excluded Dutch and English Protestants.[9] Full political participation, however, was reserved for noblemen like Antonio and Bassanio, members of an elect set of families who derived their initial wealth and status from trading rather than land. As an urban aristocracy, this class of merchant-princes stood above the *cittadini*, yet bore a special relationship to them, having been raised out of their ranks at an early date in the city's history and often being bound to them through intermarriage.[10] Major offices rotated by election among this group, who thus constituted a kind of democracy within the aristocracy. The *populo* (or *populo menutu*), composed of a highly mobile and heterogeneous population of servants, laborers, and artisans (represented in *The Merchant of Venice* by Launcelot), lay at the base of the official Venetian populace).[11] Edward Muir attributes the relative tractability of the *popolani* to the "egalitarian attitude of the courts" and to the sacral quality of the city's civic pageants and festivals; Brian Pullan points as well to the strength and resilience of the city's charitable organizations and the public policy initiatives associated with them, including the availability of low-interest loans to the poor required in charters with the Jewish community.[12] Finally, existing within the borders of Venice in their own segregated neighborhoods were the established groups of resident aliens, including German and Turkish merchants as well as the Jews. Each of these groups had a recognized corporate identity in the life of the city and contributed to its commercial success, maintaining its own national membership and regulating civil activities and disputes within the watermarked bounds of its separate quarters. These incorporated bodies of legally recognized resident aliens achieved a form of citizenship that functioned both inside Venice (as part of its geography of neighborhoods, guilds, and confraternities) and outside its jurisdiction, governing themselves according to laws and customs imported from outside.

The status of the Jews, however, was not strictly covalent with that of the other foreign groups. On March 29, 1516, the Venetian Senate enacted the following decree:

> *The Jews must all live together in the Corte de Case, which are in the Ghetto near San Girolamo; and in order to prevent their roaming about at night: Let there be built two Gates on the side of the Old Ghetto where there is a little Bridge, and likewise on the other side of the Bridge . . . which Gates shall be opened in the morning at the sound of the Marangona, and shall be closed at midnight by four Christian guards appointed and paid by the Jews at the rate deemed suitable by Our Cabinet.*[13]

Eventually there would be two ghettos, one for the "German Nation" of Jews of long residence in Venice, and one for the Spanish and Portuguese Jews, many of them *conversos* and *marranos*. The latter group had especially close ties with Rumania, the Balkans, and the Ottoman Empire; indeed, many were Turkish subjects, with a special legal status (Calimani 45, 46).[14] The Levantine Jews were more often brought before the Inquisition in Venice than the German ones, not because they professed to be Jews, but because they professed to be Christians in ways that rendered their allegiances suspect. Like the *universitas judeorum* of Marlowe's Malta, the Venetian ghettos were part residential quarter (guaranteeing a relative permanence of address and self-rule in a civic history marked by repeated expulsions) and part prison (with a curfew, guards, boarded windows, restricted exit and entry, and so on). The ghettos of Venice became models for Christian communities across Europe concerned to sequester the Jewish element, as well as destinations chosen by Jews in search of relative safety, prosperity, and civil autonomy in Diaspora.[15]

In reconstructing what he provocatively calls "the Ghetto Republic," historian David J. Malkiel has argued that the Venetian *università,* itself an umbrella organization of several national groups with their own distinctive charters and sets of rights, borrowed some of its own constitutional features from that of the Venetian republic.[16] Malkiel argues for a general shift in the sixteenth century from a homogeneous Jewish community organized around the plutocratic figure of a single banker-founder to a diverse community governed by a body of officials elected from the different corporate groups of the larger *università:* in the course of the sixteenth century, "The structure of the banker and entourage was ultimately replaced by that of a political community."[17] The Jewish circle of citizenship, drafting its procedures from elements of Jewish, Roman, and Venetian law, was itself composed of many interior circles (German and Italian, Levantine, Spanish, and Portuguese); indeed, Malkiel argues that the ethnic diversity of the Jews in Venice "was the most powerful internal dynamic in the construction and operation of Venetian Jewish self-governance."[18]

Shakespeare, of course, would have known few if any of these fine points. His achievement instead was to visualize Shylock's entrance into the public space of Venice from a milieu distinctively marked as Jewish. An exception in the scene of Gentile Venice, Shylock is normative with respect to Judaism and the daily operation of the Jewish community incorporated as a legal foreign body in the Christian commonwealth. The normative quality of Shylock's Judaism separates him sharply from the extremist profile of his literary antecedent, Barabas, whose criminal consciousness made him an exception with respect to all norms, Jewish or Christian. Shakespeare, on the other hand, makes Shylock *part of a world,* trained in certain habits of exegesis and governing his life according to socially validated rules.[19] In creating a *normative Jew* living as a *tolerated exception* in a Christian state, Shakespeare draws on the historical resources of Pauline typology, with its emphasis on the legal integrity and historical function of Israel in the unfolding drama of redemption. As we saw in chapter 1, Paul was determined to discount the legal observances of contemporary Judaism in order to broaden membership in Christ in the current moment of messianic crisis, yet he remained equally committed to granting historical significance to the Jews as a people governed by special laws. The mimetic achievement of *The Merchant of Venice,* as well as its unresolved dilemmas, largely derive from Shakespeare's ability to retranslate these two poles in the Pauline legacy in relation to the institutions of classical politics recovered within and behind them.

In his first scene, Shylock defends usury through recourse to a biblical prooftext, the story of Jacob in the house of Laban:

SHYLOCK: *When Jacob grazed his uncle Laban's sheep—*
This Jacob from our holy Abram was,
As his wise mother wrought in his behalf,
The third possessor; ay, he was the third—

ANTONIO: *And what of him? Did he take interest?*

SHYLOCK: *No, not take interest, not as you would say*
Directly interest. Mark what Jacob did.
When Laban and himself were compromised
That all the eanlings which were streaked and pied
Should fall as Jacob's hire, the ewes, being rank,
In end of autumn turnèd to the rams,
And when the work of generation was
Between these woolly breeders in the act,
The skillful shepherd peeled me certain wands,
And in the doing of the deed of kind
He stuck them up before the fulsome ewes,
Who then conceiving did in eaning time
Fall parti-colored lambs, and those were Jacob's.
This was a way to thrive, and he was blest;
And thrift is blessing, if men steal it not. (1.3.69–88)

Shylock's style of exegesis deliberately excludes all references to the New Testament and its systematic reinscription of Old Testament motifs.[20] Instead, his emphasis falls on what we could call the "practical reason" embedded in the story, the pointers it contains for handling the social and economic challenges of everyday life in an ethical, Torah-based manner. Shylock's reading of the Jacob story is by no means a straightforward "literalism" or "legalism," much as his argumentation will devolve into such later in the play; to the contrary, his examination of the conundrums of urban life through recourse to the pastoral vocabulary of ancient Israel requires the systematic substitution of one set of terms for another. As such, Shylock's hermeneutics are not out of keeping with the project of early midrash, which "measure[s] the distance between Mishnah [the legal core of the Talmud] and Scripture and aims to close it."[21] Much as Shylock uses the Jacob narrative to explain and legitimate the practice of moneylending, many midrashim gloss Biblical stories in response to legal rulings or problems, striving to coordinate the narrative and the prescriptive dimensions of Torah by asking "Scripture to tell them how they were supposed to conduct themselves at the critical turnings of life."[22]

These exegetical techniques come out of and in turn help define the laws constituting a specific national group. Shylock's opening excursus on the genealogy that links him through the ages to "our holy Abram" expands upon Shylock's reference earlier in the same scene to "our sacred nation" (1.3.43). In Shylock's hermeneutics, what makes his "nation" "sacred" is the Book that establishes election on the basis of a revealed law, a set of "statutes and ordinances" (Deut 4:1,5) confirmed and unfolded in the Torah's narratives of generation and livelihood and given substance in the daily workings of Jewish communities. Here as elsewhere in the play, the word *nation* in the singular translates the peculiar status of the Jews as an *ethnos,* a stranger-people defined by both a religious code and a genealogical imperative that sets them apart from the "nations" united in Christ (see 3.1.53, 81). In this regard, it is striking that the story Shylock chooses to tell is about the appropriative manipulation and marking of the fruits of physical generation through an external act. As an indirect allegory of *ethnos*—the demarcation of a flock that will become the property of Jacob/Israel—the scoring of a shaft symbolizing procreation leads to the mottling and subsequent separating of the animals on grounds that are physical without being fully natural. Similarly, circumcision "pills the wand" in order to register the infant in the nation, imposing a definitive and permanent bodily sign through an act of deliberate *techne.*[23] Shylock's exegetical exercise defines the Jews as a "sacred nation" not only of brothers (defined by blood), but also of *readers,* a community bound by a common set of revealed texts and shared habits of interpreting them.

Pauline discourse provides a model of historical reconstruction ready at hand for Shakespeare's mimetic goal—namely, to depict not a criminal Jew à la Barabas, but an ordinary Jew who enters the public stage of Venice from another public sphere. Recall Paul's words in Romans, reminding his mixed audience of Israel's special historical destiny: "They are Israelites, and to them belong the sonship, the glory, the covenants, the giving of the law, the worship, and the promises; to them belong the patriarchs, and of their race [*sarx:* flesh] . . . is the Christ" (Rom 9:4–5). As we saw in chapter 1, Paul's contribution to the Western discourse of nations encompasses not only the extension of the Christian message to all mankind, but also the preservation within that universal message of a unique place for the Jewish people and Scripture. That place is defined above all *historically,* as a monumental yet circumscribed foundation for the Christian epoch that replaces the Hebrew one by retroactively occupying the prophetic lines laid out by it. In *The Merchant of Venice,* Shakespeare grants a qualified authenticity, a fixed yet potent integrity—the bounded coherence of an historical period—to this Bible and the interpretive modes associated with it, and he does this by virtue of the historicizing or "civil-izing" vision of the Jewish *ethnos* implicit in Pauline typology. If typology grants Shylock's voice its provisional autonomy, it also severely limits its validity; in Lars Engle's acute analysis, "Shylock loses control of the Jacob story as soon as he introduces it: he becomes Laban, his daughter and idols stolen, or Esau, bereft of blessing and compelled to witness a younger people thrive."[24] The larger point I want to make is not simply that Shylock's Jewish hermeneutics are rejected by the Christian techniques that dominate the play, but rather that the very possibility of imagining a specifically Jewish habit of reading itself exists within the typological framework as an essential if restricted part of its historical vision.

The interpretive community represented by Shylock in act 1 is a group that also eats, drinks, and prays. When Bassanio invites Shylock to dinner in the same scene, the Jew's response deftly conceptualizes the intersecting spheres of civil life in the play:

> SHYLOCK: *May I speak with Antonio?*
>
> BASSANIO: *If it please you to dine with us.*
>
> SHYLOCK: *Yes, to smell pork, to eat of the habitation which your prophet the Nazarite conjured the devil into. I will buy with you, sell with you, talk with you, walk with you, and so following; but I will not eat with you, drink with you, nor pray with you. (1.3.29–36)*

The interchange establishes three circles of citizenship in the play: the *civility* of the ruling class; the *civil society* of economic exchange; and the *Jewish community* created and maintained by both external mandate and internal laws. Antonio's supper party, the promised end of social gathering in the first movement of the play (1.1–2.6), epitomizes the civil conversation of the Venetian nobility, bound together by "gentle" acts of friendship, hospitality, and gift-giving that enact and ensure equity within the closed circle of the aristocratic republic.[25] Bassanio offers Shylock temporary entry into this world, but the Jew refuses. Excluded from the public civic life of Venice by virtue of his religion, Shylock, like Barabas, becomes a concentrated cipher of the divisive forces of an increasingly market-driven economy, an antisocial society that identifies, as Shylock does, a man's "goodness" not with his ethical bearing, but with his financial credit (1.3.12–15).[26] Declining Bassanio's covenantal hospitality, Shylock insists instead that the sphere properly shared by Jews and Christians is that of *civil society,* reduced to its un-civil core: buying, selling, and the walking and talking that facilitate these transactions. "Walking" implies access to some form of shared public space, while "talking" implies a minimal common language. Yet active expulsion of the

Jews by the Christians into the domain of naked capital is both reinforced and relieved by the existence of a third circle of citizenship, namely the *università*, or corporate body, formed by Venice's several Jewish groups. If Shylock will not eat, drink, or pray with the Christians, it is not simply because they won't let him (after all, Bassanio's invitation is on the table), but because the legal norms of his own milieu do not permit it. These laws separate him from the Venetians as an exception, but in relation to another set of rules that designate and regulate an alternate civic space.

The minor character of Tubal, "a wealthy Hebrew of [Shylock's] tribe" (1.3.54), steps out from the Jewish community as its normative representative. Gratiano quips with his trademark gratuitousness, "Here comes another of the tribe. A third cannot be matched, unless the devil himself turn Jew" (3.1.73–74). In relation to the Venetian nobility, the Jews are devils—exceptions to the Christian norm—but in relation to each other, they are "match'd," displaying similar behaviors dictated by the same collective rules. Whereas Barabas's fellow Jews in Malta exist as the first in a line of dupes, Tubal participates in an ongoing series of normative exchanges with Shylock: he lends him money to meet Antonio's needs (1.3.52–55), he gives Shylock news of Jessica's doings and Antonio's misfortunes (3.1), and he presumably agrees to "fee an officer" for Shylock in anticipation of Antonio's breach of contract (3.1.119). Their interchange in act 3 ends with the promise of a further rendezvous: "Go, Tubal, and meet me at our synagogue. Go, good Tubal; at our synagogue, Tubal" (3.3.121–23). The word *synagogue*, as we saw in chapter 2, indicated for the Jews in the Hellenistic and Latin Diaspora the act of assembly, the place of assembly, and the community so assembled, an increasingly important site for communal business in the post-Temple, post-priestly context of semi-autonomous self-rule in host states.[27] Although the religious sense of the term was dominant by the sixteenth century, Shylock's invitation to Tubal reactivates its political meaning; they have appointed to *meet in the place of meeting*, and there determine their next move in the legal gambit with Antonio. With Tubal, Shylock eats, drinks, and prays, but also buys, sells, walks, and talks, combining civil and civic functions within the limited sphere of Jewish self-regulation.

Shylock's refusal of Bassanio's dinner invitation asserts the problem of commensality or "table fellowship" that figured along with circumcision as one of the major conflicts between Paul and Peter in the struggles over the rites and rights of membership in the new church. As James D. G. Dunn notes, "part of the pressure on a devout Jew in the 40s and 50s of the first century AD would have been the constraint to observe the limits of acceptable table-fellowship."[28] In Galatians, Paul links dietary laws and circumcision in his reference to a conflict at Antioch with Cephas, follower of Peter: "For before certain men came from James, [Cephas] ate with the Gentiles; but when they came he drew back and separated himself, fearing the circumcision party" (Gal 2:12). Invited to eat with the Gentiles, Shylock also "draws back and separates himself," actively choosing in this case to remain within the world defined by Jewish law. Shakespeare borrows from Paul the negative judgment on the ethical, soteriological, and civil limits of such a retreat, but he equally borrows from Paul a sense of the social, emotional, and legal coherence—the lived normativity—of that world.[29]

These same features of the Pauline legacy underwrite Shylock's famous "Hath not a Jew eyes" speech (3.1.50–69), whose pathos rests on the paradox of Shylock's claim to participate in the general circle of humanity from within the particular world of the Jews. The force of his cascade of rhetorical questions is to insist on his human affinity with his Venetian compatriots: "Hath not a Jew eyes? Hath not a Jew hands, organs, dimensions, senses, affections, passions?" Yet when he asks if we are not "fed with the same food," he poses the limits of commensality drawn by both Venetian social practice (eating with Jews, along with other forms of intimate intercourse, was actively discouraged by the Venetian polity) and Jewish law. When Shylock asks further, "If you prick us do we not bleed?" he hits directly on circumcision as a contested symbol of citizenship in the two traditions. Enrolling the infant or adult proselyte into the nation of Israel by cutting the physical body, circumcision in Judaism functions as a (de)naturalizing rite. But Shylock's evocation of circumcision in this speech is closer to Paul than to Abraham: If we all bleed when we are pricked, does not our common participation in the *ethne* of the world supercede enrollment in any particular *ethnos*? Shakespeare draws on the audience's Christian knowingness to limit the impact of Shylock's plea; surely it is not Shylock, but Shakespeare, who evokes Paul, mobilizing the Epistles in order to dissolve Jewish difference in the promise of Christian humanism. Yet Paul, unlike the Gentile Church Fathers, remained "pricked" in the flesh as well as in the heart. This constitutive double scarring of the body of Pauline thought in turn *limits the limit* placed on Shylock's plea by the supercessionist force of the New Testament allusion. Not unlike Paul, Shylock is willing to lay claim to participation in something universal (call it human being) based on the deep procedural specificity of his membership in the nation of Israel. Before this truth Shakespeare refuses to flinch, though he finally has no dramatic or conceptual means to maintain it.

Home Alone

In Shakespeare's play, Shylock stumbles twice: first, when he refuses Bassanio's dinner invitation, remaining resolutely in the circumcision party; and second, when he belatedly accepts the invitation, breaking the dietary laws that hold together his community and leaving his daughter home alone. Planning her elopement, Jessica bids farewell to Launcelot:

> *I am sorry thou wilt leave my father so.*
> *Our house is hell, and thou, a merry devil,*
> *Didst rob it of some taste of tediousness.* (2.3.1–3)

In the dramatic line of *The Jew of Malta,* Jessica alludes to the medieval stage convention of the Hell's Mouth, here perhaps gesturing to the inner stage as its remainder in the public theater. If her house is Hell and her servant is a "merry devil," or stage clown, she nonetheless finds her abode "tedious" rather than horrific, implying the internal normativity of the Jews' exceptionalism in relation to Venice. Jessica goes on to separate herself from the family of Shylock:

> *But though I am a daughter to his blood,*
> *I am not to his manners. O Lorenzo,*
> *If thou keep promise, I shall end this strife,*
> *Become a Christian and thy loving wife.* (2.3.17–20)

Launcelot's change in service from Jew to Christian—a move made at the lowest level of Venetian society, by a member of its *populo menuto*—traces the same path as Jessica's proposed escape from the Jewish ghetto into Venetian society, indeed, into the special *politeia* constituted by the urban nobility. The rite of marriage is Jessica's means of civic naturalization and is bound implicitly to the act of religious conversion. As will also be the case for Othello, Jessica aims to enter into three types of covenant: the *marriage contract* (intermarriage) is the means to the *civic contract* (naturalization), and is signed and sealed by the *religious covenant* (conversion). In these transactions, marriage is at once means and end—because she desires to marry Lorenzo, she is willing to convert and leave the ghetto; at the same time, marriage to Lorenzo is her passport out of Jewish particularism into the larger Venetian and Christian polity. Marriage, moreover, as a legal ritual mediates or "marries" the civil and religious moments. Creating a ligature between two kinship groups, marriage represents the first instance of civil society. The irregularity of elopement reduces marriage to the barest minimum of civil contract, namely, consent between the two parties, without parental knowledge, communal witnessing, or the blessings of the Church. The furtive elements of theft and prodigality that attend the midnight marriage of Jessica and Lorenzo render their union *merely civil* or *barely civil,* a libertine exercise at the limits of social norms for both groups. At the same time, however, their union, insofar as it implies Jessica's conversion to Christianity, takes on a sacramental, even mystical quality in the larger typological frame of the play, her individual conversion borrowing its shape from biblical narratives (the Exodus, the marriage of Jacob and Rachel), and redolent with the messianic promise of Jewish redemption.[30]

If Jessica and Lorenzo's elopement strips marriage to its barely civil core, Shakespeare reclothes their union in the costume of carnival, evoking the forms of civic ritual, at once political and theological, that lent their aesthetic power to Venice's legendary social cohesion and stability.[31] It is no accident that their night-time absconding is coordinated with Bassanio's bon voyage party: "But come at once, / For the close night doth play the runaway,/ And we are stayed for at Bassanio's feast" (2.6.47–49). This is the same supper party that Shylock had first refused, and has then fatefully chosen to join. The festive meal represents the closed civility of the urban aristocracy (the hospitality shared by friends in the *philadelphia* of a limited republic), and the open *koinônia* of Christianity (the easy table fellowship of the Gentiles). Yet the much-promised meal is never, it seems, adequately or completely consummated in the play. The paths of father and daughter do not cross, the infidel presumably coming early and perhaps not eating, and the new convert arriving late and missing whatever seating there had been: "No masque tonight. The wind is come about; / Bassanio presently will go aboard" (2.6.63–64).

If Paul authorizes Jessica's manumission from the law, he is also, however, the preserver of an economized modicum of Jewish difference. Jessica's soliloquy in the house of her father is Pauline not only in its proposed escape from the closed ghetto to the open city, but also in Jessica's momentary contemplation of the losses incurred by her triple entry into the marital, Christian, and civic covenants. She experiences as "heinous sin" her shame for her father (recalling the Fifth Commandment) but, through her actions, subordinates the old law of the father to her new membership in Christianity. She attributes both "blood" and "manners" to Shylock, fixing him in a way of life as well as a personal demeanor, supporting Barbara Lewalski's aptly Pauline formulation that Judaism and Christianity function in the play "as theological systems . . . and also as historic societies."[32] Jessica is preparing to leave one historic society for another, enacting a typological passage whose costs are acknowledged if not lamented in this scene of formal disaffiliation.

Jessica's quasi-ritual act of disaffiliation finds precedent in both hagiographic and civic discourses. In the lives of the saints, the young believer often begins her death walk by separating herself from earlier domestic and romantic ties, echoing the call of Christ's church militant: "For I have come to set a man against his father, and a daughter against her mother" (Matt. 10:35).[33] Citizenship, especially in the critical moments of legal institution or naturalization, also involves the mortification or transvaluation of kinship ties. Jessica is a citizen-saint in her doubling of the two functions of Christian conversion and civic naturalization under the rainbow canopy of intermarriage. Having broken with her prior familial, civic, and religious circles, she sacrifices Jewish patrimony for Christian matrimony. When her father locks her in for the night, she declares, "Farewell, and if my fortune be not crossed, / I have a father, you a daughter, lost" (2.5.57–58). Exiting from the ghetto, she does not look back, spending with a prodigality worthy of Bassanio her father's money and his engagement ring ("I had it of Leah when I was a bachelor" [3.1.114]). Crossing over the double threshold drawn by Jewish and Venetian laws, Jessica can trade the ring for a monkey because the complex set of affiliations it had bound together (marital/familial, religious/covenantal, legal/communal) have been broken apart and refigured. Pauline typology provides the symbolic archway shaping and sheltering this citizen-saint's flight from "blood" to "manners," from "flesh" to "promise," from Judaism to Christianity, and from kinship to citizenship. Yet Paul's passion for Judaism—the passion that Judaism undergoes in Paul— keeps track of the travel expenses when Jessica no longer can or will, gathering the receipts of historical transformation and handing them over to Shylock as their nominal repossessor.

Citizenship on Trial

The trial scene sends us to the center of Venetian civic life. In sixteenth-century Venice, the setting would have been the Ducal Palace, on the Piazza San Marco, where the official life of the city unfurled between the Ducal Palace and the Cathedral of St. Mark, the two poles of sacred and political life mediated and manifested in the great pageants and processions that took place in the public square of the Piazza itself.[34] The Duke presides over the proceedings of act 4, but his authority is severely limited by the laws of the state. Edward Muir characterizes the Duke's authority in historical Venice: "Symbolically, he was the sovereign of Venice; legally he was merely *primus inter pares* of the patrician class; but practically he could wield whatever power his own ability and political connections provided."[35] There was much debate among sixteenth-century political theorists about the nature and extent of the Duke's sovereignty. Humanists like Contarini, who lauded Venice as a living example of a classical mixed constitution, insisted on the limited but real sovereignty of the Duke.[36] Jean Bodin, arguing from the premise that sovereignty is indivisible, insisted, contra Contarini, that no constitution, including the Venetian one, could be mixed. Accordingly, Bodin wrote of the Doge, "[H]e is a prince *(princeps)* properly so called, which is to say 'the first.' For he is nothing but the first among the gentlemen of

Venice, and has no more than the privilege of speaking last when decisions are made in any council where he is present."[37]

In the trial scene (actually a hearing, as Jay Halio points out),[38] the Doge speaks semi-privately to Antonio, exhorts Shylock to show mercy, but has no power of his own to abrogate the terms of the contract. As Shylock says, "If you deny it, let the danger light / Upon your charter and your city's freedom!" (4.1.38–39), a constitutional position confirmed repeatedly throughout the scene (e.g., 62–63, 176–77). Antonio had made the same point in his prison cell:

> *The Duke cannot deny the course of law;*
> *For the commodity that strangers have*
> *With us in Venice, if it be denied,*
> *Will much impeach the justice of the state,*
> *Since that the trade and profit of the city*
> *Consisteth of all nations. (3.3.26–31)*

Antonio links constitutionalism and capitalism: the laws of Venice insure the economic transactions continually being made among Venetian citizens and "strangers," each of whose commercial rights are protected under civil law.[39] If Antonio and Shylock reside in two very different and unequal spheres, the "gentle" civility of the urban aristocracy on the one hand and the alien world of the ghetto on the other, merchant and Jew nonetheless function as relative equals when they sign a bond or contract in the limited yet economically essential public space defined by "trade and profit." This minimalist map of the public space required by capital is not without theological resonance in Antonio's discourse: The reference to "nations," recalling the Pauline motif of equality among the *ethne*, backs the social and civil contracts of the city with the promise of a universal religious covenant. Taken together, these contracts map the historico-symbolic coherence and incipient modernity of the play's representational program. As such, it must be maintained at any cost, even the life of Antonio, whose willingness here to die for the rule of law casts him in the role of the citizen-saint.

The case that Shylock brings before the Duke is a civil one, involving breach of contract; in this situation, the Duke has no power to step above the law. When Portia makes her famous argument for mercy, she directs her appeal not to the Duke, but to Shylock:

> *'Tis mightiest in the mightiest; it becomes*
> *The thronèd monarch better than his crown.*
> *His scepter shows the force of temporal power,*

The attribute to awe and majesty,
Wherein doth sit the dread and fear of kings.
But mercy is above this sceptred sway;
It is enthronèd in the heart of kings;
It is an attribute to God himself. . . . (4.1.182–93)

Portia draws liberally on the iconography of sacral kingship familiar from political theology, but she must address this discourse to the plaintiff, not the sovereign, since the Duke is himself subject to the rule of law and cannot create an exception to it. Wielding the power of justice and mercy, Shylock emerges for a moment as a vengeful shadow of the kind of singular sovereign order displaced by constitutionalism.

In Shakespeare's Republic of Venice, the political decision that marks sovereignty has been dispersed in the circuits of the legal process, where it takes shape again in the form of circumcision, the ritual that informs Shylock's bond in the exegetical imagination of the play. As critics have long noted, Shylock's bond represents a tendentious reworking of Paul's "circumcision of the heart"; what has been demonstrated less systematically is the way in which Shylock's reappropriation is one moment in a set of procedures performed by *The Merchant of Venice* on the Pauline motif, moves that together thematize the play's philosophy of history as well as the faultlines disturbing the symbolic consistency of its world.[40] It is not enough to simply equate the literalisms of Shylock and Portia, such that the Judaism of the one renders ironic or paradoxical the Christianity of the other. Instead, each set of literalizing moves must be seen as a step in a historical dialectic, a progressive emplotment that may indeed be subsequently unsettled by the irony (or allegory) intimated by its parallel stages, but which nonetheless also serves to lay out the dominant ethical and mimetic coordinates of the play.

In Romans, Paul writes, "He is a Jew who is one inwardly, and real circumcision is a matter of the heart, spiritual and not literal" (Rom 2:29). As we saw in chapter 1, Paul's dictum encapsulates his attempt to internalize and universalize the Jewish rite of circumcision by making it into a symbol of righteousness by faith. In his rereading of Abraham's circumcision in Romans 4, Paul shifts from the performative emphasis on circumcision-as-seal *(sphragis)* in Genesis 17 to the semiotic emphasis on circumcision-as-sign *(semeion)* developed in the Prophets (Rom 4:11). In doing so, however, Paul does not (and cannot) simply dissolve the external act in the internal state. He *cannot* because it is the nature of the sign to exist as a split form. Perhaps more important, however, Paul would not even *want* to effect such a complete dissolution of the external mark, because it supports the historical differential that links and separates

Judaism and Christianity, the temporal and membership relation so important to Paul's double project of instituting a universal mission while reserving a theological function for Israel. In the recurrent, insistently temporalizing phrase of Romans, God comes to "the Jew first, and also to the Greek" (2:9, 2:10). As Auerbach points out, typology "differs from most of the allegorical forms known to us by the historicity both of the sign and what it signifies."[41] Accordingly, Paul had to acknowledge the actual performance of circumcision as a rite (its trace still visible, of course, on his own flesh), since it is only through its physical enactment—on real bodies in a discrete historical space—that circumcision can become a sign of the new Christian era that replaces it.[42]

Milton's short poem "On the Circumcision" similarly insists on the physicality of Christ's circumcision. In the poem's final lines, the infant Jesus

> . . . seals *obedience first with wounding smart*
> *This day; but Oh! ere long*
> *Huge pangs and strong*
> *Will* pierce more near his heart *[emphasis added]*.[43]

The typological impulse of the verse moves from circumcision of the foreskin to that of the heart, the one pointing upwards and inwards to the other in a figural sequence. In this poem, however, both moments require a physical piercing or pricking that occurs in time and on the flesh, since here the latter event is not so much the inner faith of Paul (though Milton certainly alludes to this as well) but the physical passion of Christ on the cross, the historical turning point around which so much typological interpretation unfurls its significations. The word *seal,* which Milton borrows from Genesis 17 as well as Romans 4, signals the performative status of circumcision in the very act of deploying it in a figural pattern of metaphoric correspondences. In Christ's Passion, taken by Milton as the archetypal "circumcision of the heart," the physical actuality and the spiritual meaning of circumcision perfectly coincide on the cross, in which the human and the divine, the temporal and the transcendent, the horizontal and the vertical—already united in the Incarnation—are torn asunder in order to be forever rejoined in the Resurrection.

In *The Merchant of Venice,* Shakespeare exploits this historical logic for specifically mimetic ends. When Shylock says in the trial scene, "I stand for judgment" (4.1.103), the quasi-allegorical signification does not obscure the memorable character cut by Shylock in the play; Shylock achieves a psychological presence not despite but because of the play's Pauline coordinates. Shylock's physical circumcision has forever fixed him in his own world, whose unique combination of normativity (as a semi-autonomous community) and exceptionality (in relation to the Republic of Venice) are equally plotted by the hermeneutics mobilized by Paul. So too, Antonio does not disappear into his Christological figurations; part of what establishes his reality on the stage is the very real threat that, as with Milton's Christ, "Huge pangs and strong / Will pierce more near his heart." What links Antonio to Christ is his location in a sacrificial scenario that foregrounds his human vulnerability, a humanity embodied (like that of Morocco or Shylock earlier in the play) by the ability of his flesh to be pierced.[44] In the case of Antonio, however, the frailty of the flesh presents not an obstacle to spiritualization, but the very passageway for it, the material tunnel that enables symbolic interiorization; the forfeited flesh of Antonio, like the sacred heart of Christ, brings into incarnational harmony the physical and the spiritual, the signifier and the signified, bound together in Paul's reading of circumcision.

Hence, if the bond as suffered by Antonio implies the Pauline symbolization of circumcision, the bond as formulated and executed by Shylock recalls the Jewish reading of *brit milah*. Shylock declares in court,

> *Till thou canst rail the* seal from off my bond,
> *Thou but offend'st thy lungs to speak so loud.*
> *Repair thy wit, good youth, or it will fall*
> *To cureless ruin.* I stand here for law. *(4.1.139–42; emphasis added)*

Shylock's emphasis on the "seal" of the bond places the contractual and performative account of circumcision from Genesis 17 over against its semiotic and symbolic retranscription in Romans 4; the seal on his bond cannot be "railed off" in the same way that the scar of circumcision remains a permanent mark of *ethnos* on the naturalized and nationalized Jewish body. As Leslie Fiedler points out, the seal of circumcision that ratifies Israel's covenant with God is what makes the Jew Jewish, his identity being contractual rather than inherited: "[A]rchetypally the Jew does not exist at all, not even for himself, until he has made his covenant with God."[45] In the play's typological economy, it is precisely Shylock's insistence on the Jewish seal that locates him at the end of the speech as the historical symbol of the old covenant: "I stand here for law." Like the seal of circumcision in Milton's poem, Shylock assumes a semiotic function in the play insofar as he insists on the performativity of contract.

Yet Shylock speaks not as an Old Testament patriarch, but rather as a modern Jew in Christian Venice; so too, the bond does not allude to circumcision per se but to its symbolic displacement toward the heart. Shakespeare stages Shylock's Judaic reading within the arena of Christian modernity in order to isolate and embody the potentially non-Christian aspects—here, the contractual basis—of capitalist society. That is, Shylock's strategy does not return him to a Judaism free of Christian revision; he cannot go back to the first, originary moment of the institution of circumcision, above all not in his interactions with the Christian community. Instead, Shylock tries to transform the Christian rereading of circumcision into a weapon to use against Christianity itself, deforming the Christian symbolization of circumcision by resubjecting it to its Jewish characteristics as contractual seal and as physical act within the public space delimited by civil contract and its litigation. Although both of these features are also maintained in Paul's rereading of circumcision, it is always in incarnational relation to the semiotic structure and spiritual telos identified with "the heart," a balance that Shylock's bond attempts to tip back toward the flesh. (The result, of course, is a distortion of circumcision in Judaism as well as Christianity.) This upsetting of the Pauline balance characterizes Shylock's "legalism" or "literalism," which names not the imagined hermeneutics of Judaism per se as an independently evolving system (more closely approached in Shylock's midrash on Jacob and Laban) but the symbolic disfigurations produced when Judaism reappears as a residual threat within the Christian scene, an arena itself constituted as the progressive reinterpretation of Hebrew motifs.

So far, then, three distinct moments measure out the cuts of circumcision in the play's exegetical historicism:

1. Circumcision of the foreskin (Genesis 17): OT
2. Circumcision of the heart (Romans 2): NT
3. Circumcision of the heart literalized (Shylock's bond): modern Judaism in Christian world

To these three moments in the historic rereading of circumcision, we should add a fourth, namely Portia's legal tactics in act 4. Modernist "anti-Portia" readers of the play have, I believe, too quickly equated Portia's legalism with Shylock's in a scene of abyssal irony.[46] Portia's legalism, however, pointedly occurs under the aegis of Christianity, not of Judaism. At the trial's turning point, Portia declares,

> *Tarry a little; there is something else.*
> *This bond doth give thee here no jot of blood;*
> *The words expressly are "a pound of flesh."* (4.1.305–8)

Portia's "jot of blood" recalls Christ's words in the Sermon on the Mount: "Think not that I have come to abolish the law and the prophets; I have come not to abolish them but to fulfill them. For truly, I say to you, till heaven and earth pass away, *not an iota,* not a dot [KJV: tittle], will pass from the law until all is accomplished" (Matt 5:17–18; emphasis added).

Spelled as "one iote" in the Geneva Bible and as "iot" in Shakespeare's Folio, both Portia and Jesus refer to the Greek *iota* [ι] modeled on the Hebrew *yodh* [י], its simple stroke constituting the most minimal letter in both alphabets and hence coming to indicate the smallest or least bit of something.[47] Jesus, reassuring his Jewish audience that he does not intend to do away with the law, goes on to effect its internalization by arguing that anger against one's brother is equivalent to violence against him. He thus renders up, according to the Geneva gloss, "the true meaning of the sixth commandement" (against killing) through an act of retroactive rereading. A law so thoroughly interiorized, however, can no longer be regulated by a public judicial institution like that of the Sanhedrin; hence Christ's "fulfillment" of the law also changes it forever.[48] Portia's reference to the "jot of blood" serves both to align Shylock's bond with the bloody letter of the law and to associate her own legalism not with Shylock's Judaism but with the internalizing "fulfillment" of the law brought about in Christ's post-Sinai Sermon on the Mount. Rather than simply identifying her with Shylock by ironically repeating his tactics, Portia's maneuver functions dialectically, as the negation of a negation, a sublation that locates the two characters on either side of a historical divide, within two distinct circles of citizenship. Whereas Shylock's bond represents the return of Judaism within and against Christianity, Portia's ruling instantiates the reformational rhythm of Christianity as the repeated overturning of its own Judaizing tendencies.

Although Portia follows Jesus, not Shylock, in promising not to change an iota of the law, her own argument conspicuously fails to complete the movement of fulfillment and internalization modeled in the Sermon on the Mount. Compare Portia's "jot of blood" with Augustine's linked theories of language and life: "Not all the parts [of life] exist at once, but some must come as others go, and in this way together they make up the whole of which they are parts. Our speech follows the same rule, using sounds to signify a meaning. For a sentence is not complete unless each word, once its syllables have been pronounced, gives way to make room for the next."[49]

Augustine, writing as always in a typological mode, insists on the temporality of both language and experience, such that the full meaning of an earlier sound or event only becomes clear when the sequence in which it appears arrives at its conclusion, retroactively revealing the meaning or spirit of the individual sounds or elements that make it up.[50] Portia's "no jot of blood," on the other hand, does not itself unfold or develop the logic it evokes, refusing to deploy the *iota* in a word or sentence that would render up its meaning. Indeed, as a "jot of *blood*," it is no longer clear that the *iota* functions as a letter at all, indicating instead a minimal quantity-without-quality, a blot, mark, or arche-writing that obscures rather than constitutes meaning. Circling back to the tropics of circumcision, the "jot of blood" names the element of physical cision, pricking, or cutting, along with its attendant marking and scarring, performed by *brit milah,* but forcibly rips that element from either its national function in Judaism or its universalization in Paul. For a moment, the letter floats free of its typological suturing, as a symptomatic jot, blot, or stain that obscures the play's historical vision.

As such, it meets up with the "seal" of the Jew's bond, uncannily identifying Portia and Shylock across the epochal divide that separates them. For the Jew (or "Iewe") is precisely such a jot (or "iot") in the figural structure articulated by the play. The Hebrew patriarch is a key element, a capital letter, in the historical sequence leading from the physical covenant with Abraham to the stone tablets of Sinai to Paul's writing "on your hearts" (2 Cor 3:3). The modern Jew, however, dislodging the Hebrew letter from its Hellenizing transcription, represents an illegible stain in Christianity's temporal schematics. Shylock's refusal to accept the typological contract also entails the return of allegory within the symbolic scene of "Shakespearean" representation—the return, that is, of a Shakespeare other than the one produced by the play's mimetic successes. This allegorical stoppage leads to the impasse of ironic mirroring, not (as some secular critics have suggested) because Portia's discourse directly resembles Shylock's, but, more complexly, because her short-circuiting of historical interiorization highlights the structural parallels between dialectically distinct eras, rendering up the rhythmic periodicity of history as the engine of its own ironization.

A similar process of abruption governs the canine insults that follow Shylock throughout the play and climax with Gratiano's courtroom invective, making the Jew into a living epithet no longer fully contained by the play's mimetic frame. Gratiano castigates Shylock:

> GRATIANO: *O be thou damned, inexecrable dog!*
> *And for thy life let justice be accused!*
> *Thou almost mak'st me waver in my faith,*
> *To hold opinion with Pythagoras*
> *That souls of animals infuse themselves*
> *Into the trunks of men. Thy currish spirit*
> *Governed a wolf who, hanged for human slaughter,*
> *Even from the gallows did his fell soul fleet,*
> *And, whilst thou layest in thy unhallowed dam,*
> *Infused itself in thee; for thy desires*
> *Are wolvish, bloody, starved, and ravenous.*
>
> SHYLOCK: *Till thou canst rail the seal from off my bond . . . (4.1.128–39)*[51]

More powerfully than any topical reference, the identification of Jews with dogs here and elsewhere in the play recollects Paul's exhortation to the Philippians, a mixed congregation of Romans, Greeks, and Jews:[52] "*Look out for the dogs,* look out for the evil-workers, look out for *those who mutilate the flesh.* For we are *the true circumcision,* who worship God in spirit, and glory in Christ Jesus, and put no confidence in the flesh" (Phil 3:2–3; emphasis added).[53]

Paul's epithet, picked up by Gratiano and others in *The Merchant of Venice,* locates the *ethnos* of the Jews outside the widening circle of humanity. Unlike Paul, however, Gratiano does not mitigate his antihumanist expletives with the typological reassertion of a "true circumcision" that would both depend on and supercede the physical circumcision practiced by "those who mutilate the flesh." Instead, not unlike Portia's "jot of blood," Gratiano "gratuitously" cuts short Paul's symbolic recuperation of circumcision, precipitating Shylock out of the play's representational order into the realm of the inhuman, the hellish ranks of the allegorical type, the embodied conceit, the livid metaphor, and the mere creature.[54]

Gratiano, however, is not given the last word on Shylock's fate in Venice. If the Duke had been essentially powerless in the court of civil law, Portia's legal argument ends by shifting the charges from civil to criminal grounds. As Shylock attempts to leave the court, Portia stays him:

> *The law hath yet another hold on you.*
> *It is enacted in the laws of Venice,*
> *If it be proved against an alien*
> *That by direct or indirect attempts*
> *He seeks the life of any citizen,*
> *The party 'gainst the which he doth contrive*
> *Shall seize one half his goods; the other half*
> *Comes to the privy coffers of the state,*
> *And the offender's life lies in the mercy*
> *Of the Duke only, 'gainst all other voice.*
> *[. . . .]*
> *Down, therefore, and beg mercy of the Duke.* (4.1.345–61)

Several distinct operations are at work here. First, Portia makes a deliberate move from civil to criminal law, from breach of contract to attempted murder. Whereas Venetian civil law had protected the "commodity of strangers"—international commercial transactions—in the minimal public sphere constituted by the economic contract, criminal law in this instance shields the rights of citizens, over against the "aliens" in their midst. The open port of Venice now retreats into its interior islands, reasserting the lines dividing the citizen and the noncitizen. Finally, the power of judgment and mercy, the sacral attribute of kings, is now forcibly taken from the civil litigant-turned-defendant and delivered to the Duke, who shifts from being the nominal figurehead of Bodin to the empowered monarch of Contarini.

Why would the sovereignty of the Duke be reasserted or restored precisely at these internal boundaries between civil and criminal law, and between the citizen and the alien? The play moves quickly at this point, and gives us few answers. It would seem, however, that when *civil contract* devolves into *mortal conflict,* the agon between the resident alien and the noble citizen produces a miniature state of emergency, a situation when someone—in this case, the Duke—must step above the merely civil law and make a decision concerning life and death, reinstituting a moment of political theology within the legal regime of Venetian constitutionalism. On the line is not human life per se (the life protected in the universal sweep of the sixth commandment, for example), but rather *the life of a citizen,* defined in opposition to the claims of the alien. And if the life of a citizen is at risk, so too is civic life, *bios politikos,* more generally. Hence half of Shylock's money will go to Antonio, as the citizen whose life has been mortally threatened, and the other half to the state, whose ability to protect citizens and citizenship has been put into crisis.

Civic life has fallen into emergency not only because a citizen might die, but because, at a deeper and more troubling level, the stark opposition of citizen and alien, of insider and outsider, threatens the philosophical and ethical viability of citizenship as a category of existence and coexistence. Reduced to a circumcised dog in the operations of Portia's argument and Gratiano's invective, Shylock suddenly stands before the law as mere life or bare life, the life of the creature, over against the civic life incarnated by Antonio. The harshness of this juxtaposition jars with the myth of Venetian constitutionalism, adorned with the attributes of social justice, corporate bodies, and international law. It also runs counter to Paul's insistence on the historical priority of the Jews, to whom "belong the sonship, the glory, the covenants, the giving of the law, the worship, and the promises" (Rom 9:4). Shylock, reduced to a mere "iot" and bare "Iewe," stands shorn of the multiple covenants, laws, and promises, the material and spiritual bequests, that had bound him *as alien* to the civic life and history of Venice through the city's corporate structure and political theology.

Portia's gambit has brought forward the legal boundary between citizen and noncitizen that defines every *politeia*—every constitutional regime of citizenship—and pushes it into the domain of the scandal, triggering a moment of violence in the law that exceeds the law. In so doing, the passage poses despite itself the following question: Can civic life survive as a valid and authentic form of existence if it operates at the expense of the alien, no longer conceived as the member of a recognized corporate community with its own distinct internal and external rights and charters, its own circle of citizenship, but now stripped of property and dignity, criminalized and dispossessed, and fundamentally alone? (In contemporary politics, we would contrast here the permanent resident with the illegal alien, the immigrant with the refugee, the tourist with the terrorist.) Civic life is not only *at stake* in the case, but also *on trial;* if citizenship has become the plaintiff, it is also, on a deeper level, the defendant, brought before the law on counts of exclusion and expropriation—not directly or explicitly, but in the very bareness of the felt contrast between the citizen and the alien, the latter standing stripped of corporatist protections and Pauline promises alike.

Portia's radical exposure of Shylock to the sovereign force of the state is not unlike the "murder of the moral person and annihilation of the juridical person" that Arendt attributes to the production of the refugee in modern politics.[55] Such a scenario cannot be tolerated for long. The Duke, in his new guise as empowered sovereign, immediately extends mercy before Shylock even has a chance to request or refuse it:

> *That thou shalt see the difference of our spirit,*
> *I pardon thee thy life before thou ask it.*
> *For half thy wealth, it is Antonio's;*
> *The other half comes to the general state,*
> *Which humbleness may drive unto a fine.* (4.1.366–70)

The Duke's act of mercy reasserts the "difference of spirit" between Christian and Jew, not, however, in order to reinforce the sudden scandal of the opposition between citizen and alien drawn by Portia, but rather to resituate that couple within a recognizable political and theological economy. To speak of a "difference of *spirit*" is to remind us, *to remind Venice,* that Christian and Jew represent, in Lewalski's helpful phrase, "theological systems" that are also "historical societies,"[56] civil circles that coexist, though always inequitably, in an incorporated political order. As such, the Duke's judgment aims to alleviate the public emergency brought about by the fundamentally anti-Pauline spectre of the "juridical annihilation" of the Jew. Far from begging for mercy, Shylock rejects the Duke's offer:

> *Nay, take my life and all! Pardon not that!*
> *You take my house when you do take the prop*
> *That doth sustain my house. You take my life*
> *When you do take the means whereby I live.* (4.1.372–75)

Shylock will not let the scandal disappear so quickly. Still in shock from the sheer force of legal dispossession, he refuses to be reduced to mere life, insisting instead (and here he echoes Marlowe's Barabas) that life is a *life form,* that life is not life without livelihood and the civil networks it implies.[57] This is not merely an individual, but also a communal claim. After all, the charter between the Jewish community and Venice was formulated on the premise of Jewish solvency; just as Shylock's money props his house, his house props the ghetto republic. Without capital, he does indeed become the homeless, rightless, de-covenanted refugee of Portia's discourse. Moreover, there is surely a reference to Jessica as well here, as another "prop" that has been taken from him and whose loss leaves him unsupported and hence less than alive.

As if accepting some piece of Shylock's argument, Antonio counters with another deal:

> *So please my lord the Duke and all the court*
> *To quit the fine for one half of his goods,*
> *I am content; so he will let me have*
> *The other half in use, to render it*
> *Upon his death, unto the gentleman*
> *That lately stole his daughter.*
> *Two things provided more: that for this favor*
> *He presently become a Christian,*
> *The other, that he do record a gift*
> *Here in the court of all he dies possessed*
> *Unto his son Lorenzo and his daughter.* (4.1.378–88)

Antonio here rescinds the money owed to him in damages; he will retain use of the funds for his projects, but as a trustee for Jessica and Lorenzo, on the condition that Shylock convert to Christianity and that his remaining wealth pass to his daughter and son-in-law when he dies. A few lines earlier, Portia's recourse to criminal law had opposed the citizen and the alien in the sharpest possible way. The Duke's judgment accepted the legal distinction between citizen and alien, but quickly redrew this "difference of spirit" within the more familiar corporate landscape of the polity. Antonio's settlement aims to suspend the difference, by inviting the Jew into the civic circle through the same act of conversion and naturalization that had covenanted Jessica to Lorenzo, marrying her to the city. Antonio's offer re-props Shylock's house, by restoring funds for Shylock's own use and siphoning the rest of it back to his daughter. By linking these twin buttresses to the act of conversion, Antonio in effect rezones the "house" of Shylock, moving his *oikos* from the ghetto to more general quarters in the city.

This offer Shylock accepts. The word *content,* repeated three times in the course of this momentous transaction, measures out the naturalization of Shylock from alien creature (Portia) to resident alien (the Duke) to Christian convert and proto-citizen (Antonio). Laying out the terms of the final deal, Antonio says, "I am content." Portia then asks of Shylock, "Art thou contented, Jew?" and he replies, "I am content" (4.1.396–91). The word *content* implies quantities that can be measured according to a common scale—the terms of the civic order that has now begun to include both men, in their extremism, within the recalibrated norms of the city. The circumcised dog has been drawn not only back into the circle of humanity, but also toward the circle of Venetian citizenship itself. The converted and repossessed Shylock will have the wealth and the right to pursue commercial practices other than money-lending in the city. A Papal Bull of 1542 urging the active conversion of the Jews had stipulated that neophytes be made citizens of whatever place in which they were baptized;[58] whether or not some form of political citizenship is offered to Shylock at this point, a serious barrier to property ownership and trade has just been lifted, and some capital to pursue these interests remains his.[59] In some virtual space and time not quite imagined by the play except perhaps in the extraordinary blank check of its title, Shylock may indeed become, like many of his "New Christian" compatriots, a Merchant of Venice.

Yet there is no ecstasy in Shylock's contentment.[60] Indeed, as most recent readers have insisted, it is a contentment that borders on discontent: Shylock goes on to say, in what will be his final words in the play,

> *I pray you give me leave to go from hence;*
> *I am not well. Send the deed after me,*
> *And I will sign it. (4.1.392–95)*

In a recent essay, Hugh Short, arguing for the felt sincerity of Shylock's conversion, writes that Shylock "is not well, but he is on the road to health."[61] Short's reading offers a useful corrective to the current anti-Venetian consensus on the play, but he errs in separating the Christian narrative of conversion from the civic narrative of naturalization. In my reading of the play, Shylock may be content with naturalization, but he departs fundamentally discontented with its cost; his *livelihood* may be restored, but his *life form* is forever altered. And in this discontent, he remains at odds with Jessica, who has achieved a more complete, but also a more profligate, covenanting with Venice. Jessica, cast in the romance image of Marlowe's Abigail, marries into both Christianity and citizenship, rescinding her Judaism in favor of a new Christian-civic synthesis sealed in the rite of marriage, at once civil transaction and holy sacrament. Although Shylock, like Jessica, must also leave his Judaism at the gates of the city, unlike Jessica he remains both single and singular. His markedly solitary condition at the end of the play points to the lingering exceptionality of the citizen-saint as the discontented remainder, the Jewish *iota,* that both dots and blots—completes and decompletes—the Christian-civic synthesis embraced by his daughter.

Jessica against Shylock: Shakespeare could only reconcile these two versions of the citizen-saint in the terms of romance, mapping the Senex of New Comedy onto the Old Man of Christian typologics.[62] Their juxtaposition, however, suggests other patterns of solution that would emerge in the later development of liberalism. These solutions generally involve decreasing, but never eliminating, the civic buy-in for political participation (lower price of admission) while expanding, but not infinitely, the scope of the civic circle (a larger, but still limited, guest list). Certain variations in the liberal conversation also entail breaking the intimate bond between culture and citizenship by embracing the formal, procedural, and legalistic dimensions of citizenship at the expense of the more fantasmatic appeal of patriotism and national belonging. In a diverse democracy, citizenship can never gather every participant's social affiliations and yearnings into a mesmerizing bundle of cultural identifiers, and must settle instead for a minimal number of naturalization requirements that can admit the greatest number and variety of people at the lowest cultural cost. Political philosopher Will Kymlicka has called this the "thin culture" or "societal culture" of liberal pluralism, which he opposes to the dangers of a "thick" nationalist culture based on ethnic purity.[63] The "thinner" the public culture (the more minimal the requirements for admission and participation), the "thicker" (the more vigorous and variegated) the resulting spheres of local life, and the richer the possibility for affiliations in overlapping communities. Liberalism, that is, substitutes a *discontented contentment,* a provisional and procedural inscription in the polity, for a mystical or ecstatic union sealed by imaginary forms of national identification.

If Kymlicka is right, Shylock, with his mixed feelings and multiple memberships, rather than Jessica or Antonio, emerges as the strongest forerunner of modern citizenship at the close of act 4. If conversion can be purely formal, a social arrangement without spiritual content, then naturalization too can be permanently unnatural, preserving a necessary distance between every citizen and the collective. The discontent that continues to resonate in Shylock's publicly acknowledged contentment proclaims in its very hollowness the possibility of a *politeia* that would attenuate and distend but never fully de-couple the intimate bond between naturalization and conversion, citizenship and death, in the laws and legends of the Western state. Shylock's legal and psychological condition at the end of the play demonstrates the extent to which naturalization in a diverse polity not only can but should remain structurally incomplete, maintaining memories of suspended modes of affiliation that never dissolve completely into a new identity. In my reading, Shylock undergoes not so much a forced conversion as a nominal or procedural one; his reluctant consent is measured and limited, like the rule of law itself. It is worth asserting that however ambivalent we may feel about Shylock's conversion, there is *nothing tragic* in his destiny. We would prefer that Shylock had been offered citizenship without conversion, yet such a choice is only conceivable from across the historical divide of Jewish emancipation, whose success was predicated on the dissolution of the traditional corporate privileges of Europe's Jewish communities. Before emancipation, naturalization was unthinkable without conversion, not only because Christianity was so hegemonic, but because being a Jew meant belonging to a separate political entity (a legacy from Roman law). While it is easy to deplore Shylock's conversion as a forced one, that is because the formal emancipation of the Jews into citizenship is so thoroughly entrenched in our contemporary modes of affiliation that we are no longer cognizant of the systematic transformations in the nature of Jewish collective life that emancipation itself entailed—namely, the replacement of corporate self-rule (the many estates and bodies of Europe's *anciens regimes*) by political representation in a larger entity (the modern state). When Portia strips Shylock of his corporate privileges and Antonio offers naturalization in its place, the play begins not only to imagine the foundations of Jewish emancipation, but also to calculate its costs. Emancipation, too, can be framed as a loss of sorts—another scene of death into citizenship—but, like Shylock's life story, it, too, is not simply a tragedy.[64]

FOUR

Othello Circumcised

Othello, one of Shakespeare's middle tragedies, has often been taken as a rewriting of *The Merchant of Venice:* both are set in the mercantile city-state of Venice, both employ clearly marked "others" as central characters, and both use the theme of conspicuous exogamy to heighten the conventional comedic situation of young lovers blocked by an old father.[1] Whereas *The Merchant of Venice* exhibits a comic structure sharply typological in its countering of Jewish justice and Christian mercy, *Othello* uses a more submerged but no less powerful set of related scriptural coordinates, in which the hero enters into Christian fellowship and the Venetian polity through intermarriage and public service. A fundamental religious ambiguity vexes the racialization of Othello throughout the play; although his professed Christianity authorizes Othello's place in Venice, the play never decisively determines whether he has converted from a pagan religion or from Islam. I argue that the black Gentile of a universal church militant undergirds *Othello*'s opening narrative of international romance, but that this divine comedy of pagan conversion is continually shadowed by the more troubling possibility of Othello's entrance into Christianity via its disturbing neighbor, Islam. This secondary scenario situates the Moor in both greater proximity with and greater resistance to Christian Revelation than the pagan, conceived as a blank slate more open to a transformative Christian reinscription. Moreover, Shakespeare locates these issues within the citizenship structure of Venice. Following precedents in Roman and Venetian law, Othello makes his bid for inclusion in Venice through manumission, intermarriage, and military service, yet these acts provide him with only provisional membership—a green card as it were—among the ranks of the Venetian *cittadini.* It is only when he kills himself through a sacrificial act of recircumcision that Othello joins the civic body, enacting the *death into citizenship* that describes the career of the citizen-saint within the dispensation outlined by the acts and epistles of Paul.

Shakespeare borrows his staging of civic rites from Paul's division of humanity into Greek, Jew, and barbarian, national differences fashioned in relation to the Jewish, Hellenistic, and Roman circles of citizenship that Saul of Tarsus crossed in his life and work. As we have seen in the previous chapters, the universality of Christian fellowship is both produced and limited by the dialectic between the open embrace of the Christian message on the one hand and the internal national coherence represented by the Jews on the other, a tension that provides a foundational mapping of Western ethno-political consciousness. In the typological schemes of the Renaissance, Islam represents a double scandal, the catastrophic bastardization of both Christian universalism—through the seductive danger of the Islamic world mission—and Jewish particularism, represented by Muslim allegiance to ritual laws and to an Abrahamic monotheism without Christ.

Disclosing the play's reliance on the Pauline discourse of nations necessarily reorients color-based approaches to the play, in which the scandal of "monstrous" miscegenation inherited from the nineteenth-century racial imaginary has come to govern *Othello's* economy of differences.[2] Indeed, if we insist on grafting the typically modern question of Othello's color onto the problem of Othello's religion, the results might not fall where we expect them. Looking west and far to the south, toward pagan Africa and the New World, Othello would appear darker-skinned, barbarian, and perhaps more capable of a full conversion because of his religious innocence. Looking east, toward Arabia and Turkey, and to the northern parts of Africa, Othello would become a Muslim-turned-Christian, probably lighter-skinned than his Gentile counterpart, inheritor of a monotheistic civilization already marked by frequent contacts with Christian Europe, and hence more likely to go renegade. Whereas for the modern reader or viewer, a black Othello is more subversive, "other," or dangerous, in the Renaissance scene, an Othello more closely resembling the Turks whom he fights might actually challenge more deeply the integrity of the Christian paradigms set up in the play as the measure of humanity. Critics have rightly decried the nineteenth-century movement to "whiten" or "Orientalize" Othello.[3] It is certainly not my intention to return to such a project; rather, I insist that this move in the nineteenth century already took place within a racialized discourse, whereas in *Othello* religious difference is more powerfully felt, or at least more deeply theorized, than racial difference, which was only then beginning to surface in its virulent modern form. Rather than deciding what color Othello "really" is, I argue that the play initially draws moral and physiological "blackness" away from the diabolical and bestial imagery manipulated by Iago into the more positive circuit of the Gentile barbarian, a recuperation that in turn is undercut by the potential attraction between the "Moor" and the "Mohammedan." Shakespeare's play renders visible the blind spot of *ethnos* that mortgages the inclusive vision of Christian humanism, a blind spot marked above all by the inerasable yet nongenetic scar of circumcision in Shakespeare's Venetian plays. At the end of the play, modern citizenship takes shape at the troubled intersection of Jewish particularism, Christian universalism, and their uncanny mirroring in Islam. Like Shylock, Othello undergoes in his final moments on-stage a process of (re)conversion and naturalization that re-enrolls him in the commonwealth, but at the cost not only of prior religious and national affiliations but of his very life. Dying into citizenship, the incorporation of Othello's foreign body into the Venetian polity serves to separate *dēmos* from *ethnos,* the formal aspect of citizenship from both its collusion with and its effacement of particular religions and ethnicities.

Greek, Jew, and Barbarian

The Merchant of Venice, I suggested in the previous chapter, marries the forms of medieval typology with the verisimilar imperatives of classical comedy and the themes of emergent secularism in order to create a mimetically convincing yet symbolically girded representational mode. In *Othello,* Shakespeare further submerges his typological materials by dividing Shylock's Judaism among several characters and among competing historiographical myths. In the marriage plot, Brabantio, in assuming the generic mantle of *senex* from his predecessor in *The Merchant of Venice,* also inherits some of Shylock's typological baggage. Iago cries out to Brabantio, "Look to your house, your daughter, and your bags" (1.1.81), a line that clearly recalls Solanio's report of Shylock's cry, "'My daughter! O, my ducats! O, my daughter'" (*Merchant* 2.8.15). The Duke's promise to Brabantio, "the bloody book of law / You shall yourself read in the bitter letter / After your own sense" (1.3.69–71), momentarily places the literalist legalism associated with Old Testament justice at Brabantio's command. Yet Brabantio, of course, is no Jew, but one of the "brothers of the [Venetian] state," a citizen and senator in this Christian maritime republic (1.2.98). How, then, should we understand these echoes of Shylock?

By recalling the moneylender of Shakespeare's earlier Venetian play but within a thoroughly Christian scene, the figure of Brabantio instantiates the type not so much of the Jew per se as of the *Jewish Christian* (whether a convert from Judaism or a Judaized Christian Gentile) confronted by St. Paul in the Epistle to the Romans, where he addresses his message "both to Greeks and to barbarians . . . to the Jew first and also to the Greek" (Rom 1: 14–16). Paul's conciliatory evenhandedness in Romans is not to Jews and Christians per se, but to the Jewish and Gentile converts who made up the mixed congregation of the church at Rome. Despite the apparent equity exercised toward Greeks and Jews throughout the epistle, Paul's placement of a (universally attainable) faith before (culturally separatist) works would inevitably tip the balance in favor of Gentile Christians, uncommitted to Jewish law and unconnected to Jewish genealogy.

Shylock ends the play by undergoing conversion to Christianity; Brabantio enters *Othello* as a type of the Jewish Christian, uneasy with the universal fellowship promised by his faith. Brabantio excludes Othello from the "wealthy, curlèd darlings of our nation" (1.2.69), implicitly equating "nation" with *natio,* or birth. Similarly, when Brabantio refers so confidently to his "brothers of the state," we are left with the religious question, "Who is my brother?" Brabantio, like the Jewish Christians of Paul's Epistle to the Romans or the Judaizing missionaries in Galatians and Philippians, would presumably restrict the circle of brothers to the civic aristocracy of Venice, to those men who could stand for public office by virtue of the antiquity of their families in the commercial history of the city. Rather than including Othello among his "brothers of the state," Brabantio presumably concurs with Roderigo's assessment that the Moor is "an extravagant and wheeling stranger" (1.1.139), distinguishing like the usury laws of Deuteronomy 23:19-20 between members of the covenant and aliens to it.[4] So too, when Brabantio warns of the new marriage, "For if such actions may have passage free, / Bondslaves and pagans shall our statesmen be" (1.2.100–101), he effectively denies the inclusiveness of Paul's address by refusing to recognize the validity of Othello's conversion, the confession of faith that allows the Moor to pass from the position of "bondslave" or "pagan" to brother in Christ. Yet Brabantio, as a type of the Judaized Christian rather than a Jew proper, is not a villain; unlike Marlowe's Barabas, Brabantio appears narrow but not damned, clannish but not evil, myopically wed to external appearances, "to all things of sense" (1.2.65), but not without the Abrahamic gift of patriarchal hospitality that helped lead to the present crisis.[5]

Othello, by extension, initially combines two loci in Paul's national geographics; in the first, Hellenistic pair, he plays the "barbarian" to Venice's "Greeks," and in the second, Hebraic, pair, he represents the Gentile to Brabantio's Jew. As barbarian Gentile, Othello enters the play as a convert to Christianity from paganism, a position that locates him in the iconographic tradition of the African king at Christ's Epiphany. As a Christian soldier who traces his "life and being / From men of royal siege" (1.2.21–22), Othello takes shape in an exegetical as well as a biographical genealogy that casts him as a latter-day Balthazar. The Three Kings were typologically keyed to the three sons of Noah, taken as the forefathers of the world's white, black, and yellow peoples; in such a scheme, Othello-as-Balthazar becomes the epochal negation of Ham, father of the black nations. In patristic and rabbinic traditions, Ham brought the curse of blackness onto his descendants by sleeping with his wife on the ark, an anecdote oft-repeated in current historicist readings of the play. This tradition is indeed relevant to *Othello,* but as antetype rather than type of Othello himself: thus Shakespeare is careful to show Othello and Desdemona arriving from the "high-wrought flood" (2.1.2) and "enchafèd flood" (2.1.17) on *separate ships,* their married chastity redeeming rather than repeating Ham's transgression.[6]

In *The Merchant of Venice,* Jessica's elopement from the house of Shylock into the arms of Lorenzo typologically staged the historic shift from Judaism to Christianity. In *Othello,* a barbarian groom rather than a Jewish bride seals his entry into the New Dispensation—and into the ranks of Venetian citizenship—through marriage to a Christian. "Certain qualifications of residence and marriage" were required for "citizenship by grace," the aptly Pauline term for the naturalization of citizens in Venice.[7] In Roman law, moreover, military service could lead to citizenship for slaves and foreigners;[8] although mercenaries in Venice do not appear to have been offered citizenship, the Roman precedent may well inform Shakespeare's portrait of the foreign soldier.[9] In both plays, these intermarriages achieve epochal significance, dramatizing in *The Merchant of Venice* the exodus from Jewish slavery to Christian freedom, and marking in *Othello* the extension of the Christian message from European Gentiles to all the nations of the world. From this typological perspective, the union of white and black, of Greek and barbarian, far from representing a monstrosity or scandal, assumes almost cosmic significance in these early moments of the marriage. The coupling of Othello and Desdemona borders on the mystery of Gentile redemption celebrated in Colossians, where "there cannot be Greek and Jew, circumcised and uncircumcised, barbarian, Scythian, slave, free man, but Christ is all, and in all" (Col 3:11). The exultant tenor of the Pauline passage in turn finds its Old Testament sustenance in the erotic, spiritual, and racial harmonies of the Song of Songs, where the proclamation that "black is beautiful" (1:5) prefigured for Christian commentators the dream of Gentile conversion.

As Gentile barbarian, the black Othello enters the play as a living symbol of Christian universalism, a social and spiritual vision that stands in conflict with the narrowness of Brabantio's Judaizing constructions of national brotherhood. This epochal scene of Gentile conversion initially controls the play of black-white imagery in the drama. From the start, Iago uses bestial and demonic images of blackness in order to deform and prejudice Brabantio's—and by extension the audience's—reception of the news of the elopement. Iago performs this diabolical shaping of Othello as a character with his own strange links to the world of *The Merchant of Venice,* taking his place in the long line of Vices and Machiavels crystallized for Shakespeare's generation by Marlowe's grotesque portrait of Barabas.[10] Iago's famous negation of the Jewish God's unspeakable name, "I am not what I am" (1.1.67), not only flags him as the Devil of the play, but also roots him in a parodically Old Testament *ethos* of historical *ressentiment,* seasoned by the damaged pride and nurtured spite of all the Cains, Ishmaels, and Esaus passed over in the Bible for younger favored sons. Indeed, Iago's consciously crafted fantasies of intermarriage may be the force that "Judaizes" Brabantio, infecting him with the fear of the stranger and leading him to contract defensively the borders of Venetian brotherhood. It is Iago, for example, who warns Brabantio about "your house, your daughter, and your bags," as if the character of Iago were somehow responsible for raising the spirit of *The Merchant of Venice* into *Othello.* Even Iago's infamous image of bestial cross-coupling, "an old black ram / Is tupping your white ewe" (1.1.90–91), echoes the most egregious pun in *The Merchant of Venice,* that between "ewes" and

"Iewes,"[11] irradiating the play's most cited example of color-based racism with an animus of a different color.

And this other animus, evoking the typological arrangement and succession of the nations in Christian historiography, largely underwrites and organizes the more visible, specular play of black-and-whiteness in the drama. Iago's presentation of blackness as the sign of a savage, degraded, lascivious, demonic, or unredeemable nature is soon marked by the play as historically bankrupted through the epochal weight granted the marriage of Othello and Desdemona as a mystic symbol of Gentile conversion. The same theme of Christian universalism authorizes the apparently antiracist counterdiscourse that reads Othello's blackness as only skin-deep, covering a true whiteness within. When the Duke consoles Brabantio with the reassuring couplet, "If virtue no delighted beauty lack, / Your son-in-law is far more fair than black" (1.3.292–93), he speaks from a position opened up by the world mission of Christianity, which equates a person's "fairness" with the soul's faith rather than the body's color. As Eldred Jones argues, the first scenes of the play effectively take us through prejudice, introducing us to Othello through the jaundiced eyes of Iago in order to correct his contaminating language with the figure cut by Othello himself.[12] And, as G. K. Hunter has suggested, what makes possible the judicious weighing in act 1 of Iago's conventional stereotypes against Othello's natural dignity is the universalist vision of a world Christianity.[13]

The possibility of such an epochal marriage between barbarian and European Gentiles had already been intimated in *The Merchant of Venice,* where the Prince of Morocco had entered the stage as part of the parade of nations who march through the fantasy space of Belmont. Declaring his human equality through "incision" rather than distinguishing his *ethnos* through circumcision (2.1.6), Morocco is closer to the type of the African King celebrated in Epiphany narratives than to the circumcised Muslim or Jew. Thomas Middleton's 1613 masque, *The Triumphs of Truth,* which celebrated the induction of the new Lord Mayor into office, features the arrival in London of a "king of the Moors" whose conversion to Christianity epitomizes the "triumph of truth" announced in the masque's title.[14] Middleton's Moor figures his visit to London as an Epiphany narrative, "Nor could our desires rest till we were led / Unto this place, where those good spirits were bred."[15] Shakespeare's Morocco, too, evokes Epiphany imagery when he chooses the gold casket:

> *Let's see once more this saying graved in gold:*
> *"Who chooseth me shall gain what many men desire."*
> *Why, that's the lady; all the world desires her.*

From the four corners of the earth they come
To kiss this shrine, this mortal breathing saint. (2.7.35–40)

Morocco's exegesis of the motto casts himself as a Gentile king coming to honor Portia, "this mortal breathing saint," in a modern nativity scene, with the gold casket as its renovated manger; through the international theme of Epiphany, Morocco, ever concerned about his standing in this European court, persuades himself of his romantic eligibility. (As if to acknowledge this resonance, "Balthazar," the name often assigned to the African King, reappears twice later in the play, first as Portia's servant and then as her moniker in the trial scene.)

If *The Merchant of Venice* evokes the universal message of the Epiphany in its casket theme, the play manages to bracket Morocco's potential seriousness as a suitor—and by extension his claims to international inclusion—by wrapping him in bombast and identifying his Pauline bid for equality with a materialist misreading of the Epistles.[16] In the opening act of *Othello*, the marriage between a Venetian gentlewoman and a prince of Morocco—earlier imagined only in the mode of farce—appears to be finally taking place within the bounds of a Venice that just might actualize its own universal ideals. In its opening act, *Othello* brings forward the epiphany imagery that animates the civic pageants of the Middle Ages and the Renaissance and begins to realize the inclusive promise of their political theology.

Pagans and Bondslaves: Entries into Covenant

It would be easy enough, however, to love this vision of Christian humanism not wisely but too well. As more recent critics have pointed out, the play's spiritual rereading of the black-white dichotomy internalizes but does not challenge the moral hierarchy of the opposition. The chiastic inversions that blacken Iago and whiten Othello are specular rather than dialectical, leaving in place the system of values they appear to negate.[17] Perhaps less visibly, the Christian-humanist discourse through which the play encounters, frames, and inverts the black-white couple always operates as a *universalism minus the circumcised,* a set that excludes not the unconverted heathens of the New World, who still lie before the Christian states as objects of future proselytization, but rather the Jews and the Muslims, who espouse monotheisms intimately bound to Christianity by common texts, theological principles, and an Abrahamic genealogy. Forming what Islam has called *ahl al-kitab,* People of the Book, the three monotheisms are linked by shared texts, hermeneutic habits, and a single God. At key moments of historical development, the People of the Book have managed to develop instances of pluralist civil societies within larger polities, yet their differences have also led to patterns of rivalry, containment, fear, terror, and genocide.[18]

We have already seen that the play's negative discourse on blackness is subtly but consistently Judaized in the play, whether linked to Iago as the anti-Yahweh and modern Esau relentlessly spreading his insidious resentment, or associated with Brabantio, the Venetian patriarch who distinguishes too sharply between brothers and strangers; it is only against this canceled ground of Jewish types that the Christian image of the Gentile convert takes shape. It is time now to fold Islam into the play's dramatic scenario and historiographical imagination. First and most obviously, the Muslims appear in the form of the Turks, their threat to Venice serving to validate Othello's integrity as righteous Gentile; not only has the Moor joined Christianity, but he has made its security his occupation. Othello's role as defender of the faith, however, is muddied by the fact that we cannot be certain that he has converted to Christianity from paganism and not from Islam, a route that would locate Islam *inside* Othello as the past he has abjured as well as *outside* Othello as the enemy he fights. Moreover, entry into Christian brotherhood from Islam would trace a different arc from that of the Gentile barbarian, locating the pre-Christian Othello not *ante legem*—practicing a natural religion before or outside the law—but *sub lege,* submitted to the code of a strict monotheism unmitigated by Christian mercy.

Othello's recollected autobiography in act 1, scene 3 bears traces of this typological crossing of Muslim and Jew. Midway through the speech, Othello remembers telling "Of being taken by the insolent foe / And sold to slavery, of my redemption thence" (1.3.139–40). In these lines the pairing of "slavery" and "redemption" recalls the flight of the Jews from slavery into freedom in Exodus, dramatizing the passage of God's people from the bondage of Jewish law into the freedom of Christian grace in the Pauline tradition. Under Roman law, as Paul well knew, formal manumission from slavery meant not only freedom but also citizenship, sometimes via the intermediary legal act of adoption.[19] On the one hand, the biblical resonances of the lines simply reinforce the play's image of Othello as a free and open convert, intensifying rather than clouding the mythohistoric clarity of the Moor's baptism. At the same time, however, the allusion's encrypted narrative of a movement from law to grace disturbs the dominant picture of Othello as a specifically *Gentile*—pagan or barbarian—convert, who would have entered the Promised Land of the New Covenant from a position outside rather than under the law. It suggests to the contrary that Othello joined Christianity from a prior relation to the law, a relation emblematized by the Jew in Paul's letters, but figurally linked to the Muslim in the post-Pauline tradition—as in Luther's frequent association of Jews, Turks, and Papists. The overall effect of Othello's prior enslavement is to reinforce the pattern of righteous conversion and Christian militancy—of citizenship by grace—embodied by Othello, but by rerouting the implied itinerary of his autobiography according to the different providential scheme of law and its supercession.

Othello's reference to his "slavery . . . and redemption thence" lays the groundwork for his potential slide into identification with the slave, the renegade, the Jew, and the Muslim, calling into question the security of Othello's place in the world-historical expansion of the Christian mission to the Gentile nations. If he has entered the New Covenant as a Muslim rather than a Gentile, then his allegiance to Christianity is liable to be weaker; instead of the blank slate of a "free and open nature," his religiously marked body would present a surface forever scarred by "the bloody book of the law," a denatured body less amenable to religious rewriting. Brabantio's warning against "bondslaves and pagans" (1.2.101) acknowledges the two possible avenues of Othello's entry into Christianity. More than simply synonyms, the pointedly paired words represent distinct locations in the play's conceptual geography of the non-Christian world. The pagan identifies the state of the Gentile barbarian, potential recipient of the expanded Pauline mission. The bondslave names the condition of Hagar, her offspring, and his Ishmaelite progeny, following Paul's gloss that "Hagar is Mount Sinai in Arabia [who] corresponds to the present Jerusalem, for she is in slavery with her children" (Gal 4:25). If the remainder of the play charts Othello's increasing distance from the role of Christian soldier established in act 1, we must pay attention to the effects that these competing scripts for the entry into covenant might have on Othello's tragic exit from the Christian faith- and marriage-contracts. As the play progresses, is Othello, as critics have frequently suggested, increasingly *paganized*—made exotic, savage, and barbaric—or is he also *Islamicized and Judaized,* brought back into contact with a law that should have been both historically and personally dissolved by the rite of baptism? In the play, paganization describes Othello's decline into gullibility, madness, and cruelty, a process that takes place under the sign of the infamous handkerchief, its subtle fabric woven out of the iconography of the pagan gods. Islamicization, on the other hand, reverts not to anarchy *ante legem* but to tyranny *sub lege,* a transformation manifested by Othello's increasing identification with a jealous justice that must be executed at any cost, a law driven by the fiercely passionate monogamy of an immoderate monotheism.

Covenants in Crisis, or Turning Turk

Whereas the first act of the play as well as the early scenes in Cyprus establish Othello as Christian soldier and devoted husband, the middle movement of the tragedy instigates a crisis in Othello's marriage that also threatens his place in the New Dispensation. The isolation of a specifically Islamic path out of the play's broader and bolder movement of paganization is already enunciated in Othello's admonition to the brawling soldiers:

> *Why, how now, ho! From whence ariseth this?*
> *Are we turned Turks, and to ourselves do that*
> *Which heaven hath forbid the Ottomites?*
> *For Christian shame, put by this barbarous brawl!* (2.3.163–166)

The expression "turning Turk," common as early as the late Middle Ages, usually refers to a Christian's conversion to Islam, always with the sense of the renegade's opportunism or the captive's forced choice rather than the spiritual transformation of a true convert.[20] The phrase casts Turkishness not as an ethnicity into which one is born but as a religious condition that one can adopt, the state of what John Pory calls "accidental Turks": "Naturall I terme them, that are borne of Turkish parents: and them I call accidental, who leaving our sacred faith, or the Moysaicall law, become Mahumetans."[21] In *Othello,* the phrase is spoken by Othello, who, himself having turned Christian, castigates men to whom the faith is "natural" rather than "accidental," an involuntary inheritance rather than a self-transforming choice. As the play's tragic action progresses, the irony of this early interchange redoubles as Othello himself, as Daniel Vitkus has argued, appears to "turn Turk."

In its simplest, most basic, and most dramatic reading, that downward arc devolves simply as paganization; thus Othello's admonition two lines later, "For *Christian* shame, put by this *barbarous* brawl," presents a parallelism in which the word "barbarous" repeats and includes the word "Turk." In the play, the barbarization of Othello accounts for his decline into ignorance and violence. From this perspective, his fall out of covenant is a fall into lawlessness and disorder, as when Othello exclaims, "And when I love thee not, / Chaos is come again" (3.3.99–100). In this reading, the tempest that dissipates the Turkish threat once again becomes a type of the Flood, now understood as a cosmic de-creation that annihilates the world of divine and human covenants, atavistically returning to the anarchy of the era before the Noachide and Mosaic laws.

At the same time, however, "turning Turk" delineates a distinctive tragic trajectory that runs alongside the path of barbarization, paralleling, elaborating, and deviating from it. Note Othello's ambiguous gloss of what it means to turn Turk: "Are we turned Turks, *and to ourselves do that / Which heaven hath forbid the Ottomites*?" Samuel Chew explains this as a reference to the high level of discipline among Turkish soldiers, an inverse mirror of the discord in the Christian camp;[22] the lines may also refer to the drinking of alcohol, the activity that, forbidden under Islamic law, has led to the current unrest. They have, in effect, become their own enemies. Othello associates the Turkish ranks with a *greater* rather than a lesser degree of lawfulness; though Othello uses "turning Turk" to describe the present fray, assimilating it to "barbarous brawl" two lines later, the actual description of Turkish behavior in the intervening line belies the automatic absorption of Islam into a libertine paganism. Rather than a dissolution into antediluvian anarchy, "turning Turk" in this second reading implies the reversion to a position *sub lege,* enchained by a harsh justice and ritual law unmitigated by Christian mercy.

Iago reasserts the renegade scenario at the end of the same scene when he advises Cassio to elect Desdemona as his petitioner:

> *And then for her*
> *To win the Moor—were't to renounce his baptism,*
> *All seals and symbols of redeemèd sin—*
> *His soul is so enfettered to her love*
> *That she may make, unmake, do what she list.* (2.3.336–340)

Here Iago plots the tragic pattern of the play; Othello will indeed "renounce his baptism"—fall out of covenant—through his destructive love for Desdemona. Moreover, the phrase "*seals and symbols* of redeemèd sin" intimates an epochal reading of baptism by allusively linking it to St. Paul's reading of circumcision as "a *sign or seal*" of faith (Rom. 4:11). In Romans, as we saw in the last two chapters, Paul transforms circumcision from the legal ratification of a contract to an outward mark that reflects the internal condition of faith. Paul transfers the performative dimension of the seal to baptism, the new circumcision "made without hands" (Col. 2:11), which operates along an internal-spiritual rather than an external-material conception of both ritual and language. Unlike circumcision, the rite of baptism leaves no bodily trace of its operation; the transparent and reflective waters of baptism purport to dissolve the blood and erase the scar of circumcision's violently inscriptive cut.

Iago's "seals and symbols of redeemèd sin" cites baptism as an example of Christian semiosis, in which the ritual embodies or incarnates the inner state that it signifies (the word "symbol" here thus anticipates its formulation in Romantic aesthetics). In addition, the application of the phrase to Othello, a new Christian, invokes the world-historical function of baptism as the "redemption" not only of the individual soul, but also of circumcision as the sign and seal of the old law; baptism "seals" circumcision in the sense of sealing it off, a canceling water-mark that fulfills and completes the era of circumcision. Finally, Iago's activation of the typological dimension of baptism within the scenario of baptism's *renunciation* ("to *renounce* his baptism, / All seals and symbols of redeemèd sin") casts Othello not as the embodiment of history's progression from law to grace, but as the emblem of an historical regression from grace to law—a fall from baptism back to circumcision, and from a semiosis based on the fluid transparency of the *logos,* the spirit that gives life, to another based on the externality of written, bodily signs, the letter that kills.

In the unfolding tragedy, this route back to circumcision is charted by Othello's increasing identification with the law as the vehicle of anger and jealousy. If in act 1 Iago had presented himself as the anti-Yahweh, he-who-is-not-what-he-is, the play increasingly casts Othello not as a devilish negation but as a tragic parody of the Old Testament God, the Lord "whose name is Jealous" (Ex. 34:14).[23] When the soldiers' brawl arouses Othello from his bed, he finds himself ruled by rage in a trial scene in which he now takes the role of judge rather than defendant:

> *Now, by heaven,*
> *My blood begins my safer guides to rule,*
> *And passion, having my best judgment collied,*
> *Essays to lead the way. Zounds, if I stir,*
> *Or do but lift this arm, the best of you*
> *Shall sink in my rebuke. Give me to know*
> *How this foul rout began, who set it on;*
> *And he that is approved in this offense,*
> *Though he had twinned with me, both at a birth,*
> *Shall lose me. (2.3.198–207)*

The passage begins under the cloud of a passion darkening judgment, and then moves on to a classical guarantee of impartial justice: namely, the claim that even one of his own kinsmen, "though he had twinned with me," will receive punishment if found guilty. The Duke had made a similar promise in the play's first trial scene, when the Venetian judge promises Brabantio,

> *the bloody book of the law*
> *You shall yourself read in the bitter letter*
> *After your own sense*—yea, though our proper son
> Stood in your action. *(1.3.69–72; emphasis added)*

Although Othello has substituted the twin brother for the legitimate son, the sentiment, familiar in classical and Renaissance political theory, is the same.[24] In both scenes, however, this pledge to an impartial justice blind to family ties is seriously compromised: the Duke breaks his promise to Brabantio as soon as he hears that Othello, desperately needed for the affairs of state, is the one who stands accused; so too, Othello's replay of the Duke's humanist dictum occurs only after he announces that anger guides his judgment. Moreover, the passage of the maxim from one scene to the other props Othello's judicial stance on "the bloody book of the law," associating his too-passionate justice with the fierce deity of the Old Testament and projecting a justice married not to the ameliorative qualities of mercy and love, but to the negative intensifiers of anger and jealousy. Whereas in the scenario of paganization, these negative passions would represent the disorderly antitheses of lawfulness, in the Judeo-Islamic register, they function as allies to the law, passions that dangerously heighten the principled harshness implicit in justice. In Daniel Vitkus's analysis, the renegade Othello, reconverting from Christianity back to Islam, becomes a type of "oriental despotism" in the final movement of the play.[25]

Othello's identification with an angry and jealous law culminates in the play's third and last trial scene, as Othello enters the bed-chamber reminding himself that he acts as an executor of justice in a divine drama and not as a private citizen driven by the unprincipled rage of cuckoldry: "It is the cause, it is the cause, my soul. . . . It is the cause" (5.2.1–3). Earlier in the play, Othello had wanted to inflict eternal punishment on Desdemona by having her perjure herself before her death: "Therefore be double damned: / Swear thou art honest" (4.2.39–40). Now he wants her to confess her sins before she dies, confirming the rightness of the death sentence and making his justice *more just* by not letting him cut her off in the blossom of her sin. Appointing himself her confessor, Othello struggles to assume a priestly as well as a judicial function, becoming in Marlowe's coinage an "Ithamore," a Moorish son of Aaron who combines the features of the Levite and the Muslim.

Such reasoning climaxes in Othello's anguished retort to Desdemona's denials:

> *Thou dost stone my heart,*
> *And makes me call what I intend to do*
> *A murder, which I thought a sacrifice. (5.2.67–69)*

In Othello's logic, the act that would count as "murder" when committed out of anger becomes a "sacrifice" if executed in the name of justice. Othello's "sacrifice" simultaneously identifies him with the old law, and indicates the law's epochal supercession by Desdemona's obedient love, insofar as her death resonates with that of Christ and his saints. Whereas studies of race in the play tend to emphasize the movement of paganization, feminist critics have noted

Othello's increasing association with justice, usually taken as the masculinist tenets of Judeo-Christian patriarchy.[26] My point is somewhat different: Othello, not unlike Shylock, increasingly "stands for justice," an allegorizing tendency that separates the Semitic strands out of the Judeo-Christian synthesis even while grotesquely reinforcing the authority of the husband. Although Othello's increasing alliance with the law is indeed "patriarchal," I would insist on the Abrahamic (Judeo-Islamic) connotations of the concept. Othello's "sacrifice" brings to a head the Moor's submission to the obscene yet principled cruelty of a heteronomous law registered by the play as historically outdated. In fewer than twenty lines, Desdemona will be smothered, the sacrifice complete.

Othello Circumcised

In the remorseful aftermath of Desdemona's sacrificial murder, Othello's final autobiography stages his double placement in the historical narratives of paganization and Islamicization:

> *Soft you; a word or two before you go.*
> *I have done the state some service, and they know't.*
> *No more of that. I pray you, in your letters,*
> *When you shall these unlucky deeds relate,*
> *Speak of me as I am; nothing extenuate,*
> *Nor set down aught in malice. Then must you speak*
> *Of one that loved not wisely but too well;*
> *Of one not easily jealous but, being wrought,*
> *Perplexed in the extreme; of one whose hand,*
> *Like the base Indian [Iudean], threw a pearl away*
> *Richer than all his tribe; of one whose subdued eyes,*
> *Albeit unusèd to the melting mood,*
> *Drops tears as fast as the Arabian trees*
> *Their medicinable gum. Set you down this:*
> *And say besides that in Aleppo once,*
> *Where a malignant and a turbaned Turk*
> *Beat a Venetian and traduced the state,*
> *I took by th'throat the circumcisèd dog*
> *And smote him, thus.* (5.2.348–66)

The parable of the base Indian casting away the pearl situates Othello's life-story in an exotic pagan scene, in which the rejected jewel condenses the murder of Desdemona with Othello's departure from Christianity, his renouncement of the linked covenants of marriage and baptism. The first simile is swiftly followed by the reference to tears that drop "as fast as the Arabian trees / Their medicinable gum," an elaborate circumlocution for myrrh, the resinous perfume brought by the Magi to Christ's manger (Matt 2:11). As nativity gift, the myrrh manifests the economy of conversion, in which the Gentile kings bring the precious distillations of their countries in exchange for a place in the New Dispensation. In the aftermath of Desdemona's murder, the myrrh also functions as a figure of Othello's regret and repentance for having reneged on that exchange, becoming the medium of a "melting mood" that dissolves the universalist iconography of Epiphany into the scene of conversion's reversion into the strange substances that distinguish the nations. As the symbol of the Epiphany and its dissolution, the myrrh tree situates Othello in a pagan Gentile scene, darkening his skin in its allusive shade.

Yet, as critics have pointed out, the Folio text's substitution of "Iudean" for "Indian" installs Othello's tragedy within another set of mytho-historical coordinates. Since Lewis Theobald's eighteenth-century edition, editors and critics have occasionally favored the Folio reading, referring it to Judas's betrayal of Christ and to the Herod-Mariam story of jealous murder, taken from Josephus' *Jewish War* and *Antiquities of the Jews* as the material for several neo-Senecan dramas.[27] As Edward Snow points out, citing Richard S. Veit, "the word 'tribe' is never used in connection with Indians in Shakespeare. It primarily connotes 'clan' for him, often in connection with the 'tribes of the world.'"[28] Like Brabantio's (or Shylock's) restricted use of "nation," the "tribe" of the "base Iudean" implies the circumscribed world-view of an *ethnos* in which the Christian pearl finds no proper place, a rejection that stems not from the ignorance of the Indian, but from the knowledge of good and evil brought about by the law. Moreover, if we read "base Iudean" in terms of the Herod and Mariam story, a now-familiar typological scenario takes shape within the confines of the simile. Herod, an Idumean descended from Esau, is a type of the inveterate and jealous Jew as well as the latter-day Muslim, and his maligned but faithful wife Mariam, a sacrificial victim in the Christological pattern shared with Desdemona, represents the righteous remnant who makes possible the historic transition into the new era.[29]

Rather than selecting "Iudean" over "Indian," I follow Edward Snow in insisting instead that "each variant suggests a different side of Othello."[30] "Indian" describes the more broadly drawn, theatrically more powerful movement of the drama as the tragic breakdown of Gentile conversion, yet the almost effortless substitution of "Iudean" for "Indian" traces another path within the play's dominant turn of paganization. It is in this sense that "Indian" is my preferred reading, with "Iudean" bracketed after it as a variant—not because "Iudean" offers a less compelling interpretation of the drama, but because it does its work *as an auxiliary narrative.* The story of Islamicization precipitates out of the broader tragedy of paganization, not only defining a subset of the general category ("a Muslim is a kind of pagan"), but also leading to the particularization of both paganism and Islam as the starting points of separate itineraries into and out of Christianity.[31]

Othello's recollection of the Turk in Aleppo flows out of this auxiliary reading, finally naming the rite of circumcision that has haunted the theological economies of both *The Merchant of Venice* and *Othello.* As critics have often argued, Othello's reenactment of his earlier anti-Turkish heroics both identifies him with the Turk, and kills off that identification in the act of suicide, the play's final sacrifice, which serves to reassert Othello's allegiance to the Christian ethics whose standard he has borne. Yet these readings too often identify the Turk simply as a "barbaric enemy," as "the Infidel," or as one of a "proliferating series of exoticized others." To the contrary, it is my project to distinguish the Judean from the Indian, the Jew and the Muslim from the Gentile pagan, as delineating a separate if often embedded historical course from that of "exoticized others."[32] For, strong and compelling as these readings of the Turk as barbarian may be, they do not account for the way in which circumcision singles the Muslim out from a generalized exoticism.

In Othello's final speech, the cut of circumcision establishes both the object and the means of the Moor's deadly identification with the Turk. As Lynda Boose has pointed out, circumcision, rather than skin-color, is the man-made, religiously mandated trait that Othello "invokes as the final, inclusive sign of his radical Otherness";[33] through the operation of circumcision, every (male) Turk is an "accidental Turk," a subject who has "turned Turk" by being submitted to this rite. Othello enacts the earlier encounter with his drawn sword: "I took by th'throat the circumcisèd dog / And smote him, thus." The sword at once points outwards to circumcision as the trait identifying the object of his scorn, and reflexively returns it onto Othello's own body as the very means of death, as a final stroke that cuts off his life by turning the Turk into and onto himself. The suicide, then, not only murders the "circumcisèd dog" that Othello has become, but is itself a kind of circumcision, a gesture that constitutes at once a means of social reinscription and a subjectivizing signature.

On the one hand, given the sacrificial dynamics of act 5, this cut redeems the Moor in death, restoring him to the history of Venice as one who has "done the state some service" and who, like Mary Magdalene, has "loved not wisely but too well." From this perspective, circumcision functions as the emblem of typology *par excellence,* the vehicle of world-historical cancellation that allows for the reconversion of the Moor to Christianity through his sacrificial death.

Othello's suicide, that is, functions as a martyrological baptism in blood, a "seal and symbol of redeemèd sin" that in effect circumcises circumcision, completing and terminating the era of the law through the operation of sacrifice. Following the directive of Paul in Romans 2, Othello has indeed circumcised himself in the heart, reentering the Christian covenant through his expiatory death. Moreover, this sacrificial cut also signs and seals Othello's death into citizenship, his entry into the archives of state memory as a citizen-soldier. In death, Othello becomes both saint and citizen, both true Christian and acknowledged member of the Venetian Republic. And he does so through reanointing three linked covenants: he rejoins the polity by reaffirming his baptism and remarrying Desdemona, dying upon the couplet of a kiss ("No way but this, / Killing myself, to die upon a kiss" [5.2.368–69]).

On the other hand, this reinscriptive cut does not disappear into its typological sublations, instead reinstating the Hebraic function of the signature, a legally ratifying and self-identifying mark that dislodges Othello from the Christian historical order by locating him in a different covenant. If in this second scenario, Othello also performs the role of citizen-saint, each of the terms has undergone revision, linked now not to Venetian Christendom, but to the original membership protocols signed into being by circumcision, and the political-theological space that it delimits. In Lacanian terms, Othello's final circumcision both *alienates* him in the social order and constitutes the unique mark, the trace of the real, that allows him to *separate* from that order. In the play, this movement of separation articulates Islam as a distinct historico-theological position, a regime defined by the singular imprint of circumcision as the persistent "sign and symbol" of the law, and as a means of citizen-making in its own right. This (re)circumcision operates as a *point de capiton* or a *trait unaire,* a traumatic piercing of the real onto the symbolic that situates the subject with absolute uniqueness within the civic order that reshapes around it. With this traumatic gesture, Othello signs his final autobiography, inflaming as much as redeeming that ancient scar in the Pauline discourse of nations. This momentary positing of Islam as its own dispensation both exceeds the typological vision (which would reduce Islam to Christian categories of faith and nationhood) and is itself anticipated by the historiographical impulse of Pauline Christianity as a narrative of epochal relations among multiple citizenships.

Othello's departure from the Venetian order demarcates the ranks of the still-circumcised as a constitutive lack within the universal set drawn by Christianity. This movement is signaled by the phrase "circumcisèd dog," which echoes the same passage in Philippians that had informed the canine invectives of *The Merchant of Venice:* "Look out for the dogs, look out for the evil-workers, look out for those who mutilate the flesh. For we are the true circumcision" (Phil

3:2–3). In the calculus of Christian humanism, to maintain the rite of circumcision and thus to espouse a *particular* citizenship is to refuse entry into the *general* citizenship of the *ethne* at large, which in turn means negating one's own humanity. Othello's final speech signals this logic by animalizing both the malignant Turk and the hero who fatally identifies himself with him. Like the Shylock of the trial scene, Othello's subordination to the animal epithet identifies him with mere life, existing at the suffering limit of the political order. Yet, also like Shylock, Othello is ultimately reincorporated into the body politic, in his case by dying into the citizenship that before he had claimed through intermarriage and public service. In reminding his Venetian witnesses of his service to the state and his marriage to Desdemona, he requests to be remembered in their calendar of state papers, the play of *Othello* standing in for the fulfillment of this request.[34]

Finally, however, if Othello achieves a certain membership at the end of the play, his citizenship, like Shylock's, remains structurally incomplete. Shylock responds to Antonio's deal with the phrase, "I am content": in this interchange, "content" rhymes with "consent," signing his formal agreement to the new social and religious contract. Yet Shylock's contentment, I argued in the last chapter, is diminished or qualified by his palpable discomposure in the very public space to which he will in effect be converted: "I pray you, give me leave to go from hence; / I am not well" (4.1.390–91). In Othello's case, the same self-circumcising mark that recovenants Othello to Venice ("circumcising circumcision") also points to circumcision as an ongoing rite associated with acts of naturalization, delimiting Judaism and Islam as distinct and persistent world-historical movements that demand recognition on their own terms. By continuing to draw an alternate circle of citizenship within the very arc of circumcision's universalizing internalization, Othello's suicide indicates the need for conceptualizing models of multiple membership that might establish civil relations among the People of the Book.

At the end of their respective plays, Shylock and Othello emerge as citizen-saints who have undertaken challenging itineraries between civic and religious forms of membership. Both Shylock and Othello effect partial passages into a Venice affronted at almost every instance by the spectre of their inclusion, yet structurally predicated on the possibility of pluralism by virtue of its international commerce, its republican constitution, and its commitment to Pauline universalism. Crossing into the polity from places just beyond it, Shylock and Othello incarnate the "accidental" or artificial character of citizenship, bringing forward in their own stories the inherent tension within citizenship between *ethnos* and *dēmos*—between natural nativism and legal personhood, between the organic localization of nationhood to a particular place and people, and the equalizing package of rights granted to those who find themselves within its circle of citizenship regardless of their prior affiliations.[35] In both plays, the imperfect incorporation of these resident aliens into the Venetian polity serves to divorce, if only for a moment, the formal aspect of citizenship from its romance with particular cults or cultures. This momentary separation of citizenship from national culture occurs on both sides of the naturalizing passage, not only by requiring the new citizen to leave the frankincense and myrrh of his prior loyalties at the city gates, but also by beginning to test the seemingly invincible link between Christianity and civic participation on the part of the Western state.

The civic passions undergone by Shylock and Othello cannot be deemed successful by a modern eye. The costs are too high, to themselves and to those nearby. Indeed, it is precisely *the costs of citizenship* that these two plays lay at our feet, for our deliberation and judgment. Yet any assessments that we make in this regard in turn manifest a set of historical transactions in which Shakespeare's plays have participated. The measures that we apply *to* Shakespeare themselves reflect the questions posed *by* Shakespeare. Like Paul's Epistles, Shakespeare's plays are open letters, composed and performed at distinct moments in time to specific audiences in the city and the court, yet deeply indeterminate in the scope and call of their future reach. Shakespeare's two Letters to the Venetians invite us to compare competing membership routines (Greek, Jewish, and barbarian; Abrahamic, pagan, and civic), to confront the deadliness of their inherent exclusivisms, and to imagine possible models of their civil coexistence that might draw upon, and ultimately nurture, both their distinctive and their shared resources.

FIVE

Antigone in Vienna

Shakespeare's Isabella is a sister of Antigone—but "adoptedly," as Isabella says of her "cousin Juliet" (1.4.47). Antigone, of course, already has a sister, Ismene, creature of compromise in the unsecret sorority of civil norms. Both Ismene and Juliet exhibit a certain social ease and functional fluency in their respective worlds, whereas Antigone and Isabella find themselves at odds with the city—by temperament and by legal cause—as they strive to represent their brothers before a law that has condemned them. Antigone and Isabella instate the exception in relation to the norm, the saint in relation to the citizen. Both plays depict a political order caught up in a crisis by the actions of brothers, an emergency that calls their sisters into a public sphere that barely accommodates them. Yet Antigone and Isabella can be sisters only "adoptedly"—not by virtue of any influence or genetic relationship, but by the sheer force of their elective affinity within the field delimited here as the literature of citizenship. Adoption is, of course, a key model and metaphor of civic naturalization: To become a citizen of a city to which one is foreign is more than simply "like" becoming the legitimate child of parents to whom one has no biological connection. As we have seen in previous chapters, in Roman law, adoption was one of the means by which slaves could be manumitted and naturalized as citizens, a paradigm developed by Paul in his vision of manumission from slavery to the law into free sonship in Christ.[1] In the rites of adoption and naturalization, a new nativity is artificially born through a legal process supplemented by psychosocial forces of reinvestment and reinvention in the face of exile and exposure, banishment and abandon.

This chapter submits the paperwork for the adopted sisterhood of Isabella and Antigone. *Antigone,* as William Tyrrell and Larry Bennett have demonstrated,[2] bears witness to the displacement of *oikos*-based control over matters of life and death by the polis's new monopoly on public funerals; Antigone both asserts the ancient right of a woman to bury her kin and, on behalf of the new regime of citizenship and its order of equivalence, challenges the polis to fulfill the civic responsibilities it has assumed. *Measure for Measure* follows Isabella out of the convent and into the open city, where she will try to secure the future of her brother. If for Isabella chastity means exiting from social and sexual contracts of all sorts, becoming a radical integer, unbound and unmatched in the generalized promiscuity of the Viennese scene, the question remains as to the social destiny of her decision for chastity, which is not negated by her impending marriage, but rather made into the integral kernel of her emergent citizenship.

To imagine Antigone in Vienna also means posing the question of the relationship between *citizenship* and *psychoanalysis,* between the set of dramatic and interpretive patterns set into orbit by Sophocles and Shakespeare on the one hand and the conceptual world brought into being by Freud and his followers on the other. At first glance, citizenship and psychoanalysis would appear to have little to say to each other. Psychoanalysis, with its emphasis on the singularity of subjectivity, the force of fantasy, and the unsettling effects of desire and enjoyment, presents itself as the inverse and underside of citizenship, with its normative presentation of the public life and juridical definition of persons. The word *citizen* does not appear in the general index to the *Standard Edition* of Freud, nor does it figure in any substantial way in the teaching of Jacques Lacan. Yet the two discourses can be joined, adoptedly, around the dialectic between subjective alienation in the symbolic order (the institution of norms) and subjectivizing separation from symbolic systems (the creative-destructive cut of the exception). Moreover, psychoanalysis and citizenship are drawn together *by, in, and as the field of drama itself,* in its dialectic between ancient and modern, tragic and comic, classical and Christian, and civic and saintly forms of emplotment. I take up Lacan's reading of *Antigone* in his *Ethics of Psychoanalysis* in order to draft a circle of common membership for the discourses of psychoanalysis and citizenship that frames the antiphony of dramatic forms and moments chanted by Antigone and Isabella across the trenches of history.[3]

Antigone's Act

Lacan's remarks on *Antigone* center on the moment when Antigone, having sung her own dirge on her road to death, makes the following declaration:

> *Had I had children or their father dead,*
> *I'd let them moulder. I should not have chosen*
> *In such a case to cross the state's decree.*
> *What is the law that lies behind these words?*
> *One husband gone, I might have found another,*
> *Or a child from a new man in first child's place,*
> *But with my parents hid away in death,*
> *No brother, ever, could spring up for me.* (905–912)

Goethe, in his conversation with Eckerman in 1827, was appalled: How could Antigone, the living-dying paradigm of filial piety, imagine leaving the bodies of her children and husband to rot in the fields unburied?[4] Analyzing the intensity of Goethe's reaction, Lacan takes Antigone's declaration as a model of the relation between a chain of signifiers (what he will call S_2, defined by their replaceability in a line of associations and substitutions) and the singular signifier, or S_1, that anchors the shifting meanings of the signifying chain by being itself irreplaceable, not subject to any substitution. Installed by and as trauma, this singular signifier refuses to budge, forming the immoveable cornerstone of the fantasmatic architecture of the unconscious. Lacan says of Antigone's declaration that she invokes a "a right that emerges in the language of the ineffaceable character of what is—ineffaceable, that is, from the moment when the emergent signifier freezes it like a fixed object in spite of the flood of possible transformations. What is, is, and it is to this, to this surface, that the unshakeable, unyielding position of Antigone is fixed."[5] Antigone fixes on her brother as the one irreplaceable element in the world of *philôtes,* the prepolitical rituals of reciprocity that included the bonds of kinship, friendship and hospitality. She has defended these bonds in a more global manner up until this point; now she singles the brother out as the one person who cannot be replaced, and in doing so she singles herself out, becoming in Lacan's description "unshakeable" and "unyielding." Lacan goes on to link this separation of Polyneices and Antigone from all systems of exchange to language, which introduces a break, and hence a separation, between human existence and the contexts, natural or historical, from which it emerges: "That purity, that separation of being from the characteristics of the historical drama he has lived through, is precisely the limit or the *ex nihilo* to which Antigone is attached. It is nothing other than the break that the very presence of language inaugurates in the life of man."[6] Although language in its symbolic function interrelates humans to one another in systems or structures of relationship, language in its function as pure break, as S_1, produces a separation: a separation from biology, but also from the various institutions and forms of relation that give meaning to being. What is striking in Antigone's speech is how both of these functions of language are held in relationship: She speaks for the irreplaceability of her brother, a stance that irrevocably isolates her from the polis, but she does so while also allowing—and here lies the scandal for Goethe—the total fungibility of other elements in the world of intimate bonds, namely, husbands and children. If one point is unmovable, then it is precisely this anchoring point that allows her to release other forms of relation to the regime of substitution in the polis.

Joan Copjec, a major voice in American engagements with Lacan's thinking and *Antigone*'s strongest recent psychoanalytic reader, emphasizes the radicality—political, sexual, existential—of Antigone's separation from the polis, in this passage and throughout the play. According to Copjec, "the deed Antigone undertakes traces the path of the criminal drive, away from the possibilities the community prescribes and towards the impossible real. . . . It will not be for Lacan a matter of setting another place at the table, of making room for the one brother who was formerly excluded from the rites of community, but of destroying that community in the name of what is impossible in it."[7] Returning to the same passage that offended Goethe, she writes, "Antigone lets us know that her brother is unique, irreplaceable. There will never be another like him. His value to her depends on nothing he has done, nor on any of his qualities. She refuses to justify her love for him by giving reasons for it, she calls on no authority, no deity, none of the laws of the polis to sanction the deed she undertakes on his behalf."[8] Yet surely it is not the irreplaceability of the brother (hardly offensive to a Romantic reader), but rather the indifference toward virtual husbands and sons that disturbed Goethe. Lacan's emphasis falls not on the uniqueness of the brother alone, but on the relationship between the uniqueness of the brother and the equivalence of citizens.[9] It is no accident that when Lacan describes Antigone's fixation on her brother, he speaks the language of rights ("a right that emerges in the language of the ineffaceable character of what is"), as if rights, the hallmark of the citizen and a key measure of social equivalence, come forward precisely at the point where non-equivalence is asserted, but within and in relation to the signifying chain.

Polyneices' position in the signifying order of the polis exemplifies what Lacan, following Freud, calls the *Vorstellungsrepräsentanz:* "This means not, as it has been mistranslated, the representative representative (*le représentant représentatif)* but that which takes the place of the representation (*le tenant-lieu de la representation)*."[10] Although Lacan takes this concept in several directions, its relevance to *Antigone,* I would argue, lies in its demarcation of S_1 and S_2 as a coupling that implicates semiotic representation in political representation. The dead brother has fallen out of the signifying chain, has been refused burial by his city, because of his traitorous acts. These include his marriage to a foreign bride, Diopyle, daughter of the king of Argos, and his return to the city with six heroes allied with Argos, dubbed as a group "the Seven against Thebes." In the dictum of Creon, "it is announced that no one in this town / may give [Polyneices] burial or mourn for him."[11] One brother will be buried with public honors by the polis, and the other shall be left to rot outside its walls. By radically decoupling the brothers at the level of symbolic mourning, Creon's decree installs the rule of citizenship in the place of *philôtes.* Antigone's defiance, however, will not so much reassert *philôtes* as a conservative reaction-formation, delivering the swan-song of the aristocracy as it will elevate *philadelphia,* love of one's wombmate, into the banner of citizenship itself (the sense that the term will assume in the later history of political philosophy). This, I would argue, is the content of what Copjec calls the singularity of Antigone's act,[12] which I locate not in the subversive or anticommunitarian thrust of Antigone's defiance, but rather in her separation and sublimation of a civic potentiality from the very bosom of aristocratic *philôtes.* In my reading, that is, Antigone is neither a conservative reactively reasserting ancient *nomoi* based on outmoded forms of kinship relations (Hegel), nor a radical anarchically resisting state power (Butler);[13] rather, if despite herself and at the greatest cost, she is a foundational figure in the articulation of citizenship in both its contradictions and its promises.

In the course of his commentary on *Antigone,* Lacan refers to his own literary conversations with Lévi-Strauss. Although Lacan's approach to psychoanalysis builds in part on structuralist conceptions of language, kinship, and social order, in French classical studies, the structuralist approach to myth and tragedy would develop largely apart from psychoanalysis, culminating in the work of Marcel Detienne, Pierre Vidal-Naquet, and Jean-Pierre Vernant, their student Nicole Loraux, and English and American scholars such as Charles Seaford, Froma Zeitlin, Charles Segal, William Tyrell, and Larry Bennett. Tyrrell and Bennett, in an important study entitled *Recapturing Sophocles' "Antigone,"* also focus on this speech and Goethe's response as a crux in the play's original social meanings and its misprision in Christianizing, sentimentalizing, and Romantic appropriations (from which they aim to "recapture" the play). Their analysis corroborates Lacan's basic insight into the relation between movable and unmovable signifiers in the play, but does so by focusing on the evolution of specific political institutions and rituals rather than on a general schema of signification or subjectivity. Moreover (and here lies my project), to emphasize citizenship in this regard is both to recover a historically specific discourse that establishes the original intelligibility of classical tragedy and to deploy a transportable, transferable category whose historical destiny is still unfolding.[14] Posing the question of psychoanalysis and citizenship does not mean applying a universal form of explanation (Lacan) to a local instance (Athenian civic myth and ritual); rather, it means mobilizing within citizenship itself the dialectic of the particular and the universal, the individual case of citizenship and the impulses toward both normative expression and internal critique immanent within citizenship as a discourse. The difference made by psychoanalysis is insistence on the singular place of sexuality, desire, and enjoyment in shaping both the exploitative and the utopian dimension of every social arrangement, including civic ones; again and again, the paradoxes that animate citizenship rest on the vicissitudes of gender, sexuality, and kinship in a civic world that founds itself on their neutralization, equalization, or cancellation.

Antigone is a foundational example. Her language is everywhere permeated with the vocabulary of *philôtes,* whose aristocratic, tribal, and prelegal forms of relation have come into epochal conflict with the new policies of the polis. In the aristocratic *oikos,* each member of the kinship group is the recipient of a unique bundle of obligations that must be fulfilled by specific persons or their substitutes in the great web of *philôtes;* each nexus of ritualized social links, materialized in the form of gifts, records the status of the heroic individual in relation to others of his same class, though not necessarily of his own region. Far from presenting a narrow, house-bound set of contacts, guest-friendships could connect far-flung families via rituals of hospitality, exogamy, and the exchange of gifts.[15] With the rise of the Greek polis, the networks of *philôtes* that linked the ancient heroes in positive and negative rituals of reciprocity could come into conflict with *politeia,* translated as citizenship, citizen-body, constitution, or state—although they were also of course in myriad ways integrated into the life of the city.[16] In the democratic *politeia,* citizens are by definition equal and equivalent, substitutable for each other and for the polis, on whose behalf they must be willing to die, one by one and side by side, their deaths in turn demarcating and defending the limited boundaries of the citizenship group.[17] Whereas foreign marriages cemented aristocratic alliances under predemocratic systems of social regulation, the Athenian constitution would reserve citizenship only for those born of two Athenian parents. Whereas *philôtes* describes an open set linking elite stakeholders in complex status relations, *politeia* describes a closed set that equalizes differences among its members while heightening distinctions between those inside and those outside its circle. Notice that it is not a question of intrinsic value against exchange value, or of unique individuals versus interchangeable roles, but rather of two different ways of organizing social relations. The singularity of Polyneices, and of the sister who cast her lot with his, will emerge precisely at the intersection of *philôtes* and *politeia,* passing from one sphere to the other, and hence ultimately binding them together via their exclusion from both.

Tyrrell and Bennett argue that when Antigone delivers her troubling speech about brothers, husbands, and sons, she has already begun the work of crossing over to the values of the polis, both by staging her death as a marriage, an act that signals a certain integration into the social forms of the city, and, in this speech, by partially submitting the bonds of *philôtes* to the new exigencies of citizenship.[18] Antigone's declaration echoes key themes from the genre of the public funeral oration, which replaced *oikos*-based rites of mourning for fallen soldiers with civic rituals that emphasized the equality of citizens in death.[19] Buried in collective tombs by civic tribe in a public cemetery rather than in family graves attached to specific households, and with strict sumptuary laws in place regulating private displays of grief, this transfer of mourning obligations from family to state helped break the hold of the great aristocratic clans in newly democratic Athens. In the process, it also restricted women's roles in overseeing life-cycle events, limiting not only their political roles but also their social capital.[20] As such, the institution of the public funeral enunciated in the clearest possible form what I call "dying into citizenship": not only the idea that the equality of citizens is most perfectly realized in death, which visits all alike, but also that the polis, in burying the dead on behalf of families, mortifies local forms of tribal allegiance and sexual labor in order to interpellate subjects as generalized citizens in a new symbolic order.[21] Lacan is right to say that "at bottom the affair concerns the refusal to grant Polyneices a funeral."[22] What needs to be further specified, however, in dialogue with political anthropology, is the nature of that foreclosed funeral, caught in the historic transfer of funeral rites from *oikos* to polis.

Acknowledging the democratic rule of substitution in relation to sons and husbands on the battlefield, Antigone accedes to the civic order of the new polis. And yet (as Copjec insists),[23] in Antigone's discourse, the brother remains unfungible. Antigone's argument here is resolutely based on kinship: If both her parents are dead, no future brothers can be produced. In this, the very logical armature of her insistence on her debt to the dead brother locates her in the economy of the *oikos*. The brother, of course, is a favored emblem of citizenship: one need think only of the French Revolution's trinity of liberty, equality, and fraternity to intuit the lateralizing linkage, hand in hand, shoulder to shoulder, of brotherly love as a counterimage to the singular rule of the Father, his obscure and even obscene commands issuing from above. Freud's *Totem and Taboo* provides the psychoanalytic counterpart and commentary on the competing vectors of father-hate and brother-love, of monarchical sovereignty and republican constitutionalism, in the family romance of Western political philosophy.[24] To this table of political mythemes we would have to add the fundamental scene of aristocracy, namely the *aristeia*, or one-on-one combat, of great heroes that rules, for example, much of the *Iliad*'s epic action. Closer to *Antigone* is Aeschylus's *Seven Against Thebes*, which relates the agon between Polyneices and Eteocles, and ends with Antigone's resolve to bury the brother excluded from public rites. At the heart of the play's liturgical rhythm is the heraldic matching of Theban hero against foreign one, culminating in Eteocles' decision to take arms against Polyneices: "King against king, and brother against brother, / foe against foe we'll fight" (674–75).[25] When two brothers fight to the death, epic agon becomes tragedy and scandal: the combat of Polyneices and Eteocles represents the self-destruction of epic *arête* from within, the battle of battles that serves to cancel the very conditions of aristocratic order.

The individual excellence of the epic hero, armed and identified with his great heraldic shield, will be supplanted by the regime of the hoplites, the army of citizen-soldiers who were trained to fight together in an unbroken line of identical and overlapping shields, a living chain of political signification. Before they became hoplites, young men trained for the army and for citizenship as *ephebes*—the group represented in *Antigone* by Haemon.[26] John Winkler has speculated that the Chorus (in some plays representing a group of men, and at other times representing a group of women) was recruited from the ranks of the *ephebes*, and that tragedies were written and performed with the civic education and initiation of this special class in mind. The ephebes took an oath of loyalty to the polis that began by affirming the integrity of the battle line: "'I will not disgrace the sacred weapons [*hopla*] and I will not desert the comrades beside me *[parâstaten]* wherever I shall be stationed in a battle line.'"[27] The comrade, or *parâstaten*, is literally "he who stands beside," the neighboring soldier whose overlapping shield cannot be disengaged without destroying the entire phalanx and hence putting the integrity of the city itself at risk.

From combat face-to-face to comradeship side-by-side: The line of the hoplites breaks up and realigns the fratricidal couple. Polyneices, his name meaning "many battles," is the switch point between two types of military discipline and the social regimes they represent. Polyneices and Eteocles came to arms because Eteocles, ruler of Thebes after Oedipus, broke their agreement *to take turns ruling*, assuming instead continuous power for himself. In the *Politics*, Aristotle defines the citizen as "one who shares in governing and being governed" (1283b), an image of reciprocity and interchangeability put into place by the agreement, we might even say the contract, between the two brothers. Polyneices, insisting on his rights to share in the governance of the city, is not only the traitorous enemy of the polis, committing the crimes of radical exogamy and external invasion, but is also the city's first defender of citizenship as a principle of pure exchange and reciprocal rule.[28]

In Aeschylus's play, Polyneices bears a shield inscribed with an image of Justice, depicted as an armed woman leading a man behind her, with the inscription, "I will bring him home / and he shall have his city and shall walk / in his ancestral house" (647–49). Eteocles will derisively deny that Justice will "stand his ally" (*parastatein*), a phrase that redrafts the heraldic image from one of *leadership* to one of *comradeship*. This allegorical woman reflects the historic function of Antigone herself in the civic world crystallized by her act. She brings her exiled brother home to his city *(polis)* and to his ancestral house *(patrôiôn dômatôn)* by burying him against its law. As Warren J. and Ann M. Lane have argued, "[S]he attempts to bury her brother in the spirit of a war comrade and condemns her uncle's corruption in the spirit of a political equal."[29] Her act, by no means describing a simple arc of *nostos*, or return, divides this un-familiar, *unheimlich* home into several zones: the doubled and conflicting spaces of democracy and aristocracy as well as the cities of the dead and of the living. By insisting on Polyneices' right to civic burial but performing those rites as female next-of-kin according to ancient household custom, the sexual and military status of Antigone shifts between Amazonian warrior en route from a lost epic scene and Athenian comrade and hoplite in the *agora* of the now. The first model acknowledges Antigone's femininity, but as an archaic, outmoded, and even dangerous force (what Lacan calls her "terrible splendor"),[30] while the second neutralizes her gender but also grants her equality by placing her within the ranks of the *ephebes,* themselves in a state of social and sexual transition.

Reflected in the shield of Aeschylus, Antigone's act performs several operations in relation to citizenship: she reasserts the continued priority of *philôtes,* even while ceding certain rights to the polis; she insists on the irreplaceability of one signifier, while accepting the exchange of all others; and she does so by fixing on the brother as the conflicted essence of both the *oikos* and the polis, the *vel,* or negative intersection, of the two regimes. It is, I would argue, precisely this doubled, contradictory role that gives Polyneices—and Antigone through her bond to him—their fixed, overdetermined character, both in the city and more than the city, breaking its laws but also ultimately supporting them by returning them to the principle of pure equivalence in relation to a single signifier, the signifier of singularity per se, that animates the symbolic order of the polis. Singularity, reducible to neither the particular nor the universal, keeps the ranks of pure equivalence open to the transformative possibility of act, innovation, and event without falling back into epic archaism.[31] Moreover, this singularity is charged through the play and its subtexts with the ambiguity of sexuality represented by the incestuous legacy of the house of Laius. After all, as psychoanalysis has insisted, these are not brothers and sisters in the usual sense, but the children of Oedipus and Jocasta. In the civic ritual known as Greek tragedy, their incestuous overdetermination of kinship destroys the very conditions of aristocracy in order that the polis might inherit its organizing place.

Choosing to bury Polyneices rather than marry Haemon, Antigone collapses the exogamous drive of *philôtes* into a kind of incest. Yet her relation to Polyneices in no way repeats the household's originary incest, since the sexualization of her relation to Polyneices occurs within and for the evolving language of social relationship in the polis. It is no accident that Lacan finds in Antigone an exemplar of sublimation, defined by Freud as the "satisfaction of the drive through the inhibition of its aim."[32] If the aim of the drive is incest, its sublimated satisfaction comes not in replacing the brother with a more acceptable object (Haemon), but in realizing the goal of lying down with the brother in such a way that the object itself is transformed—in this case, from forbidden lover to fellow soldier. In mourning her brother as a political act, the sister becomes the *parastâtes,* the shielding hoplite, of the fallen soldier, suturing the chain broken by his fratricidal death and his refused mourning by taking her place beside him. When she says, for example, that "it was a brother [*adelphos,* of the same womb], not a slave [*doulos*] who died" (515), she asserts the citizenship rights of Polyneices by contrasting his status with that of the ultimate noncitizen, the slave.

So too, when she declares in her next line that "Death yearns for equal law [*homos . . . nomos*] for all the dead" (517), Antigone asserts a *citizenship of the dead,* a polis of the underworld, that takes as its very *politeia,* or constitution, the mortifying element that haunts citizenship in this world. Finally, in the same interchange with Creon, she speaks the line that will endear her forever to generations of Christian readers: "I cannot share in hatred, but in love [*outoi sunechthein, alla sumphilein ephun*]" (523). But what love is this? We are certainly far from either the *eros* of the philosophers or the *agape* of the Church; evoking the obligations of *philoi,* the phrase would seem rather to pull Antigone back into the cave of kinship. In their on-line translation of *Antigone,* Tyrrell and Bennett render the line, "It is not my nature to side with an enemy but with a *philos*";[33] the military language of "taking sides" here draws the *philos* toward the polis, the brother toward the citizen. In siding with her brother, the sister becomes the *parastâtes,* the neighboring hoplite, of her brother, himself taken as last hero and first citizen on the Theban scene.

In siding with her brother, Antigone brings about the fall of the play's antagonist, namely Creon, who tyrannically places himself above the city he represents by failing to honor the city's fallen dead. Arguing against the Hegelian thesis that Creon represents a form of right, J. Peter Euben surmises, "Even if the male citizens in the audience were initially outraged at Antigone's audacity and Haemon's defiance of his father, when Creon's 'Shall I be ruled by a woman?' and 'Shall I be ruled by the young?' becomes 'Shall I be ruled by the people?' and a claim that he owns the city and must be obeyed in all things, their outrage might well become redirected. They might even reflect on what they now saw as a precipitous agreement about gender and age."[34] By placing political resistance in the hands and voice of a woman, Sophocles tests the regime of citizenship at its limits; whereas suppression of her position might initially appear legitimate, Creon's slide toward a more general tyranny forces us to reevaluate Creon's initial rejection of Antigone's claims on the basis of gender. The sexual exception becomes the voice of civic norms, forcing the polis assembled both within and without the play to begin to broach the question of equity and equality between the sexes. Antigone does not simply recall Creon to the political order he has tyrannically corrupted, but recalls the political order itself to examine its foundations—not in order to restore predemocratic values, but in order to stretch democracy itself.

Antigone's exit, leading in the next stasimon to the fall of Creon, creates the conditions for the normative choral speech, manifesting the survival of the polis, that ends the play. At the conclusion of *Antigone* (pace Copjec), the community is far from destroyed. Rather, purged of the extremes embodied by

Antigone and Creon, the Chorus remains on stage to deliver their "Exodos" or final ode:

> *Our happiness depends*
> *On wisdom all the way.*
> *The gods must have their due.*
> *Great words by men of pride*
> *Bring greater blows upon them.*
> *So wisdom comes to the old. (1347–52)*

Far from reaching the sublime heights achieved in some of the play's earlier passages, the Exodos is a brief song of and about commonplaces.[35] Wearing the masks of old men, but likely chosen from the ranks of the *ephebes*, the Chorus physically mediates and moderates the extremes of youth and age, as well as femininity and masculinity, represented by Antigone and Creon in the play. Cautioning against the "great words" spoken by the play's protagonists, their choral discourse of mediocrity has been brought into equilibrium by the very sacrificial action of the play: this platitudinous speech is the product and telos of the play's dramatic movement. A modern reader might remark on the falling-off, might want to end on a more existential or subversive note, but it is to this purged, chastened, and collective discourse that *Antigone*, and Antigone, deliver us. It is imperative, I would argue, that we hear in this speech the social and aesthetic processes, the sublime expenditures, the painful public and private work, that allow sociality to emerge as something other than a straightjacket, that permit rules and procedures, norms and forms, to become blueprints for new creation.

The speech of the Chorus is born from Antigone's act. In burying her brother against the edict of the city and consequently meeting her own death in the tomb of her family *Até*, Antigone *dies into citizenship* in several senses. First and foremost, her act has a sacrificial dimension: Antigone dies into and for a citizenship that cannot include her except in death. By removing the extremity of her own being and words from the scene, by forcing Creon's fall, and by asserting the equality of bodies in death, Antigone's death stabilizes the norms upon which citizenship is based. Forever absent from the real life of the city, she dies into its civic archives, her *kleos* preserved through the commemorative mourning of the Chorus. Moreover, as Tyrrell and Bennett have argued, the ritual and legal formula for this death into citizenship is marriage, which tames and binds the savage girl to the social order as she leaves it, neutralizing the threat of her unbound sexuality (92–121).[36]

Yet this symbolic scenario, one which ultimately re-alienates Antigone in the symbolic order from which she had initially separated, cannot exhaust Antigone's function in the play or in the history of citizenship it sets into motion. Here Copjec's reading is right on target. Glossing Lacan, Copjec writes that Antigone "immortalizes the family *Até,* that point of madness where the family lineage is undone or overturns itself. . . . If Antigone is fated by her family *Até,* it is in this paradoxical sense: she is *destined to overturn her fate through her act.*"[37] If her fate is the family curse of incest, she overturns or sublimates her fate through her act, traversing the fantasy of sexual union with her brother by taking her place beside him as his comrade in the tomb. To regloss psychoanalysis in terms of citizenship: If her *fate* is determined by the implosion of aristocratic kinship through an incestuous desire that has preceded and produced her, Antigone's *act* is to transform that broken home, riddled with the caves and cellars of failed mourning and destructive desire, into the foundation of a *politeia* whose normative equalizations will forever harbor the memory and possibility of extraordinary action as their very condition. Her act keeps open a space for singularity, for a new form of *arête* beyond epic heroism, housed between the regular intervals of the ranks of the hoplites as their sublime placeholder.

The name given to this possibility by the Chorus is *autonomy:*

> *Untouched by wasting disease,*
> *Not paying the price of the sword,*
> *Of your own motion [*autonomos*] you go. (819–21)*

Copjec glosses the Chorus's characterization as a form of exception to the law: "She gives herself her own law and does not seek validation from any other authority."[38] If autonomy is indeed the ethical stance produced by Antigone's act, we must, however, clarify its mode of production in relation to both the authority of unwritten law (which she claims to support) and the authority of the state (whose edict she breaks). Tyrrell and Bennett note that the image of a freely chosen early death is borrowed from the genre of the public funeral oration, delivered as a consolation to the families of fallen soldiers.[39] As such, the lines implicitly equate Antigone with the ranks of hoplites who have died for their city, imaginatively transferring Antigone's corpse from the family tomb of mourned kin to the public cemetery where the hoplites receive their collective burials. If, as Copjec claims, "Antigone does not seek validation from any other authority," it is because the very gesture of attributing autonomy to Antigone replaces the ritual authority of obligations to *philoi* with the equality of citizens in death. And what is autonomy if not the attribute of the citizen, he who rules and is ruled in turn, who makes his own law by reciprocally submitting to the rule of others and assuming rule in turn? Such autonomy, however, is not ruled by extremes, aberration, or excess, but by norms—the limited and yet all the more heroic autonomy achieved by the Chorus in their exodus from *ephebeia* into *politeia*.

Lacan locates Antigone "between two deaths" —between real death and symbolic death, between the death of the body and death into (or, more radically, out of) social memory.[40] To read psychoanalysis with citizenship is to refine and relocate this ethical topography in terms of the polis. Antigone is between two deaths-into-citizenship. On one side lies a symbolic death into citizenship, her sacrificial disappearance into the historical memory of a polis freed of her dangerous criminality. On the other side lies a more emancipatory death into citizenship, the holding open of a space for autonomy, of future acts and new singularities, that render the equalizations of democracy something other than deadening. We find Antigone reflected between the great ecphrastic shield of the epic hero and the interlocking shields of the hoplites, asserting the terrible splendor of her own singularity, last in the royal line, in order to project the possibility of autonomy into the phalanx of the future.

Isabella's Decision

Both Antigone and Isabella stand in a troubled relationship to the *oikos* and the *polis*. Antigone's name has been glossed as "born to oppose" and "against generation";[41] she rejects marriage to Haemon in favor of fulfilling her duties to her dead brother, a choice whose incestuous lining recalls their parents' own unhappy coupling while transposing it to the new civic order. Isabella, too, enters on a path leading her away from marriage and reproduction; her name, meaning "God is my oath," emphasizes her dedication to a life of chastity that removes her from the sexual exchanges and substitutes her biological family for a spiritual one.[42] As the force of Angelo's propositions invades her psychic world, brutalizing her capacity for social imagining, for creative interaction, Isabella's isolation exponentially increases even as she finds herself at the city's pulsing center. At sea in the city, Isabella has lost all recourse to a system of justice that has revealed its obscene face to her. Even the doors of the convent, archive and altar of the chastity on which she has staked her being, are effectively closed to Isabella, given her new sexual knowledge and her repudiation of the principle of mercy that charges the chaste prayers of the nuns with a social mission.

Yet both Antigone and Isabella will find some relation to the city by the end of their respective plays. Antigone's exodus into a mortifying kinship became the basis, though in a sacrificial mode, of a refunctioning of *philadelphia* toward *politeia*, of brotherly love toward a citizenship whose call to equal rights in death breaks the tyrannical jurisdiction of Creon and creates the conditions for the moderate speech of the Chorus. What is the sexual, social, and political destiny of Isabella's unknown decision in a Vienna symbolically reconstituted by her proposed marriage to the Duke? By leaving her response in question, I argue, the play ends with the startling spectacle of *consent in reserve,* bringing forward, suspending, and illuminating the element of mutual agreement that had signed the precontract of Claudio and Juliet, and releasing it to irradiate the entire civic field. In and between these foundational sister plays in the imaginative history of the civic psyche, the citizen-saint comes forward as *she who invests the regular intervals of citizenship with the ongoing potential for radical singularity.* She does so, moreover, via a certain "anti-gonal," or antigenerative stance, raising the possible withholding of sexual union into the marker of that singular, uncoupled potential within the bonds of civility.

Isabella's decision to maintain her chastity at all costs—beginning with her momentous declaration at the end of act 2, "More than our brother is our chastity" (2.4.186) and culminating in her "kind of incest" speech—plays the same troubled role in critical evaluations of Isabella as Antigone's variable weighing of kinship does for the conversation begun by Goethe. At first glance, the heroines' choices are inversions of each other: Whereas Antigone stresses the absolute irreplaceability of her brother, Isabella willfully breaks ties with Claudio, electing her own chastity rather than the body of her brother as the one immoveable quantity in a world defined by fluid circulation. Indeed, one critic goes so far as to say that "Isabella commits nothing short of fratricide."[43] Yet what binds Isabella and Antigone in the literature of citizenship is their fixation on a pure quantity or measure borrowed from an archaic order of sociality (*philôtes,* monasticism), in order to sublimate it into the exceptional kernel that founds a domain of new civic norms. For Antigone, *philadelphia* lies between *philôtes* and *politeia,* the absolute singularity of the brother becoming the anchoring point in the endless line of fraternal hoplites. For Isabella, chastity represents both the core of her commitment to the vanishing world of the cloister, and the wild card or bargaining chip—will she or won't she?—that brings forward consent as a genuine question in her proposed entry into civic life via marriage at the end of the play.

Isabella's choice of chastity over Claudio has been the object of extensive interpretation, much of it either explicitly psychoanalytic or colored by post-Freudian concerns. In his introduction to the Arden edition of the play, J. M. Lever characterizes her behavior as "hysterical," a diagnosis echoed by Darryl Gless and Arthur Kirsch.[44] For these critics, Isabella protests too much, her explosive anger and morbid imagination revealing the warping power of eros repressed.[45] Is it fair to say that Isabella's commitment to chastity over charity is simply the function of repression and inhibition, or does her choice, in all its furious destructiveness, manifest instead the force of sublimation? In the *Ethics* seminar, Lacan insists that Freud "attaches sublimation to the *Triebe* [drives] as such," in distinction from desire; sublimation concerns not the dialectic of desire in the shifting objects marked by the signifying chain, but comprises the insistent, determined focus on a single object removed from the play of substitutions and "elevated to the dignity of the Thing." In sublimation, the object itself, that is, undergoes transformation, not by being substituted for something higher or better, but by being separated out from all other relationships and posited as the anchor of a newly configured world. Lacan refers in this regard to "creationist sublimation," and he goes on to indicate

> *the necessity of the moment of creation* ex nihilo *as that which gives birth to the historical dimension of the drive. In the beginning was the Word, which is to say, the signifier. Without the signifier at the beginning, it was impossible for the drive to be articulated as historical.*[46]

The "Word" is the singular signifier, S_1, which, in its very absence, in its radical excision from the signifying chain, establishes the equivalence of the remaining signifiers. Isabella's decision, I argue, installs chastity as the sublime object that resides in the creative void left by this singular signifier. As such, her decision changes forever the function and meaning of chastity in the world she prepares to join at the end of the play.

Isabella's choice is a decision in the etymological sense of a cut: her choice irrevocably cuts her off not only from Angelo (whom her counterpart marries in the immediate source texts), but also from Claudio, from her dead mother, and from the convent, to which she makes no motions of return. The cut of her decision, moreover, entails a violence that is more than metaphorical, even if it remains purely potential: "[H]ad he twenty heads to tender down / On twenty bloody blocks, he'd yield them up / Before his sister should her body stoop / To such abhorred pollution" (2.4.181–83). The horrific image of consecutive decapitations visualizes the sweep of the de-cisive cut, again and again, fantasmatically investing it with executive force. Chastity is the object salvaged by the cut of the decision, but it is also *the cut itself as object*, as named and articulated void, insofar as chastity names nonrelation as such, Isabella's willed exit from sexual circulation and its fluid exchanges. Like Antigone, she finds herself at this moment *anti-gonal*, both "against generation" and "borne to oppose."

Finally, Isabella's resolve is a decision in Carl Schmitt's sense of being made without reference to precedents or norms: "Looked at normatively, the decision emanates from nothingness."[47] Although we might imagine many codes and examples to which Isabella could refer in making her declaration (including a multitude from the lives of the saints), they are strikingly absent from her discourse at the moment of the decision itself. Here Isabella differs from Lucrece, who searches the tapestry of Troy for precedents, and commits her own deed within a fabric of once and future exempla. Isabella's decision that breaks free from precedent extends to Shakespeare's interaction with his sources; Shakespeare innovates his received materials by scripting Isabella's refusal of Angelo's proposition, a bargain accepted and consummated by her previous counterparts in Whetstone and Cinthio. *Shakespeare's* decision serves to highlight *Isabella's;* he brings forward the exceptionality of her choice in a social scene ruled by compromise. Here I differ from Darryl Gless, who places Isabella's chastity on the side of the Old Law, works-righteousness, and the repressive rule of the superego (134–41).[48] Contra Gless, I would insist that in deciding for chastity, in response to the brutalizing proposition of the law's corrupted representative, Isabella's drive transforms the meaning of its object, raising it into the reservoir not of an outmoded legalism, but of a new freedom in relation to the law. The superego here is not the Church but Angelo himself, as the obscene voice of the sovereign law. According to Copjec, "Satisfaction of the drive by sublimation testifies to the autonomy of the subject, her independence from the Other."[49] If sublimation tempers passions, it is not sensual enjoyment, but the commands of "the cruel superego" that are escaped.[50] Sublimation is not spiritualization: if Isabella's conception of the sexual act retains its lurid, even perverse core, she has effectively transferred that charge onto the function and significance of the decision itself, without relieving it of its fundamental link to *jouissance*. Chastity is enjoyment by other means.

In his reading of modern tragedy as a species of martyr play, Benjamin points to chastity as the precise counterpart to the tyrant's executive decision:

> *The function of the tyrant is the restoration of order in the state of emergency [*Ausnahmezustand*]: a dictatorship whose utopian goal will always be to replace the unpredictability of historical accident with the iron constitution of the laws of nature. But the stoic technique also aims to establish a corresponding fortification against a state of emergency in the soul, the rule of the emotions. It too seeks to set up a new, antihistorical creation—in woman the assertion of chastity—which is no less far removed from the innocent state of primal creation than the dictatorial constitution of the tyrant.*[51]

Benjamin spells it out for us: *Chastity is to the martyr what the decision is to the tyrant.* Isabella's recommitment to virginity in the face of Angelo's offer bears all the creationist marks of the sovereign decision: it is violent, exceptional, and emanates from a void, flying sublimely free from precedent, but toward potential catastrophe, and within a state of emergency. Angelo has placed himself in tyrannical fashion above the law, "Bidding the law make curtsey to [his] will, / Hooking both right and wrong to th'appetite / To follow as it draws" (2.4.176–78). In asserting her chastity, the martyr of *Trauerspiel* stakes out for herself a measure of the sovereignty monopolized by the tyrant. Isabella's decision for chastity is equivalent to what the Chorus calls Antigone's autonomy: a drive to reserve a sovereign moment, within the subjected subject, and in the process to begin to become both subject and citizen in the modern sense, conceived as *autonomos,* not fully alienated in an externally imposed law. It is no accident that the passage culminating in her decision begins with the question of political speech: "To whom should I complain?" (2.4.172). In the void opened up by this unanswerable question—a complaint about the impossibility of complaint—Isabella makes a sovereign decision that, unbeknownst to her, sets her on a course toward the realization of public petition and grievance in act 5.

This emergent citizenship, for Isabella as for Antigone, and indeed for the discourse of citizenship writ large, occurs at the expense not only of tyranny (its oppressive Other), but of kinship (its origin and ground). Autonomy means freedom from both the mother and the father. When Isabella embarks on the path of the decision, she puts herself at odds with the last familial ties remaining to her. In her infamous confrontation with Claudio in prison, she evokes incest in order to disestablish the kinship ties doubled by incest. This break with kinship takes the form of an act of defiance: "Take my defiance: / Die, perish" (3.1.145–46). *Measure for Measure* invites us to read *defiance*—a word that appears frequently in readings of Antigone—on analogy with *affiance:* "betrothal, engagement, willed affiliation." In casting her lot with Polyneices, Antigone deaffiliates from Ismene and from Haemon as well as from Creon; in resolving herself for chastity, Isabella divorces her brother and impugns the fidelity of her mother. In the process, she unmoors herself from the matrix of kinship, community, and vocation that had previously supported her. This de-fiance is chastity doubled, intensified, and raised into a quasi-legal act, further sharpening the cutting edge of the decision that separates her from Vienna. Yet, like Antigone's before her, Isabella's de-fiance, her breaking faith with familiar forms of filiation, also becomes the springboard for new styles of civic binding, which will take shape in response to but also beyond the absolute sovereignty of the Duke, the play's other superego. This is comedy, not tragedy; the marriage rituals that had solemnized Antigone's symbolic reintegration into the city, but only through death, will here take center stage in the play's final act, with its invitation to four weddings and no funeral. In both plays, defiance as willful de-affiliation is the cut or interval around which a new modality of the political can emerge. Born of the negation of *philôtes* on the part of its feminine representative, in both plays the political takes shape as a creative-destructive potentiality not fully measured by the regulated ranks of the *politeia* that houses it. Or, to shuffle the vocabularies of *Antigone* and *Measure,* a certain de-fiance, both at odds with and in the name of inherited bonds, is at the root of the figure cut by the woman who is *autonomos,* the citizen-saint who wills her own law within and as the space of modern citizenship.

Claudio and Juliet's Contract

If Isabella, like Antigone, embodies the exception, Claudio and Juliet, like Ismene and Haemon, are at home in the world of norms. Legal theorist Robert C. Ellickson defines norms as "order without law."[52] Lars Engle, in important new work on norms in Shakespeare, writes that "literary normativity involves a social readership which responds to literature by adjusting a structure of norms, whether by reinforcing or weakening existing norms (the more probable scenario) or, more radically, by destroying old norms and introducing new ones."[53] Like Ismene, Claudio's normative status is signaled by his role as a sibling, embodying the fraternal function in and for the world of civil norms. To talk about Claudio and Juliet's behavior as "normative" may sound counterintuitive—after all, they are under arrest for a crime of sexual deviance. It is important here to distinguish norms from prescriptive moral codes or from laws; norms arise out of human interaction as modes of social self-regulation and compromise among competing interests and expectations, and as such always involve an element of experiment and transformation. It is the nature of norms that they be constantly generated, tested, and revised. Claudio and Juliet are "normative" in the sense that their navigation of the emotional and economic territory of sexual coupling in Vienna as well as their frank, unheroic, deeply situational responses to the basic creaturely givens of life, death, and sex establish an identificatory middle measure for an audience perplexed by the extremes of Isabel and Angelo. Moreover, their selective adaptation of existing legal standards and practices threatens to "normalize" irregular practices into accepted ones. This innovative nature of their union brings them before the law, which, in judging their relationship, is in turn exposed to the sovereign implications of their civil experiment.

Indeed, the union of Claudio and Juliet is so "normal" when evaluated against English practice that Claudio's arrest and capital sentence for impregnating Julietta has been described as "story-book law" and as "preposterous" and "absurd."[54] Claudio states his case to his friends on the street as he is led off to jail in act 1, scene 2:

> *Thus stands it with me: upon a true contract*
> *I got possession of Julietta's bed.*
> *You know the lady; she is fast my wife,*
> *Save that we do the denunciation lack*
> *Of outward order. This we came not to,*
> *Only for propagation of a dower*
> *Remaining in the coffers of her friends,*
> *From whom we thought it meet to hide our love*
> *Till time had made them for us. But it chances*
> *The stealth of our most mutual entertainment*
> *With character too gross is writ on Juliet.* (1.2.142–52)

Theirs was a secret consensual union, between two adults, without witnesses from family or neighborhood, and performed outside the sanction of the Church. As such, it is an exercise or experiment in civil society, taken as those forms of public association that elude the direct supervision of the state and its church, but also occur beyond the household or *oikos*. The verbal declarations implied by Claudio's reference to a "true contract" were signed and sealed by sexual union, which has now become a visible signature of consent on Julietta's body: "The stealth of our most mutual entertainment / With character too gross is writ on Juliet" (1.2.135–36). Although marriage founds a household and hence institutes a new set of kinship and dependent relations, in English marriage law, it begins as an agreement between two persons, and all that was legally required for a marriage to be valid was the declared consent of both parties, in words and in physical deed.[55] These minimal requirements have been met, and now, in their very minimalism, stand before the law of Vienna. Their marriage is not a "decision" in the creationist sense unfolded with reference to Isabella; far from occurring against a void, the union of Claudio and Juliet has taken place with clear reference to precedents, both legal and social, even when they have read those earlier cases and procedures selectively and with an eye to pragmatic adaptation.

In a milieu in which a libertine like Lucio is impregnating prostitutes and then refusing to acknowledge his offspring, the union of Claudio and Juliet, characterized by economic pragmatism as well as mutual consent, would seem to be a poor test-case for Angelo's legal reforms. Yet perhaps what attracts the Duke's deputy—and the play's author—to the case is the intuition that the "true contract" performed by Claudio and Juliet bears on the nature of sovereignty itself. The state must intervene not only because it is concerned with the proper functioning of civil society, but because the very relation of civil society to the state is potentially challenged by this contract. Their union, lacking the "denunciation" of "outward order," dangerously separates the purely contractual dimension of marriage from its sacramental and communal mediations. As a so-called "hand-fast" marriage, this union takes the strikingly lateral and reciprocal gesture of hand-holding as its corporeal icon. (Juliet is, he says, "fast" my wife—meaning either "almost" or "securely," but evoking also the hand-fast agreement that has joined them.) By choosing this path to marriage, Claudio and Julietta not only separate their union from direct supervision by the state and its church, but they also instantiate, in the equality and mutuality of their bond, an image of civil relation distinct from the one that authorizes absolute sovereignty.

Victoria Kahn has demonstrated how "the language of the marriage contract was appropriated by both royalists and parliamentarians in their debate over the conditions of legitimate sovereignty."[56] In relating *Measure for Measure* to the prehistory of this debate, I will indicate three milestones here—Aristotle, Paul, and Locke—that anchor the play in the literature of citizenship, conceived as general economy rather than local history. In the *Politics,* in a chapter on household management (*oikonomika,* laws concerning the *oikos*), Aristotle isolates for a moment the civil and civic dimension of marriage from the realm of the household:

> *A husband and father, we saw, rules over wife and children, both free, but the rule differs, the rule over his children being a royal [*basilikos*], over his wife a constitutional rule [*politikos*]. For although there may be exceptions to the order of nature, the male is by nature fitter for command than the female, just as the elder and full-grown is superior to the younger and more immature. But in most constitutional states the citizens rule and are ruled by turns, for the idea of a constitutional state implies that the natures of the citizens are equal, and do not differ at all. Nevertheless, when one rules and other is ruled we endeavour to create a difference of outward forms and names and titles of respect. (1259b)*

The *oikos,* it would appear, is itself a mixed polity, instituting kingship in relation to children and constitutionalism in relation to wives. Paternal rule is royal because "a king is the natural superior of his subjects, but he should be of the same kin or kind with them, and such is the relation of elder and younger, of father and son" (1259b). Kinship, however, is missing in marriage, whose exogamous synapse moves out of kinship into a civil bond, if only to reenclose that civil moment within the circle of family life. This *civil* relationship, moreover, achieves a *civic* dimension insofar as it implies rule among equals. Contrary to the situation in "most constitutional states," power in marriage does not in fact rotate; nonetheless, the perceived equality of the partner on grounds other than fitness for command forever builds the suspended possibility of rotation into their relation, creating special grounds for respect (which we might define as the political dimension of civility).[57] In this passage, Aristotle grapples with what he saw as the unassailable natural differences between men and women, while also intuiting a component of equality between the sexes that rendered the husband's rule "constitutional" (*politikos*) rather than despotic.[58]

Aristotle's embedding of constitutionalism at the very heart of the *oikos* provides conceptual grounds for using the marriage contract to displace the hegemony of monarchy and aristocracy, each sustained by kinship metaphors that would use the natural superiority of the husband and father to legitimate the extended authority of the king or the chief. In the Western political tradition, the legal contract of marriage carries a conflicted political charge. Embodying, as it does for Aristotle, both constitutional and monarchical valences, the marriage contract could be used either to conceptualize the willing subjection of the body-politic to the King (on the analogy of the wife to her husband), or to assert contractual and consensual relations among members of a self constituting civil society. Locke, for example, near the end of the century that *Measure for Measure* opens, will define marriage as a "Conjugall Society" in order to break the patriarchal analogies deriving the king's authority from that of the first father, Adam.[59]

Locke's civil reading of marriage is oriented by his rereading of the Fifth Commandment, a touchstone for the patriarchal metaphors of political theology.[60] In his *Patriarcha* of 1680, Robert Filmer had taken the Fifth Commandment, to honor one's father, as the touchstone of an absolutism grounded on paternal authority as revealed in scripture. In his own reading of the Fifth Commandment, Locke neatly rotates the verticality governing Filmer's analogic thinking onto the horizon mapped by the marital couple as a first instance of civil society. Breaking with a long tradition of socially conservative readings of biblical treatments of marriage, Locke insists that the joining of father and mother implies equality between the two partners, a liaison witnessed in the grammar of the commandment, in the contract of marriage, and, ultimately, in the networks of civil association in which that contract will figure for Locke.[61]

As the Locke example already indicates, the ecclesiastical, pastoral, and symbolic entry of Jewish and Christian rites and regulations into the scene further deepens the mix in the postclassical West, lending support to both hierarchical and consensual models of union. To return for a moment to Paul: the comments on household management transmitted to the Ephesians in his name present a picture dominated by a hierarchical image of the body-politic, but softened and lateralized by the idea of neighbor-love that closely follows. The Pauline author begins by saying, "Wives, be subject to your husbands, as to the

Lord. For the husband is the head of the wife as Christ is the head of the church, his body, and is himself its Saviour" (Eph 5:22). Yet he goes on immediately to transpose the verticality of this image, enjoining the husband to "love his wife as himself." Echoing the Levitical ideal of neighbor-love (Lev 19), the dictum institutes the husband as neighbor to his wife, effectively civil-izing—bringing into the domain of social relation rather than sovereign power—the bond of husband and wife.[62] Such lateralization receives more radical figuration (though in a more metaphoric, less pastoral context) in the declaration of equality delivered to the Galatians: "There is neither Jew nor Greek, there is neither slave nor free, there is neither male nor female; for you are all one in Christ Jesus" (Gal 3:28). In this transcendent passage, Paul brings together motifs of Jewish citizenship (circumcision) with those of Roman citizenship (manumission) along with marriage, a common if contested naturalization rite in many civic traditions. The effect is one of sublime equalization of social and sexual relations in the new citizenship in Christ, if only within the limited circle of the congregation and in the context of faith rather than the pragmatics of social life.

The more conservative lines from Ephesians, cited in the "Homily on the State of Matrimony" read after weddings and subject to witty play by Pompey, were part of the many-piled fabric of biblical and political commonplaces from which Shakespeare cut his dramatic cloth.[63] To Paul's set of corporate analogies were added the king as head of the body politic, effectively rendering the people as his wife.[64] If the brother is a key figure in the family romance of constitutionalism, here he cedes the place of honor to the bride in sovereignty as marriage plot. The bride is *she who consents to submit,* who enters freely and equally into a contract that will henceforth install a law above her. The conditions and limits of that law—the retention of any rights and immunities, the possibility of divorce, and the problem of custody—then become the subject of political, social, and sexual definition, debate, and even war.

In sidestepping the denunciation of outward order, Claudio and Juliet would not have been subjected to the sermon on matrimony, nor would they have had to exchange vows dictating Juliet's obedience to Claudio. The "Conjugall Society" they institute establishes provisional equality among partners in a consensual relation that harmonizes affective and economic interests, becoming a building block for civil society more broadly conceived. Hand-in-hand versus head-to-body: The true contract firmly installs this marriage in the civil rather than the sovereign sphere, eluding regulation by church and state and withdrawing the semiotic energy of the marriage metaphor from the symbolic operations of sovereignty. Their union threatens to establish horizontality itself as a norm, indeed, as the norm of norms, as a measure for measures, a principle of social equivalence with the potential to realign the civil and civic fields in their interlinked entireties. With the true contract of Claudio and Juliet asserted as the slim occasion of the play's dramatic action, the Duke's proposal at the drama's close must address itself both to the sublime exceptionality of Isabella's chastity and to the irregular normativity of her brother's "true contract." Moreover, the Duke must formulate this address at both the level of the individual proposal, tendered by Vincentio to Isabella, and at the level of the sovereign relation, extended by the Duke toward the city itself.

The Duke's Proposal

Isabella's divorce from Claudio—and with him, from the variable norms of the city at large—does not go unwitnessed. What future, what possible end, can Isabella's de-fiance have in Shakespeare's Vienna? Such a question must occupy the Friar-Duke as he overhears the divisive interchange between brother and sister. In response to the horror and the promise of her radical integrity, the Duke steps in with a plan. The device of the bed-trick saves Claudio's life and preserves Isabella's virginity by "performing an old contracting," and it will lay the grounds for rebinding Isabella to the life of the city through the new contracting proposed by the Duke.[65] If the bed-trick is a means toward reestablishing norms (though not itself a norm), these norms return in innovated form, forever altered by the horizontal relations of the true contract on the one hand, and by the exceptional singularity of Isabella's antinormative chastity on the other. Isabella's indeterminate response to the Duke's proposal, occurring at the end of the arc opened up by the calling of Claudio before the law, bears not only on her own pursuit of happiness, but on the real and symbolic life of the city reanointed and remapped by the proposed marriage.

The weddings meted out as punishments by the Duke in act 5 serve to reregulate a civil society that has separated too quickly from broader ecclesiastical and municipal frameworks. He orders Angelo to marry Mariana, under the offices of the Friar: "Go take her hence and marry her instantly. Do you the office, Friar, which consummate, / Return him here again" (5.1.385–87). The "consummation" in its physical sense has already occurred; here the outward order of the church-state alliance appears in denuded form, as the pure operation of a public "office"; Angelo's consent to the union has been procured retroactively, through the extraordinary fiat of the bed-trick. The sentence of Lucio, as many have noted, is even more of a mandate from above, carrying the weight of corporeal and capital punishment ("The nuptial finished, / Let him be whipped and hanged" [5.1.523–24]), and leading to protest on the part of the groom: "Marrying a punk, my lord, is pressing to death, whipping, and hanging" (5.1.53–44). Here, Lucio's consent is actively subtracted from the scene, marriage becomes imprisonment by other means, and the proposed union reasserts marital hierarchy, but in inverted form, with Kate Keepdown very much on top. Finally, the Duke directs Claudio, "She, Claudio, that you wronged, look you restore" (5.1.536), presumably directing him to marry her in a proper ceremony, "restoring" the vertical relation between husband and wife within the shelter of an absolute sovereignty rebuttressed by the marital metaphor that had momentarily escaped it. Within this tableau of the ingathering and reregulation of sexual exchange, the Duke's proposal to Isabella represents the final elevation of sovereign over subject, yet at the same time is irrevocably transformed by the play's earlier experiments with the lateral links of civil normativity.

The word *citizen* appears twice in the brief scenes leading up to act 5. Friar Peter remarks, "Twice have the trumpets sounded. / The generous and gravest citizens / Have hent the gates" (4.6.12–14), and then "citizens" are listed in the stage directions among the group gathering for the final act. In Shakespeare's English the term *citizen* did not generally have a political or national significance. Although it was sometimes used to refer to the inhabitants of the land, it usually carried a more local, municipal meaning, referring to city-dwellers who were economically independent members of a profession, trade guild, or mystery, and hence eligible to participate in the corporate governance and civic rituals of the city. Whereas *citizen* in modern English (echoing the Greek *polites*) implies formal political equality in a system of laws, *citizen* in Elizabethan and Jacobean England was primarily an economic category bounded by status or estate, below the nobility and above the many dependents in one's business, workshop, or household as well as peasants and masterless men.[66] In *Measure for Measure, citizen* is a *civil* category, pertaining to economic life, with correlated *civic* functions pertaining to corporate self-governance—at work most prominently in the figure of Elbow, who has monopolized the "place" or "office" of Constable, designed to rotate among the citizens of his ward or parish (2.1). In choosing to stage his play in a duchy, Shakespeare narrows the difference between subjects (of a realm) and citizens (in a municipal corporation), making the two groups substantially overlap. The "city's institutions" evoked in the Duke's first speech refer to both governmental and urban functions, the offices of state as well as the formal and informal exchanges of civil society. And marriage is one such institution, a foundational feature of civil society that lends its symbolic resources to both the legitimation and the testing of sovereignty.[67]

It is such citizens as these, inhabitants of a municipality who are also subject to their Duke, that assemble before the gates to witness the retransfer of power from Angelo to Vincentio. The proclamation that "if any crave redress of injustice they should exhibit their petitions in the streets" (4.4.9–10) addresses citizens in something other than an economic dimension, calling on them to bring forward their complaints before and against the law. The Duke will at the very end of the scene issue a similar proclamation with respect to Lucio: "Proclaim it, Provost, round about the city; / If any woman wronged by this lewd fellow—/ As I have heard him swear himself there's one / Whom he begot with child—let her appear, / And he shall marry her" (5.1.518–23). If on the one hand such a call magnifies the sovereignty of the Duke, evoking his sublime embodiment of a quasi-divine justice, it also begins to call forth a political sense of citizenship, as a formalized set of political rights, including rights of petition and assembly, from within the bosom of its medieval corporate foundations. That these petitions should occur before the city gates emphasizes the element of transition, historical passage, even emergency, that lends the scene its sense of moment. (It is no accident that in the Anglo-American and French traditions at least, many of the great documents of constitutional crisis and reform occur in the form of petitions.[68]) The Duke will not reenter the city itself until he has reassumed his sovereignty from Angelo; the moment of transfer is also a moment of potential transformation, framing the being and meaning of the city itself in its aperture.

Act 5 is staged, theatrically and symbolically, against the background of civic pageantry. We need go no further than the "Magnificent Entertainment" commissioned by the City of London to celebrate James's accession, marked by his ceremonial procession through the capital before opening his first Parliament. Performed on March 15, 1604, and designed by Thomas Dekker and Ben Jonson, the procession presented London shedding its civic status in favor of a courtly one, and becoming a "bridal chamber" and "wedding hall" for James as a "glorious bridegroom."[69] Brian Gibbons notes that "Shakespeare and eight fellow actors wore the livery of grooms of the king's chamber in the process," and describes *Measure* as Shakespeare's first response to the "new monarch's tastes and interests."[70] The "Magnificent Entertainment" stands in a long line of civic rituals that combined the tropes of political theology with those of city theater, run corporate-style by the guilds and mysteries of the town. Royal entries celebrated the inauguration of a new reign, while "reconciliations"—much less common—effected a kind of second entry, healing a state of emergency that had opened up between monarch and city. In both forms of pageant, spousal imagery abounds: the king appears as a *sponsus* or bridegroom greeted by an allegorical Maid of the City; the city itself appears as a *hortus conclusus* or a heavenly Jerusalem. Often staged during the Christmas season, these spectacles wed the *adventus*, or military entry of the Roman Emperor, to the Advent of Christ.[71]

As Josephine Bennett noted many years ago, *Measure for Measure* is a Christmas play, "chosen, in 1604, for presentation in court to open the Christmas revels" (2). Although James's own London entry had occurred the previous spring, the play's advent themes, culminating in Act 5's solemn reentry, marries James's accession to the older liturgical conventions. Ruled by the counterfeit Angelo, the city has been in effect headless, or governed by a counterfeit head; in returning to power, in making his royal entry, the Duke must *remarry the city,* becoming its symbolic head and restoring order to the civil monster. The Duke's proposal takes place before the city gates, and in front of the assembled body of citizens. In such a scene, Isabella functions not only as a private person, but as a civic representative, as the feminine allegory of the city itself. The Duke's proposal, then, signifies his (re)marriage to the city, in the form of his anticipated marriage to Isabella. As a forthrightly Jacobean production, the sovereign dimensions of this proposal, occurring as they do in a sequence of other subsumptions of civil and uncivil experiment, must surely dominate.[72] The Duke reassumes headship of the body-politic by assuming headship of his bride-to-be, Isabel, the one relation confirming and consolidating the other in a symphony of marital mediations. Yet, even apart from the question of Isabella's response, the Duke's proposal itself does open onto the lateral plateau of the marriage contract emblematized by the hand-fast wedding of Claudio and Juliet.

The proposal occurs in two waves, the first flowing immediately from the unmuffling of Claudio: "If he be like your brother, for his sake / Is he pardoned, and for your lovely sake / Give me your hand, and say you will be mine, / He is my brother too. But fitter time for that" (5.1.401–4). Although the Duke speaks in imperatives, he evokes the language of hand-holding, if in a rather "one-handed" way. He emphasizes the lateral effects of the proposed marriage: If they marry, Claudio "is my brother too." This suggests not only the creation of new "in-law" kinship bonds, but also a general "brothering" of the social order, along civil lines. In *Measure for Measure* as in *Antigone,* "brother" is an overdetermined category, standing between kinship (as its last outpost) and citizenship (as its first instance), *philôtes* becoming *philadelphia.* The Duke will become brother of his subject by marrying Isabella, a gentlewoman but surely of no great status, marriage becoming the mechanism for a more lateral and contractual linkage of the Duke to the city via its institutions.

In the first wave of his proposal, the Duke as it were demands consent ("*Give* me your hand, *say* you will be mine"), but then retreats, sensing reticence or even shock on her part: "But fitter time for that." After a brief address to Angelo, he calls Lucio forward for trial by marriage. The work of pardoning done, he delivers final messages to the principals still on stage, and then turns back to Isabel:

Dear Isabel,
I have a motion much imports your good,

Whereto if you'll a willing ear incline,
What's mine is yours, and what is yours is mine.—
So, bring us to our palace, where we'll show
What's yet behind, that's meet you all should know. (5.1.545–50)

Here his language more clearly invites consent; he speaks in the hypothetical about her receptiveness rather than presuming it ("If you'll a willing ear incline"), and he promises something resembling community of property: "What's mine is yours, and what is yours is mine." Having made the motion toward contract, the group proceeds toward "our palace," sanctuary of sovereignty, lead by the Duke but also *assembled* by him, becoming a body that might ultimately claim sovereignty itself.

In royalist arguments about sovereignty, the element of consent in marriage—deemed irrevocable—serves to legitimate the rule of the monarch: "[T]he point of the analogy was to naturalize and romanticize absolute sovereignty by making it seem that the subject, like the wife, was both naturally inferior and had consented to such inferior status out of affection. Yet while such a contract was predicated upon consent of the governed (the wife), once it had been agreed to, the contract was irrevocable."[73] If the Duke's proposal implies the importance of consent (while also presuming the answer), Isabella's response, or rather marked *nonresponse*, brings forward and suspends that request for consent, presenting it to us as a quantity forever in reserve.[74] This remarkable withholding of consent draws out the lateral movement of the Duke's proposal, extending its civic potentiality into the inner offices of the palace itself.

Such reserve is totally in keeping with both the personal ethos and the symbolic figure cut by Isabella in the play. Part of the dramatic and political function of Isabella's earlier decision for chastity is to render the question of her consent more than perfunctory, to keep it open as question. Another character put in the same position— a Hero or a Helena, a heroine more in love with marriage—might more quickly be presumed to consent. Isabella, however, is another matter. Having already turned down Angelo's indecent proposal, she must now consider the Duke's legitimate turn on the same theme. If the general momentum and political climate of the play and its performance pushes her toward a marriage that remains nonetheless unconsummated, and hence incommensurate, we can imagine that she will bring into such a union (of bride and groom, of sovereign and city) some portion of the de-fiant chastity that had set her apart from the city in the earlier movement of the play. Isabella is, in my expression, a citizen-saint, not only a novice sister who is poised to choose life in and indeed *as* the city, as its genius loci, over cloistered virtue, but one who will inject into any new civic position she might assume a continued stake in sexual singularity, an autonomy of being within the community of property evoked by the Duke.

If Antigone dies into citizenship, Isabella *marries into citizenship,* in several senses. Marriage is the legal and ritual means of her registration in the civic body, rebinding her to the social order from which she had separated. This marriage, precisely in its status as a request for consent, proposed in the conceptual gateway of civic reentry and sovereign transfer, is also a marriage that *produces citizenship,* that draws a sovereignty that had modeled itself on the vertical vector of the marital relation into the civil dimensions of the marriage contract. If Isabella marries into citizenship, citizenship also opens her way to marriage, insofar as she enters the public space of act 5 as a speaker before the law, first as a plaintiff and then later, on Angelo's behalf, as a defense attorney. These exercises in public speech rebuild her capacity for social relationship without reducing her to a sexual function. She has in this sense already begun to become a citizen before the proposal further addresses her in this capacity.

The play's fundamental binding (sovereign or civil?) of marriage and citizenship places the question of feminine desire—its orientation, its retreat and reserve, its peculiar laws—at the gates of modern citizenship. Both *Antigone* and *Measure for Measure* insistently link a femininity resistant to sexual exchange—an anti-gonal sexuality— to operations that can only be called political: defiance, petition, and complaint, acts of public speech that call forth the speaker as the victim of an injustice who becomes, through her very voicing of injustice, capable not only of achieving redress, but of challenging the legitimacy of the state itself. The English Bill of Rights of 1689 would assert "the right of the subjects to petition the king," building on rights requested in actual petitions issued in earlier conflicts (including the Magna Carta itself as well as the Petition of Right addressed by Parliament to James's son Charles in 1628).[75] In literature, is not woman the consummate bearer of the petition and the complaint? One need think here only of the genre of the lover's complaint, although in *Measure for Measure* it is Mariana's visualization of dejected eros more than the defiant sexual singularity of Isabella that is most relevant. It is no accident that Isabella and Mariana appear on stage together, two faces of feminine desire exercising their collective right to petition. Each has been moated off from the life of the city, Isabella by her acts of de-affiliation, and Mariana by wedding her own sexual dejection; each reenters the social scene during the moment of political transfer, becoming a citizen before the gates of the city. This is Isabella's first recoupling, as she takes sides with (*parastatein*) Mariana, forming the first link in a lateral chain of citizen-sisters. Laurie Shannon has written evocatively of the "associative" rather than solitary function of chastity in Renaissance discourses of female friendship, which could exercise and institute a "consensual social bond or body that is not inherently subordinating."[76] If Isabella's informal, adopted cousinage with Mariana and Juliet, as well as her attraction to the more regulated life of the convent, had aligned certain forms of social capital with the world of women, here the special resources of *philôtes* among women are called forth and rendered political.

The twinning of Isabella and Mariana within the play mirrors, if only distantly and through adoption, the twinning of Isabella and Antigone across the epochs of the literature of citizenship. In both *Antigone* and *Measure for Measure*, the normative intervals of citizenship, as embodied by Haemon and Ismene, Claudio and Juliet, are themselves secured by the singularity of the exception. The "weaker" positions of each play's secondary characters do not act as foils against which the more exalted heroism of the greater characters shine, nor is the exorbitant heroism of the exceptional figures found lacking when measured against the choral norms of their ordinary siblings. Rather, the extraordinary acts of Antigone and Isabella have as their consequence, if not as their aim, the preservation and expansion of the equality, reciprocity, and pragmatism of citizenship exemplified by their less-famous siblings. They do so by inserting something immeasurable—the chance for autonomy, which includes the possibility of withholding consent—within the irregular rhythms of adaptation and compromise that order the daily life of their respective cities.

Exodos *on Urban Planning*

In the antiphonal song Antigone sings with the Chorus on her road to death, she proclaims herself "alive to the place of corpses, an alien [*metic*] still,/ never at home with the living nor with the dead" (850–51). *Metic* was a formal legal term for resident alien, designating a denizen but not a citizen of the polis. In the Theater of Dionysus, seating was arranged by *phyloi* or civic tribe, the groupings created under the reform of Kleisthenes (509–508 BCE) to lessen the hold of the great kinship corporations that organized the polis before democracy. Ten *kerkides*, or wedges, of seating were reserved for the ten tribes, the division of the theater reflecting the new zoning of the city; one larger central sector seated the Boulê, or city council, and the *ephebes*, the tragedies' privileged audience; finally, two segments at either end of the amphitheater were open for *metics* and tourists.[77] Tyrrell and Bennett speculate that Antigone first enters the play from one of the gangways, not from the central *skene*, passing the *metics* and tourists, moving in front of the assembled *phyloi*, and finally speaking to Ismene at stage center, before the assembled council and the cohort of *ephebes*.[78] In the speech preceding her death-march, a walk that will take her back down the gangways again, Antigone identifies herself with the *metics* seated on the outside wedges, who as noncitizens would have no representatives on the jury that would award prizes at the end of the theatrical festival.[79] Like the exiled Polyneices, and like the unnamed criminal of the play's most famous choral ode, the so-called "Hymn to Man," Antigone is at this moment in effect *apolis,* without a city.[80] Yet, insofar she undergoes a symbolic marriage and rejoins her soldier-brother in death, the *metic* is naturalized, crossing before and even into the central wedge of the *ephebes,* but only by dying. The space of the theater itself provides a map of the symbolic subject positions traversed by Antigone in the course of the play.

Measure for Measure, though performed for the king, was also part of the Kings' Men's public repertory; its venues were both courtly and suburban.[81] Like Sophocles' *Antigone,* and more immediately like Marlowe's *Jew of Malta,* the settings traversed by the actors link the map of the city to the space of the theater. The world depicted in *Measure for Measure* falls into several zones: the civic center, ruled by palace and prison, law and its enforcement; the liberties, outside the walls of the city and harboring a dangerously deregulated economy; the convent, also outside municipal jurisdiction but following its own strict laws; and the moated grange, a kind of private or lay convent attached to "St. Luke's" (3.2.267). As we saw in the rezonings of Marlowe's Malta (chapter 2), the liberties became environments for economic, sexual, and artistic experiment—the site, that is, of theaters and brothels—as a result of the dissolution of the monasteries, the original "liberties," so called because of their subjection to papal rather than royal or municipal jurisdiction. Appropriated to the Crown and then reparceled for cash, these areas retained their special legal status. In Marlowe's play, the Jew's house becomes a convent, evoking the typological conversion of the synagogue into the church, but also pointing forward to the conversion of Catholic holdings into secular ones. In *Measure for Measure,* convent and liberty exist in the same temporal frame, yet when Isabella leaves the convent for the city, its doors effectively lock behind her, its minimal stage props and place markers stowed away until the next performance. Her departure from the convent stages a larger typological exit from the peculiar spaces, genres, and icons of Catholicism. In the forward movement of the play, the saint becomes both a subject (to her sovereign-husband, who reflects Shakespeare's monarch in the private stage at Whitehall) and a citizen (of a Vienna rezoned by her own advent to public speech before its gates). This double passage travels through the world of the modern liberties, profligate heirs of papal immunities, accidental outcome of royal authority, and laboratory for the invention of new norms and forms of civil society. Among these different spaces, and between the world depicted on the stage and the locations of the stage itself—at Whitehall and at the Globe, in the seat of sovereignty and in the liberties—civil norms are publicly performed, instantiating and recreating the grounds of collective life in the shadow of sovereignty. In both *Antigone* and *Measure for Measure,* though at very different moments in its history, the literature of citizenship is fundamentally a *theater* of citizenship, a public place—a place in which "the public" as such is produced—whose legal, ritual, economic, and social realities undergo continual exchange and typological refunctioning in response to those represented on the stage.

SIX
Creature Caliban

SIX ✱ Creature Caliban

What is a creature? Derived from the future active participle of the Latin verb *creare,* "to create," *creature* indicates a made or fashioned thing, but with the sense of continued or potential process, action, or emergence built into the future thrust of its active verbal form. Its tense forever imperfect, *creatura* resembles those parallel constructions, *natura* and *figura,* in which the definitive determinations conferred by nativity and facticity are nonetheless opened to the possibility of further metamorphosis by the forward thrust of the suffix *-ura* ("that which is about to occur").[1] The *creatura* is a thing always in the process of undergoing creation; the creature is actively passive, or, better, *passionate,* perpetually becoming-created, subject to transformation at the behest of the arbitrary commands of an Other. The creature presents above all a theological conceptualization of natural phenomena. In Judaism and Christianity (and indeed it is only via the Latin of late antiquity that the word enters the modern languages), the word *creature* marks the radical separation of Creation and Creator.[2] This separation in turn can articulate any number of cuts or divisions: between world and God;[3] between all living things and those that are inert, inanimate, or elemental; between human beings and the "other creatures" over which they have been given rule;[4] or, in more figurative uses, between anyone or any thing that is produced or controlled by an agent, author, master, or tyrant.[5] In modern usage, *creature* borders on the monstrous and unnatural, increasingly applied to those created things that warp the proper canons of creation. It can even come to characterize the difference between male and female, or between majority and minority: *Creature* as a term of endearment is generally used of women and children, and *creatura* itself might be said to break into formed and formless segments, with *creat-* indicating the ordered composition of humanity and the *-ura* signaling its risky capacities for increase and change, foison and fusion. In various moments in the theological imagination of the West, "creatureliness" has served to localize a moment of passionate passivity, of an abjected, thing-like (non)being, a being of subjected becoming, that precipitates out of the divine Logos as its material remnant.

Caliban is such a creature. Although the word appears nowhere in *The Tempest* in conjunction with Caliban himself, his character is everywhere hedged in and held up by the politico-theological category of the creaturely. As Stephen Greenblatt remarks, "The Caliban of Act V is in a very real sense Prospero's creature," a designation that describes Caliban's radical subjection to and separation from Prospero, as well as the peculiar bond of responsibility implied by those relations.[6] As a solitary Adam on an island to which he is native but not natural, Caliban first stood apart from the rest of creation as "his own king." Now enslaved to a Master-Maker, he finds himself locked within the swarming ranks of "scamels," filberts, and the nimble marmoset, a natural marvel in a world of marvels. As such, he becomes an emblem of what Giorgio Agamben has called "mere life," pure vitality denuded of its symbolic significance and political capacity and then sequestered and abandoned within the domain of civilization as its disavowed core.[7]

If we place Caliban in the circuit of Pauline membership protocols that organize the civic space of Marlowe's Malta and Shakespeare's Venice, his creatureliness comes forward as a way out of the limitations placed on universal fellowship by the persistence of circumcision in modernity. By typologically locating Caliban in the world before the covenant with Abraham, the political theology of the creature avoids the impasse between universalizing and particularizing readings, an impasse immanent in Paul and his legacy and still at work in critical responses to Caliban.[8] As part of primal Creation, Caliban shares the universe of Adam, thwarting attempts by both characters and readers to exclude him from the common fellowship of humanity. At the same time, his creaturely monstrosity foils any reading of this community that would raise Caliban into an exemplar of basic drives. The play includes him within the cosmos of Adam, but as its chaotic exception. If the creature Caliban both invites and jettisons universalizing readings, the same is true for the particularizing impulse. As monstrous exception to the human norm, Caliban's creatureliness expels him into the conceptual space occupied by ideas of national and racial membership, eliciting a long line of culturalist readings of Caliban's oppression. Yet Caliban's exceptionality, both deeply singular and highly indeterminate, also stymies his naturalization within that space, preventing him from becoming the articulate representative of a single race or culture, be it Atlantic or Mediterranean. The creature Caliban subsists within an unredeemed Creation not yet divided into nations, forming the forgotten ground of a heterogeneous universalism irreducible to the economies of a normative humanity on the one hand and the semiotic coherence of individual cultures on the other.

At once monstrous and human, brutely slavish and poignantly subjective, the creature Caliban dwells at the vexed crossroads of (general) humanity and (specific) culture. As such, Caliban's creatureliness *precedes* humanism, since the universe of creatures is measured by neither the totality of humanity nor the authenticity of a culture, but by the infinity of life forms that include the human within their teeming ranks. Caliban's creatureliness may also *exceed* the increasingly troubled solutions of secular humanism in its historicist variants, pointing to another universalism defined by the singularity of each of its members. Unlike Ariel, who is a native spirit, Caliban is a stranger in a strange land, born to a mother forced into exile from Algiers and forced to make a place for himself on these new shores, both before the play begins and after it ends. As such, he comes forward as an unlikely but potent figure of the citizen, as the one who must undergo naturalization, repeatedly called to renounce or revalue the precious indices of particularity in relation to universal measures. In the uncoupled intensity of both his sexual and his political yearnings—and here he may share something with the wild child Antigone and her adopted cousin Isabella—Shakespeare's creature reserves a plaintive core for the citizenship protocols that will reassemble in the century to come around the very themes that animate *The Tempest* (including contract, consent, and divine violence in the state of nature). In this desert scene of emergent political forms, Caliban joins the uneven ranks of Shakespeare's citizen-saints, materializing the perennially minoritarian element—in the double sense of being both a (legal) minor and an (ethnic) minority—that continually besets the majoritarian contract of citizenship as its seemingly inevitable product, but also as its insistent prod.

Approaching the Creature

The German-Jewish philosopher Franz Rosenzweig (1886–1929) initiated twentieth-century reflections on Creation as a category of critical reflection rather than scientific or religious controversy. His magnum opus, *The Star of Redemption,* locates Creation as one point in a triad completed by Revelation and Redemption. Creation, Rosenzweig insists, is an ongoing process: "For the world, its required relationship to the creator was . . . not its having been created once and for all, but its continuing to manifest itself as creature." The creature, writes Rosenzweig, is the subject of a special consciousness: "[B]eing created would thus mean for it manifesting itself as creature. This is creature-consciousness, the consciousness not of having once been created but of being everlastingly creature."[9] *Everlastingly creature:* in this phrase, Rosenzweig unfolds the philosophical consequences of the *-ura,* finding in it the expression of a continuously subjected subjectivity in relation to a Creator who remains sublimely other from it.

In *The Origin of the German Tragic Drama* (1927), Walter Benjamin transcribed Rosenzweig's existential analysis of the creature into a political category embedded in the absolutisms of Reformation and Counter-Reformation Europe. Benjamin identifies the creaturely with the peculiarly Baroque perception of human finitude, everywhere infused with the sense of both the *necessity* and the *evacuation* of theological frameworks:

> *The baroque . . . had . . . a clear vision of the misery of mankind in its creaturely estate. If melancholy emerges from the depths of the creaturely realm to which the speculative thought of the age felt itself bound by the bonds of the church itself, then this explained its omnipotence. In fact it is the most genuinely*

> *creaturely of the contemplative impulses, and it has always been noticed that its power need be no less in the gaze of a dog than in the attitude of a pensive genius.*[10]

Following Rosenzweig, Benjamin identifies the creaturely with a peculiar form of consciousness, impelled by idealism yet forever earth-bound by the weight of corporeality, at once sullen angel and pensive dog. On the one hand, the creature is *too much body,* collecting in its leaden limbs the earthenness and passionate intensity of mere life uninspired by form. On the other hand, the creature suffers from *too much soul,* taking flight as "speculation," as reason soaring beyond its own self-regulating parameters toward a second-order materiality of signifiers unfixed to signifieds. In Benjamin's analysis, "melancholy" identifies the psychosomatic foundations of this creaturely consciousness, its violent yoking of an excessive, even symptomatic mental production to the dejected gravity of an unredeemed body. Benjamin encounters this creaturely melancholy in "the gaze of a dog" precisely because the creature, caught between mud and mind, dust and dream, measures the difference between the human and the inhuman while refusing to take up permanent residence in either category.

In Benjamin's discourse—and here he builds explicitly on the work of the conservative jurist Carl Schmitt—the creature represents the flip side of the political theology of absolute sovereignty developed in the latter sixteenth and seventeenth centuries. In Schmitt's analysis, the king is like God in the creative-destructive potential of his decisive word, his juris-diction.[11] By extension, his subjects are his creatures, the objects of his continual sovereign activity, a power that comes to the forefront during states of emergency, when the normal functioning of positive law is lifted in favor of the sovereign's executive decisions. In English, *emergency* is defined by the state of *emerging,* a condition in which forms are no longer fixed, when new—potentially dangerous, revolutionary, or counter-revolutionary—forms of political life can arise. In German, the *Ausnamezustand* (literally, "state of exception") is ruled by the idea of exception. The *Ausnahmezustand* is that condition in which what is outside the law—the exception to the rule—comes to define the very essence of the law, through the cut of the sovereign's de-cision. In the state of emergency, the sovereign stands outside of a legal order that includes him as the necessity of its own suspension.

In Benjamin's resolutely materialist analysis of political theology, the sovereign, unlike God, is himself a creature: "[H]owever highly he is enthroned over subject and state, his status is confined to the world of creation; he is the lord of creatures, but he remains a creature."[12] The creature is finally both sovereign and subject, both mind and matter, both tyrant and martyr, but he suffers the two modalities in a wildly disjunct form which refuses to resolve into a reciprocal or homogeneous economy. The creature is never simply sovereign over himself, in a situation of stable autonomy in which the terms would balance each other in a just distribution: His self-rule is tyrannous, and he suffers that rule as mere creature. His reason takes flight as speculation; his law is that of the state of emergency, not the state of nature; and his body forever speaks in the hagiographics of dismemberment, torture, deformity, and symptom.

The Genesis of Caliban

Almost all the geographical indicators of *The Tempest* flag Caliban as an Old World figure, born on an unnamed island between Tunis and Naples, perhaps somewhere off the coast of Sicily, from an Algerian mother and an undetermined father.[13] In this mapping, Caliban might appear to be a sorry cousin of Othello, a young man of North African descent and Punic features who finds himself the unwilling inhabitant of a Mediterranean island newly under Italian control. In this reading, "Cannibal" rhymes with "Hannibal," deriving Caliban from a long line of Semitic ancestors, from Sidonian Dido to Algerian Sycorax. Yet the language of Old World Moorishness rolls off of the tempest-tested gabardine of Caliban, who insistently emerges in the world of the play and its criticism as a New World rather than Old World figure. Part of this effect surely derives from the sheer force and power of the play's creative reappropriations by anticolonial writers beginning in the nineteenth century as well as the renaissance of historicism in our own moment.[14] It is not only an accident of the play's reception, however, that leads to this critical disabling of Caliban's Mediterranean genealogy. I would argue that it is also a function of the biblical typing that silhouettes Caliban as creature, both exiled to an island of Edenic nature (caught in the region of mere life, of purely animate being), and forever exiled from it, insofar as his melancholic capacity for both depressive pain and poetic speculation separates him from the natural world he emblematizes.

Caliban enters the play under the sign of the creature:

This island's mine, by Sycorax my mother,
Which thou tak'st from me. When thou cam'st first,
Thou strok'st me and made much of me, wouldst give me
Water with berries in't, and teach me how
To name the bigger light, and how the less,
That burn by day and night. And then I loved thee
And showed thee all the qualities o' th'isle,
The fresh springs, brine pits, barren place and fertile—
Cursed be that I did so! All the charms

> *Of Sycorax, toads, beetles, bats, light on you!*
> *For I am all the subjects that you have,*
> *Which first was mine own king; and here you sty me*
> *In this hard rock, whiles you do keep from me*
> *The rest o'th' island. (I.ii.333–47)*

Stephen Orgel cites the Geneva Bible as the proof text of Caliban's language lesson: "God then made two great lights: the greater light to rule the day and the less light to rule the night" (Gen 1:16).[15] The allusion places Caliban in the order not of history, but of creation, the pristine landscape of the world's birthday. In learning to name "the bigger light and . . . the less," Caliban becomes a type of Adam, *ha-adama,* man of earth, naming the elements of God's creation in a childlike, naively concrete language.[16] Caliban and Adam's shared connection to the earth marks their creaturely status. These primal men are made from dust, fashioned by a divine potter-sculptor, forever emerging (*crea-tura,* about-to-be-created) from the base matter of the elements into the more fixed forms of animate life: "Thou earth, thou" (1.2.314), "a thing most brutish" (1.2.356), "a thing of darkness" (1.2.356; 5.1.275). Throughout the play, Caliban appears as a *thing* made of *earth,* characteristics that mark the elemental quality of the Adamic creature. Caliban's earthen core recalls the first fashioning of conscious life out of an inert yet infinitely malleable substance, as if the very plasticity of mud prompts the idea of conscious life, the inanimate crossing over into the animate as its inspiration, its material intuition. In this scenario, the Golem precedes and informs the human; the manikin is father to the man.

In his history of the island, Caliban, like Adam, names the objects of creation, yet, unlike his antetype, must be taught this language rather than discovering it within himself. Whereas Adam's naming project places him at the head of creation, Caliban's language lesson places him within creation, as one creature among others, a creature who, unlike Adam, bears no obvious resemblance to his Creator. Caliban is mere creature, a creature separate (like Adam) from the Creator, but (unlike Adam) not reflected back to the Creator as his image. The uncertainty throughout the play as to Caliban's shape—"a man or a fish? Dead or alive?" (2.2.25)—reflects this fundamental lack of reflection, this inchoate muddiness at the heart of Caliban's oddly faceless and featureless being, caught at the perpetually flooded border between metamorphic mud and mere life, without the solidifying breath of an instilled form.[17] Naming, language, serves to bring some order to this emergent world, this state of "emerg-ency," and it is perhaps in search of such clarity that Caliban is taught to name not "every living creature" (Gen 1:29), as Adam does, but rather the "bigger light and . . . the less," as if the swarming dominions of bird and beast would too quickly absorb Caliban back into their creaturely folds and idolatrous potential.

Yet sun and moon, purveyors of illumination and models of Logos, also install within the scene of education the possibility of inveterate rivalry. Rashi, one of the great medieval Rabbinic commentators on the Bible, adduced the following midrash from the passage: "They were created of equal size, but that of the moon was diminished because she complained and said, "It is impossible for two kings to make use of one crown."[18] Abhorring equality, the moon suffers diminishment at the hands of her Maker. Sun and moon, Prospero and Caliban, Creator and creature, king and subject: the image of the two lights inserts an unequal couple within the apparent innocence of the recollected lesson, an incipient movement toward rivalry and protest that structures the entire speech. The moon's diminished light glimmers in Caliban's closing reminder that Prospero's sovereignty depends on its reflection back to him in the form of his subject's unwilling recognition: "For I am all the subjects that you have, / Which first was mine own king." In the place of divine similitude, the special stamp of Adam, Caliban is left with the baser mimesis born from rivalry and the quest for recognition. The language lesson lessens the "mooncalf" Caliban (2.2.111), indicating his diminished place within Prospero's sovereign remapping of the island.

Symptoms Taken for Wonder

Caliban is left, that is, with resentment, the creaturely passion that burgeons from the hinge of the hierarchical coupling between sun and moon. It is, of course, a passion previously tapped and tested by Shakespeare: Resentment describes the chip on the ugly shoulder of Richard III, the incalculable debt of Shylock, and the motiveless malignancy of Iago, each finding Marlovian precedent in Malta's Jew. And close behind each of these figures is Lucifer, clothed in the secular garments of the stage Vice and Machiavel. Lucifer, the Morning Star, reflectively intensifies Rashi's eclipsed moon in his hatred of subordination and in his precipitous diminishment from original brightness to darkness visible. In his earlier plays, Shakespeare had consistently fashioned Luciferian resentment as an emblem of market modernity, predicting Nietzsche's analysis of *ressentiment,* in which culture itself in its higher forms reworks an essentially economic relation: "[T]he feeling of guilt, of personal obligation, had its origin, as we saw, in the oldest and most primitive personal relationship, that between buyer and seller, creditor and debtor."[19] In Shakespearean drama, resentment is a mark of villainy under the law, the sign of a soulless legalism, a kind of second-order secularized Judaism, that separates the modern ethos of markets, contracts, and

Realpolitik from the (nostalgically reconstructed) civility of dying feudal institutions of life and love. To restore grace, in its theological and aesthetic registers, to the legalized, economized world of a dispersed and generalized resentment is a dream that animates any number of Shakespeare's plays, from *The Merchant of Venice* to *The Winter's Tale*.

The Tempest changes tack by locating resentment not within but before the law, as the passion of a prehistoric world that takes shape at the shores of the economic as such. In *The Tempest,* resentment belongs to the protosocial world of the creature, a (living) thing, but not yet an object of exchange, subsisting at the threshold of commerce and conversion. The creature does not respond to the exigencies of exchange so much as function as a first quantity of subjected, "created" value that sets the possibility of exchange into motion as such. In *The Tempest,* power requires a moment of enforced inequality for its mobilization. The name of this originary expropriation is slavery, which maintains a creaturely preserve of bare life within a system of sovereignty and covenant, the latter represented in the play by Prospero's contractual relation to Ariel. Prospero defends the necessity of maintaining Caliban within the *oikos* of the master: "He does make our fire, / Fetch in our wood, and serves in offices / That profit us" (1.2.314–16). The reduction of Caliban to his labor places the creature at the heart of an economy governed by the necessities of life, the economy of the Wood-Cutter. At the same time, founded on the very purity of that reduction, Prospero's enslavement of Caliban implies the possibility of an economy of exchange, of "offices / That profit us."

Caliban's counternarrative recounts this originary expropriation: [H]e who was once "mine own king" is now "all the subjects that you have." His own self-rule, his prior self-possession, can only be conceived on the model of sovereignty that he experiences under Prospero, in which the latter's kingship depends on the former's exacted recognition. The institution of sovereignty through the enforced establishment of difference creates the conditions for resentment, a passion that looks forward to the possibility of usurpation and backward to the positing of a self-kingship that would be free from (and yet remains fundamentally modeled on) the dialectic of recognition within a hierarchical couple. Resentment brings Caliban to speech at the level of the symptom, a psychosomatic phenomenon that articulates and inflames the creaturely edges of his being. The pinches and cramps that Prospero visits upon Caliban need have no magical or physical source at all; they may simply manifest the passion born of enforced service, the stinging nettles of resentment as it flowers on the body of the creature inhabiting the edge of symbolization. The aches and pains caused by Prospero's commands are the bodily registration and primitive equivalent of Hamlet's "stings and arrows of outrageous fortune." They are the passionate inscription on the body of Caliban, projected outwards as a magical force, of the slave's rejection of his master's rule, the moon's continued hatred of the sun. "Thou shalt have cramps, / Side-stitches that shall pen thy breath up" (1.2.328–29). The phenomenology of the *cramp* that *pens up breath* with its suturing *side-stitches* describes the suffocating, claustrophobic response, the oppressive sense of internal constraint, that occurs in reaction to Prospero's archaic, noncontractual rule over Caliban. Caliban's pains materialize in the form of the symptom, the protosymbolic dimension of a constraint that as yet bears no epochal force because neither master nor slave is partner to an agreement. Shylock's resentment emblematizes morality under the law—he is the arch-accountant of slights and grudges—and thus takes shape as bonds, contracts, and scriptural commentary. Caliban's resentment is fundamentally preliterate; he can speak but not read; he suffers not under the law, but rather outside the law. Lacking access to legal types of accounting, the creature keeps track of servitude in the only writing available to him: the cramped script, the tatooing side-stitches, of the symptom.

Caliban's bodily suffering of resentment comes to speech in two more articulate forms of discourse: as curse and as counternarrative. The punctual, invective quality of the curse as well as its nagging, repetitive strain and its capacity for vivid if profoundly localized expression place it one step away from the symptom, as an act of minimal verbalization of the hieroglyphs of pain, a first gesture toward an act of imaginative creation around the insistent *nihil* of bodily distress. Caliban's counternarrative represents a fuller, more coherently symbolized articulation of bodily resentment into rational speech; in counternarrative, the abrupt, pointed, explosive trajectory of the curse unfolds in the fuller form of history. Yet counternarrative also remains a limited form of political discourse in the play. Part of the pathos of Caliban's position vis-à-vis Trinculo and Stephano is his inability to communicate his counternarrative to them:

> CALIBAN: *Wilt thou be pleased to hearken once again to the suit I made to thee?*
>
> STEPHANO: *Marry, will I. Kneel and repeat it. I will stand, and so shall Trinculo.*
>
> Enter Ariel invisible.
>
> CALIBAN: *As I told thee before, I am subject to a tyrant,*
> *A sorcerer that by his cunning hath*
> *Cheated me of the island.*
>
> ARIEL: *Thou liest.*

> CALIBAN (to Trinculo): *Thou liest, thou jesting monkey, thou!*
> *I would my valiant master would destroy thee!*
> *I do not lie. (3.2.37–46)*

In a repeated pattern throughout the scene, Caliban attempts to relate his counternarrative, only to be interrupted by the invisible sound of Ariel mimicking the skeptical voice of Trinculo. The result is inarticulate fist-fighting rather than the creation of a new political community around a shared narrative and set of values. Ariel's ventriloquized intervention triggers Caliban's inversion of his story's key terms: Prospero appears first as "tyrant" and "sorcerer," only to flip over into the "valiant master" who will destroy the doubting Trinculo. If the symptom instantiates Caliban's bodily transcription of Prospero's law, the voice of Ariel represents the phantasmatic de-materialization of that same law, its ghostly dissemination into every cove and corner of the island, including the mind and soul of Caliban himself, who is indeed "Prospero's creature": a puppet and a slave, who supports Prospero's sovereignty in the very attempt to rebel against it.

Symptom, curse, and counternarrative: These are the forms of opposition that the passion of resentment takes in the discourse of Caliban. Although they cover a full range of articulate speech and open up the possibility of the creature's own creativity, they share the structure of reaction-formation and as such do not lead Caliban into successful conspiracy, let alone toward a genuine political program or philosophy. Yet there is a more positive dimension to Caliban's speech: the passion of wonder that characterizes the creature's reaction to Creation. In the discourse of the creaturely, the image of cosmos or microcosmos, a totality that subsumes the singularity of the creature in the order of a limited or general Creation, is never distant. The reflex of wonder leaps from the sublime variety of creatures to the larger synthetic unity of a Creation formed by a Creator; in *The Tempest*'s most famous lines, Miranda's "wonder" at "such goodly creatures" finds rest in the cosmic clarity of the "brave new world" they surely represent. Caliban (not unlike Miranda) is a *wonder who wonders,* a creature capable of an affective response to the world around him.[20]

The key passage here is Caliban's most elaborated poetic response to the island:

> *Be not afeard. The isle is full of noises,*
> *Sounds, and sweet airs, that give delight and hurt not.*
> *Sometimes a thousand twangling instruments*
> *Will hum about my ears, and sometimes voices*
> *That, if I then had waked after long sleep,*
> *Will make me sleep again; and then, in dreaming,*

The clouds methought would open and show riches
Ready to drop upon me, that when I waked
I cried to dream again. (3.2.137–45)

Caliban imagines a rain that would be the creative and fructifying antidote to the violence of Prospero's flood.[21] In its positive evocation of place, Caliban's wonder also corrects the negative animus behind the passion of resentment. The passage thus opposes Caliban both to Prospero and to a version or aspect of Caliban himself, and it does so through crafting a response to the physical attributes of the island. The passion of wonder affectively relates the creature to the rest of Creation, finding a home for him there through the re-creative resources of poetic language. An emergent historical dimension structures Caliban's poetry of wonder, since the register of dream introduces an element of linguistic mediation and temporal recollection into the ekphrastic presencing that tends to characterize the poetry of place. When Caliban declares, "when I waked, / I cried to dream again," he represents the beauty of the island as a fundamentally lost dimension of his relation to it, a relation interrupted by the expropriative entry of Prospero onto the scene, but also made available to language by that same emergency. Wonder, that is, occurs across the divide carved out by resentment; it does not precede it, as its lost ground, but rather succeeds it as its refraction and aftermath, an imaginative arch thrown across the destructive breach of the tempest.

Caliban's poetry thus indicates, in a more elaborated, more world-creating form, the creative potentials of the creature himself: the *creat-ura* is a created thing who is himself on the verge of creating. It is still, however, only an incipient creativity (the emergence or potential marked by the *-ura*), located at the origins of civilization, at the border of the real and the symbolic. Thus the passage evokes the classical motif of the Aeolian harp, in which the wind blows through chimes or strings in order to make a random natural music; in this, it is the primitive antetype of the "miraculous harp" of Amphion, whose reasoned music had raised the walls of Thebes (2.1.88). The two harps echo each other, but in different keys: whereas Amphion's harp is tuned to the political sphere, the Aeolian harp remains within the natural world it passively indexes. So too, Caliban's *poetry of place* is not yet a *politics of the polis*. If Aristotle defines man as the *zoōn politikon*, the creature lives at the hinge of this formula, between the zoo and the polis, at home in the taxonomy of neither. Here Caliban's wonder differs from Miranda's, whose marvel—first at Ferdinand, then at the other Italians—takes place as the response to the possibility of intersubjective relations, whether in the form of marital union or of a larger community. It is an established determinant of her character that she is a *human* creature, and her wonder serves to link her to the brave new world of a humanity reconstituted in the wake of Prospero's tempest. Caliban's humanity, on the other hand, remains a question rather than a given in the play. This question is traced by the limited vector of Caliban's wonder: He is a mere creature who wonders at creation without a reflex toward the Creator and also without recourse to a subjective or sexual relation. However full the island is to him, he remains alone on it. The very plentitude of the island masks its fundamental emptiness for him, the lack of a subjective partner for him within its foisoning copia. Caliban's loneliness is a further sign of his imprisonment, of his exile *from* the island *on* the island, but it also may represent the possibility of another type of subjectivization, another model of humanity resident in the motif of the creature, that exists somewhere just beyond the conceptual limits of the play.

Man or Fish?

In the epochs of Christian history, the creature lies before or outside the law. In *The Merchant of Venice* and *Othello*, the dominant types of ethnic alterity were identified with the epoch *sub lege*, under the law, their exclusive and hence excluded contracts marked by the Judeo-Islamic signature of circumcision. The floating world of *The Tempest* reaches back to the epoch of the Flood, *ante legem*, in which unredeemed Creation suffers a sea change on the road to law and grace. Like the Flood, the tempest creates a state of emergency in which primitive instincts emerge in a clarified form, leading to the reassertion of positive law and the reinclusion of the sovereign within its normative order.[22] Caliban's island is postlapsarian, faulted by sin and potential monstrosity and not yet brought into the higher significations of Revelation and Redemption.[23] The creature, existing before the law yet in desperate need of its discipline, offered a fitting emblem for the new peoples discovered across the Atlantic, since the *figura* of the *creatura* includes within its swampy matrix the possibility for both noble savagery and incorrigible drives, for prelapsarian innocence and postlapsarian lawlessness, as two faces of the epoch *ante legem*.[24]

Prospero's storm threatens Creation much as God's Flood does, and the rainbow announcing the marriage masque evokes among other motifs the contract of reconciliation sent by God at the end of the Flood. In the rainbow, God signs a covenant not only with all humanity, but with all creatures: "And the bow shall be in the cloud; and I will look upon it, that I may remember the everlasting covenant between God and *every living creature of all flesh* that is upon the earth" (Gen 9:16; emphasis added). Accompanying this broader promise are the Noachide commandments, a set of seven laws addressed to all humanity that locate mankind within the order of living creation (Gen 9:1–7). In this, they differ significantly from the Ten Commandments, at once more comprehensive in scope and number, yet more limited in their address, pertaining initially only to the nation of Israel (Ex 20:1–14; Deut 6–18). Suzanne Last Stone cites the importance of the Noachide laws for theories of citizenship that might serve to link the forgotten pluralism of ancient Israel to the deeply vexed conditions of modern Israel: "The admission of non-Jews (and Jewish women) as equal partners in the polity would seem to require a bolder theory, one that affirms the equality of all persons under the law." Stone goes on to cite Hermann Cohen, the German-Jewish neo-Kantian, whose rapprochement of Athens and Jerusalem represents one important line in liberal political theology: "'The Noachide,' [Cohen] writes, 'is a citizen.'"[25] Re-signing the work of Creation itself (of which the Ark, with its encyclopedic collection of animals, is a kind of summa), God's rainbow covenant with all creatures provides a comprehensive basis for Jewish, Christian, and Islamic universalisms.

Yet even within the biblical text itself, as well as in the traditions it has spawned, God's covenant with a universe of creatures almost immediately gives way to the first division of the world into the primeval branches of the nations or *ethne*. From Noah's three sons, Shem, Japheth, and Ham, stem the subsequent genealogies of mankind, the so-called Table of Nations, whose roll of generations is marked for the first time by national difference: "These are the families of the sons of Noah, after their generations, in their nations [*hagoyim*]; and of these were the nations divided in the earth after the flood" (Gen 10:32).[26] Moreover, this table is divided into three unequal parts: the progeny of Ham, whose sins may have included intercourse with his wife on the ark, was cursed by his father with slavery: "Cursed be Canaan [son of Ham]; A servant of servants shall he be unto his brethren" (Gen 9:25). In all three monotheisms, Ham's curse provided an etiology of blackness as well as a proof text for slavery based on descent; taken together, the two would provide a powerful rationale for race-based slavery.[27] If the arc of the rainbow embraces the creature as the constitutive element of an everlasting covenant, the institution of slavery identifies the creature with his function as mere life, as pure labor deprived of rights, within a system of national division. The Flood thus represents a watery dividing line between the shifting shores of universalism and particularism as they have been variously imagined, reconfigured, and reduced in the ethno-political legacies of monotheism.

From the broadest of universalisms—a covenant with all creatures—to the narrowest of particularisms—the establishment of slavery based on descent via a sexual crime: This mapping of the Flood and the successive waves of its exegesis also describes the history of Caliban on his island. "First mine own king" and now decried as a "savage and deformed slave" of "vile race" by his masters,

Caliban's passage from freedom to bondage occurs as the result of a sexual crime, the attempted rape of Miranda. Shakespeare had explored some of this typological territory earlier, when he cast Othello as an historical recollection of Ham. Othello and Desdemona arrive in Cyprus, across the "enchafèd flood" (2.1.17), *in separate ships,* a decision that prevents Othello from repeating Ham's crime of intercourse on the ark. Whether understood positively, as the typological redemption of Ham's curse, or negatively, as its inveterate repetition, the Ham-ish face of Othello binds his fate with that of Africa and its peoples, and hence with the history of the world after the Flood. Unlike Othello, Caliban appears to like sex in the rain; at the very least, his attempt on Miranda's honor occurred in the environs of a cave, linked since the *Aeneid* with tempestuous passions of a Sidonian savor.[28] Yet, whereas Othello's links to Ham place him within the order of law and history, Caliban resides just outside the rainbow world of ethnic groups, as primal cause rather than historic symptom of the continental divides brought about by Ham's transgressions. As creature, Caliban straddles the universalist and particularist faces of the Flood, at once included in God's contract with the infinitude of life (but as the measure of difference between the human and the inhuman) and deposited at the scandalous origin of national differentiation (but without clear identification with any stem or continent). In the epochal mapping of the play, the creature Caliban exists somewhere over the rainbow, on the far side of the law, an emblem of mere life who treads water in a flooded Eden fallen from grace and not yet civilized by covenant.

Caliban's enslavement, like that of Ham's progeny, is the consequence of a sexual act; in Prospero's account, Caliban sought "to violate the honour of" Miranda (1.2.346–47). Caliban's response is ambiguous, neither a denial nor a confession, since his terms for conceiving of sexuality are at odds with those of Prospero:

> *Oho, Oho! Would't had been done!*
> *Thou didst prevent me; I had peopled else*
> *This isle with Calibans.* (1.2.352–54)

For Prospero and Miranda, Caliban's response reinforces their view of his unregenerate nature, his status as mere creature, outside the borders of the human community. His desire to reproduce links him to the animals, whom God grants the blessing of increase: "And God blessed them, saying, 'Be fruitful, and multiply'" (Gen 1:22). Yet Caliban's morphological proximity to the human makes his advances on Miranda all the more heinous, placing him below even the bestial, in the category of the monstrous. According to Prospero, Caliban is

a devil, a born devil, on whose nature
Nurture can never stick; on whom my pains,
Humanely taken, all, all lost, quite lost!
And as with age his body uglier grows,
So his mind cankers. (4.1.188–92)

Caliban's physical deformity mirrors his moral limitations, which, in Prospero's analysis, are inborn and native to him. In this, he resembles not so much the "swarms of living creatures" (Gen 1:20) who are characterized by their buzzing multiplicity, their dizzying embodiment of pure increase, as the sublime singularity of Leviathan.[29] Leviathan, the rabbis suggested, was first created as part of a couple ("the great sea-monsters," in the plural, of Genesis 1:21); the female was later slain in order to prevent their disastrous reproduction (Rashi 1: 5).[30] Caliban as Leviathan, as monstrous creature at the limits not only of humanity but of the canons of creation as such: in this perspective, Caliban's enforced celibacy is designed to prevent this singular Leviathan from begetting a whole swarm of them.

Yet Caliban's desire to have "peopled the island / With Calibans" also evokes the Adamic dimensions of a more recuperative typological reading. After all, Caliban's turn to Miranda is not unlike Adam's desire for a helpmeet. Having named "every living creature"—having brought into discourse the fullness of Creation—Adam nonetheless finds himself alone, the very abundance of other creatures pointing to his own isolation (Gen 2:19). So too, Caliban, unique in his ability to apprehend the beauties of the island, is not only *at one* with the island, a part of Creation, but also, like Adam, *alone* on the island, apart from Creation. To "people" the island with Calibans is to find himself in another, to realize his potential humanity by entering into the sexual couple of man and woman. It is significant here that Caliban does not speak of mere "increase" (with its etymological link to "creature"), but rather of *peopling*, rhetorically linking himself to the human kindness from which Prospero and Miranda would exclude him.

So, too, Genesis distinguishes creaturely increase from human coupling. Although the phrase, "Be fruitful and multiply" occurs in connection with both animals and humans, the rabbis noted that God simply "blessed" the animals with this dictum, whereas he directly addressed Adam and Eve in the form of a command: "God blessed them *and God said unto them,* 'Be fruitful and multiply'" (Gen 1:28). This apparently minor variation emphasizes the fact of God's linguistic utterance, a scene of heteronomous command that forever reorients and displaces the sexual act it mandates by removing it from the realm of the merely creaturely. What is in effect *descriptive* in the animal context (though it is an inaugural or creative description) becomes *legislative* in the human context, a demand from the Other that forever separates human being from biological *jouissance*.[31]

Caliban's urge toward Miranda both links him to Adam's blessing and identifies him with Adam's fall. In both cases, the turn toward woman is a move not only toward fuller humanity, but also toward humanity defined as creatureliness, as marked by material urges and baser passions. Woman represents the creatureliness of man; in her capacity for increase, she separates out the *-ura* of the *creat-ura*, its capacity for generation and metamorphosis. In Genesis, the urge toward woman marks the beginning of the fall into a secondary creatureliness defined by its increasing distance from the Creator: Genesis moves from the order of mere creatures (swarming beasts and single monsters) to the human creature created in God's image, to the epoch of fallen creatures who copulate between Eden and Flood. In the typological imagination, such a fall in turn implies the hope of redemption, and this chance distinguishes Adam from Leviathan, the human creature from the monstrous one, the rule from its exception. Read in this light, Caliban's desire to "people the island with Calibans" affiliates rather than divorces Caliban and Adam, inviting Shakespeare's creature into the fold of "people" as such, a common humanity marked by both passion and possibility. The arc of such a reading echoes in Prospero's grudging recognition of Caliban, "This thing of darkness I acknowledge mine," in which Prospero accepts both a commonality with and a responsibility for his creature.

The common humanity implied by this recognition, however, fails to account for, and points in its incompleteness to, the particularism implied by Caliban's desire to have "*peopled* . . . this isle with Calibans." "People" indicates not only "people as such"—humanity taken as a whole—but also *a people*, an *ethnos*, *gens*, or nation of Calibans that would take its place among other *ethne*. Caliban, born on one side of the rainbow (before the law, and before the ethnic divisions instituted by Noah's sons), desires through his Ham-ish actions to cross over to the other side of the rainbow: to a world of covenant and contract, but also to a world of peoples, in which his language and *bios*, or in Miranda's phrase his "vile race," would take on an historical identity. It is perhaps in this space of an imagined particularism that the order of the circumcised called up in the play through the various markers of Semitism (Algiers, Tunis, Carthage) might finally take root. In the speculative space of an island peopled by Calibans—a utopic Calibania—the potential kinship between Othello and Caliban might finally gain some dramatic currency, some mimetic viability.

This achieved particularism is the endpoint of Greenblatt's analysis, where it takes the name of "culture."[32] "It is precisely the particularism of "culture," set against a universalism presumed bankrupt, that neo-historicist readers of Shakespeare have attempted to salvage, whether in the guise of Othello's blackness, Shylock's Judaism, or Caliban's indigenous claims. In the process, however, the universal potentialities of the plays' conceptions of these positions are necessarily ignored, reduced, or secularized. Yet, if Caliban desires to found a people of Calibans, he nevertheless remains radically singular, the first and only citizen, the *princeps,* of his commonwealth. Like Frankenstein's monster, no female Leviathan joins him at the end of the play, and no brave new world springs from their loins. Shakespeare is interested in Caliban precisely insofar as he embodies the antediluvian moment before *ethnos,* insofar as he does not and cannot cross over in the post-Noachide Table of Nations. If in Miranda's vocabulary, Caliban is of "vile race," his moral and physical deformities marking him for slavery, in conception and composition he remains one of a kind, a lonely monster rather than the representative of a nation or a race, a strange exception born in a state of emerg-ency. It is here, in this singularity, at once Adamic and monstrous, that another universalism might accrue, one which would acknowledge and maintain the difference of the creature without resolving that difference into an identity, whether subsumed in the macrocosmic totality of "humanity" or the local habitation of "culture."

By maintaining Caliban as creature, Shakespeare manages to isolate within the idea of the human, forever divided between universalist and particularist strains, an elemental category of bare sentience that refuses to resolve into the homogenizing ideal of the one pole or the identitarian tendency of the other. That is, in response to the forced choice between universalism and particularism, the creature takes shape as their negative intersection, equal to neither. As an Adamic figure, the creature resides in a concertedly prenational, universal scheme; by definition, the creature belongs to Creation, not to nation. As such, the creature would appear to belong in the general field of universal humanity. At the same time, however, the creature is not equal to Adam. The creature Caliban partakes of Adam's earthenness, but is deprived of the *imago dei.* The creature Caliban shares Adam's sexual passion, but remains, like Leviathan, perennially alone. The creature Caliban takes up the burden of Adam's labor, the curse of the fall, but as slave, as pure labor separated from human freedom, does not partake in Sabbath rest. In the chronologic of Creation, we could say that Caliban lives in a perpetual five-day week, created on the fifth day along with the "great sea-monsters" (Gen 1:21), but remaining fundamentally unpartnered by the helpmeet created on the sixth day, and finding his burden forever unalleviated by the cessation of labor created on the seventh. This five-day creature cannot become a model or paradigm for the humanity of other creatures; he does not represent the genetic origin or primal design of either a universal or a particular stem. He is forever undergoing creation, forever *creatura creaturans;* he falls within the field of general humanity, but only as the exception to its rule. This exceptionality in turns exiles him to the particularism of *ethnos*, yet the lack of a sexual relation, of a means of peopling—his both originary and enforced singularity—denies the creature permanent residence there as well.

The world of creatures constitutes an infinity rather than a totality, since it is made up of a series of singularities that do not congeal into a single set. It is here, in this singularity, at once Adamic and monstrous, that another universalism, a universalism after culturalism, might accrue, one that would acknowledge the difference of the creature without resolving that difference into the identity of an *ethnos*. By maintaining Caliban as creature, Shakespeare manages to isolate within the category of the human, with its potential for both universalist and particularist determinations, a permanent state of emergency. As such, the creature materializes a profane moment within the idealism of theology, and thus defines in its very primitivism a possible face of modernity, understood not as the negation but as the remainder of a theological vision. If we want to find a new universalism in the play (as I believe, urgently, we must), it is not by reasserting that "Caliban is human," but rather by saying that "all humans are creatures," that all humans constitute an exception to their own set, whether conceived in general or particular terms. This is by no means a solution that Shakespeare works out in this play or any other. Yet Shakespeare's play is part of the conversation about universals and particulars that grips us still. His decisive crystallization of a certain material moment within the theology of the creature might help us find a postsecular solution to the predicament of modern humanity, trapped in the increasingly catastrophic choice between the universalism of global capital on the one hand and the tribalism of ethnic cleansing on the other.

How, then, do we read Caliban's final lines in the play, "I'll be wise hereafter, / And seek for grace" (5.1.294–95) in relation to the paradigms and promises of citizenship? The reference to grace indicates the play's drive to translate Caliban from an era *ante legem* to a situation *sub grazia*, skipping the period of the law entirely. In the constellation of political theology posited by Franz Rosenzweig, Caliban would move from Creation to Redemption, sidestepping Revelation, with its link to law and nation. Like the conversion of Shylock at the end of *The Merchant of Venice*, however, Caliban's anticipated conversion feels rushed and dramatically unprepared for, yielding a quotient of discontent for its characters and their audience. In both plays, the typological reading remains structurally incomplete and imperfect, the proposed redemptions of their comic villains bearing the marks of a *forced* choice, in which entrance into a new totality occurs at the cost of a felt singularity. This incompleteness, however, is not an aesthetic or ethical failing on the part of the playwright or his characters; rather, it is precisely the point, the product and symbol of the plays' dramatic action and typological movement. In the case of Shylock, the legal formalism of his conversion manifests the condition of the naturalized citizen, who builds a home in the polity out of the remains of his former affiliations. Member of no city and part of no social group, Caliban is surely not the prototype so much as the antitype of the modern citizen; if no man is an island, the creature surely can be. Yet the island vacated by the Italians has suffered a sea change by the play's close, forever altered by the drama's various failed experiments—by Gonzalo's imperfect utopia, Stephano and Trinculo's abortive rebellion, Caliban's disastrous courtship, and Prospero's enforced regime. Caliban's closing statement is a plea for forgiveness and redemption, but also a bid for inclusion, for entry into some form of the human fellowship instantiated, if only negatively, by the departing Italians. To "seek" for grace suggests an element of uncertainty and process, of sustained subjective work on Caliban's part. "Grace," moreover, implies (new) covenant, and hence reintroduces in a theological key the element of contract and consent that was missing from both Caliban's attempted violation of Miranda and Prospero's subsequent rule over Caliban.

As the play closes, Caliban, himself the child of an immigrant and refugee, yet born on the island and in that sense its native son, must begin to remake, renaturalize, his relation to the place. His search for grace will not occur in any church or state of Prospero's making, but rather on the deserted shores of this abandoned island; his resources will include the flotsam and jetsam of political realia left over from the play's dramatic action in tandem with his own considerable poetic, creative, and nominative powers. Following these lines of thought, we can, in a move that is only apparently phantasmatic, draw Caliban's resolution to "seek for grace" into the train of the later phrase memorialized by Thomas Jefferson, "the pursuit of happiness," whose insertion into the Declaration of Independence revised the liberal trinity of life, liberty, and property for an America henceforth held accountable to its exacting vision. Happiness, like grace, projects a wider situation, a fundamental givenness or happenstance, whose social scope diverges from the infantile pleasure principle of pure self-interest. *To seek for grace* is to *pursue happiness:* this tendentious redrafting is not meant to secularize Christian redemption (by replacing "grace" with "happiness") so much as recall the messianic impulse within liberalism (by insisting on happiness as a greater good than property, insofar as happiness both includes and renders social the individuating drive of ownership).[33] In the affinity between "grace" and "happiness" lies the unlikely fellowship between political theology and the literature of citizenship, between religious redemption and secular emancipation, between the sublime suspension of the Sabbath and the productive rhythm of the work week. In the region bordered by theological grace and political happiness, *creature* Caliban might reach his majority as *citizen* Caliban, not by overcoming but by giving voice to the creature's condition as a minor—childish, *unmündig*, hopelessly particularized, and hence recalcitrant to, yet therefore all the more demanding of, political and aesthetic representation.

SEVEN

Samson Dagonistes

"Sovereign is he who decides on the exception": with this magisterial, even sovereign, declaration, Carl Schmitt inaugurates his 1922 book, *Political Theology: Four Chapters on the Theory of Sovereignty.*[1] With the performative force of a decree, Schmitt's definition organizes a field of discourse around the singular stroke of its formulation. In the same chapter, Schmitt goes on to describe the arc of the sovereign's decision in terms that explicitly recall the doctrine of creation *ex nihilo:* "That constitutive, specific element of a decision is, from the perspective of the content of the underlying norm, new and alien. Looked at normatively, the decision emanates from nothingness."[2] Like God's first creative acts, the sovereign's exceptional decisions involve a movement *ex nihilo,* out of a void, insofar as they are not bound by any normative reference to the law. Moreover, insofar as his decision is almost always a decision for violence of one kind or another, it threatens to resubmerge creation in the *nihil* from which it emanated. As we saw in the last chapter, Walter Benjamin's 1927 *Origin of the German Tragic Drama* returns Schmitt's theory of sovereignty and the state of emergency to the Baroque discourse from which Schmitt frequently takes his bearings.[3] In that text, Benjamin follows Schmitt in comparing the sovereign to the Creator, yet he also reminds us that the sovereign never stands outside of Creation: "[H]e is the lord of creatures, but he remains a creature [er ist der Herr der Kreaturen, aber er bleibt Kreatur]."[4] Unlike God, the sovereign cannot know the import or rectitude of his act; hence his decision, instigating an act of decreation, or annihilation, involves a quotient of risk, potentially immeasurable in scope, that can affect the security of the sovereign and his subjects as well as his enemies. Illuminated by catastrophe, the Baroque "drama of the creature"[5] takes the form of tragedy, or rather its postclassical variant, the *Trauerspiel* or mourning play, centered on the trials of the tyrant-martyr, the sovereign-saint.

Victoria Kahn has argued that "*Samson Agonistes* is Milton's—and Samson's—attempt to think the exception in the realms of politics and theology."[6] Milton, unlike Shakespeare, was neither romanced by the spectacle of sovereignty nor enmeshed in its patterns of patronage. Nonetheless, the relations among creatures and creation, decisions and their destinies, and law and its limits arguably plot the fundamental exegetico-political coordinates of his poetry. Recent critics have argued that *Samson Agonistes,* published as an addendum or supplement to *Paradise Regain'd* in 1671, reworks Milton's disappointment and disillusion over the failure of the English Civil War; in the words of Sharon Achinstein, the play explores "how individual experiences of loss could be shaped by post-Restoration non-conformists into a collective experience."[7] In Milton's lifetime, and with his active participation and witnessing, the civil, constitutional, and monarchic tropes that generally functioned in Shakespeare's dramas *in potencia* have undergone the genuine trauma of emergency, revolution, and its failure.[8] In *Samson,* I argue, Milton searches for forms of sovereignty beyond the state. In the career of Samson, a Biblical *shophet,* or judge, from the premonarchic history of Israel, Milton encounters an instance of the sovereign decision not yet captured by its statist institutionalizations. In Milton's typological treatment of Samson, the terrifying exceptionality of the judge derives its force from the creature as a figure of theological abjection and permanent emergency, without the mediation of instituted office provided by the king's second, mystical body.

His life defined by intermarriage and multiple memberships, Samson comes forward as one heir to Shakespeare's citizen-saints in the very extremity of his political (self-)expenditure at the crossroads of divergent typological patterns. Much that functioned at the level of symbol and allegory in Shakespeare—biblical tropes and allusions, the founding metaphors of political theology and social contract—are laid bare in Milton. In *Samson Agonistes,* the Bible forms not just an allusive framework but the explicit content of the work itself, and its magistrate-hero is not simply "like God" in the generalized way of, say, the Duke in *Measure for Measure,* but appears as one of Israel's judges from the pages of Scripture itself. In addressing the political theology of Milton's play, my goal is not to determine Samson's affinity with either Christ or Satan, but rather to link the language and logic of creatureliness that animates the figure of the fallen Samson in Milton's play with the peculiar form of sovereignty manifested by the figure of the judge.[9] In the devolving drama of the citizen-saint, Samson, both creature and judge of creatures, embodies the element of violence eluded or evaded in most accounts of citizenship internal to liberalism. Samson's final act puts into motion what Benjamin has called "divine violence,"[10] in contrast with both the law-making and the law-enforcing functions of force in natural and positive law. Divine violence is unmoored from any particular political end (though it has political consequences), and, unlike Schmitt's sovereign decision, it does not resolve so much as precipitate a state of emergency. Such a situation of radical uncertainty renders future political forms radically contingent, presenting the possibility of forms of sovereignty beyond or outside of monarchy. With brutal clarity, Milton neither glorifies nor condemns such violence, but rather explores its conditions and calls us to judge it.

Creature Samson

Milton even more than Shakespeare is the poet of the creature and Creation. Following Genesis, Milton conceives of man as the creature whose fashioning completes the active work of creation on the sixth day: "There wanted yet the Master work, the end / Of all yet done: a Creature who not prone / And Brute as other Creatures, but end'd / With Sancity of Reason, might erect / His Stature, and upright with Front serene / Govern the rest, self-knowing."[11] Adam and Eve *stand out* from the general order of creation in so far as they *stand up*, "Godlike" in their vertical capacity for reason and sovereignty over nature [*PL* 4: 290]). Yet even while crowning creation, they nonetheless remain within its capacious set, subject to their Author and Maker, the autonomy of humanism countered by the heteronomy of createdness. In *Paradise Lost*, Adam and Eve speak for the totality of creatures in their song of praise: "On Earth join all ye Creatures to extol / Him first, him last, him midst and without end" (*PL* 5: 164–65), a hymn that swells to include not only plants and animals but the sun and stars, air and elements, the very "Mists and Exhalations" that spray the canvas of new creation with their painterly effects. The fall of Adam and Eve in turn threatens to degrade Creation itself: "Us his prime Creatures, dignifi'd so high, / Set over all his Works, which in our Fall, / For us created, needs with us must fail, / Dependent made" (*PL* 9: 940–43). Adam and Eve fall back into the Creation they had earlier crowned, effecting a sea-change in the creaturely folds of a cosmos that includes them still as the natural sovereigns of creation, but now in a state of permanent labor and war. Satan himself is a creature who stands apart from Creation by attempting to stand above it, to deny his created origins.[12] In the poem's sublime choreography of ascents and descents, Satan derides the presumption of the Adamic "creature formed of earth" (*PL* 11: 148) as he prepares to enter the body of a serpent, himself becoming-creature as he constrains himself "[i]nto a Beast," mixing his aspiring essence "with bestial slime" (*PL* 9: 164–68). In a stunning tableau of *creatura creaturans*, of a foisoning matrix of emergent morphologies, the "dire form" of the serpent, its prone body and hissing voice eclipsing the defining attributes of the human, infects the legion of fallen angels, mutating them all into creatures of that anti-Creation called Hell (*PL* 10: 543–44).

"Betray'd, Captiv'd," with both his "Eyes put out,"[13] Samson's opening complaint describes his threefold reduction to the state of a mere creature. His betrayal is sexual; shorn on the lap of Dalila, his devastating loss of strength stems from his sexual weakness, the "impotence of mind" (52) that allows him to reveal the secret of his strength. Like Caliban though from the opposite direction (Caliban is a pagan creature who desires a Christian girl, while Samson is an Israelite with a weakness for Gentile women), Samson's sexual urges cross the respected limits of the proper marriage group, leading to his emasculation and eventual enslavement. The language of the creature accompanies his radical demotion: under Dalila's hands, he is "[l]ike a tame Wether," shorn "of all my precious fleece" (538); returned to Israel, he imagines himself a "burdensome drone"

(567). Dalila herself enters under the sign of the creature ("But who is this, what thing of Sea or Land?" [710],) and Samson's betrayal by Dalila replays Adam's betrayal by Eve, insistently referring Samson's story to the order of Creation.

Yet with regard to the creature, the real weight of Dalila's betrayal falls not so much on emasculation or castration as on the radical decoupling of Samson, his return to an Adamic state of absolute loneliness, a primary depression born of genetic incompleteness.[14] Walter Benjamin writes, "Adam, as the first born, pure creation, possesses the creaturely mournfulness; Eve, created to cheer him, possesses joyfulness."[15] The divorce of Samson and Dalila, like the temporary separation of Adam and Eve or the solitude of Caliban, is a sign of Samson's helpless dissolution into the swamp of creation and his attempt to create a provisional shelter of and for his solitude within its boggy fens. In the *Divorce Tracts,* Milton conceptualizes the act of Creation not as a cosmic wedding but as a divine divorce, a primal separation of light from darkness: "[B]y his divorcing command the world first arose out of chaos."[16] To be single, without a helpmeet (either outside marriage or within an unhappy one), is for Milton the sign of an unfinished or decompleted creature who renders darkness visible in the sheer weight of his ponderous melancholy, but who is linked thereby to the negative genius of God's creative decision *ex nihilo.*[17]

In the cascading sequence of creaturely reduction suffered by Samson, sexual betrayal and decoupling leads to foreign captivity, which economizes Samson's heroic strength into pure labor, sign of the fall: "O glorious strength / Put to the labor of a Beast, debas't / Lower than bondslave!" (36–38). A bondslave operates under a contract, with fixed terms set to his work, whereas Samson's load is infinite and non-negotiable. (Recall here the difference between Ariel's contractual service, timed to end at the conclusion of *The Tempest* itself, and Caliban's enslavement.) Having been, in his words, a "Bondslave" to Dalila ("But foul effeminacy held me yok't / Her Bondslave" [409–10]), he now grinds interminably in the mills of the Philistines. Jeffrey Shoulson points out that the rabbis envisioned the shorn Samson as a kind of sex worker: "'[E]very Philistine would bring his wife to [Samson] in the prison-house so that she might be impregnated by him.'"[18] Although such a fate is not developed by Milton in *Samson Agonistes,* he uses a similar image in the *Divorce Tracts* when he describes the evils of an unhappy marriage as "grind[ing] in the mill of an undelighted and servile copulation."[19] The midrash and its Miltonic parallel conceptualize the link between Samson's sexual fall and his enslavement and reembodiment as pure labor; separated from the conversation provided by domestic union, sexuality becomes animality. Samson's labor is fundamentally alienated and divided, with Creation again providing a reference: Whereas in Paradise, Man was distinguished from "other creatures" by his "daily work of body or mind / Appointed" (*PL* 4: 614–19), Adam and Eve take their first steps toward the fall when they agree to "divide [their] labors" (*PL* 9: 214).[20] Betrayed by a woman, Samson's coglike labor, separated out from his being and then identified with it, reifies him into a kind of automaton, a primitive Golem at work in the mills of a military-industrial complex that has swept his primitive strength up into its higher-order functioning.[21]

But it is his blindness that most clearly casts Samson's lot with that of the creature:

> *O loss of sight, of thee I most complain!*
> *Blind among enemies, O worse than chains,*
> *Dungeon, or beggary, or decrepit age!*
> *Light the prime work of God to me is extinct,*
> *And all her various objects of delight*
> *Annull'd, which might in part my grief have eas'd,*
> *Inferior to the vilest now become*
> *Of man or worm; the vilest here excel me,*
> *They creep, yet see . . .*
> *[. . .]*
> *O first created Beam, and thou great Word,*
> *"Let there be light, and light was over all":*
> *Why am I thus bereav'd thy prime decree? [67–83]*

The contrast between man and worm, between the upright creature and the crawling and swarming ones, echoes a basic duality in the zoology of Genesis.[22] Blinded and helpless, Samson judges himself lower than a worm, forever divided from the first act of Creation and its informing Word by the catastrophic loss of sight and light. This vermicular life is a form of death: "Myself my Sepulcher, a moving Grave, / Buried, yet not exempt / By privilege of death and burial / From worst of other evils, pains and wrongs, / But made hereby obnoxious more / To all the miseries of life, / Life in captivity / Among inhuman foes" (102–9). Reduced to permanently disabled yet infinitely laboring life—what Giorgio Agamben, following Hannah Arendt, has termed "bare life"—his strength and physical being have been exiled from the social and prophetic frameworks that had given them meaning and then recaptured and concentrated as pain, subjection, and labor, corporeal effects that materialize the power of the state over him. Lacan writes of the sexual drive that "it has no day or night, no spring or autumn, no rise and fall";[23] a similar constancy of thrust, of imposed and relentless energy without hope of relief, links Samson's blinded condition to the vicissitudes of the drive.

Samson's body is that of a fallen giant, echoing the fall of the angels in *Paradise Lost:* "See how he lies at random, carelessly diffus'd, / With languish't head unpropt, / As one past hope, abandoned, / And by himself given over; / In slavish habit, ill-fitted weeds / O'erworn and soil'd" (118–23).[24] His ruined hugeness recalls the classical etiologies of mountains formed from earthquakes that will erupt again in the poem's final epic simile (1646–50), dissolving or "diffusing" him into the elemental landscape of Creation. Creature Samson is vegetable as well as mineral, his "ill-fitted weeds" describing his disheveled state while rhizomatically merging his great prone body into the unweeded garden of Canaan itself. Samson is "abandoned" in the sense that he has let himself go, but also in the sense that God appears to have forgotten his prophet; moreover, this state of abandon also defines his condition as mere life, subsisting not as a political subject, citizen, or resident alien in Gaza, but as a captive quantity held within its order as an enemy element. As Giorgio Agamben writes, "The matchless potential of the *nomos,* its originary force of law, is that it holds life in its ban by abandoning it."[25] Betrayed, captive, and blinded, Samson finds himself confined within a certain limit or ban, but *as abandoned,* deprived of the intimate bands and bonds of a symbolically integrated form of life.[26] Like Caliban and also like Satan, Samson is akin to Leviathan, who appears in the new-created landscape of *Paradise Lost* as the "Hugest of living Creatures, on the Deep / Stretcht like a promontory" (*PL* 7: 413–14; cf. 1: 200–203). Like Caliban, he is a distant cousin of Polyphemos, that other blinded giant reduced to a state of enforced infancy by the trick not of sex but of wine. The reference to giants throughout the play evokes the pre-Noachide world of Genesis, when the Nephilim, "mighty men that were of old, the men of renown," walked the earth (Gen 6:4). Creature Samson suffers from giganticism: overgrown and archaic, a migrant worker from the outback of folklore, disabled by his very strength, bigger than life and hence an emblem of bare life, of living matter reduced to the pure quantities of labor and pain.

Yet this body in ruins is also a mind tormented by that mix of speculation and regret called despair. Samson's retreat beneath the tree of pastoral leisure grants "Ease to the body some, none to the mind / From restless thoughts, that like a deadly swarm / Of Hornets arm'd, no sooner found alone, / But rush upon me thronging, and present / Times past, what once I was, and what am now" (18–23). Evoking the swarm of bees in the carcass of the lion, these multitudinous creatures now reappear as emblems of the mental activity of the creature, tormented by a teeming swelter of recriminations that crowd out all peace of mind with the mosquito hum of temporality itself ("what once I was, and what am now"). Dragged lower than the creeping worms by his physical disablement, he finds himself just as cruelly buffeted upwards on the limber fans of thought, conceived in its creaturely capacity as the buzzing drone, the gray noise, of ceaseless cogitation. In Samson's own analysis, the mere creature is he who *creeps in body* and *swarms in thought;* the first attribute prostrates the erect posture that separates man from other creatures, while the second releases man's rational functions into the bug's life of pure speculation. The insectile dispositions of creeping and swarming, moreover, counter the sublime singularity of Leviathan with the multitudinous character of infinite ecrudescence, evoking the fetid fecundity of the unformed populace that represents the resistant precondition of state-imposed power. Behind the capture, harnessing, and disabling of Samson looms the larger spectre of the multitude itself, hobbled, blinkered, and put to work.

Harapha derides Samson's debased condition, confined to "the common Prison, there to grind / Among the Slaves and Asses thy companions" (1161–62). Gone is the distinction of the hero, and in its place is the numbing commonality of slaves and asses, fellow beasts of burden in the ceaseless turns of the mill. Harapha will refuse to fight Samson precisely because of his creaturely degradation: "With thee a Man condemn'd, a Slave enroll'd, / Due by the Law to capital punishment? / To fight with thee no man of arms will deign" (1224–26). Samson is no longer *Agonistes,* capable of joining in one-on-one heroic combat in an epic *aristeia;* instead he is, in my coinage, Samson *Dagonistes,* a laboring, mutilated, living-dead creature aswarm with thoughts of despair who subsists at and as the prone horizon of the human itself. Emmanuel Levinas describes the creature in terms of a primal passivity: "The self as a creature is conceived in a passivity more passive still than the passivity of matter, that is, prior to the coinciding of a term with itself."[27] Thrown and fallen, dejected and abjected, bound and abandoned, Samson finds himself (or fails to find himself) cast back into a passivity and a passion heavier than matter itself, and as old as time.

Samson, Judge

In *Paradise Lost,* Dagon almost rhymes with Caliban: "Dagon his name, Sea Monster, upward Man / And downward Fish" (*PL* 1: 462–63). Yet Samson's world, unlike Caliban's, has been fundamentally remapped by the revelation of the law at Sinai. This is not the era of the Flood, *ante legem,* but the early years in Canaan, after the wars of Joshua but before the period of the kings. Milton is insistent on the legal dimensions of the era Samson represents, effectively couching every reference to Creation within the later jurisdiction of Sinai and its first formalizations after the conquest of Canaan. Samson's imprisonment, writes Derek Wood, "images bondage [to the law] from the start"; the play as a whole, Wood argues, "dramatize[s] the mentality of those raised in the state of religion under the Law."[28] Milton differs from his sources in making Samson's betrayal by Dalila not simply sexual but marital, not a mere "love quarrel" but "wedlock-treachery" (1008–9) and "matrimonial treason" (959). Milton insists here on the civil nature of the bond between Samson and Dalila, its instantiation of a founding particle of civil society, transcribing the Edenic pre-text into a covenantal and even contractual key. Moreover, as an *inter*marriage, their bond brings up the dilemma of double allegiances and multiple memberships, with Dalila choosing "the bonds of civil duty" (854) to her own *ethnos* over those of matrimony and her husband's community.

So, too, the Festival of Dagon is a kind of anti-Sabbath: "This day a solemn Feast the people hold / To *Dagon* their Sea-Idol, and forbid / Laborious works, unwillingly this rest / Their Superstition yields me" (*PL* 1: 12–15). God completed his positive work of creation on the sixth day, but on the seventh day, he created rest itself, a divine cessation from activity that reserves and sanctifies a portion of the *nihil* from which Creation primally divorces itself. The observance of the Sabbath as a weekly festival recalls the work of creation, but is instituted at Sinai; the "Superstition" of the Dagonalia implies a superabundance of laws and rituals enforcing rest, projecting both a pagan antitype and a parodic mirror of Jewish legalism and its afterlife in Christian ceremonialisms. The fall of the temple in turn evokes a kind of de-Creation: "What noise or shout was that? It tore the Sky" (1471); "Noise you call it or universal groan / As if the whole inhabitation had perish'd?" (1511–12). From the Sabbath of the first creation to the Shabbat Shabbaton of an instituted law and liturgy to the radical de-Creation of Apocalypse: Samson's last weekend encapsulates a universe of types that place him before, beneath, and beyond the Law.

Finally, there are the references to circumcision, familiar to us by now as physical marks of the law that perform the act of civic enrollment in the nation of Israel. The Chorus represents Samson's slaughter of the Philistines at Ramath-lechi as a kind of mass enforced circumcision, in which "a thousand foreskins fell, the flower of *Palestine*" (144). Shorn by Dalila, Samson himself, not unlike Othello, is twice circumcised, doubly submitted to the law. As scourge of the Philistines, Samson's haphazard incursions are figured as a kind of extralegal or de-legalized circumcision that expose this neighboring people to the emergent rule of Israel. Under Samson's hands, the violent stroke of circumcision, its act of physical de-completion, overtakes its symbolically integrative function as a rite of conversion and naturalization. (Samson's felling of foreskins may recall the strategic use of circumcision to weaken the Shechemites after the rape of Dina in Genesis 34.) When Samson in turns suffers trimming at the hands of Dalila, the motif of circumcision continues to sharpen the brutal edge of the law at the expense of its symbolic functioning, the excess of the saint overwhelming the rule of equivalences promised to the citizen. Unlike the recuperative arc of Othello's double circumcision, which ultimately serves to register the military hero in the archives of the Venetian polity, the shearing of Samson's hair cuts him off from membership in either Israel or Palestine, de-naturalizing circumcision's naturalizing function. In *Samson,* the circuit of this second, anticircumcision draws the zone of captivity and concentration in which mere life can be, in Agamben's phrase, "abandoned." The turn of the mill follows the turn of the knife, drawing the circle not of free membership through civic inscription, but of banishment to the interior through military conscription.

But if Samson is a creature of the law, he is sovereign as well as subject in relation to it. Hailing from the Book of Judges, he manifests the primitive form of leadership that characterized the early years of the Israelite conquest of Canaan. James Harrington, in his *Prerogative of Popular Government* (1658), wrote, "The shophet or judge of Israel was a magistrate, not, that I can find it, obliged under any certain term, throughout the book of Judges; nevertheless, it is plain that his election was occasional and but for a time, after the manner of a dictator."[29] Harrington's analysis is largely confirmed by modern commentators. J. Albert Soggin, for example, describes the rule of the judges as follows: "[T]heir power came to be seen as an exceptional measure, reserved for periods of extreme danger and thus justified by the state of emergency. At least in the view of the texts, this led to a centralization of power, albeit temporary and provisional, to the detriment of the traditional independence of the tribes of Israel." Soggin goes on to compare the institution of the judge to that of the dictator in the Roman republic, and refers as well to the tradition since Max Weber of interpreting the rule of the judges as a species of charismatic power.[30] Gideon, "the prototypical *shofhet,*" refuses to be a monarch, insisting instead on God's unmediated rule: "I will not rule over you myself, nor shall my son rule over you; the Lord alone shall rule over you" (Jgs 8:23).[31]

The rule of the judges, then, is characterized by *exceptionality* and *emergency,* as well as by an inherent tension between the unity of Israel as an *am,* or nation, gathered together as a confederated body during periods of Canaanite insurgency, and the decentralized autonomy of the individual tribes. Moreover, the premonarchic period was one in which Israel's conquest of Canaan remained incomplete and contested, leading to various leagues with Canaanite city-states that lay interspersed with Israelite settlements.[32] Harrington uses the terms "occasional," "election," and "dictator" to describe the temporary yet extravagant sovereignty of the judges, who step forward out of the loose bands of the tribes to impose provisional unity in a state of emergency. Ruling by coup, the judgment of the judge exhibits an early form of the sovereign decision. The judge's "election" (Harrington's term) is both from above—God visits his judges with the charismatic gifts of the prophets—and from below, in so far as they come not from a group of elders or other recognized authority figures in the structure of the tribe, but from the populace, even from its margins:[33] as one modern commentator notes, "Jepthah was a prostitute's son [Jgs 11:1), Gideon was the youngest of his family [Jgs 6:15] and Deborah of course was a woman."[34] In his *Two Treatises of Government,* Locke also emphasizes the elected and occasional character of the judges, as well as Jephtha's lowly status as "a Bastard of their Family."[35] The repeated experience of judgeship, traumatic both in the conditions that gave rise to it and the violent events that unfolded beneath its shifting banner, would eventually give way to kingship. The office of the king would attempt to institutionalize the temporary accumulation of military power around the judge into a more permanent form of government that included hereditary rule, more elaborated judicial and administrative functions, and a capital in Jerusalem.

Within the sequence of exceptions constituted by the rule of the judges, Samson is himself an exception: According to modern commentators, "He is described as a Nazirite rather than as a judge, and his exploits are often more in the nature of practical jokes than of heroic acts of deliverance"; and "Samson's authority was hardly that of a judge."[36] Part of Samson's exceptionality derives from his mixed literary lineage; finding his place in a book of history, this judge-without-judgment who comes to exemplify the sublime caprice of the decision is more at home among the foxes and lions of myth and folklore than in the national archives of leadership. In *Samson* criticism, Hercules arises frequently as a comparison, given the childlike, even whimsical character of his stories of strength, his kinship with the monsters he kills, and his unexpected apotheosis as a major figure in Greek and Roman tragedy and in imperial cults. Hercules was a culture-hero who killed monsters in order to clear the ground for civilization, but was forced to display his ghastly trophies outside the city-walls for fear that the monster-killer would turn monster himself. (I say "monster" here and not "creature" because the *creatura* is foreign to the classical vocabulary.) Hercules took the invincible skin of the Nemean lion as his primitive armor, and he dipped his arrows in the poisonous blood of the hydra; the same blood would madden him to death at the end of his career. In a similar *peripetiea* that makes its ironic turn around the body of an animal, Samson will slaughter Philistines with "the Jaw of a dead Ass" (143), only to find himself a comrade of asses at work in the mill of his enemy.

In what sense is the judge, hailing from the early epoch of the law, a creature, brought into being at the dawn of Genesis? In what sense does the judge materialize the creaturely aspect of sovereignty more generally—of sovereignty, moreover, caught between its monarchical and its popular manifestations, its vertical and horizontal axes? Is the judge man or fish? Prone or upright? Creeping and swarming, like the multitude, or erect and singular, like the anointed king? Bound in common cause with his companions, or decoupled from every social relation? In *Samson Agonistes*, written in the early years of the Restoration, Milton, I would suggest, is attracted to the placement of Judges before Kings, as both an archaic step in the history of sovereignty, and as the remnant of an alternative to the political theology of absolutism. In the play, typology functions only insofar as it hangs suspended: If Samson presents a type of Christ, he remains, as Derek Wood has argued, "exiled from light,"[37] tragically separated from knowledge of any higher historical development that might give retroactive meaning to his suffering being.[38] In the political register, the judge cannot know that kings will follow next in the history of sovereign forms, and the judge himself remains as much the creature of a tribal multitude as the forerunner of a future political order.

The choral ode preceding the entrance of Dalila gives the play's clearest general account of judgeship:

> *God of our Fathers, what is man?*
> *That thou towards him with hand so various,*
> *Or might I say contrarious,*
> *Temper'st thy providence through his short course,*
> *Not evenly, as thou rul'st*
> *Th'Angelic orders and inferior creatures mute,*
> *Irrational and brute.*
> *Nor do I name men of the common rout,*
> *That wandering loose about*
> *Grow up and perish, as the summer fly,*
> *Heads without name no more remember'd,*
> *But such as thou hast solemnly elected,*
> *With gifts and graces eminently adorn'd*
> *To some great work, thy glory,*
> *And people's safety, which in part they effect:*
> *Yet toward these, thus dignifi'd, thou oft,*
> *Amidst their height of noon,*
> *Changest thy count'nance and thy hand, with no regard*
> *Of highest favor past*
> *From thee on them, or them to thee of service. (667–87)*

The ode begins as a general reflection on the condition of man: Whereas God evenly rules "Angelic orders and inferior creatures mute"—the strata of creation immediately above and below humanity—man is subject to more "various" and "contrarious" treatment. The initial focus on man as exception to the norms of creation shifts quickly to those singular men who stand out from the multitude, "the common rout" who, like the inferior creatures of the ode's opening, "Grow up and perish, as the summer fly." God "elects" these men with charismatic "gifts and graces" to "effect" their own wills for the "safety" of their people. Here we see Harrington's key terms at work: the judge is "elected" by God, but for "the people's safety," a reference to security that finds the occasion of sovereignty in the state of emergency. The "people" secured by the judge, moreover, renames and reworks the "common rout," whose swarming namelessness is transformed by the judge, if only for a brief time, into something like a national unity.

In Manoa's speech, Samson's hair becomes an emblem of this unifying function: "And on his shoulders waving down those locks, / That of a Nation arm'd the strength contain'd . . . Garrison'd round about him like a Camp / Of faithful Soldiery" (1493–99). Combining many strands into one well-ordered head that in turn leads an organized political body, Samson's hair represents military discipline and national unity, the many coming together in the one, a head with a name. Yet, to return to the choral ode, these accidental leaders are elected by God only to be "degraded" (687) at the height of noon, "their carcases / To dogs and fowls a prey" (695), falling back into and even beneath the order of "inferior creatures mute." Manoa's portrait of well-ordered locks commanding well-ordered troops is belied by the guerilla, even terrorist, character of Samson's warfare, as well as by his relative ineffectiveness as a galvanizing force. Tribes do not so easily rally into a nation: Samson blames "*Israel's* Governors, and Heads of Tribes" for failing to acknowledge his victories, to the point indeed of handing him over bound to their enemies (241–76). Samson specifically criticizes the tribal structure of Israel for its inability to bind itself to the singular point of power instantiated by the judge. It is interesting in this regard that the Chorus does not represent the totality of Israel as a nation, but only the Danites, *"certain friends and equals of his tribe"*:[39] "thy friends and neighbors not unknown" (180). Milton would seem to be explicitly interested here in the prepolitical condition of Israel at this early point in its history, a civil society but not yet a state. Whereas Samson would seem to want to raise the tribes of Israel into some higher form of federation, his own being and practices are too primitive, too destructive, too lacking in judgment, but perhaps also too multitudinous, to effect such a change. Graham Hammill defines the multitude in the context of Marlowe: "[T]he multitude is at one and the same time the opposite of the well-regulated populace and that group's precondition."[40] The judge is the one who both brings order to the multitude and comes from their ranks; his rule being temporary, his fall also effects that of the people itself back into the multitude.

Samson's Decision

But what characterizes Samson as judge is not his fall from fortune's favor—conventional at best, and more characteristic of kings than of judges in the Christian political imaginary—but rather the terror of his decision. It is the act of judging that makes the judge a judge—not, however, as part of a juridical or administrative process, which does not seem to have been a central part of the biblical *shophet*'s vocation, but rather a decision for violence, mobilizing the military sense of *shophet*.[41] Both Stanley Fish and Victoria Kahn associate Milton's Samson with the drama of the decision. Milton, writes Fish, shifts "the emphasis of the story from the so-called climactic act (which he renders radically mysterious) to the decision to move into the space in which that act becomes a possible one, a decision that is itself marked by a radical uncertainty. . . . Like Abraham, Samson goes out, or rather goes along, and he goes along to he knows not what." Kahn writes similarly, "Samson's about-face in going to the temple suggests that, while rules can be instantiated, and examples imitated, an exception must be decided."[42] Samson becomes a judge, in Harrington's precise exegetico-political sense, by arriving at a decision that places him outside any law, Philistine certainly, but Hebrew as well. In going along to the temple of Dagon, Samson becomes more than anywhere else in his whole biography of exceptions an emblem of the exception, in its violence, its antinomianism, its blindness, and its creative-destructive potential, referring itself backward to Genesis (but under the stroke of primal divorce, of the most terrifying separation) and forward to Apocalypse (but in the form of suspended and unredeemed typology).

Relevant here is a passage from Benjamin's "Critique of Violence," an essay that interested Carl Schmitt:[43] "[T]he question 'May I kill?' meets its irreducible answer in the commandment, 'Thou shalt not kill.' . . . It exists not as a criterion of judgment, but as a guideline for the actions of persons or communities who have to wrestle with it in solitude and, in exceptional cases, to take on themselves the responsibility of ignoring it."[44] This is surely Samson's situation when he decides to raise himself up again as judge in the final act of his life. The Decalogue has been delivered; now Samson must become "deliverer" (another epithet of the *shophet*), and this entails not breaking the commandment against killing so much as suspending it, choosing to make an exception to it. Samson's decision is not just any judgment, but a judgment for violence—for an act of violence, moreover, that bears no evident relation to the ends of either law-making or law-enforcing, the types of force traditionally legitimated in natural and positive law respectively.[45] Samson's decision invokes what Benjamin calls "divine violence," "violence outside the law," "pure immediate violence," what appears in the final words of his essay as "sovereign violence."[46] It is sovereign not because it founds the state (constituting power) or preserves the state (constituted power), but because it exists in fundamental tension with law as such. Samson gathers from his very debasement as creature a motivating contact with creation itself as a principle of exceptional violence, of primal sundering and sublime divorce, out of and around a *nihil*.[47] In rising to a decision, the creature resembles his Creator, the One who, the Chorus has told us, "made our Laws to bind us, not himself, / And hath full right to exempt / Whom so it pleases him by choice" (309–11). Yet Samson remains a creature, not knowing whence comes the motivation for his act or whither tends its violence. As Benjamin writes of *Trauerspiel,* "In the ruler, the supreme creature, the beast can re-emerge with unsuspected power."[48] When Samson decides for violence, his act could be Satanic or divine; the point, as Kahn and Fish have both demonstrated, is that Samson doesn't know, that he must act "of his own accord,"[49] that is, without accordance or concordance with a law that would determine its meaning and legitimacy.[50] In this sense, true decision is, like Samson himself, always blind.

Even the Decalogue—and here is where Benjamin's reading of the Ten Commandments is pertinent—cannot tell the judge how to judge. The Decalogue is not "a criterion of judgment"—a code for deciding what is right and wrong, legal and illegal—but rather "a guideline for the actions of persons or communities" who find themselves in the predicament of having to decide on an exception to those rules. The decision of the judge refers the order of law back to the founding trauma of creation *ex nihilo;* under his prophetico-military jurisdiction, the revelation at Sinai is shot through with the terrible light of Creation. The judge works in the penumbra of Sinai, in the terrifying halo of its thunderous revelation, but not in the mode of application or enforcement. It is worth keeping in mind here that the word *commandment* does not appear in Exodus 20 in connection with the giving of the law at Sinai. Rather, the phrase "ten words" (*aseret ha-devarim*) occurs in Exodus 34:28 to refer to the contents of the two tablets; the Greek *deka logoi* (or English Decalogue) is thus a more accurate rendering. We could say here that God's giving of the law itself has the character of a decision, collating the speaking of the ten words of the covenant with the speaking of the world into being in Genesis. The dictated law in turn both *binds* and *abandons* those who, like Samson, are called to act in its name, but of their own accord: they are bound to the law, as its executors, but abandoned to their own judgment in relation to its words.

We in turn are called to judge Samson's act. Samson's destruction of the Temple of Dagon stands in ambivalent relation to the possibilities and realities of state power. On the one hand, he has desired to "serve [his] Nation" (566) by drawing the tribes of Israel into a greater unity, and berates them for their refusal to see him as other than a "private person" and a "League-breaker" with the Philistines (1208–9). Yet he does finally act alone, not private so much as privatized, unaccompanied by any friend, shorn of all Hebrew regalia, and dressed in the colors of the Philistines ("as a public servant brought, / In their state Livery clad" [1615–16]). Samson's final act fails the classical criteria of heroism in either its aristocratic or its democratic form. Despite his epithet, Samson does not die in the one-on-one combat of epic agon; although Manoa comes to retrieve his son as Priam had for Hector, Samson has no "Antagonist" (1628) and dies by no "glorious hand" (1581). Yet he also fails to command a phalanx of hoplites joined together in a chain of equivalence in defense of a *politeia*—or, in more properly Israelite terms, he fails to bring together a set of tribes united by common covenant and the signature of circumcision against the Philistines.[51] Instead, he reclaims his strength from its captivity as pure labor, and uses it to destroy the structure of publicity itself. It is an act that occurs within the instinctive realm of the creature, as the reflex and the recall of the drive, but not as its sublimation.

In this, his destiny remains distinct from, even the inverse of, that of Antigone, who represents the deadly purity of the drive, but also the chance of its sublimation. Although both move inexorably toward live burial, to the fate that Lacan calls the second death,[52] Antigone is sentenced by the state to a capital punishment whose precise end point and meaning she is able to transform in order to recapture the space of the *politea* from its tyrannical repression. Samson's final act, on the other hand, mounts an assault on the very possibility of a public sphere (free assembly and congregation being the true target of terrorism). Hannah Arendt defines "total terror" as the destruction of the space between men, the collapse, that is, of the possibility of a public sphere.[53] What Dennis Kezar has aptly termed "Samson's death by theatre" could also be described as Samson's death by—and *to*—public space.[54] Earlier, Samson had carried the very gates of the city on his back; now he devastates the heart of the city itself by pulling down the sustaining pillars of its central hall, at once a "Theatre" (1605), a temple, and a site of "great Assembly" (1315). Samson destroys the civic conditions of Gaza itself, both its material support and the space for collective assembly, recreation, and ritual that it had sheltered.

Yet if the Temple of Dagon is a public space, its organization is strictly hierarchical:

The building was a spacious Theater
Half round on two main Pillars vaulted high,
With seats where all the Lords and each degree

> *Of sort, might sit in order to behold,*
> *The other side was op'n, where the throng*
> *On banks and scaffolds under Sky might stand.* (1605–10)

Unlike either the loosely federated structure of *b'nai Israel* or the Theatre of Dionysius, organized by civic *phyloi,* seating at the Temple of Dagon is organized by caste, by "each degree of sort." In this case, hierarchy has its dangers, since the roof falls only on the elite, "Upon the heads of those who sat beneath, / Lords, Ladies, Captains, Counsellors, or Priests. . . . The vulgar only scap'd who stood without" (1651–59). Samson is "with these inmixt," ending his judgeship by dying into the confused ruin of institutionalized and hierarchical rule, but without synthesis or fusion with its underlying architecture of order. Earlier, creature Samson had decried his blindness as a kind of living death, a burial alive, "Myself my Sepulcher, a moving Grave" (102). His destruction of the temple of Dagon brings the metaphor of live burial crashing down on himself and the Philistine elite, short-circuiting death and interment in one sublime implosion. In relation to the Philistine state, he is both captive subject and sovereign power; in Benjamin's terms, he is a tyrant (but without being ruler of any state), and a martyr (but without being victim of any execution).[55]

The common people survive destruction, though now, deprived of leadership during the impending state of emergency, they will surely dissolve into "the common rout" that "grow and perish, as the summer fly" (675–76), becoming multitudinous once more. In this sense, Samson's act is both a massacre and a countermassacre, if we follow Graham Hammill's definition of massacre as that phenomenon of state violence, directed against the insurgent resistance of a popular collective, that enters into political discourse in the sixteenth and seventeenth centuries as a feature of modern sovereignty. "Massacre," Hammill writes, "implies not just slaughter but also desecration," often involving the refusal of burial or exposure of corpses as well as their physical killing: "The statist fantasy of massacring the multitude attempts to place the multitude between these two deaths [physical and symbolic], positing and taking aim at a kind of life beyond life."[56] Samson's act is a massacre insofar as he inflicts massive violent death on an assembled group of people within a sacred space that is itself destroyed, becoming a tomb, or rather antitomb, for those buried alive inside it. Yet this act of violence is not performed by a state against an insurgent populace, but rather by a solitary prisoner against a foreign state; by restricting his massacre to the elite, Samson in effect releases the "mass" within "massacre" into a state of emergency that might bear further ills for the Philistine government. Coming out of the Hebrew multitude, in the populist tradition of

Judges, Samson maintains a link with the Philistine multitude even while destroying their public space and massacring their public representatives.

Creature he remains. The penultimate choral ode celebrates Samson's death in a veritable eruption of animalia:

> *His fiery virtue rous'd*
> *From under ashes into sudden flame,*
> *And as an ev'ning Dragon came,*
> *Assailant on the perched roosts,*
> *And nests in order rang'd*
> *Of tame villatic Fowl; but as an Eagle*
> *His cloudless thunder bolted on their heads.*
> *So virtue giv'n for lost,*
> *Deprest and overthrown, as seem'd,*
> *Like that self-begotten bird*
> *In the* Arabian *woods embost,*
> *That no second knows, nor third,*
> *And lay erewhile a Holocaust,*
> *From out her ashy womb now teem'd,*
> *Revives, reflourishes, then vigorous most*
> *When most unactive deem'd,*
> *And though her body die, her fame survives,*
> *A secular bird ages of lives. (1685–1707)*

The passage makes its ascent from the homely to the sublime, the "ev'ning Dragon" that kills the farmhouse chickens metamorphosing into the Eagle and finally into the Phoenix. Derek Wood argues that Samson's "fiery Virtue" is "a pre-Christian 'virtus'—or physical might,"[57] not yet redeemed by its Christian translation and spiritualization; the image that initiates the sequence presents a feral baseline untamed by the higher forms of the mythical bestiary that soars above it. Samson Agonistes is Samson Dragonistes, a snake in a hen house, a creeping creature who, insinuating death into "nests in order rang'd," might well inflict more damage not by the number of birds he kills, but by his ability to terrify the surviving flock into a swarm of confusion. Although the sequence promises Samson the form of literary survival known as fame, it does so by incanting his kinship with the creaturely; unlike the Phoenix, he is not "self-begotten," but rather a created thing: blind and violent, mortal and lethal.

Samson does not die into citizenship, as Antigone and Othello do. Reclaimed from the ruins of the temple, Samson dies back into the tribe for burial in a family tomb. Manoa makes resolutely un-Periclean funeral arrangements for his dead son:

> *I with what speed the while*
> (Gaza *is not in plight to say us nay)*
> *Will send for all my kindred, all my friends*
> *To fetch him hence, and solemnly attend*
> *With silent obsequy and funeral train*
> *Home to his Father's house: there I will build him*
> *A Monument, and plant it round with shade*
> *Of Laurel ever green, and branching Palm,*
> *With all his Trophies hung, and Acts enroll'd*
> *In copious Legend, or sweet Lyric Song.*
> *Thither shall all the valiant youth resort,*
> *And from his memory inflame thir breasts*
> *To matchless valor, and adventures high:*
> *The Virgins also shall on feastful days*
> *Visit his Tomb with flowers, only bewailing*
> *His lot unfortunate in nuptial choice,*
> *From whence captivity and loss of eyes.* (1728–44)

Sending for "all [his] kindred, all [his] friends," Manoa activates the resources of social capital stored in and as the bonds of civil society in order to give his son local burial. Yet in the biblical books that follow, this *death into kinship* will eventually bear fruit in the *birth of kingship,* when the children of Israel, weary of emergency, elect to subject themselves to a king, despite the warnings of their last judge, Samuel. The "copious Legend" and "sweet Lyric Song" that transmit Samson's story to future generations of young men and young women (conceived as separate interpretive communities) might be imagined to act as some form of intermediary or catalyst between the era of judges and the reign of the kings. Via the fame of the Phoenix, of local cult and poetic praise, the judge, in the vulgar barnyard cruelty of his exceptional powers, places the creaturely essence of sovereignty at the threshold, the very "Gates . . . and massy Bar," of the future state.

Yet is the king the only inheritor of the judge in Milton's vision? Victoria Kahn's essay on Samson and political theology usefully salvages reason of state for the revolutionary as well as the absolutist cause. Kahn aptly distinguishes Dalila's Hobbesian politic acquiescence to authority from Samson's exercise of judgment apart from any determinate authority.[58] Samson's decisive assault on the very architecture of political hierarchy and its social formalisms is surely relevant here; like the more articulate and programmatic antistatist visions of Gideon or Samuel, but in a more brutal and externalized key, Samson's act rejects vertical forms of public organization, exploding them for the Philistines, but debasing them for Israel as well. This attack on hierarchy is mirrored in his creaturely being, his tendency in both his heroic and his degraded state toward rhizomatic and prostrate, creeping and swarming forms of existence and affiliation, even or especially when he tries to erect himself above himself, "to quit himself / Like Samson" (1709–10). His Medusan head of "redundant locks" (568) mirrors both the order of a well-regulated people and the eclectic and electric energy of the unruly multitude. There is something Robin-Hoodish in Samson's challenge to Harapha to come arrayed in "gorgeous arms" against Samson's "Oak'n staff" (1119, 1123), and Samson has already shifted into politic irony when he accepts the Public Officer's orders by pretending to cede to absolute sovereignty: "Masters' commands come with a power resistless / To such as owe them absolute subjection" (1404–5). Such passages remind us of the populist and even demagogic element of the judge; he is more dictator than sovereign, more the exceptional expression of a confederated and preterritorial body politic than of a nationally unified one.

Samson's death back into kinship, then, might be something other than a falling away from the political—perhaps a discovery within tribalism of forms of confederation that might *become political,* and according to a destiny other than that of kingship. Read in this way, the "Acts enroll'd / In copious Legend, or sweet Lyric Song" that convene around his tomb might point to an early instance in the literature of citizenship, a narrative tradition deeply interwoven into civic life that "enrolls" future youth in its call to active reading and public performance, including, when necessary, choosing to will special "Acts" of tragic decision, of determining the exception. Acts and Legends: these are the traditional genres of the saint's life. "Acts" refers to actions, but also to legal proceedings—to the public trials and martyrdoms of the early saints, beginning with Stephen and Paul in the Acts of the Apostles. "Legend," meaning "something having to be read," refers to the lectionary of saints' lives in the liturgical calendar.[59] To act is to come before the law because one has decisively placed oneself against or beyond it; those who act in this manner (Antigone, Paul, Samson) find themselves under arrest and in captivity, threatened by corporeal or capital punishment, and reduced to the live burial of mere life captured and abandoned within the borders of sovereignty. Their "acts" in turn must be "read," *legenda,* their meaning decided by a community, but also by individual readers. (For Shakespeare, the emphasis falls on the former, and for Milton and also for Marlowe, on the latter.) In Victoria Kahn's formulation, "Milton puts the reader in Samson's position of deciding the meaning of his act."[60] Acting and reading—

acting as reading and reading as acting in so far as each requires deciding the exception, making a judgment momentarily divorced from normative frameworks—establish the agenda ("things having to be done") for the interpretive community that assembles around Samson's tomb.

Act and Read: if these are the commandments delivered at the tomb of Samson, he manifests the first in all its terror, but seems incapable of the latter. In his populist and prepolitical strain, Samson finally is more Marlovian than Shakespearean, bearing comparison with both Tamburlaine and Barabas in his capacity at once to embody the bare life of the creeping, swarming multitude and to annihilate the life and life-forms of others, to reduce them to bare death, in a momentary burst of "cloudless thunder" (1696), of sovereign force stripped of the dignity and permanence of formal office.[61] Like that of Marlowe's heroes, the sovereignty achieved by Milton's Samson exists as a swollen node within the loose ligatures of uncivil society rather than a higher organization of civil forms into civic ones. Samson, like Barabas, remains a creature of civil society even—or especially—as he attempts to bring the house down on the assembled state. Here, perhaps, more than anywhere else lies his much-contested Hebraism—not the Judaism of hyperlegalism (Samson, like Barabas, has little use for the contracts dear to Shylock), but of a violent and vengeful God. Samson's Massacre at Gaza, like Barabas's Massacre at Malta, explodes sites of assembly and civility, using the very rites and sites of civil society as weapons against itself.[62]

A glimpse of the messianic illumines Samson's act—not in the typological sense given to Messianism in Christian exegesis, where the Second Coming will complete a history that at every moment points toward it (with judges becoming kings, and Jews becoming Christians), but in the sovereign sense it receives in Benjamin's modern reading of the rabbinic tradition: "Only the Messiah himself consummates all history, in the sense that he alone redeems, completes, creates its relation to the Messianic. For this reason nothing historical can relate itself on its own account to anything Messianic."[63] For Benjamin, the Messiah is an "end" not a "goal," insofar as his life creates a new meaning rather than fulfills prior predictions. If in Samson's career, the first half of "*mas*sacre" echoes the first half of "*mes*siah," it does so only insofar as echo itself is rejected as a historical principle. The destruction of the temple does not derive historical meaning from precedents in or before Samson's life but functions as a fundamentally new moment; as such, Milton's Samson is finally not typological (a figure of Christ), or even typological in a terminally suspended way ("exil'd from light"), but *anti-typological,* arresting the recuperative movement of typology in the sheer violence of his act.

What Hammill says of *Tamburlaine* could be equally applied to *Samson:* "Marlowe introduces a distinction precisely where sovereignty overlays the multitude with bare life, actualizing the collective apart from sovereignty in its albeit fragile potentiality."[64] That is, Milton, like Marlowe, and unlike Shakespeare, is interested in separating the collective from sovereignty via the multitude, bypassing or even collapsing the legal formalism of citizenship and the constituted people it represents. Put otherwise, Marlowe and Milton are poets of the exception, whereas Shakespeare is the poet of the norm—not a norm that forces conformity or is imposed from above, but that emerges out of and indeed *as* social process, as those sets of human *conventions* that arise out of moments of *convening*, with the acts of deliberation and compromise that such convening invites.[65] Although all of *Samson Agonistes* is talk, there are no true conversations, no moments of genuine exchange or encounter; Samson's internal transformations remain as abrupt and mysterious as the changes he visits on the world around him. It follows that the future to come remains illegible as well. The judge is dead. Who lives after him: the sovereign, the citizen, or the multitude? This is the question with which Milton leaves us, chastened by the restoration of monarchy but neither resigned to its inevitability nor assured of its alternatives.

EPILOGUE

The Literature of Citizenship: A Humanifesto

In Pedro Almodóvar's film *Talk To Her* (2002), Benigno, a male nurse, emotionally and sexually crippled by an oppressive childhood spent alone with his aging mother, falls in love with his comatose patient, a former neighbor and local ballet student who has been hit by a car. Benigno follows her to the hospital and becomes her devoted nurse. Against all reason and without hope of any response, he talks to her with immeasurable patience and earnestness. In speaking to her, he grants her the dignity of a subject; by sleeping with her, however, he debases her body and her personhood. His acts eventually impregnate her; although he is able to hide her condition for several months, he is ultimately exposed, thrown out of the hospital, and arrested. Humiliated, Benigno kills himself in jail. Meanwhile, still comatose, the young woman gives birth to the child, who dies; the trauma of labor, however, shakes her out of her coma. This modern sleeping beauty awakens on the far side of a kiss to the dance of life and the chance for civil conversation, but forever separated from her most unlikely prince.

The film submits consent, the cornerstone of liberal theories of both the state and marriage, to the most extreme probation, not in order to abandon it as bourgeois myth, but in order to reclaim it in its radicality as sheer hypothesis, ungrounded in any confirmable act yet all the more vehemently asserting itself as the essence of authentic human relation. Consent in the film is not rejected so much as sublimated—made sublime, resituated on another plane than that of daily life and ordinary communication, raised, in Lacan's definition, to the dignity of a Thing.[1] In *Talk to Her,* the possibility of the woman's consent sleeps in the twilight zone between the citizen and the saint, between the consenting partner in the socio-sexual contract required by liberal theories of law and the suffering, unconscious enjoyer of unsought attentions familiar from the archives of the mystics. The film asks us: Can consent be registered in some mode other than the signature of verbal or gestural affirmation—in an immobilized body, beyond consciousness, through the very force of the other's love, or through the sheer addressivity of speech?[2] As in Locke's theory of social contract, consent functions in the film as hypothesis, as fiction, operating most powerfully precisely when it involves a citizen who is legally incompetent, *unmündig,* physically and mentally unequal to the equality guaranteed her by the law (see Gillian Brown 19–23). In such cases, the citizen's consent has to be guarded, protected, sheltered (by the law), but also called forth, evoked, elicited, invented (by the lover). In this scenario, Almodóvar's Benigno bears affinities with Shakespeare's Caliban (recall his solitary childhood, his attempted rape of the unconsenting Miranda, his uncoupled singularity, his vegetable love), but also with the Duke at the end of *Measure for Measure,* whose unanswered proposal brings forward consent as a suspended quantity, a terminal question mark or permanent hypothetical posed by both femininity and the social body to sovereignty.[3]

As such, Almodóvar's film belongs to what I have called in this book "the literature of citizenship." In this epilogue, I would like to propose the literature of citizenship as a field of scholarly inquiry but also of artistic capacity that might draw humanists toward matters of public interest and consequence without diluting the integrity of what we do. The literature of citizenship clears a forum for mediating among—but also charting the infinite divide between—universal and particular, canonical and multicultural, national and transnational, debates and methods in the increasingly fractured and uncivil settings of our classrooms, hallways, and meeting places. We know all too well that our internal arguments, usually carried out at a high level of abstraction and with a great deal of seriousness, often come back to us from public onlookers in the form of cruel and destructive jokes. The crisis in the humanities—in public funding, in public interest, and in support on our own campuses—is *our problem,* not so much in the sense that we have caused it (there are multiple systemic factors at work), as in the sense that no one is going to fix it for us. Work on the literature of citizenship may open an avenue for more constructive dialogue with public audiences who find themselves increasingly disengaged from academic discourse, offering the chance to integrate not only the work of several disciplines (literature, history, and the social sciences), but also the efforts of several institutions, including the university, secondary schools, and community organizations, in innovative collaborations that can help each of us articulate our individual and collective goals and values within a new civic space.[4]

What follows, then, is a "humanifesto," a manifesto for the humanities. It is a public statement of principles that also serves as a call to action, a forcible making-appear of a set of relationships or practices for the purpose of their further realization. And it is concerned to encourage the humanities to *manifest themselves,* to unfold their work within public spheres of discourse. The conceptual and pragmatic frameworks of citizenship offer not only a theme for such manifestation, but also a genealogy and a set of conditions—a past with a future—for developing this work in an intellectually coherent and historically grounded way. The endeavor I am suggesting is actually a modest one—I am certainly not proposing the literature of citizenship as a new major or discipline, but rather as a topic for humanistic study within the university and as a theme for collaborative projects between the university and other institutions, in the form of public symposia, seminars for teachers, community poetry or oral history projects, service-learning initiatives, and so on. Precisely by linking work inside the university with work outside of it, however, these minimal enterprises could have a dynamizing effect on other aspects of our teaching and scholarship and help us better unfold, open up, *render manifest*, the work we do in relation to other public discussions and institutions.

The literature of citizenship, it would seem, has always been with us, certainly in the West and probably globally as well. It is a commonplace of humanistic inquiry that a key function of literature has been initiation into the group—what Michael Bernstein called "the tale of the tribe." But is the literature of citizenship a variant of the tale of the tribe, or rather its opposite—its refusal, its retort, its sublation? In an essay entitled "Myth Interrupted," Jean-Luc Nancy analyzes the tale of the tribe as itself a myth whose hold on Western consciousness must be (and indeed repeatedly, constitutively, has been) interrupted: arrested, suspended, exposed as fiction so that other forms of less imaginary communion can take place. Nancy begins his essay by evoking the primal scene of socialization through literature: "There is a gathering, and someone is telling a story. We do not know yet whether these people gathering together form an assembly, if they are a horde or a tribe. But we call them brothers and sisters because they are gathered together and because they are listening to the same story."[5] Nancy goes on to critique this tableau as the myth of myth, the fantasy of a "full, original speech, at times revealing, at times founding the intimate being of a community." The interruption of this myth would also entail "the interruption of community," of the dream of the fusion of its members in a single voice or general will. Such a suspension, Nancy argues, would reveal the "disjunctive or hidden nature of community," the insistent resistance to the collective consolations of the great national stories that runs through and against hegemonic community formations, in turn founding an alternate form of community that takes shape as a force-field of responsive and passionate yet ever-distinct, uncommon singularities joined together by exceptional forms and acts of consent.

Following Nancy, though drawing his insights onto a path leading back to liberalism and classical politics, I would submit that the literature of citizenship is precisely *not* the tale of the tribe, even when it appears as a neighbor at work in the same social fields. If literature is *that which breaks from myth* (as, say, writing rather than speech, as univocal rather than collective expression, or as irony rather than confirmation), and citizenship is *that which breaks from tribalism,* (above all in those rites of naturalization that sacrifice ancient kinship bonds to new civic ones), then the literature of citizenship must tell a story and do a work other than that of assembling a tribe in the mesmerizing circle of its performance.[6] This is why, in the Western tradition, we would do better marking the origins of the literature of citizenship in tragedy than in epic, in Sophocles rather than in Homer. Classical tragedy, as we saw in chapter 5, bears witness to the destruction of the great aristocratic houses and their epic myths within the arena of the new polis. The pattern of tragedy, in which "the destruction of the royal household end[s] in benefit for the polis,"[7] reflected the conditions of tragic performance as a civic ritual. Seating in the Theater of Dionysus was divided into ten wedges, or *kekrides,* for each of the ten "tribes," or *phyloi,* instituted under Cleisthenes' reforms of 507. But these regroupings, unlike the four kinship divisions that preceded them, were drawn from a precise combination of coastal, inland, and urban districts, creating new citizen groups united by neither blood nor regional ties.[8] These *phyloi* were not so much tribes as anti-tribes, brought into existence through a legal process of rezoning. And it was these new civic tribes that "competed among themselves for honors in serving the people, particularly in the choral competitions at the festival of the City of Dionysia" — that is, in the annual civic ritual that produced Greek tragedy.[9] Greek tragedies, with their *mythoi* of imploded kinship, were submitted to public judgment by civic "tribes" whose political affiliations had themselves been created through radical acts of detribalization.

A social instance, a public sphere, is called forth in the literature of citizenship, but the modes of equality and participation it promises remain formal and artificial, a function of legal and institutional definition, irreducible to either the first nature of kinship or the second nature of culture (myth being the structural mediation between nature and culture). We could say that citizenship, unlike the community imagined by myth, is *never enough,* and hence always requires supplementation by other forms of communal life, including the rites of religion and family, *oikos* and cult, which nonetheless remain distinct from the forms of citizenship they variously support, reflect, or negate. The insufficiency of civic discourse—its choral platitudes, its public cheerfulness, its pomp and circumstance—is part of what the literature of citizenship thematizes, and not only to parody or critique it, but also to find in its very normativity opportunities for new drama and lyricism.

By insisting on the salutary insufficiency of citizenship, the formality of its forms, I break from the tradition of civic republicanism, which posits that human being is most fully realized in civic activity: In the words of J. G. A. Pocock, one of the tradition's most articulate and learned contemporary spokesmen, "Citizenship is not just a means to being free; it is the way of being free itself."[10] Pocock goes on to oppose this positive political definition of citizenship, derived from the Greek experience, to the negative legal definitions that date from the Roman period, when "a 'citizen' came to mean someone free to act by law, free to ask and expect the law's protection, a citizen of such and such a legal community."[11] Although civic republicanism offers a rich vision of political life that certainly motivates much of my thinking in this book, it achieves actuality most effectively in local arenas involving groups already unified by a shared set of values and interests. Jürgen Habermas has taken issue with both the liberal investment in negative rights and the republican emphasis on positive liberties in favor of what he calls "deliberative democracy," a model that relocates the republican ideal of human self-realization through public speech and action within a juridical framework whose procedures facilitate and enforce the compromises that are required by complex and diverse societies. According to Habermas, "The political interests and values that stand in conflict with each other without prospects of consensus are in need of a balancing that cannot be achieved through ethical discourses—even if the outcomes of bargaining processes are subject to the proviso that they must not violate a culture's agreed-upon basic values."[12]

Although Habermas's account of the public sphere has been legitimately criticized for its overconfidence in the transparency and rationality of communication and the ideal speech situation, his work has been useful for this project on two counts.[13] First, deliberative democracy takes as its starting point an irreducible social heterogeneity—quite the opposite of transparency—as the very essence of the pluralist public sphere: The procedures of deliberative democracy are required precisely when the intractability of distinct ethical positions precludes the possibility of consensus. When ethical agreement is permanently on hold, differences need to be resolved (through arbitration, negotiation, and compromise) rather than dissolved (through mutual identification). *Arbitration* brings forth the specter of the *arbitrary:* Useful to my project is the extent to which the aspect of decision orients Habermas's notion of deliberation, retaining an element of sovereign exception, grounded in the heterogeneity of the modern social body, in the normative flow of liberal debate, in contradistinction to the more uniform polity of republicanism.[14] Of equal importance to my argument is Habermas's distinction between *citizenship,* as an inherently formalist and procedural discourse, and *culture,* taken as a set of imaginary identifications that collude all too easily with nationalism. In Habermas's view, citizenship in modernity represents not the fullest flowering of a national political community, but rather a means of adjudicating among competing cultures via norms that establish the rules of deliberation for its diverse participants.

Citizenship is not culture; indeed, its norms represent an alternative to culture, understood as either a national community or as the form taken by particularized minority positions excluded or marginalized by that national vision. In the assessment of Seyla Benhabib, one of Habermas's most original students, "deliberative-democratic politics in its strong proceduralist form . . . immunizes politics against the forces of cultural and ethical life."[15] In a related tack, liberal political philosopher Will Kymlicka has argued for a "thin" or "societal culture" (rather than a "thick" nationalist culture) as the minimal common ground of pluralist polities: "In order to make it possible for people from different ethno-cultural backgrounds to become full and equal members of the nation, and to allow for the maximal room for individual dissent, the terms of admission are relatively thin—say, learning the language, participating in common public institutions, and perhaps expressing a commitment to the long-term survival of the nation."[16] Many humanists react with horror or at least skepticism to the very term *citizen,* which may at first glance appear to be the watchword of a conservative agenda. For many of us, the term evokes the policing of territorial borders, the enforcement of a nationalist mentality, and the prescription of a narrow set of social behaviors. Yet, read from the democratic perspectives opened up by Habermas, Benhabib, and Kymlicka, citizenship can offer a provisional ground of equivalence and a forum for deliberation and compromise for persons from diverse groups without equating politics with particular religious, cultural, or sexual identities.

The possible translation of this political discourse to humanistic inquiry and literary study is clear. As a liberal institution, the humanities both set out a common canon or core of knowledge, however amorphously and contentiously defined, and support regions of research and teaching that are often oriented toward articulating the interests and identities of particular national, linguistic, ethnic, religious, or socio-sexual groups. This book both reflects and reflects on these dynamics. I have taken a canonical figure, Shakespeare, whose plays have been central to civic culture in England, America, and their former colonies.[17] In reading Shakespeare, we find ourselves dead center in the canon that has been used for centuries to define the civic and national life of many groups. From this centrist position, I have moved outward to examine what could be called Shakespeare's "multicultural" plays—especially *The Merchant of Venice, Othello,* and *The Tempest*—plays that in recent years, under the impact of new historicism, multiculturalism, and postcolonialism, have been decanonized (exposed as ideology or recycled as counterculture) and recanonized (within alternative definitions of the disciplines that themselves have moved toward the center of the academy).[18] Rather than simply affirming the "other voices" in these plays, however, I have tried to trace their navigation, calculation, and re-visioning of the tension between local and general memberships. Although this book unfolds in the wake of multicultural reclamations of Shakespeare, my readings are more attuned to calls for recognition, inclusion, and the recalibration of norms, and hence to the creation of limited universals, than to demands for separate worlds. I have attempted to stage generative scenes of civic invention within some of the most vexed and troubling moments of Shakespeare's plays, whether it is

Shylock's conversion or Othello's suicide, Isabella's prospective marriage or Caliban's suit for grace. In seeking social recognition within the inherently insufficient regime of citizenship, these deeply particularized characters are not subsumed within a greater collective whole (Hegel's view of citizenship in relation to civil society), but rather are de-completed, not fully taken up in the local and general memberships that continue to define them, and hence secure a measure of subjective freedom in relation to the several circles they inhabit.

Part of the task of a literary study of citizenship is to reclaim the idea of the citizen from its functionalizations and instrumentalizations, but also from its devaluations and diminutions. This includes investigating models of multiple citizenship, of informal or extralegal forms of citizenship, and of what Étienne Balibar has called "citizens without citizenship," which means breaking "the sacrosanct equation of citizenship and nationality."[19] In this, Balibar echoes Habermas's claim that "citizenship was never conceptually tied to national identity," even if national feeling and republican politics were fused at the revolutionary origin of the modern nation-state.[20] The literature of citizenship must address the practical exigencies and imaginative worlds of noncitizens or paracitizens—whether legally disenfranchised (as aliens, prisoners, detainees, or minors) or excluded de facto from large parts of civic life by economic and educational inequity, inner migration, and the general dissociation of faculties that attends the rising dysfunctionality of the public sphere. Rather than dismissing citizenship as a concept, humanists can research and even foster forms of civic participation that might temper some of the exclusionary and oppressive functions of the nation-state by drawing new actors, new texts, and new approaches into civic life and discourse, and by renewing our bonds with older ones in reconfigured scenes of academic life. Such discussion can occur around key moments of foundation, revision, and response to citizenship ideals, recoverable in strong instances of the political tradition from Sophocles and Aristotle to Mandela and Havel, Balibar and Habermas. This approach links the classic liberal emphasis on education as a means of access to full citizenship (which implies that citizenship itself is a given) to an open discussion about the history, limits, and future of citizenship as part of the evolving content of that education, and of citizenship itself.

Citizenship, I submit, represents a limited public alternative to the cultural identifications, whether local or national, that otherwise sustain us, instituting a break with or mediation of tribal tales, above all in a diverse society such as the United States. There were already signs and symptoms of such diversity in the Athenian laboratory where citizenship in its Western form first took shape. Early in the *Politics,* Aristotle defines the state in terms of its origins and its end: "When several villages are united in a single complete community, large enough to be nearly or quite self-sufficing, the state comes into existence, originating in the bare needs of life, and continuing in existence for the sake of a good life" (1252b).

Here and elsewhere, Aristotle emphasizes the plurality that constitutes the community: *several villages* are required to make a single complete community. Aristotle, of course, presumed a certain baseline homogeneity among the villages that make up a community and become a polis. Yet the reference to plural villages may recall the inland, coastal, and urban zoning of the Athenian *phyloi,* and hence a constitutional as well as an organic linking of communal forms. Himself a *metic,* or foreigner, in Athens, Aristotle repeatedly defends the mixed and plural nature of the polis and supports constitutional over nativist definitions of citizenship.[21] Note as well the unmarked yet crucial transition in the passage from "community" to "state": at some point, a loose civil alliance becomes a more articulated civic body. This process of coalescence and articulation occurs via the concrete activities required to meet "the bare needs of life," activities that of necessity involve social interaction and cooperation. At a certain point, this sociality becomes an end rather than a means—it points toward the idea of "the good life." The good life (*eu zên,* living well) remains a material form of *zoē* (life), intimately engaged with material needs; the social modes of the good life stretch up and out from the living ground of *zoē* as both its shelter and its fruit. It is at this same dynamic node, we might imagine, that the "community" becomes a "state," eliciting some higher form of organization—a body of laws, a system of magistracies, a set of civil procedures. And, finally, it is at this point that the two senses of *politeia* meet and divide. *Politea,* which can be translated as "constitution," "commonwealth," or "polity," has its origins in *polites,* or citizen, and originally bore the meaning "citizenship."[22] *Politeia* flips between the *objective* structures of government and the *subjective* modes of participation in them, naming the dialectic between "constitution" as legal structure and "constituency" as a body of human actors who derive their social being from institutions that will survive their individual participation.

Moreover, students of the *Politics* have long noted that *politea* refers to both constitutions in general and to the constitution of which democracy in Aristotle's critical view represents a degeneration.[23] The term gives unity to a set of phenomena—the available types of government—and also derives a norm from them, that of constitutional rule by citizens. The word *citizen* itself similarly travels between a taxonomy of forms and a single definition. Thus Aristotle admits that citizenship must be defined in relation to specific constitutional types ("He who is a citizen in a democracy will often not be a citizen in an oligarchy"), but then goes on to give a procedural definition of the citizen that crosses these contexts: the citizen "in the strict sense" is he who "shares in the administration of justice, and in offices" (1275a). Citizenship as a category is both rooted in local practice, in the life of a polis or city with its own institutions, and embodies a standard that breaks away from its particular instantiations precisely because its formal definition does not gather into its reach all aspects of social life.

The *polites* mediates between the particular example and the universal norm, the communitarian vision and the compromises of due process, the individual participant and the institutions that regulate public exchange. Each of these traumatic transitions—from particular identities to universal ideals, from the life of the community to the laws of the state, from citizenry to constitution—requires an act of abstraction, reflection, and formalization. Here the humanities broadly understood have played a constitutive role, in enabling and conceptualizing these movements in and as social thought and in capturing their vicissitudes and fallout through the imaginative resources of art and literature. In the *Politics,* Aristotle writes that "there is a science for the master and a science for the slave"—areas of technical expertise covalent with what have become management and engineering on the one hand and vocational training on the other. He goes on to distinguish these from "philosophy and politics," reserved for those "in a position which places them above toil" (1255b). Although it is easy to mock Aristotle here for his rationalization of the slave economy and his defense of the leisure of the theory class, it is more important at the present moment to foreground Aristotle's demarcation of the liberal arts as a space of freedom from the very forms of mastery upon which that freedom is so fragilely based. Now as then, the sciences of management and the labor they organized pay for the leisure of the arts and the humanities, but in that leisure lies the chance of rethinking social relations. Should we undermine the liberty of the liberal arts (whether by cutting its funding from above, or berating it as ideology from below), or rather open up the leisure of thought—the promise of the humanities—to masters and slaves, bureaucrats and workers alike, with the hope of transforming, modifying, or redistributing the debilitating dialectic of despotism? To change, shift, or alter the technocratic thrust of education and to reclaim leisure from its commodifications are no small tasks. If they require strategic alliances and compromises—in short, all the resources of deliberative democracy—citizenship as topic and structure, as matter and form, as a once and future idea for pragmatic and speculative experiment, may provide one ground on which to advance the negotiations.

Skeptics further to my left will counter that the mediating and reflective functions of the humanities simply serve to render capital immanent to the state. In this view, what Aristotle called the good life is merely *a life of goods,* of economic instrumentalizations and subjective colonization.[24] To this analysis I would like to counter that the transitional moment between exigency and reflection, between labor and thought, or, in liberal terms, between the protection of property and the pursuit of happiness, has and can be a moment of subjective and intersubjective emancipation. Of course the university is never really external to the social field, but this truism need not lure us into believing that the kind of thought supported by the university is a mere fiction, an ideological trick. Reflection describes a bend or fold on a surface of relations that contains yet is distinct from it, drawing a new line, a new topology, on its continuous planes. The university functions not only as an organic development of the public sphere—the factory of its normative reproduction—but also as a possible break or cut in the social fabric, the laboratory or studio in which new thought about the social can arise. It is this possibility that can engage us when we think about humanities in the public sphere. The thankless task of "publicizing the humanities," often delegated to development officers and the support staff of humanities centers, needs to be drawn away from the demands of marketing and image spin—the ever-popular film series, or the perennially under-attended public forum—and toward the goal of rendering visible the twinned conditions of sociality and thought through concrete acts of engagement with various publics. When audiences are transformed into constituencies, reflection can become genuinely collaborative, involving the determination of shared vocabularies around the production of common goods. (Multilateral curricular design undertaken by schools and universities is a cogent example.) The creative cuts of critical reflection may be the most important phenomena, beyond any archive of objects or ideas (or perhaps as the essence of that archive), that the humanities have to share with "the public." More ambitiously, the humanities need to recover these interventions in the forms of public life that flourish outside our walls. Deliberating the particular and the universal can take many shapes (from the contestatory to the prescriptive) within various forms of discourse that describe both the object and the forms of public partnerships in the humanities (creative expression and performance, critical analysis, documentary witnessing, public debate, archiving and recording, and so on). That is, the reflective moment can itself become the basis for action and interaction with our neighbors and colleagues in the public sphere.

Although I began with Greek tragedy and philosophy, it would be a mistake to identify the literature of citizenship exclusively with any one set of literary works or genres, or to tie it to a political or literary history stretching from ancient to modern times. The literature of citizenship assembles not only a group of texts that take their themes and modes of production from civic life, but also a way of approaching texts, of reading them for the styles of deliberation and debate, of address and redress, of bargaining and compromise, that they depict or instantiate. The literature of citizenship encompasses, then, not only such classically literary works as Greek tragedy, but also various forms of para- or subliterary works, including law codes and legal cases; oratory and rhetoric; open letters and occasional writing; prison notebooks and *samizdat;* and those forms of journalism and public discourse that engage constituencies in debate or reflect on that debate in ways designed to promote further discussion and action. It is worth noting that these nonfictional genres are increasingly an official part of high school language-arts training, though often within a narrowly pragmatic mandate of technical mastery (the business letter, the public document, the information manual) that misses key opportunities for critique, comparison, and new creation.[25] The literature of citizenship offers a means of gathering together diverse genres, modes of comprehension, and deliberative skills in an intellectually rigorous format that can draw its methods and models from the established discourses of rhetoric, civics, and literature. And such work can occur both in and between universities (where future teachers are trained) and secondary schools (which aim to send their students on to university classrooms). Developing an approach to the literature of citizenship would provide one means of linking the kinds of materials that are currently animating interdisciplinarity and innovation among humanities faculty (historical documents, works of rhetoric and argument, nonverbal artifacts, theory and criticism, new media, and cross-cultural texts that fall outside traditional genres) to the real needs, interests, and mandates of teachers and students in the public schools.

The literature of citizenship might take citizenship as its theme; more important, however, this literature assembles its readers as a body of listeners gathered together in a space (virtual or real) that implies a public, even ritual, dimension, yet refuses to resolve its discrete members into interchangeable equivalences. The modes of the public speech (e.g., the funeral oration of Pericles or the inaugural poems of Frost and Angelou); the covenant or contract constituting a people through an act of agreement on shared principles (the Ten Commandments, the Bill of Rights); public theater, staged before the diverse yet momentarily unified citizenry of a municipality (Sophocles, Shakespeare, New York's African Theatre); the transformation and redistribution of narrative and dramatic forms in cinematic and electronic media; and the open letter or epistle addressed to a community of listeners within an identified civic locale such as Corinth, Birmingham, or Prague: all of these instances of directed expression stake out specific valences and variations on the literature of citizenship, which is itself not a fixed concept so much as an open field defined by the activities and responses of its users.[26] By dramatizing the scandal of naturalization—its murderous sacrifices, its forced conversions, its troubling marriages, its captured creatures, its censored voices, its structural incompleteness—the literature of citizenship is never simply civic, never fully coterminous with the public spaces that it maps. Although the literature of citizenship necessarily touches on the genres and modes of rhetoric and public speech, its character *as literature* may come forward at those points where it stumbles on a forgotten signpost of lost or competing affiliations within the well-lit space of publicity. In the strophe and antistrophe chanted by the citizen and the saint, the public deliberation of Habermas calls forth the inoperative community imagined by Nancy.

And it is precisely around these limit points of scandal and sacrifice that the literature of citizenship provokes collective and individual processes of evaluation, deliberation, and debate—especially concerning the definition of the citizen as such. The literature of citizenship taps into a key assumption of liberal democracies—namely that literary study has a civic dimension—without accepting the flag-wrapped packaging that characterizes so much civic delivery in the schools, the media, and official discourse.[27] The civic dimension of literary study has become so ingrained in secondary education that it has become largely invisible and undervalued at the university, an object of ignorance or ridicule rather than recovery and collaboration. One task of a renewed literature of citizenship is to reopen the civic envelope of liberal education in order to separate its critical and creative potential from its ideological functionalizations. The consequences just might include remapping the divisions among educational sectors and the segregated spheres of public life in ways that are intellectually urgent and, yes, genuinely civic—real politics, not *Surrealpolitik* (or, business as usual in the academy). Talk to her, *talk to them*—who knows what forms, moods, and shapes of consent might awaken in response?

NOTES

INTRODUCTION

1. On Hercules as a culture-hero who clears the ground for the life of the polis but cannot join it, see Karl Galinksy, *The Herakles Theme* (Oxford: Oxford University Press, 1972). On Othello as a type of Hercules, see Robert Miola, "Othello *Furens*," *Shakespeare Quarterly* 41 (spring 1990): 49–64.
2. See William Blake Tyrrell and Larry J. Bennett, *Recapturing Sophocles' "Antigone"* (Lanham: Rowman and Littlefield, 1998), on *Antigone* as a tragedy that stages the transition from aristocracy to democracy for its Athenian audience. Tyrrell and Bennett are building on the larger argument about tragedy and the *polis* put forward by Richard Seaford in *Reciprocity and Ritual: Homer and Tragedy in the Developing City-State* (Oxford: Oxford University Press, 1994). On the role of tragedy in the civic education of the *ephebes*, see John Winkler, "The Ephebes' Song: *Tragôidia* and *Polis*," *Representations* 11 (summer 1985): 6–43. These readings are developed further in chapter 5.
3. Here and subsequently, Aristotle's works are cited parenthetically in the text from *Complete Works*, revised Oxford translation, ed. Jonathan Barnes (Princeton, NJ: Princeton University Press, 1984).
4. John Rawls makes a similar point when he separates the question of justice from the true and the good: "The aim of justice as fairness as a political conception is practical, and not metaphysical or epistemological. . . . To secure [political] agreement we try, so far as we can, to avoid disputed philosophical, as well as disputed moral and religious, questions. We do this not because these questions are unimportant or regarded with indifference, but because we think them too important and recognize that there is no way to resolve them politically. Thus, justice as fairness deliberately stays on the surface, philosophically speaking"; see "Justice as Fairness in the Liberal Polity," in *The Citizenship Debates*, ed. Gershon Shafir, 57 (Minneapolis: University of Minnesota Press, 1998).
5. On the genre of the funeral oration and its significance for the literature of citizenship, see Nicole Loraux, *The Invention of Athens: The Funeral Oration in the Classical City*, trans. Alan Sheridan (Cambridge, MA: Harvard University Press, 1986).
6. The speeches of the National Convention leading up to the trial of Louis XVI have been collected by Michael Walzer in the volume *Regicide and Revolution* (Cambridge: Cambridge University Press, 1974). Walzer links these debates—as the *conventionnels* themselves did—to the death of Charles I.
7. Max Weber, "Citizenship in Ancient and Medieval Cities," excerpted from *General Economic History*, in *The Citizenship Debates*, ed. Gershon Shafir, 43–49 (Minneapolis: University of Minnesota Press, 1998).
8. See especially Giorgio Agamben's *Homo Sacer: Sovereign Power and Mere Life*, trans. Daniel Heller-Roazen (Stanford, CA: Stanford University Press, 1998), which figures in my readings of *The Merchant of Venice*, *The Tempest*, and *Samson Agonistes*.
9. See Walzer, *The Revolution of the Saints: A Study in the Origins of Radical Politics* (New York: Atheneum, 1970) and *Regicide and Revolution*.
10. On Shakespeare and political theology, see important recent work by Debora Shuger, *Political Theologies in Shakespeare's England* (Hounsmills, Hampshire: Palgrave, 2001); and Victoria Kahn, "Political Theology and Reason of State in *Samson Agonistes*," *South Atlantic*

Quarterly 99 (fall 1996): 1065–97. Richard Halpern has explored Shakespeare and the Jewish question to great effect in *Shakespeare Among the Moderns* (Cornell University Press, 1997). Kathleen Biddick has recently published a book-length study of "the typological imaginary" that resonates with many themes of this book (*The Typological Imaginary: Circumcision, Technology, History* [Philadelphia: University of Pennsylvania Press, 2003]). Graham Hammill has embarked on major new work on Moses and political theology from Machiavelli to Freud. For another contemporary reflection on political theology, see William T. Cavanaugh, *Theopolitical Imagination* (London: T. and T. Clark, 2002). Gordon Kipling and Sergio Bertelli have done important new work on the iconography of sacred kingship in the civic pageantry and public life of Renaissance cities and states; see Kipling's *Enter the King: Theatre, Liturgy, and Ritual in the Medieval Civic Triumph* (Oxford: Clarendon Press, 1998) and Bertelli's *The King's Body: Sacred Rituals of Power in Medieval and Early Modern Europe*, trans. R. Burr Litchfield (University Park: Pennsylvania State University Press, 2001).

11. Carl Schmitt, *Political Theology*, trans. George Schwab (Cambridge, MA: MIT Press, 1985), 5.
12. On Shakespearean normativity, see significant new work by Lars Engle in "Shakespearean Normativity in *All's Well That Ends Well*," forthcoming, *Shakespeare Yearbook* 2004.
13. Robert Ellickson, *Order Without Law: How Neighbors Settle Disputes* (Cambridge, MA: Harvard University Press, 1991), 127.
14. Karl Marx, "On the Jewish Question," in *The Marx-Engels Reader*, 2nd ed., ed. Robert C. Tucker, 46 (New York: W. W. Norton, 1978).
15. The concept of civil society has had its champions on both the left and the right. For a more conservative sampling of views, see Don Eberly and Ryan Streeter, eds., *The Essential Civil Society Reader* (Lanham, MD: Lexington Books, 2002). For a more progressive sampling, see Virginia Hodgkinson and Michael Foley, *The Civil Society Reader* (Hanover, NH: University Press of New England, 2003). For a collection of contemporary liberal approaches to civil society (emphasizing problems of minority rights), see Simone Chambers and Will Kymlicka, *Alternative Conceptions of Civil Society* (Princeton, NJ: Princeton University Press, 2002).
16. See James Strong, *Strong's New Exhaustive Concordance of the Bible* (Iowa Falls, IA: World Bible Publishers, 1980), Hebrew entries 5712 and 5713.
17. In a brilliant piece of reverse typology, Marx declares, "From the beginning, the Christian was the theorizing Jew; consequently, the Jew has become the practical Christian. And the practical Christian has become a Jew again." He ends by calling for a final divorce between civil society and Judaism—in other words, the overthrow of capital: "The *social* emancipation of the Jew is the *emancipation of society from Judaism*" ("Jewish Question," 52). On the Jews of Marx, Marlowe, and Shakespeare, see Stephen Greenblatt's landmark early essay, "Marlowe, Marx, and Anti-Semitism," *Critical Inquiry* 5 (1978): 40–58.
18. Marx, "Jewish Question," 35, 31.
19. Michael Walzer, "Equality and Civil Society," in *Alternative Conceptions of Civil Society*, ed. Simone Chambers and Will Kymlicka, 34–49 (Princeton, NJ: Princeton University Press, 2002).
20. Ibid., 38.
21. See Will Kymlicka, *States, Nations and Cultures* (Amsterdam: Van Gorcum, 1997), 13–27. Kymlicka contrasts "ethnic nations" like Germany to "civic nations" like the United States: "*Civic* nations, like the United States, are in principle open to anyone who lives in the ter-

ritory, so long as they learn the language and history of the society. They define membership in terms of participation in a common societal culture, open to all, rather than ethnic grounds. So ethnic nationalism is exclusive, civic nationalism is inclusive. . . . But both involve the politicization of ethnocultural groups. Both construe national membership in terms of participating in a common societal culture, and both use public policy to uphold and perpetuate that societal culture. The use of public policy to promote a particular societal culture or cultures is an inevitable feature of any modern state" (27). Kymlicka's statist orientation, in contrast to Walzer's emphasis on civil society, comes forward in his insistence on the role of public policy in shaping the common culture of "civic nations."

22. Walzer, "Equality," 43.
23. Ernesto Laclau, *Emancipations* (London: Verso, 1996), 17. See also Michael Hardt and Antonio Negri, who write that "in the eighteenth century religion was the field of social conflict that produced the most dangerous threat to stability" (*Labor of Dionysus: A Critique of the State-Form* [Minneapolis: University of Minnesota Press, 1994], 235).
24. Brook Thomas, *American Literary Realism and the Failed Promise of Contract* (Berkeley and Los Angeles: University of California Press, 1997), 7. Gillian Brown has made a similar case about the role of consent in Locke and his legacy in revolutionary America. Rather than criticizing the Lockean tradition for its exclusions, she suggests that "those Americans excluded, either explicitly or implicitly, from the eighteenth-century narratives of individualism—women, Indians, slaves, Catholics, Jews, Muslims, and later immigrants to the continent—have continued to demonstrate the applicability of Locke's ideas to those whose perceived oddity has disqualified them from the full benefits of society"; see *The Consent of the Governed* (Cambridge, MA: Harvard University Press, 2001), 11.
25. Etienne Balibar, *We the People of Europe,* trans. James Swenson (Princeton, NJ: Princeton University Press, 2004), 8.
26. For the political anthropology of democracy, see Philip Brook Manville, *The Origins of Citizenship in Ancient Athens* (Princeton, NJ: Princeton University Press, 1997).
27. See David Novak, "Land and People: One Jewish Tradition," in *Boundaries and Justice,* ed. David Miller and Sohail Hashmi, 213–36 (Princeton, NJ: Princeton University Press, 2001); Kenneth Reinhard, "Freud, My Neighbor," *American Imago* 54, no. 2 (summer 1997): 165–95; and Suzanne Last Stone, "The Jewish Tradition and Civil Society," in *Alternative Conceptions of Civil Society,* ed. Chambers and Kymlicka, 151–70. For the outlines of a parallel enterprise in Islamic studies, see Abdulaziz Sachedina, *The Islamic Roots of Democratic Pluralism* (Oxford: Oxford University Press, 2001); and Hasan Hanafi, "Alternative Conceptions of Civil Society: A Reflective Islamic Approach" in *Alternative Conceptions of Civil Society,* ed. Simone Chambers and Will Kymlicka, 171–89 (Princeton, NJ: Princeton University Press, 2002).
28. See Julia Reinhard Lupton, *Afterlives of the Saints* (Stanford, CA: Stanford University Press, 1996).
29. Cited in Lawrence Manley, *London in the Age of Shakespeare* (University Park: Pennsylvania State University Press, 1986), 89.
30. I am grateful to Steven Miller for his articulation of the open letter as a way of understanding the literary effectivity of Paul and his legacy.
31. Martin Heidegger, *The Question Concerning Technology, and Other Essays,* trans. William Lovitt (New York: Harper & Row, 1977), 35.
32. G. K. Hunter, *Dramatic Identities and Cultural Tradition: Studies in Shakespeare and His Contemporaries* (Liverpool: Liverpool University Press, 1978); Barbara Lewalski, "Biblical

Allusion and Allegory in *The Merchant of Venice,*" in Sylvan Barnet, ed., *Twentieth-Century Interpretations of "The Merchant of Venice,"* ed. Sylvan Barnet, 33–54 (Englewood Cliffs, NJ: Prentice Hall, 1970); Nevill Coghill, *Collected Papers,* ed. Douglas Gray (Sussex, England: Harvester Press, 1988); Eric Auerbach, *Scenes from the Drama of European Literature* (Minneapolis: University of Minnesota Press, 1984); Northrop Frye, *Anatomy of Criticism: Four Essays* (Princeton, NJ: Princeton University Press, 1957).

33. Jacques Lacan, *Seminar XI: Four Fundamental Concepts of Psychoanalysis,* ed. Jacques-Alain Miller, trans. Alan Sheridan (New York: W. W. Norton, 1981), 177.
34. On the figure of the "consensual child" in the Lockean tradition, see Brown, *Consent of the Governed.*

CHAPTER I ✱ Citizen Paul

1. James D. G. Dunn reminds us that "[a]t this stage of its growth, the new movement of Jesus' followers would almost certainly still think of themselves as a development *of* and *within* the religion of the Jews (a form of eschatological, messianic Judaism" (*Jesus, Paul, and the Law* [Louisville, KY: Westminster/John Knox Press, 1990], 136). Giorgio Agamben, writing from a philosophical rather than New Testament perspective, has made the same point even more forcefully, arguing that institutional forms of religion, both Jewish and Christian, have neutralized "le judaïsme de Paul" by removing him from his messianic context (*Le temps qui reste,* trans. Judith Revel [Paris: Bibliothèque Rivages, 2000], 10–11).
2. See Loraux, *Invention of Athens.*
3. See Tyrrell and Bennett, *Recapturing Sophocles' "Antigone";* and Karl Galinsky, *The Herakles Theme* (Oxford: Oxford University Press, 1972).
4. For useful surveys of these debates, see Colin G. Kruse (writing from within New Testament studies), *Paul, the Law, and Justification* (Leicester: Apollos, 1996), 27–53; and Daniel Boyarin (writing from the perspective of the new Jewish cultural studies), *A Radical Jew: Paul and the Politics of Identity* (Berkeley and Los Angeles: University of California Press, 1994), 39–56. See also William R. Stegner's entry, "Paul the Jew," in *Dictionary of Paul and His Letters,* ed. Gerald Hawthorne et al., 503–11 (Downers Grove, IL: InterVarsity Press, 1993).
5. Colin G. Kruse cites the important work of E. P. Sanders: "In Sanders' oft-quoted words: 'In short, *this is what Paul finds wrong in Judaism: it is not Christianity*'" (Kruse, *Paul,* 36).
6. Boyarin, *Radical Jew,* 32. Boyarin's cultural approach has found fruit in recent literary reevaluations of typology from Jewish points of view. See Lisa Freinkel, *Shakespeare's Will* (New York: Columbia University Press, 2001); and Lisa Lampert, *Gender and Jewish Difference from Paul to Shakespeare* (Philadelphia: University of Pennsylvania Press, 2004).
7. Weber, "Citizenship," 46.
8. James D. G. Dunn argues for the importance of commensality as a racial and national issue in the early church: "[P]art of the pressure on a devout Jew in the 40s and 50s of the first century CE would have been the constraint to observe the limits of acceptable table-fellowship" (*Jesus, Paul, and the Law,* 137). For a view of the Antioch incident that insists, contra Dunn, on *halakhic* precedent for table fellowship among Jews and Gentiles, see Peter J. Tomson, *Paul and the Jewish Law* (Van Gorcum, Assen/Maastricht: Fortress Press, 1990), 221–58.
9. Books on Paul and the law or Jesus and the law almost invariably equate law with Jewish law, and in turn identify this law with a national particularism opposed by Paul's universalism. See, for example, Alan Watson, *Jesus and the Law* (Athens: University of Georgia

Press, 1996); Robert Banks, *Jesus and the Law in the Synoptic Tradition* (Cambridge: Cambridge University Press, 1975); Dunn, *Jesus, Paul, and the Law;* and Hans Hübner, *Law in Paul's Thought,* trans. James C. G. Greig, ed. John Richies (Edinburgh: T. and T. Clark, 1984). An exception is Stephen C. Barton, "'All Things to All People'" (in *Paul and the Mosaic Law,* ed. James D. G. Dunn, 271–85 [Grand Rapids, MI: William B. Eerdmans, 1996]), which argues that "Paul's stance in relation to the law has to be set in the context of the world of ancient politics and political rhetoric" (271).

10. J. G. A. Pocock, "The Ideal of Citizenship Since Classical Times," in *The Citizenship Debates,* ed. Gershon Shafir, 37 (Minneapolis: University of Minnesota Press, 1998).
11. John Crook, *Law and Life of Rome* (Ithaca, NY: Cornell University Press, 1967), 37.
12. See the *Institutes* of Gaius: "Free people are also either Roman citizens, or 'Latins' . . . or peregrines (and if peregrines either citizens of some particular peregrine community or of none" (summarized in Crook, *Law and Life of Rome,* 36).
13. Crook, *Law and Life of Rome,* 36–41. See also J. P. V. D. Baldson, *Romans and Aliens* (London: Duckworth Press, 1979): "Together with the enfranchisement of slaves, the greatest increase in the Roman citizen body from the time of the civil wars which ended the Republic to AD 212 was a consequence of service in the armed forces, the army and navy. Indeed the fighting services were a great factory for the production of Roman citizens both from inside the Empire and, surprisingly enough . . . from outside it" (85).
14. Jane Gardner, *Being a Roman Citizen* (London: Routledge, 1993), 7–51; David Noy, *Foreigners at Rome: Citizens and Strangers* (London: Duckworth with the Classical Press of Wales, 2000), 24.
15. See Mark Reasoner, "Citizenship, Roman and Heavenly"; and F. Bruce, "Paul in Acts and Letters," in Hawthorne et al., *Dictionary of Paul,* 140 and 682.
16. See Reasoner, "Citizenship, Roman and Heavenly," 140; and Noy, *Foreigners at Rome,* 24.
17. Reasoner, "Citizenship, Roman and Heavenly," 140.
18. Meyer Reinhold, *Diaspora: The Jews among the Greeks and Romans* (Sarasota: Samuel Stevens, 1983), [illegible]4.
19. See James Walters, *Ethnic Issues in Paul's Letter to the Romans* (Valley Forge, PA: Trinity Press, 1993), 44. The limits of this policy are evident in the revolt in Judea that began in 65 CE and in the increasing tension between Judea and Rome over religious matters. See Dunn, *Jesus, Paul, and the Law,* 133–36.
20. Boaz Cohen, *Jewish and Roman Law,* 2 vols. (New York: Jewish Theological Seminary, 1966), 1: 23. There is also evidence that Rome "did not restrict the right to judge and punish to civil cases alone, but also recognized the authority of the Jewish courts in criminal cases" (Aharon Oppenheimer, "Jewish Penal Authority in Roman Judea," in *Jews in a Graeco-Roman World,* ed. Martin Goodman,187–88 [Oxford: Clarendon Press, 1998]).
21. Reinhold, *Diaspora,* 34.
22. Cited in Oppenheimer, "Jewish Penal Authority," 191.
23. Cohen, *Jewish and Roman Law,* 1:28–29.
24. T. Paige, "Philosophy," in Hawthorne et al., *Dictionary of Paul,* 715.
25. From the *Institutes,* quoted in Cohen, *Jewish and Roman Law,* 1: 26.
26. See Bruce, "Paul in Acts and Letters," 681.
27. Scott Bartchey made this point to me in a conference on Paul at UCLA (spring 2002).
28. Bruce, "Paul in Acts and Letters," 681.
29. Philip Brook Manville (*The Origins of Citizenship in Athens* [Princeton, NJ: Princeton University Press, 1997]) defines the polis in relation to *politea* (constitution, commonwealth,

citizenship) in the context of ancient Athens: "For the Greeks, membership in the state and the state itself were closely related. In fact, the state—the *polis*—was its citizens, as for example, the Athenian general Nikias reminded his troops in Thucydides' account of the Sicilian campaign in the year 412: '*Andres gar polis, kai ou teichē oude nēes andrōn kenai*' ('Men make the polis, not walls or a fleet of crewless ships': Thuc. 7.77.7)" (6).

30. Crook, *Law and Life of Rome,* 37.
31. In Christian tradition, Stephen's mission and destiny are closely linked to Paul's, since Stephen lead the early Church away from its emphasis on the Temple and Jerusalem, anticipating aspects of Paul's Gentile mission: "Yet the Most High does not dwell in houses made with hands" (Acts 7:47).
32. Hawthorne et al., *Dictionary of Paul and His Letters,* 548, 707–8.
33. Ibid., 707–8.
34. Noy, *Foreigners at Rome,* 24–25.
35. Here *politeia* bears its original meaning, as citizenship, rather than as the commonwealth or constitution that organizes the citizenry into an effective body. The King James Bible renders *politeia* as "freedom."
36. Arthur A. Rupprecht, "Roman Legal System," in Hawthorne et al., *Dictionary of Paul,* 549.
37. The editor of the *New Jerusalem Bible* (ed. Henry Wansbrough [New York: Doubleday, 1985]) notes, "Since Festus has disclaimed jurisdiction, Paul cannot escape trial before the Sanhedrin except by claiming the Roman citizen's privilege of trial before the imperial tribunal" (1841).
38. Bruce, "Paul in Acts and Letters," 687.
39. I follow Wayne Meeks's dating of the Epistles; see *The Writings of St. Paul* (New York: Norton, 1972), 3.
40. These parallel uses of circumcision are cited and refuted in Ramban's thirteenth-century commentary on Genesis (*Commentary on the Torah,* trans. Charles Chavel [NY: Shilo Publishing House, 1973], 1: 220); Ramban in turn draws on a slightly comic discussion of the same problem in the Talmud, *Tractate Shabbat* 108a.
41. Ramban, *Commentary on the Torah,* 1: 219. Cited hereafter simply as Ramban.
42. The *Soncino Chumash* (ed. A. Cohen [London: Soncino Press, 1983]) provides this paraphrase of Sforno (Gen 17:13, p. 80).
43. "Rabbi Simeon b. Eleazer said: Beth Shammai and Beth Hillel agree that when one is born circumcised, the blood of the covenant must be made to flow from him, because it is a suppressed foreskin" (*Genesis Rabbah,* trans. H. Freedman [London: Soncino Press, 1983], 1: 396–97). The ruling is especially striking since Shammai and Hillel often disagree, with Hillel presenting the more liberal opinion.
44. The *Genesis Rabbah,* for example, glosses this passage by way of a story about two Hellenistic Egyptian proselytes, "sons of King Ptolemy," who each have themselves circumcised after reading this scene. One is rewarded by being saved by an angel in battle (1: 395–96).
45. David Novak, "Land and People: One Jewish Tradition," in *Boundaries and Justice,* ed. Miller and Hashmi, 226 (Princeton, NJ: Princeton University Press, 2001).
46. See *The Eerdmans Bible Dictionary* (Allen C. Myers, revision editor [Grand Rapids, MI: William B. Eerdmans, 1987]), for example: "Through circumcision a person became a member of Israel's community and received the right to participate in public worship" (218). David Daube notes that in Judaism, "Conversion . . . means naturalization and vice versa" (*Ancient Jewish Law* [Leiden: E. J. Brill, 1981], 1).

47. In the analysis of Jacques Lacan, circumcision effects "the downfall of biological origin," a severing of the *infans* from the bliss of maternal union and corporeal unity (*Television*, trans. Denis Hollier et al. [New York: W. W. Norton, 1990], 74).
48. Rashi, *Chumash with Targum Onkelos, Haphtaroth and Rashi's Commentary*, ed. A. M. Silberman (Jerusalem: Feldheim, 1934), 1: 67.
49. As Ramban, following Rashi, points out, the Torah specifically links the commandment to circumcise to the promise of generations: "The *vav* [and] of *ve'atah* [and you] connects the verse with the preceding matter [in Verse 4]: '*As for Me behold My covenant is with thee*, and as for thee, thou shalt be careful to keep it.' And what constitutes this 'keeping' of it? *This is My covenant, which you shall keep, between Me and you*—this applies to those who were then alive; *and thy seed after thee*—this applies to those who are yet to be born" (Ramban citing Rashi, 1: 219).
50. In a recent dissertation, Steven Miller has argued for the heteronomous element in Jewish covenant and in every act of political contract. He argues that "[a]t no point can the heteronomy of the commandment be derived from the supposed autonomy of the promise" (*The Fulfillment of the Law* [PhD diss., University of California, Irvine, 2002], 35). Although my project is to rebind heteronomy to the liberal tradition, I have learned a great deal from Miller's articulation of the strong position.
51. See Rashi, *Chumash*, 1: 66; and Ramban, 1: 218–19.
52. Daube, *Ancient Jewish Law*, 3.
53. "The rites all symbolize separation, be it from her origin, be it from her prisoner's condition" (Daube, *Ancient Jewish Law*, 4). On the conflation of marriage and funeral ceremonies in the context of *Antigone* and the pathos of citizenship, see Tyrrell and Bennett, *Recapturing Sophocles' "Antigone*," 97–122.
54. In New Testament studies, E. P. Sanders, rescuing Paul from the Lutheran tradition, coined the phrase "covenantal nomism" to describe the function of the Law in first-century Judaism: "The 'pattern' or 'structure' of covenantal nomism is this: (1) God has chosen Israel and (2) given the law. The law implies both (3) God's promise to maintain the election and (4) the requirement to obey. (5) God rewards obedience and punishes transgressions. (6) the law provides for means of atonement, and atonement results in (7) maintenance or re-establishment of the covenantal relationship. (8) All those who are maintained in the covenant by obedience, atonement, and God's mercy belong to the group which will be saved. An important interpretation of the last point is that election and ultimately salvation are considered to be by God's mercy rather than human achievement" (*Paul, the Law, and the Jewish People* [Philadelphia, PA: Fortress Press, 1983], 422).
55. Jubilees 24:11, cited in Jeffrey R. Wisdom, *Blessing for the Nations and the Curse of the Law* (Tübingen: J. C. B Mohr [Paul Siebeck], 2001), 71. Wisdom gives a comprehensive survey of the "blessing for the nations" promise in the Torah, the New Testament, and postbiblical literature, upon which my comments here are based.
56. According to most modern scholars of Paul, the Jewish community in Rome, including those who had converted to Christianity, had been exiled by Claudius around 49 CE and returned to the city with the accession of Nero in 54 CE, a return that may have led to tensions between Gentile and Jewish Christians in the Roman church at the time of Paul's letter (Meeks, *Writings*, 67). Hans Hübner summarizes and rejects this argument, taking what seems to be a minority position, namely, that Paul's more tolerant attitude toward Jewish law in Romans (as compared to Galatians) reflects a change of heart rather than of rhetorical situation (*Law in Paul's Thought*, 5).

57. On Paul's appropriation of the universalist strand from Jewish thought, see W. D. Davies, *Paul and Rabbinic Judaism: Some Rabbinic Elements in Pauline Theology* (New York: Harper, 1967), 58–85.
58. Hübner, *Law in Paul's Thought,* 56.
59. The translation in the King James version makes the point more polemically, opposing the Law *(nomos)* to the letter *(gramma):* "And shall not uncircumcision which is by nature, if it fulfil the law, judge thee, who by the letter and circumcision dost transgress the law?"
60. New Testament scholars following the line of James D. G. Dunn concur that the phrase "works of the law" refers not to works-righteousness in general (the classic Protestant interpretation) but, more narrowly, to "the social function of the Law as marking out the people of the law in their distinctiveness" (Dunn, *Romans 1–8,* cited in Richard Hays, "Three Dramatic Roles: The Law in Romans 3–4," in Dunn, *Paul and the Mosaic Law,* 152–53.
61. The great twentieth-century theorist of Judaism as a civilization is Mordecai Kaplan, whose book *Judaism as a Civilization* (Philadelphia, PA: Jewish Publication Society, 1994) lies at the base of the Reconstructionist movement of Judaism, which treats Jewish Law *(halakhah)* as "folk-ways."
62. See Erich Auerbach on the importance of Paul to the establishment of biblical typology as one of Christianity's fundamental aesthetic and historiographical principles ("Figura," in *Scenes from the Drama of European Literature* [Minneapolis: University of Minnesota Press, 1984], 49–53). Auerbach writes of Pauline typology, "What the Old Testament thereby lost as a book of national history, it gained in concrete dramatic actuality" (51).
63. *Eerdmans Bible Dictionary,* 919.
64. Stephen Barton, "'All Things to All People,'" 283. In Barton's political and sociological conception of Paul, the image of master-builder (1Cor 3:10–17) is more apt than that of missionary, since it captures Paul's task of "upbuilding a church made up of people from a disconcertingly wide range of social backgrounds" (281–84).
65. Ibid., 273.
66. A. C. Hamilton, ed., *The Faerie Queene,* by Edmund Spenser (New York: Longman, 2001), 139.
67. Carol V. Kaske, "Spenser's Pluralistic Universe," in *Contemporary Thought on Edmund Spenser,* ed. Richard C. Frushell and Bernard J. Vondersmith, 147 (Carbondale: Southern Illinois University Press, 1975).
68. The three mountains take shape against each other within the perimeter of an epic simile, an emblematically "classical" convention. In Homer and Virgil, the epic simile often functions to inset detachable pastoral pictures within the heroic movement of epic, a tendency toward momentary fixation and idyllic enframing brilliantly appropriated and intensified by Spenser's stanzaic form (see Angus Fletcher, *The Prophetic Moment* (Chicago: University of Chicago Press, 1971), 130–31; Kaske, "Spenser's Pluralistic Universe, 147). The contrastive operation of simile, which so often counterbalances or interrupts more than clarifies epic action, melds the formal transmissibility of the classical padeia with the historical rhythm of Pauline typology in order to coordinate Judaism, Christianity, and classicism as three moments in a devolving world-historical poetics of inspired verse.
69. Reasoner, "Citizenship, Roman and Heavenly," 141. The theme has patristic origins: Chrysostom insisted that all Christians are *peregrine,* strangers/pilgrims in relation to earthly cities: "'If you are a Christian, no earthly city is thine. . . . Though we may gain possession of the whole world, we are withal but strangers and sojourners in it all. We are enrolled in heaven; our citizenship is there'" (cited in Peter Riesenberg, *Citizenship in the*

Western Tradition [Chapel Hill: University of North Carolina Press, 1992], 90). Augustine provides another *locus classicus* for this heavenly *translatio:* "For the City of Saints is up above, although it produces Roman citizens here below, in whom the city is on pilgrimage [*in quibus perigrinatur*] until the time of its kingdom should come" (*Of Christian Doctrine,* trans. D. W. Robertson [Indianapolis, IN: Bobbs-Merrill, 1958], 15.1). For these Fathers of the Church, those who are true citizens in the City of God are merely pilgrims, *peregrini,* in the City of Men: the Roman legal category for free foreigner, with its implications of local citizenship, becomes associated with a state of permanent exile and pilgrimage on this earth.

70. Agamben, *Le temps qui reste,* 10.

CHAPTER 2 ✷ Marlowe's *Jew of Malta*

1. Hawthorne et al., *Dictionary of Paul,* 293–94.
2. Cited in Margaret Williams, *The Jews among the Greeks and Romans* (Baltimore, MD: Johns Hopkins University Press, 1998), 107–8.
3. See Williams on the Jews of antiquity: "The phrases we meet with regularly in Jewish inscriptions from early Ptolemaic Egypt are 'the Jews in/of such and such a place'" (*Jews among the Greeks and Romans,* 27).
4. Ibid.
5. See Godfrey Wettinger, *The Jews of Malta in the Late Middle Ages* (Malta: Midsea Books, 1985), 6; and Williams, *Jews among the Greeks and Romans,* 31.
6. See Wettinger, *Jews of Malta,* 116–39. On Malta's relation to Spain as depicted in Marlowe's play, see Emily Bartels, who argues "that it is not just the Turks but also the Spanish who are imperializing over Malta" (*Spectacles of Strangeness: Imperialism, Alienation, and Marlowe* [Philadelphia: University of Pennsylvania Press, 1993], 90).
7. Stephen Greenblatt, *Renaissance Self-Fashioning from More to Shakespeare* (Chicago: University of Chicago Press, 1980), 204. Greenblatt first developed his reading of Marx and Malta in a 1978 essay that appeared in *Critical Inquiry.* The basic insights of that essay are distilled in *Renaissance Self-Fashioning.* The earlier essay has been reprinted in Richard Wilson, *Christopher Marlowe* (London: Longman, 1999), and in Greenblatt's own collection, *Learning to Curse* (New York: Routledge, 1990).
8. As John Gager in a recent book on Paul reminds us, "We should not read Paul's conversion as if it implied a transfer out of Judaism; he has no concept of Christianity or of his gospel as a new religion" (*Reinventing Paul* [Oxford: Oxford University Press, 2000], 46). In *Le temps qui reste,* Giorgio Agamben has also emphasized the Jewish character of Paul's Messianism.
9. Citations from Marlowe are taken from *The Complete Plays,* ed. Mark Thornton Burnett (London: J. M. Dent, 1999). Text references are to act, scene, and line.
10. The choice of conversion was also offered the historical Jews of Malta in 1492, in lieu of expulsion (Wettinger, *Jews of Malta,* 128).
11. Recall, for example, the very different figures of the hero cut by Achilles, dying young on the battlefield in the name of honor, and Odysseus, surviving into middle age thanks to the navigational deftness of his situational intuitions; thus Max Horkheimer and Theodor Adorno take Odysseus as *homo oeconomicus,* the type of bourgeois reason (*Dialectic of Enlightenment,* trans. John Cumming [New York: Continuum, 1986], 61). In a different his-

torical register, think as well of the affective "gray zone" inhabited by some survivors of the Holocaust, faced with the horror of forced choices that forever ransom any future freedom.

12. In Malta, Graham Hammill has argued, the Jews instantiate a form of "accursed" life that is "excluded from the everyday laws of the polis but included within the sphere of sovereign judgment. Ferneze intensifies this situation when he reduces Barabas to a life without subsistence *and* includes him as such in the polis" ("'The ruine of a multitude,'" [Paper presented at the annual meeting of the Modern Language Association, 2003], 6).
13. In a further irony at the expense of the Christian governor, Ferneze also echoes the words of Caiphas, the Jewish high priest, in a meeting of the Sanhedrin that precedes the scene before Pilate (e.g., John 11). For commentary on Marlowe's use of this material, see James Sims, *Dramatic Uses of Biblical Allusions in Marlowe and Shakespeare* (Gainesville: University of Florida Press, 1966), 19.
14. Greenblatt comments, "Most dramatic characters—Shylock is the appropriate example—accumulate identity in the course of the play; Barabas loses it" ("Marlowe, Marx, and Anti-Semitism," in Wilson, *Christopher Marlowe,* 305).
15. Cf. 1.1.104–5. For a discussion of the blessings of Abraham in Jewish and Pauline traditions, see the section in chapter 1, entitled "Of Circumcision and Citizenship: Second Cut," and also Jeffrey Wisdom, *Blessing for the Nations and the Curse of the Law* (Tübingen: J. C. B Mohr [Paul Siebeck], 2001).
16. In his commentary on Galatians, Luther frequently links "the Jews, the Turks, and the fanatics," since "those who do [works] are not Christians: they are hirelings, whether they are called Jews, Mohommedans, papists, or sectarians" (*Works,* ed. Jaroslav Pelikan [St. Louis, MO: Concordia, 1959], 26: 26, 10). He develops the analogy further: "The monk, for example, imagines this to himself: 'The works I am doing are pleasing to God. God will look upon my vows, and on their account He will grant me salvation.' The Turk says: 'If I live this way and bathe this way, God will accept me and give me eternal life.' The Jew thinks to himself: 'If I obey the Law of Moses, I shall find God gracious to me, and so I shall be saved' (26: 28).
17. The period *ante legem* dates from Adam to Moses, *sub lege* from Moses to Christ, and *sub gratia* from Christ onwards; this is the iconographic organization of the fresco cycles in the Sistine Chapel (Howard Hibbard, *Michelangelo,* 2nd ed. [New York: Harper & Row, 1974], 99–125).
18. John Pory, "A summarie discourse of the manifold Religions professed in Africa," addendum to *History and Description of Africa,* by Leo Africanus (London: George Bishop, 1600), 3: 1001–71,
19. In Islam, circumcision is a custom rather than a law, though I have not seen this point acknowledged in the Elizabethan literature on Islam, which generally assimilates the Muslim practice to the more familiar Jewish one.
20. Bernard Lewis, *Race and Color in Islam* (New York: Harper & Row), 1–28.
21. Norman Daniel writes of Arab genealogy in Christian exegesis: "Ismael was the savage or rustic ass; Muhammad descended from him through the idolator Nabajoth, progenitor of Moabites, Madianites and Idumaeans. The authentic Islamic genealogies of Muhammad had a medieval European public" (*Islam and the West* [Edinburgh: Edinburgh University Press, 1960], 128). On the reading of Pharaoh and Herod as Muslims, see Samuel Chew, *The Crescent and the Rose: Islam and England during the Renaissance* (New York: Octagon Books, 1965), 390, 395.
22. Hans Hübner argues that the law in Gal 4 applies to Gentiles as well as Jews, who were equally enslaved by law before the coming of Christ (*Law in Paul's Thought,* 33). Whether or

not Hübner is right about Paul's original meaning, Luther's assumption that the passage refers specifically to the Israelites under Mosaic law is more relevant to the post-Pauline context: "Although a schoolmaster is very useful and really necessary for the education and training of boys, show me one boy or pupil who loves his schoolmaster! For example, did the Jews love Moses warmly and willingly do what he commanded?" (*Works* 26: 345).

23. Meeks, *Writings*, 18n.
24. Crook, *Law and Life of Rome*, 41.
25. Conversion and marriage often occurred in tandem. Geoffrey Wettinger recounts an episode in Malta involving a *conversa* aptly named "Paula" who married a Christian in 1496, four years after the Expulsion (*Jews of Malta*).
26. In Romans, Paul writes of the younger twin's ascendancy over the elder: "[W]hen Rebecca had conceived children . . . she was told, 'The elder shall serve the younger.' As it is written, 'Jacob I loved, but Esau I hated'" (Rom 9:10–13).
27. See Ruth Lunney, *Marlowe and the Popular Tradition* (Manchester: Manchester University Press, 2002), 107–8.
28. Patrick Cheney, *Marlowe's Counterfeit Profession* (Toronto: University of Toronto Press, 1997), 145.
29. Erwin Panofsky, *Early Netherlandish Painting*, 2 vols. (1953; reprint, New York: Harper and Row, 1971), 1: 133–40.
30. See Augustine, *Of Christian Doctrine*: "Just as the Egyptians had not only idols and grave burdens which the people of Israel detested and avoided, so also they had vases and ornaments of gold and silver and clothing which the Israelites took with them when they fled, as if to put them to a better use. . . . In the same way, all the teachings of the pagans contain not only simulated and superstitious imaginings and grave burdens of unnecessary labor . . . but also liberal disciplines more suited to the uses of truth" (40.60).
31. Garrett Sullivan, "Geography and Identity in Marlowe," in *The Cambridge Companion to Marlowe*, ed. Patrick Cheney (Cambridge: Cambridge University Press, 2004), 237.
32. Stephen Mullaney, "The Place of Shakespeare's Stage in Elizabethan Culture." Encyclopedia Britannica Online: eb.com.
33. See William Leigh Godshalk, *The Marlovian World Picture* (The Hague: Mouton, 1974): "It may not be unfanciful to see a connection between the actual convent (with its unchaste nuns) and the metaphoric convent (Bellamira's bawdy house)" (209).
34. Hammill, "'The ruine of a multitude,'" 6.

CHAPTER 3 ✸ Merchants of Venice

1. On the relation between *The Jew of Malta* and *The Merchant of Venice*, see James Shapiro, "'Which is *The Merchant* here, and which *The Jew*?' Shakespeare and the Economics of Influence," *Shakespeare Studies* 20 (1988): 269–79, as well as older pieces by M. C. Bradbrook, "Authority, Truth, and Justice in *Measure for Measure*," in *William Shakespeare's Measure for Measure*, ed. Harold Bloom, 7–21 (New York: Chelsea House, 1987), 7–21; "Shakespeare's Recollections of Marlowe," in *Shakespeare's Styles*, ed. Philip Edwards, Inga-Stina Ewbank, and G. K. Hunter (Cambridge: Cambridge University Press, 1980); and Maurice Charney, "Jessica's Turquoise Ring and Abigail's Poisoned Porridge," *Renaissance Drama* 10 (1979): 33–44.
2. Auerbach, "Figura," 11–76; and Walter Benjamin, *Origin of the German Tragic Drama*, trans. John Osborne (London: New Left Books, 1963).

3. Barbara Lewalski ("Biblical Allusion and Allegory in *The Merchant of Venice*," in *Twentieth-Century Interpretations of "The Merchant of Venice,"* ed. Sylvan Barnet, 33–54 [Englewood Cliffs, NJ: Prentice Hall, 1970]) provides a thoroughgoing typological analysis of the play using Dante's theory of allegory, an analysis that beautifully demonstrates the symbolic resources of allusion in the play but does not address their politics or economics. See also Nevill Coghill ("The Theme of *The Merchant of Venice*," in Barnet, *Twentieth-Century Interpretations*, 108–13); John Colley ("Launcelot, Jacob, and Esau: Old and New Law in *The Merchant of Venice*," *Yearbook of English Studies* 10 [1980]: 181–89); and Douglas Anderson ("The Old Testament Presence in *The Merchant of Venice*," *English Literary History* 52 (spring 1985): 119–32). Stephen Greenblatt, on the other hand, reads Marlowe's Barabas as a figure of secular society, retroactively installing Marx's *On the Jewish Question* in the Renaissance scene (see "Marlowe, Marx, and Anti-Semitism"; and *Renaissance Self-Fashioning*, 204–7). Stephen Cohen's reading of *The Merchant of Venice* develops a similar line; thus he argues that "Shylock's Jewishness in the play is less theological than cultural," since Judaism "functions in the play as a derogatory marker for a group . . . characterized by its economic self-interest and its willingness to further that interest by opposing itself to the dominant social ideology: the rising class" ("'The Quality of Mercy: Law, Equity, and Ideology in *The Merchant of Venice*," *Mosaic* 27 [winter 1994]: 41–42). In my estimation, Leslie Fiedler ("'These Be Christian Husbands,'" in *Shylock*, ed. Harold Bloom, 63–90 [New York: Chelsea House, 1991]); Lars Engel ("'Thrift Is Blessing': Exchange and Explanation in *The Merchant of Venice*," *Shakespeare Quarterly* 37 [spring, 1986]: 20–37); Marc Shell (*Money, Language, and Thought* [Baltimore, MD: Johns Hopkins University Press, 1982]); and Richard Halpern (*Shakespeare among the Moderns* [Cornell University Press, 1997], 159–226) are the critics who most successfully combine theological and modernist readings of Shylock; see also new work on *The Merchant of Venice* and the Pauline tradition by Lisa Lampert (*Gender and Jewish Difference from Paul to Shakespeare* [Philadelphia: University of Pennsylvania Press, 2004], 138–67).
4. Richard Halpern makes a similar point (*Shakespeare among the Moderns*, 160). On debates about Jewish emancipation (their entry into general citizenship) in relation to the decline of the autonomy of incorporated Jewish communities (alternate citizenship), see Oscar Janowsky, *The Jews and Minority Rights, 1898–1919* (New York: Columbia University Press, 1966).
5. On the fortunes of converted Jews in Renaissance Venice, see Brian Pullan, *The Jews of Europe and the Inquisition of Venice, 1550–1670* (London: I. B. Tauris, 1997), 201–312.
6. Alberto Tenenti, "The Sense of Time and Space in the Venetian World of the Fifteenth and Sixteenth Centuries," in *Renaissance Venice*, ed J. R. Hale, 17–46 (London: Faber and Faber, 1974).
7. Dennis Romano, *Patricians and Popolani: The Social Foundations of the Venetian Renaissance State* (Baltimore, MD: Johns Hopkins University Press, 1987), 10.
8. Oliver Logan, *Culture and Society in Venice, 1470–1790* (New York: Charles Scribner's Sons, 1972), 4, 6; Edward Muir, *Civic Ritual in Renaissance Venice* (Princeton, NJ: Princeton University Press, 1981), 38–39.
9. Brian Pullan, "Social Hierarchies in the Republic of Venice," in *Orders and Hierarchies in Late Medieval and Renaissance Europe*, 160–61 (Toronto: University of Toronto Press, 1999).
10. Romano, *Patricians and Popolani*, 7. Brian Pullan cites Jean Bodin: "[I]n order to preserve their aristocratic form of state, the Venetians threw open certain minor offices to the people, intermarried with them, created a state debt to give them a vested interest in the

regime, and totally disarmed them" (cited in Brian Pullan, *Rich and Poor in Renaissance Venice* [Oxford: Basil Blackwell, 1971], 8).

11. Pullan, "Social Hierarchies," 152–53; Muir, *Civic Ritual*, 42.
12. Muir, *Civic Ritual*, 43; Pullan, *Rich and Poor*, 540–78.
13. Riccardo Calimani, *The Ghetto of Venice*, trans. Katherine Silberblatt Wolfthal (New York: M. Evans, 1987), 33.
14. Ibid., 45, 46.
15. Robert C. Davis reminds us that the Venetian "ghetto," though the first with that name, was not the first such community in Europe: "[T]his dubious honor belongs, rather, to Jewish enclaves in any number of cities within the Holy Roman Empire, the best known and longest lasting of which was that in Frankfurt-am-Main, established in the 1460s" (Robert C. Davis and Benjamin Ravid, eds. *The Jews of Early Modern Venice* [Baltimore, MD: Johns Hopkins University Press, 2001], x). My main source throughout for the history of the Jews in Venice is Calimani (see n. 12 above), but see also Cecil Roth, *Venice*, Jewish Communities Series (Philadelphia, PA: Jewish Publication Society of America, 1930), as well as the new collection (cited above) of essays edited by Robert C. Davis and Benjamin Ravid. Helpful also is sustained commentary by Brian Pullan in *Rich and Poor in Renaissance Venice*. On the politics and civic culture of Venice in the Renaissance, see especially Muir, *Civic Ritual*, and Logan, *Culture and Society*. On Venice and Shakespeare, see David McPherson, *Shakespeare, Jonson, and the Myth of Venice* (Newark, NJ: University of Delaware Press, 1990).
16. David Malkiel, "The Ghetto Republic," in *Jews of Early Modern Venice*, ed. Davis and Ravid, 117–42 (see preceding note).
17. Ibid., 123.
18. David Malkiel, *A Separate Republic: The Mechanics and Dynamics of Venetian Jewish Self-Government, 1607–1624* (Jerusalem: Magnes Press, Hebrew University, 1991), 13.
19. In forthcoming work (*From Jew-Devil to Jew-Sissy* [Ashgate]), Matthew Biberman provocatively conceptualizes the difference between Barabas and Shylock as that between the "Jew-Devil" of the medieval imagination (the image is from Joshua Trachtenberg's seminal work, *The Devil and the Jews: The Medieval Conception of the Jew and Its Relation to Modern Antisemitism* [New Haven, CT: Yale University Press, 1943]) and the "Jew-Sissy" who would become the norm in modern capitalist societies.
20. Note, for example, Shylock's reference not to "Abraham" but to "Abram," the name used by the first patriarch until the institution of circumcision (Gen 17:5); the unconverted, precontractual name "Abram" situates him in a moment before covenantal transformation, announcing Shylock's Bible as a text not yet marked by the epochal shift of the New Covenant.
21. Jacob Neusner, *Introduction to Rabbinic Literature* (New York: Doubleday, 1994), 11.
22. Jacob Neusner, *A Midrash Reader* (Minneapolis, MN: Fortress Press, 1990), 76. This account of midrash in terms of practical reason is, of course, an extremely limited one that ignores the theological concerns of rabbinic discourse; it is, however, about as much as one can imagine Shakespeare being able to absorb or intuit from received accounts of Jewish writing that might have been circulating at the time. The crucial point is the role of midrash in mediating between law and narrative—between rules for current conduct and the revealed history of the nation. On the relation between law and narrative in the Hebrew Bible, see Calum Carmichael, *The Origins of Biblical Law* (Ithaca, NY: Cornell University Press, 1992).

23. Although it is highly unlikely that Shakespeare himself would have known or used such a source, it is interesting that the compilers of *Genesis Rabbah*, produced in the fifth century CE, included an etiology of race as part of the exegesis of the Jacob and Laban incident: Of the ewes watering in front of the pilled sticks, Rabbi Hoshaya said, "The water turned to semen within them, so that they merely required the image of the young. (It once happened that an Ethiopian, married to an Ethiopian, begot a white-skinned son by her. Thereupon the father took the child and went to the Rabbi, asking him, 'Perhaps he is not my son.' 'Did you have any pictures [of men] in your house,' he asked. 'Yes,' he replied. 'Black or white?' 'White,' he answered. 'This accounts for your white-skinned son,' he assured him)" (*Genesis Rabbah* 2: 674). The midrash assumes an Ethiopian community both black and Jewish; in accordance with pre- and protoracial anecdotes from other traditions and periods, it also presents color as a characteristic not genetic in nature.
24. Lars Engle, "'Thrift Is Blessing': Exchange and Explanation in *The Merchant of Venice*," *Shakespeare Quarterly* 37 (spring 1986): 32.
25. In the aristocratic republic of Shakespeare's Venice, friendship has ties to both aristocratic *philôtes* [kinship love] and a more democratic or republican *philadelphia* [brotherly love], classical strands of civic discourse developed at more length in chapter 5 in relation to *Antigone*. On friendship and republican virtue in Renaissance literature, see Laurie Shannon, *Sovereign Amity: Figures of Friendship in Shakespearean Contexts* (Chicago: University of Chicago Press, 2002). On the importance of the "love feast" in developing sociality in Venice's many confraternities, see Romano, *Patricians and Popolani*, 4.
26. See Barber, "The Merchants and the Jew of Venice," in Barnet, *Twentieth Century Interpretations*, 49.
27. Williams, *Jews among the Greeks and Romans*, 27; cf. Malkiel, "Ghetto Republic," 117.
28. Dunn, *Jesus, Paul and the Law*, 137.
29. In the same passage in Galatians, Paul writes about his own resilient commitment to Judaism with a passion we too easily forget: "We ourselves, who are Jews by birth and not Gentile sinners, yet who know that a man is not justified by the works of the law, even we have believed in Christ Jesus" (Gal 2:15).
30. Jessica's theft of her father's wealth recalls the departure of the Jews from Egypt bearing "jewels of silver, and jewels of gold, and raiment" taken from their Egyptian neighbors (Ex 12:35). This was a favorite topos of Christian humanism, dating from Augustine's *On Christian Doctrine*, which uses the passage to justify the selected borrowing of pagan wisdom for Christian use (40.60). Just as the Israelites took with them only the ornamental and utilitarian artifacts of the Egyptians, leaving behind all signs of idolatry, so the Christians should purify classical culture of its pagan elements by picking out its scientific and moral truths. In Shakespeare's Pauline recycling of the motif in the episode of Jessica's elopement, the Jews become the emblem of slavery to the Law, and Jessica's theft of her parent's wealth finances her marriage and manumission into citizenship in Christ. Lewalski's typological reading refers the world of the play to "an anagogical significance treating the ultimate reality, the Heavenly City"; she reads Shylock's conversion in terms of the conversion of the Jews that will mark the Apocalypse ("Biblical Allusion and Allegory," 35, 47). This motif has been explored most thoroughly by James Shapiro in *Shakespeare and the Jews* (New York: Columbia University Press, 1996), esp. 131–65.
31. The masterwork on the forms and functions of civic ritual in Venice remains Edward Muir's *Civic Ritual in Renaissance Venice*. For a parallel exploration of northern urban ritual

in a largely medieval frame, see Gordon Kipling, *Enter the King: Theatre, Liturgy, and Ritual in the Medieval Civic Triumph* (Oxford: Clarendon Press, 1998).

32. Lewalski, "Biblical Allusion and Allegory," 39.
33. On the disaffiliation of the saints, see Lupton, *Afterlives of the Saints*, 114.
34. Muir, *Civic Ritual*, 154.
35. Ibid., 20.
36. Pullan, *Rich and Poor*, 5.
37. Against Contarini's view, Bodin writes, "Contarini passed the same judgment on the Venetian state, saying that it is a mixture of the three forms of state just like Rome and Sparta. For the royal power, he says, is in the duke of Venice, the aristocratic in the senate, and the democratic in the Great Council. . . . Contarini was very much mistaken. . . . It is certain that at present [Venice] is a true aristocracy. For of the fifty-nine thousand three hundred and forty-nine Venetians who were counted twenty years ago . . . it was only [these] four or five thousand gentlemen, young and old, who had a share in public life. . . . Sovereignty thus lies in a minority of the Venetians belonging to a particular group of noble families" (*On Sovereignty*, ed. Julian M. Franklin [Cambridge: Cambridge University Press, 1992], 98–99). Elected for life from among the nobility, the Doges resided at the Palace during their tenure, but did not "possess a court" in the manner of other European rulers, having control only over the "adornment of their private apartments" (Logan, *Culture and Society*, 150).
38. Jay Halio, *The Merchant of Venice: A Student Casebook to Issues, Sources, and Historical Documents* (Westport, CT: Greenwood Press, 2000), 45.
39. In Leslie Fiedler's analysis, Shakespeare exploits "the link . . . which joins together scriptural and legal notions of the bond, identifying both with nascent capitalism" ("These Be Christian Husbands," 81). Historian Dennis Romano notes that the idea of the public good that evolved in Renaissance Venice "equated the public good with the free flow of people and goods on the streets and canals of the city" (*Patricians and Popolani*, 25).
40. Leslie Fiedler, for example, briefly notes the connection ("These Be Christian Husbands," 78), an exegetical line developed much more fully in James Shapiro's excellent historical work on the play (*Shakespeare and the Jews*, 126–28).
41. Auerbach, "Figura," 54. On these grounds, one would have to take issue with the recent claim by John Cunningham and Stephen Slimp that "By 'Jew,' however, typology and theology speak not of the race of Jews or of any individual Jew" ("The Less into the Greater: Emblem, Analogue, and Deification in *The Merchant of Venice*," in *The Merchant of Venice: New Critical Essays*, ed. John Mahon and Ellen MacLeod Mahon, 228 [New York: Routledge, 2002]). This judgment runs counter to Paul and to his greatest reader within literary criticism, Auerbach.
42. James Shapiro cites a number of commentaries which insist on both the externality and internality of circumcision. In a 1611 gloss, for example, Andrew Willet wrote that circumcision of the flesh and circumcision of the heart were "two parts of one and the same circumcision which are sometimes joined together, both the inward and the outward" (*Shakespeare and the Jews*, 128).
43. John Milton, *Complete Poems and Major Prose*, ed. Merritt Y. Hughes, 81 (Indianapolis, IN: Bobbs-Merrill, 1957).
44. Morocco challenges any suitor to "make incision for [Portia's] love" (2.1.6–7), and Shylock, of course, asks the infamous question, "if you prick us do we not bleed?" (3.1.58–59), a

query that implicitly places circumcision at the exact interface between Jewish particularism and Christian universalism.

45. Fiedler, "These Be Christian Husbands," 81.
46. Harold C. Goddard writes of Portia's ruling, "Now the Jew is caught in his own trap, now he gets a taste of his own medicine. . . . Like Shylock, but in a subtler sense, she who has appealed to logic 'perishes' by it" ("Portia's Failure," in Bloom, *Shylock*, 32, 34). A. C. Moody writes that the play is about "the essential likeness of Shylock and his judges" ("An Ironic Comedy," in Barnet, *Twentieth Century Interpretations*, 101). See also Renè Girard, who emphasizes the ironic "undifferentiation" between Jews and Christians in the play ("'To Entrap the Wisest,'" in Bloom, *Shylock*, 295).
47. See *Eerdmans Bible Dictionary*, 528, and *The Oxford English Dictionary*.
48. Shakespeare returns to the problem of publicly enforcing the internal code of the Mount in the oddly Venetian Vienna of *Measure for Measure*. See Darryl Gless, *Measure for Measure, the Law, and the Convent* (Princeton, NJ: Princeton University Press, 1979).
49. Augustine, *On Christian Doctrine*, 4.10.
50. See Freinkel, *Shakespeare's Will*, for a resonant rereading of Augustine in relation to Shakespearean poetics.
51. Historical critics have pointed out the possible topical connection to the hanging of the wolfish physician Lopez, and secular defenders of Shylock have suggested that the Venetians' bestialization of the Jew shows the limits of their own humanism. I have not encountered, however, an exposition of the connection to Philippians. On the Lopez affair, see John Russell Brown's introduction to his edition of *The Merchant of Venice* (London: Methuen, 1955), xxiii.
52. Hawthorne et al., eds., *Dictionary of Paul*, 707.
53. G. F. Hawthorne's modern gloss associates the group labeled as "dogs," "evil workers," and "mutilators" not "as Judaizers—that is Jewish *Christians*—but rather as Jews, Jewish missionaries in particular, who aggressively pushed for converts at Philippi, even with force" (*Dictionary of Paul*, 711).
54. It is no accident that Shylock's insistence on the "seal" of the bond occurs in response to Gratiano's canine diatribe. Shylock only appears to resist that abjecting gesture when he responds with the reassertion of his bond and his self-identification with the law, since it is precisely as the bearer of the enforced and persistent "seal" of circumcision that he becomes an "inexecrable dog" in the sense of Philippians. As such, the interchange repeats the pattern of an earlier passage, in which Shylock retorts to Antonio: "Thou call'st me dog before thou hadst a cause, / But since I am a dog, beware my fangs" (3.3.6–7). Here, the reference to Philippians is perhaps even more pronounced, since Shylock's "beware my fangs" recalls the Hellenized "cave canem" of Paul's remarks. In the interchange, Shylock becomes the type that he is cast, a metamorphosis legible both within and beyond the dictates of psychological development.
55. Hannah Arendt, *The Origins of Totalitarianism* (San Diego, CA: Harcourt Brace, 1973), 455.
56. Lewalski, "Biblical Allusion and Allegory," 39.
57. I am borrowing here the distinction excavated by Giorgio Agamben between animal life, or *zoē*, and *bios*, "which indicated the form or way of living proper to an individual or a group" (*Homo Sacer*, 1). Agamben (himself reworking Arendt's analysis of the refugee cited above) argues that "the entry of *zoē* into the sphere of the *polis*—the politicization of bare life as such—constitutes the decisive event of modernity and signals a radical transforma-

tion of the political-philosophical categories of classical thought" (4). I am suggesting that Portia's criminalization of Shylock's civil suit attempts to force this transformation, and that Shylock refuses it.

58. Pullan, *Jews of Europe*, 252.
59. Pullan indicates that was meant by citizenship in this case is not clear. Certainly all converts did not become full citizens of Italian cities; many *marranos*, for example, remained subjects of the Ottoman Empire. Pullan provides an extremely rich picture of the landscape of Jewish conversion in Renaissance Venice through the lens provided by the Inquisition and its records. See *The Jews of Europe and the Inquisition of Venice* (London: I. B. Tauris, 1997), esp. 201–312.
60. Shylock's contentment is worlds away from that of Othello reunited with his bride on the shores of Cyprus: "It gives me wonder great *as my content* / To see you here before me . . . . If it were now to die, / 'Twere now to be most happy . . . ." (2.1.182–89; emphasis added).
61. Hugo Short, "Shylock Is Content: A Study in Salvation," in Mahon and Mahon, *The Merchant of Venice*, 211.
62. Cunningham and Slimp, "Less into the Greater," 228.
63. Will Kymlicka, "Territorial Borders: A Liberal, Egalitarian Perspective," in Miller and Hashmi, *Boundaries and Justice*, 258, 259. Kymlicka has developed these arguments in an extraordinary series of interventions over the past decade and a half, including *Liberalism, Community, and Culture* (Oxford: Oxford University Press, 1989), *Multicultural Citizenship* (Oxford: Clarendon Press, 1995), and his edited collection, *The Rights of Minority Cultures* (Oxford: Oxford University Press, 1995).
64. Hannah Arendt has analyzed with great suggestiveness what she calls the "equivocalities of emancipation"—the resistance on the side of both Jewish and Gentile communities in post-Enlightenment Europe to the loss of Jewish exceptionalism (the privileges of the incorporated Jewish communities of the *ancien regime*, but also the difference between the wealthy "court Jews" and their poorer brethren) implied by legal emancipation into citizenship. For Arendt, the subsequent legacy of emancipation is equivocal indeed, tied up both with the great achievements of the (largely assimilated and nonpracticing) Jewish intelligentsia and the destruction of the Jews in the camps. See *Origins of Totalitarianism*, 11–88.

CHAPTER 4 ✱ Othello Circumcised

1. Leslie Fiedler, *The Stranger in Shakespeare* (New York: Stein and Day, 1972), 139–45.
2. The groundwork of this orientation was laid by the historical criticism of Eldred Jones in *Othello's Countrymen: The African in English Renaissance Drama* (London: Oxford University Press, 1965) and G. K. Hunter in *Dramatic Identities and Cultural Tradition: Studies in Shakespeare and His Contemporaries* (Liverpool: Liverpool University Press, 1978), as well as the political and psychoanalytic myth criticism of Leslie Fiedler (see *Stranger in Shakespeare*). Virginia Mason Vaughan provides a useful survey and synthesis of the argument to 1994 (*Othello: A Contextual History* [Cambridge: Cambridge University Press, 1994]). In a later wave of essays, the black-white opposition has been most fruitfully explored by Arthur Little ("'An essence that's not seen': The Primal Scene of Racism in *Othello*," *Shakespeare Quarterly* 44 [fall 1993]: 304–24) and Jonathan Crewe ("Out of the Matrix: Shakespeare and Race-Writing," *Yale Journal of Criticism* 8 [fall 1995]: 13–29). Karen Newman,

Patricia Parker, and Michael Neill have focused on monstrosity and miscegenation in, respectively, "'And wash the Ethiop white': Femininity and the Monstrous in *Othello,*" in *Shakespeare Reproduced: The Text in History and Ideology,* ed. Jean E. Howard and Marion F. O'Connor, 143–59 (New York: Methuen, 1987); "Fantasies of 'Race' and 'Gender': Africa, *Othello,* and Bringing to Light," in *Women, "Race," and Writing,* ed. Margot Hendricks and Patricia Parker, 84–100 (London: Routledge, 1994); and (two works by Neill) "Unproper Beds: Race, Adultery, and the Hideous in *Othello,*" *Shakespeare Quarterly* 40 (winter 1989): 383–412, and "'Mulattos,' 'Blacks,' and 'Indian Moors': *Othello* and Early Modern Constructions of Human Difference," *Shakespeare Quarterly* 49 (winter 1998): 361–74. Stephen Greenblatt, in *Renaissance Self-Fashioning,* as well as Parker, Newman, and Emily Bartels, in "Making More of the Moor: Aaron, Othello, and Renaissance Refashionings of Race," *Shakespeare Quarterly* 41 (winter 1990): 433–54 have excavated travel narratives as sources and models of *Othello*'s protocolonial practice, a dimension emphasized from a postcolonial angle by Ania Loomba in *Gender, Race, Renaissance Drama* (Manchester, UK: Manchester University Press, 1989). Bartels assumes that Othello was originally a Muslim, but does not develop the tensions between race and religion, a dynamic on which Lynda Boose has reflected suggestively in "'The Getting of a Lawful Race': Racial Discourse in Early Modern England and the Unrepresentable Black Woman," in Hendricks and Parker, *Women, "Race," and Writing,* 35–54. An early version of this chapter appeared in *Representations* 57 (1997): 73–89. Since then, several important new readings of the play have appeared, including Janet Adelman's psychoanalytic reading of race in *Othello* ("Iago's Alter Ego: Race as Projection in *Othello,*" *Representations* 48 [1997]: 125–44); Daniel Vitkus's account of conversion ("Turning Turk in *Othello:* The Conversion and Damnation of the Moor," *Shakespeare Quarterly* 48 [summer 1997]: 145–76); Michael Neill's mapping of the Moor ("'Mulattos,' 'Blacks,' and 'Indian Moors'"); and Eric Griffin's Spanish reading of the play ("Un-Sainting James: Or, Othello and the 'Spanish Spirits' of Shakespeare's Globe," *Representations* 62 [spring 1998]: 58–99). Ania Loomba has published a thoughtful response to the 1996 version of this chapter ("'Delicious Traffick': Racial and Religious Difference on Early Modern Stages," in *Shakespeare and Race,* ed. Catherine M. S. Alexander and Stanley Wells, 203–24 [Cambridge: Cambridge University Press, 2000]). Although I agree with many of the refinements that she offers there, I would continue to contest the treatment of religion by Loomba and others as homologous with "culture" and hence as one in a series of possible markers of difference (e.g., "national, religious, cultural and economic anxieties"; "national culture in linguistic, religious, and ethnic terms" [218]). The culturalist approach to religion, I submit, flattens the conceptual and temporal complexity as well as the universal ambitions (for better and for worse) implied by religious discourses. A cultural approach to religion can make little sense, for example, of the Pauline tradition, which does not simply exemplify a religious identity ("Christianity") but mobilizes an interrelated set of geographical, historical, hermeneutic, juridical, and subjective positions and processes, as well as possible programs for their transformation and sublation.

3. Neill, "Unproper Beds," 385.
4. The distinction between "brother" and "stranger" established in Deuteronomy is of course crucial to the intergroup economy of *The Merchant of Venice;* whereas the Jew distinguishes "brother" and "stranger," prohibiting the lending of money to the one but permitting it to the other, the Christian is supposed to take all men as his brothers (Shell, *Money, Language, Thought,* 51). On the civic nobility of Venice, see Logan, *Culture and Society,* 24–26.

5. In this, I am giving scriptural precedent and shape to David Bevington's thoughtful and measured evaluation of Brabantio's character ("Introduction," in *Othello,* by William Shakespeare, ed. David Bevington, xxi [New York: Bantam Books, 1980]). On Abraham as a type of hospitality, see Genesis 18:1–8 and Hebrews 13:1–2. The latter passage links the love of the brother to duties toward the stranger: "Let brotherly love continue. Do not neglect to show hospitality to strangers, for thereby some have entertained angels unawares." (The editors of *The Oxford Annotated Bible* gloss "strangers" as "Christian brethren from other places"—for example, Othello in the house of Brabantio.)
6. On the relation between the sons of Noah and the Magi, G. K. Hunter cites Bede's commentary on St. Matthew: "Mystice autem tres Magi tres partes mundi significant, Asiam, Africam, Europam, sive humanum genus, quod a tribus filiis Noe seminarium sumpsit" (*Dramatic Identities,* 50). For the patristic tradition on Ham, see Augustine, *City of God,* ed. David Knowles (Harmondsworth: Penguin, 1972), 16.11; for the rabbinic tradition, see *Genesis Rabbah,* 2: 36–37. On the Ham story as a primal scene of Renaissance racism in *Othello* criticism, see Newman, "Femininity and the Monstrous," 146–7; Anthony Barthelemy, *Black Face, Maligned Race: The Representation of Blacks in English Drama from Shakespeare to Southerne* (Baton Rouge: Louisiana State University Press, 1987), 3; and Little, "Primal Scene of Racism," 308. I have not seen mention, however, of the way that Shakespeare stages the "flood" near Cyprus as the typological antidote to the Old Testament story, effectively replacing Ham with Balthazar. In addition, there is a civic dimension to Epiphany imagery: scenes of Epiphany share a special place in both English and Continental civic pageantry, providing a sacred script for the presentation of gifts that mark the ascension of a new monarch (in the great royal entries) or the induction of a new Lord Mayor in civic ceremonies produced by and for the city as a corporate entity. Gordon Kipling writes as follows of the royal entries: "Just as the Magi bestowed gifts on the Christ-child to symbolize their faith in, and their willing submission to, the *christus* of God, so the gifts of citizens on the occasion of their sovereign's *adventus* symbolize both their fealty and their willing submission to 'the Prince of God among us'" (*Enter the King,* 117).
7. Logan, *Culture and Society,* 26.
8. Claude Nicolet, *The World of the Citizen in Republican Rome,* trans. P. S. Falla (Berkeley and Los Angeles: University of California Press, 1980), 93–94.
9. Extraordinary military service was, however, a means for Venetian citizens to enter the nobility, thus enjoying greater civic participation.
10. The genealogy linking Iago, Shylock, and Barabas has been revisited, for example, by Harold Bloom in *The Western Canon* (New York: Harcourt Brace, 1994), 173–82.
11. Shell, *Money, Language, Thought,* 49.
12. Jones, *Othello's Countrymen,* 87–93.
13. Hunter, *Dramatic Identities,* 49.
14. The King declares his typological itinerary:

> *However darkness dwells upon my face,*
> *Truth in my soul sets up the light of grace;*
> *And though, in days of error, I did run*
> *To give all adoration to the sun,*
> *The moon, and stars, nay, creatures base and poor,*
> *Now only their Creator I adore.*
> *My queen and people all, at one time won*

> *By the religious conversation*
> *Of English merchants, factors, travellers,*
> *Whose truth did with our spirits hold commèrce,*
> *As their affairs with us. (Thomas Middleton,* The Triumphs of Truth, *in* Jacobean Civic Pageants, *ed. Richard Dutton, 153 [Staffordshire, UK: Keele University Press, 1995].)*

The King's narrative recounts the classic passage of the Gentile barbarian from a life of promiscuous, "barbaric" idolatry to full and humanizing access to the Christian "light of grace," its shining presence belying the darkness of his skin. Like the nativity star, the King's desire draws him to see the birthplace of the merchants who had led to the conversion of his people to *sumpolites* in Christ. The pageant that makes up *The Triumph of Truth* likely resembled the exotic train of goods and peoples, often within or in relation to an urban scene, that decorates so many Renaissance Epiphany paintings.

15. Chew discusses the masque; see *The Crescent and the Rose,* 463.
16. Whereas Paul does indeed claim that in Christ, "there cannot be Greek and Jew, circumcised and uncircumcised, barbarian, Scythian, slave, free man" (Col 3:11), the means of equalization is their common faith in Christ. Morocco's criterion, on the other hand, is the redness of the blood; although not exactly an "externall thing," it partakes in the purely physical interiority of bodily organs rather than the spiritual inwardness of faith, remaining continuous in kind if not in color with the physical "complexion" that covers it.
17. See Jonathan Crewe, "Out of the Matrix: Shakespeare and Race-Writing," *Yale Journal of Criticism* 8 (fall 1995): 13–29.
18. On the People of the Book and theories of civil society immanent in Islamic legal and social thought, see Sachedina, *Islamic Roots of Democratic Pluraslism,* and Hanafi, "Alternative Conceptions of Civil Society."
19. For typological readings of Exodus, see Augustine, *City of God,* 16.43 and *On Christian Doctrine,* 2.40.60. On manumission and adoption as legal tropes for spiritual redemption, see Galatians 4:4: "But when the time had fully come, God sent forth his Son, born of woman, born under the law, to redeem those who were under the law, so that we might receive adoption as sons." Galatians 3 and 4 link manumission and adoption to universal fellowship in Christ: "There is neither Jew nor Greek, there is neither slave nor free, there is neither male nor female, for you are all one in Christ Jesus" (Gal 3:28).
20. See Chew, *Crescent and the Rose,* 145, 154; Vitkus, "Turning Turk in *Othello,*" 152–54. Daniel remarks on the use of the phrase during the late Middle Ages, when "we find the phrase *effici Turci* for 'become Muslims'; and a convert to Islam may be turned *Turcatus*" (*Islam and the West,* 130). See Michael Neill on the ironies of the use of the phrase in this passage ("*Othello* and Early Modern Constructions of Difference," 365).
21. John Pory, "A summarie discourse," 1015.
22. Chew, *Crescent and the Rose,* 108.
23. In an unpublished lecture, "Othello's Jealousy and the Triangle of Desire," Joseph Chaney has productively linked Othello's jealousy to that of the "Judeo-Christian God." In *Afterlives of the Saints,* I have explored extensively the relation between idolatry, adultery, and jealousy in the typological framework of *The Winter's Tale.*
24. One *locus classicus* is Niccolò Machiavelli's discussion of Lucius Junus Brutus's execution of his own sons after the expulsion of the Tarquins (*Il Principe e Discorsi sopra la prima deca di Tito Livio,* ed. Sergio Bertelli [Milan: Feltrinelli Economica, 1960], 381).

25. Vitkus, "Turning Turk in *Othello*," 171.
26. Boose, "Racial Discourse in Early Modern England," 372–73.
27. Critics who prefer "base Iudean" include Richard S. Veit ("'Like the Base Judean': A Defense of an Oft-Rejected Reading in *Othello*," *Shakespeare Quarterly* 26 [1975]: 466–69), and Gordon Braden, who reads *Othello* in the context of Herod-Mariam dramas (*Renaissance Tragedy and the Senecan Tradition* [New Haven, CT: Yale University Press, 1985], 153–71). Edward Snow provides a powerful defense of retaining both readings: "Each variant suggests a different side of Othello: 'Indian' makes him the traveller, the adventurer, full of exotic lore with which to entrance an audience; 'Judean' makes him the self-consciously converted Christian. . . . [T]hey reflect the divided consciousness that is implicit throughout the final speech: 'Indian' attempts to excuse what he did as a naive mistake, an act of unwitting folly; 'Iudean' makes him guilty of deliberate treachery, a betrayal for which no expiation is possible" ("Sexual Anxiety and the Male Order of Things in *Othello*," *English Literary Renaissance* 10 [autumn 1980]: 412). Fiedler makes a strong case for "Iudean," but then chooses "Indian" instead (*Stranger in Shakespeare*, 195–96). On the Herod-Mariam story, see Barry Weller and Margaret W. Ferguson's recent edition of Elizabeth Cary's *The Tragedy of Mariam, the Fair Queen of Jewry* (Berkeley and Los Angeles: University of California Press, 1994).
28. Snow, "Sexual Anxiety," 412.
29. Dympna Callaghan provides a related reading of the Herod-Mariam story in her interpretation of Elizabeth Cary's *Tragedie of Mariam;* Callaghan, however, emphasizes not the typological split between the intransigent modern Jew and the successful Jewish convert (the Esau-Jacob pair) but the "racialization" or blackening of Herod and the concomitant whitening of Mariam. Crudely put, in Callaghan's reading, racial difference precedes and governs religious difference; in my reading, religious difference precedes and governs racial difference. See "Re-reading Elizabeth Cary's *The Tragedie of Mariam, Faire Queene of Jewry*," in *Women, "Race," and Writing*, ed. Hendricks and Parker, 163–77.
30. Snow, "Sexual Anxiety," 412.
31. The figure of the base Judean also draws the myrrh tree into its associative circuit. In Matthew, the Epiphany story takes place in the context of Herod's responses to Jesus' birth; hearing that the Wise Men had come to see the "king of the Jews," Herod summons them and requests a report, an episode that eventually leads to the Massacre of the Innocents. The opening line of Matthew's chapter on Christ's nativity juxtaposes Herod and the Wise Men: "Now when Jesus was born in Bethlehem of Judea, in the days of Herod the king, behold, wise men from the East came to Jerusalem" (Matt 2:1). In Othello's diptych of images, the two similes function like the two halves of Mark 2:1. The figure of the "base Iudean" announces "the days of Herod the king," and the weeping myrrh recalls the "wise men from the east," the Gentile kings who understand the value of the treasure that the Jewish king refuses to recognize. In this second, "Iudean" reading of the passage, the resinous and resonant stuff collected from these "*Arabian* trees" reflects back to Othello not the dark face of Balthazar away from the manger, but the lighter skin of the Idumean Herod mourning his massacre of an innocent.
32. See, respectively, Braden, *Renaissance Tragedy*, 169; Loomba, *Gender, Race, Renaissance Drama*, 48; and Parker, "Fantasies of 'Race' and 'Gender,'" 98. Another example of the pagan reading of the play is Ania Loomba's judgment that "Othello moves from being a colonised subject existing on the terms of white Venetian society . . . towards being marginalised, outcast and alienated from it in every way; . . . he becomes simultaneously the

Christian and the Infidel, the Venetian and the Turk" (*Gender, Race, Renaissance Drama,* 48). Notable exceptions to the pagan reading of the Turk include Edward Snow's salutary comments on the "Indian/Judean" crux noted above, and Lynda Boose's extremely suggestive comments on circumcision in Shakespeare: "Does 'non-Christian' sufficiently account for the way that 'the Turk and the Jew' so often get phrased together as oppositional examples of some kind of similar Otherness? . . . In Othello's concluding lines, speaking through the strangely bifurcated discourse in which he simultaneously occupies the positions of subject and object, conqueror and transgressor, Christian and Turk, what he invokes as the final, inclusive sign of his radical Otherness is not an allusion to his skin color" ("Racial Discourse in Early Modern England," 40). My only cautionary note here would be to suggest that in Aleppo, the Christian was unlikely a "conqueror," and more likely a guest in a Muslim city reacting to the treatment of a fellow Venetian—the expression of the member of a minority responding to an ethnic insult, and not of a colonial administrator inflicting discrimination; cf. Chew, *Crescent and the Rose,* 245–46.

33. Boose, "Racial Discourse in Early Modern England," 40.
34. Here I differ from Daniel Vitkus, who insists on the "damnation" of Othello at the end of the play. Vitkus concludes, "A baptized Moor turned Turk, Othello is 'doubly damned' for backsliding. Sent out to lead a crusade against Islamic imperialism, he 'turns Turk' and becomes the enemy within. . . . Othello enacts his own punishment and damns himself by killing the Turk he has become" ("Turning Turk in *Othello,*" 176). I argue instead for the reinscriptive power of Othello's final act, in which he reenters the civil, religious, and marital covenants through death ("dying into citizenship"). I would like to thank my student Craig Carson for analyzing Othello's final speech in terms of "dying into citizenship" in the context of a graduate seminar on Shakespeare.
35. On *ethnos* and *dēmos* in the history of citizenship, see Étienne Balibar, *We, the People of Europe,* trans. James Swenson (Princeton, NJ: Princeton University Press, 2004), 8–9.

CHAPTER 5 ✹ Antigone in Vienna

1. In Roman law, for example, adoption was one of the legal means by which slaves were manumitted and made into citizens, and it was an act that required in principle the participation of the full community (Jane Gardner, *Being a Roman Citizen* [London: Routledge, 1993], 10–12). Paul, picking up on the Roman model, uses adoption as a metaphor for the transition from slavery under the law to manumission in Christ, a deal secured through his act of redemption (Gal 4:5–7.) Paul writes, "So through God you are no longer a slave but a son, and if a son then an heir" (Gal 4:7).
2. Tyrrell and Bennett, *Recapturing Sophocles' "Antigone."*
3. Jacques Lacan, *Seminar VII: The Ethics of Psychoanalysis, 1959–60,* ed. Jacques-Alain Miller (1982), trans. Dennis Porter (New York: W. W. Norton, 1992). Sophocles' *Antigone* is cited parenthetically in the text from the edition edited by Richard Braun (New York: Oxford University Press, 1973).
4. Lacan, *Ethics of Psychoanalysis,* 255.
5. Ibid., 279.
6. Ibid.
7. Joan Copjec, *Imagine There's No Woman: Ethics and Sublimation* (Cambridge, MA: MIT Press, 2002), 40–41.

8. Ibid., 41.
9. Furthermore, although Copjec is absolutely right that Antigone assigns no intrinsic value, no heroic *arête,* to Polyneices, Antigone does indeed provide a rationale for staking her claim on this one, namely, that with parents dead no other brothers may issue from the womb that produced them.
10. Jacques Lacan, *Seminar XI: Four Fundamental Concepts of Psychoanalysis,* ed. Jacques-Alain Miller, trans. Alan Sheridan (New York: W. W. Norton, 1981), 60.
11. Lacan, *Ethics of Psychoanalysis,* 204–5.
12. Copjec, *Ethics and Sublimation,* 22.
13. See G. W. F. Hegel, *Philosophy of Right,* trans. T. M. Knox (Oxford: Oxford University Press, 1942); and Judith Butler, *Antigone's Claim: Kinship between Life and Death* (New York: Columbia University Press, 2000).
14. Joan Copjec, in her intensive Lacanian engagement with Antigone, makes a similar point at the outset of her study: "But if the form of Athenian tragedy is local, tied not only to a specific place, a particular and precisely datable time, and a unique set of social problems, it would seem, then, according to the historicist-relativist thinking of our day, to offer nothing that might help us think through the juridical and ethical issues raised by the modern city" (*Ethics and Sublimation,* 13).
15. One of the best introductions to the social world of archaic Greece remains M.I. Finley's *The World of Odysseus* (New York: Viking Press, 1954). Some of the same ground is revisited in a more concertedly literary vein by Richard Seaford, *Reciprocity and Ritual: Homer and Tragedy in the Developing City-State* (Oxford: Oxford University Press, 1994). Both Finley and Seaford rely on Marcel Mauss's anthropology of the gift (*The Gift,* trans. I. Cunnison [1925; reprint, New York: Norton, 1967]).
16. Philip Brook Manville, *The Origins of Citizenship in Athens* (Princeton, NJ: Princeton University Press, 1997), 6.
17. On the ongoing tension between the internationalism of *xenia* and the boundaries of the *politeia* in democratic Athens, see Manville: "Though by then polis loyalty had mostly superseded such 'private networks' born in an earlier age, it never completely dissolved them—with the effect that 'traitorous acts' performed by aristocrats such as Alkibiades on behalf of foreign guest friends could be treated with ambivalence by Athenian contemporaries" (*Citizenship in Athens,* 25–26).
18. On the motif of marriage to death in *Antigone,* see Rush Rehm, *Marriage to Death: The Conflation of Wedding and Funeral Rituals in Greek Tragedy* (Princeton, NJ: Princeton University Press, 1994).
19. Tyrrell and Bennett, *Recapturing Sophocles' "Antigone,"* 115–17; cf. Nicole Loraux, *The Invention of Athens: The Funeral Oration in the Classical City,* trans. Alan Sheridan (Cambridge, MA: Harvard University Press, 1986).
20. Pericles tells the parents of dead soldiers, "[T]hose still of age to have children must take strength from hopes of other sons. On the personal level, those who come later will be a means of forgetting those who are no more, and the city will benefit doubly, both in not being left short and in security" (Thucydides, *The Peloponnesian War,* trans. Steven Lattimore [Indianapolis, IN: Hackett, 1998], 96).
21. In the words of Tyrrell and Bennett, "The *polis* needs warriors for its defense; in this respect, individuals are interchangeable, replaceable, and of less worth than the welfare of all. To that end, parents must surrender their children to fight and die on its behalf" (Tyrrell and Bennett, *Recapturing Sophocles' "Antigone,"* 115).

22. Lacan, *Four Fundamental Concepts,* 279.
23. Copjec, *Ethics and Sublimation,* 23–24.
24. Freud, Sigmund, *Standard Edition of the Complete Psychological Works of Sigmund Freud,* vol. 11, trans. James Strachey (London: Hogarth Press, 1974).
25. Aeschylus, *Aeschylus II: Suppliant Maidens, The Persians, Seven Against Thebes, Prometheus Bound,* ed. David Grene and Richmond Lattimore (Chicago: University of Chicago Press, 1956); line nos. from *Seven Against Thebes* cited in text.
26. For a related view of Haemon as a representative of "deliberative democracy" in the play, see J. Peter Euben, *Corrupting Youth: Political Education, Democratic Culture, and Political Theory* (Princeton, NJ: Princeton University Press, 1997), 147.
27. Cited in John J. Winkler, "The Ephebes' Song: *Tragôidia* and *Polis,*" *Representations* 11 (summer 1985): 7; cf. Tyrrell and Bennett, *Recapturing Sophocles' "Antigone,"* 87–89.
28. Lacan captures the dark side of this transition, bound up as it is with the arts and disciplines of war, when he attributes to the first choral ode the image of "Polyneices and his shadow strangely enough as a huge bird hovering above the houses. The image of our modern wars as something that glides overhead was already made concrete in 441 B.C." (*Ethics of Psychoanalysis,* 266). The civil warrior is dead. Long live the citizen-soldier—and the forms, moods, and shapes of state-sanctioned violence that he supports with his being.
29. Warren J. and Ann M. Lane, "The Politics of *Antigone,*" in *Greek Tragedy and Political Theory,* ed. J. Peter Euben, 164 (Berkeley and Los Angeles: University of California Press, 1986). In the same vein, Lane and Lane argue, "Like a Homeric hero or citizen soldier, Antigone will dare a noble death in the defense of the body of her slain friend against possible despoilment by the enemy. She vows to succeed or die beside him in the effort. Antigone conceives of her burial of Polyneices as a glorious engagement in battle" (174).
30. Lacan, *Ethics of Psychoanalysis,* 247.
31. On the singularity of the act, see Copjec: "Clearly, *singularity* is distinct from *particularity,* which is also localized, but which we commonly and rightly associate with things that fade with time and distance, with the ephemeral, things that do not endure. This notion of singularity . . . is tied to the *act* of a subject" (*Ethics and Sublimation,* 23).
32. Cited in Copjec, *Ethics and Sublimation,* 30.
33. William Tyrell and Larry Bennett, trans., *Antigone,* by Sophocles. Available on-line at www.stoa.org/diotima/anthology/ant/antigstruct.htm.
34. Euben, *Corrupting Youth,* 155.
35. "Our happiness depends / on wisdom all the way. / The gods must have their due. / Great words by men of pride / bring greater blows upon them. / So wisdom comes to the old." (1347–52).
36. Tyrrell and Bennett, *Recapturing Sophocles' "Antigone,"* 92–121.
37. Copjec, *Ethics and Sublimation,* 43, 45.
38. Ibid., 41.
39. Tyrrell and Bennett, *Recapturing Sophocles' "Antigone,"* 105.
40. Lacan, *Ethics of Psychoanalysis,* 270–87.
41. See the introduction to Sophocles' *Antigone,* ed. Richard Braun, 7; and Seaford, *Reciprocity and Ritual,* 349.
42. See Marc Shell, *The End of Kinship: "Measure for Measure," Incest, and the Ideal of Universal Siblinghood* (Stanford, CA: Stanford University Press, 1988).
43. Darryl J. Gless, *Measure for Measure, the Law, and the Convent* (Princeton, NJ: Princeton University Press, 1979), 139.

44. See p. 75 of the introduction in J. W. Lever, ed., *Measure for Measure,* by William Shakespeare (London: Methuen, 1967); Gless, *Measure for Measure, the Law, and the Convent,* 178; and Arthur Kirsch, "The Integrity of *Measure for Measure,*" *Shakespeare Survey* 28 (1975): 96, 97.
45. Janet Adelman provides a more sympathetic feminist rendering of Isabella that nonetheless ends in the same place: Isabella "allies herself with the male voices condemning female contamination, as though to distance herself absolutely from the mother she attacks" (*Suffocating Mothers: Fantasies of Maternal Origin in Shakespeare's Plays* [New York: Routledge, 1992], 132). Jacqueline Rose, responding to such charges, argues that Isabella's perceived sexual deficiency becomes the displaced target of complaints about the play's aesthetic and ethical ambiguity: "Isabella," Rose writes, "is 'hysterical' and 'unwomanly,' not through any lack of humanity (her refusal to relent), but because of the aspersion she casts on the proper sexual ordering of humanity itself. . . . The sexual scandal shifts generations and becomes the mother's sexual crime" ("Sexuality in the Reading of Shakespeare: *Hamlet* and *Measure for Measure,*" in *Alternative Shakespeares,* ed. John Drakakis, 108 [London: Methuen, 1985]).
46. Lacan, *Ethics of Psychoanalysis,* 110, 112, 212, and 213.
47. Carl Schmitt, *Political Theology: Four Chapters on the Concept of Sovereignty,* trans. George Schwab (Cambridge, MA: MIT Press, 1985), 32.
48. Gless, *Measure for Measure, the Law, and the Convent,* 134–41.
49. Copjec, *Ethics and Sublimation,* 44.
50. Ibid., 9.
51. Walter Benjamin, *Origin of the German Tragic Drama,* trans. John Osborne (London: New Left Books, 1963), 74, 55.
52. Ellickson distinguishes among the following kinds of codes: "The rules that emanate from first-party controllers will be referred to as *personal ethics;* those from second-party controllers, as *contracts;* those from social forces, as *norms;* those from organizations, as *organization rules;* and those from governments, as *law*" (*Order Without Law,* 127).
53. Engle, "Shakespearean Normativity," 1.
54. See Margaret Scott, "'Our Cities' Institutions': Some Further Reflections on the Marriage Contracts in *Measure for Measure,*" *ELH* 4 (1982): 792; and Josephine Waters Bennett, *Measure for Measure as Royal Entertainment* (New York: Columbia University Press, 1966), 18.
55. On marriage law in *Measure for Measure,* see, for example, Scott, who insists on the Catholic, and hence foreign, "story-book," and patently absurd character of the law that condemns Claudio to death. Scott notes that the Council of Trent in 1563 had declared handfast marriages invalid. Until this point, "throughout Christendom, both church and state recognized 'the consent of two parties expressed in words of present mutual acceptance' as 'actual and legal marriage' ("'Our Cities' Institutions,'" 795). Margaret Loftus Ranald argues to the contrary that "for the purposes of their plays, Shakespeare and his contemporaries merely transferred English legal practice to foreign settings" ("'As Marriage Binds, and Blood Breaks': English Marriage and Shakespeare," *Shakespeare Quarterly* 1 (1979): 69). Whether or not there is something specifically Catholic about Angelo's resurrected law (and I find the idea provocative), it seems clear that to members of Shakespeare's audience, and to English lawyers of the time, the union between Claudio and Julietta may have been "irregular" (legally and socially), but it would have been valid.
56. Victoria Kahn, "Margaret Cavendish and the Romance of Contract," *Renaissance Quarterly* 50 (1997): 533.

57. Aristotle goes on to say that the woman has a "deliberative faculty" but "without authority," while the slave has no deliberative faculty at all, and that of the child is "immature" [1260a]. The woman stands between the noncitizen (the slave) and the potential citizen (the child); she is a free person but not a political participant, not a citizen in the full sense. With respect to the political dimension of civility, one might look to Locke's commentary on the Fifth Commandment, where he distinguishes "honor" for parents from "obedience" to them: "'Tis one thing to owe honour, respect, gratitude and assistance; another to require an absolute obedience and submission" (John Locke, *Two Treatises of Government*, ed. Peter Laslett (Cambridge: Cambridge University Press, 1970), *Second Treatise*, S. 66.
58. Constance Jordan provides a comprehensive reading of the original significance and later fortunes of Aristotle's definition of marriage as a form of *politeia* in "The Household and the State: Transformations of the Representation of an Analogy from Aristotle to James I," Modern Language Quarterly 54, no. 3 (September 1993): 307–26.
59. Locke, *Two Treatises*, 318–321. Substantial commentaries on marriage and family in Locke include studies by Gordon Schochet (*Patriarchalism in Political Thought: The Authoritarian Family and Political Speculation and Attitudes Especially in Seventeenth-Century England* [Oxford: Basil Blackwell, 1975], 14–16) and Carole Pateman (*The Sexual Contract* [Stanford, CA: Stanford University Press, 1988]). On marriage in Athenian society and literature, see Kirk Ormand, *Exchange and the Maiden: Marriage in Sophoclean Tragedy* (Austin: University of Texas Press, 1999).
60. Schochet, *Patriarchalism in Political Thought*, 14–16.
61. Peter Laslett (Locke, *Two Treatises*, 187n) comments on the radicality of the passage: "In denying, as he seems to do here, that the Fifth Commandment has anything to do with political obedience, Locke was repudiating far more than the principles of Filmer. He was attacking a tradition of Christianity, and particularly of Protestant Christianity. Luther, for example, develops his whole doctrine of political and social authority as a commentary on the Fifth Commandment (*Von den Guten Werken*, 1520 [1888]), and Tyndale argues in a precisely similar manner in his *Obedience of a Christian Man*, 1528 (1848)." For a strong literary reading of Lockean consent, see Brown, *Consent of the Governed*.
62. In Galatians, addressing not the principles of *oikonomika* but the nature of membership in Christ, Paul makes a more radical claim: "There is neither Jew nor Greek, there is neither slave nor free, there is neither male nor female; for you are all one in Christ Jesus" (Gal 3:28).
63. Pompey can cut off a man's head "if the man be a bachelor . . . but if he be a married man, he's his wife's head, and I can never cut off a woman's head" (4.2.2–4). The 1563 "Homily of the State of Matrimony" is reprinted in Russ McDonald, ed., *Bedford Companion to Shakespeare: An Introduction with Documents* (Boston: Bedford/ St. Martin's, 2001), 285–90.
64. See Schochet, *Patriarchalism in Political Thought*, 81; and Gordon Kipling, *Enter the King: Theatre, Liturgy, and Ritual in the Medieval Civic Triumph* (Oxford: Clarendon Press, 1998), 237–50.
65. Space does not allow a reading of the bed-trick here. I would link Mariana to normativity; the "trick" of the bed-trick is to regularize the irregular, under the name of contract, and thus to broaden the legitimate grounds of sexual experiment in Vienna. Lars Engle, in his essay "Shakespearean Normativity," chooses another bed-trick, the conceit of *All's Well That Ends Well*, for his exploration of norms in Shakespeare. Engle describes the play as "a serious attempt to figure out how and whether these norms [of marital chastity and mascu-

line honor] serve particular interests at particular times, and how one could work within these norms, or at their edges, to live out one's desires" (9).

66. In the urban world of Stratford, John Shakespeare was a citizen in this sense: a tanner and glover, he held many civic offices, including "ale taster (inspector of bread and malt), burgess (petty constable), affeeror (assessor of fines), city chamberlain (treasurer), alderman, and high bailiff of the town—the highest municipal office in Stratford" (Bevington, *Complete Works,* l).
67. See, for example, the title of Margaret Scott's essay on marriage law in the play: "'Our Cities' Institutions."
68. Examples include the Magna Carta (1215); the Petition of Right (1628); the "declarations" and "grievances" of the Stamp Act Congress (1765), which reasserted the right to petition included in the English Bill of Rights of 1689; and the Declaration of Independence (1776). The constitutional crisis in France was precipitated by the King's need to convene the Estates General in 1789, a "convention" or assembling of representatives that included their petitions. For relevant summaries and excerpts of the English and American documents, see John J. Patrick, *The Bill of Rights: A History in Documents* (New York: Oxford University Press, 2003); for French documents, see Jack Censer and Lynn Hunt, *Liberty, Equality, Fraternity: Exploring the French Revolution* (University Park: Pennsylvania State University Press, 2001); and Lynn Hunt, *The French Revolution and Human Rights: A Brief Documentary History* (New York: Bedford/ St. Martins, 1996).
69. See Richard Dutton, *Jacobean Civic Pageants* (Staffordshire: Keele University Press, 1995), 19, 73–74. Other relevant tableaux included the allegorical portrait of Unanimity, or CONSENSUS, "intimating that even the smallest and weakest aids, by consent, are made strong: herself personifying the unanimity, or consent of soul, in all inhabitants of the City to his service" (45).
70. Brian Gibbons, ed., *Measure for Measure,* by William Shakespeare (Cambridge: Cambridge University Press, 1991), 12n, 12.
71. Gordon Kipling analyzes Richard II's reconciliation with London in 1392 (*Enter the King,* 11–12), and develops with great effect the use of Advent imagery to charge the political entry of monarchs throughout Europe with the sublime light of the Epiphany.
72. For an important earlier articulation of the "King James Version" of *Measure for Measure,* see Bennett, *Measure for Measure as Royal Entertainment.* Other more recent interventions in this vein include Stephen Cohen, "From Mistress to Master: Political Transition and Formal Conflict in *Measure for Measure,*" *Criticism* 41, no. 4 (fall 199): 431–64; Louise Halper, "*Measure for Measure:* Law, Prerogative, Subversion," *Cardozo Studies in Law and Literature* 13, no. 2 (fall 2001): 221–64; Jane Malmo, "Beheading the Dead: Rites of Habeas Corpus in Shakespeare's *Measure for Measure,*" *New Formations* 35 (fall 1998): 135–44; and Debora Shuger, *Political Theologies in Shakespeare's England: The Sacred and the State in Measure for Measure* (Hounsmills, Hampshire: Palgrave, 2001).
73. Kahn, "Romance of Contract," 521–32.
74. Compare Gillian Brown on the special bond between political consent and femininity in the Lockean tradition: "Indeed, consent relies upon the presence of the disenfranchised, who mark the condition from which a consensual society distinguishes itself. So long as consent operates, consent recalls the unentitled. The image of imperiled women informs and accompanies consent as long as the unequal status of women persists" (*Consent of the Governed,* 14).

75. Patrick, *Bill of Rights,* 15–29.
76. Laurie Shannon, *Sovereign Amity: Figures of Friendship in Shakespearean Contexts* (Chicago: University of Chicago Press, 2002), 57, 3.
77. Winkler, "Ephebes' Song," 10–11.
78. Tyrrell and Bennett, *Recapturing Sophocles' "Antigone,"* 29–30.
79. "Antigone entered by one of the gangways the spectators used to enter the theater not long before. In this way, everyone in the theater—officials, spectators, and actors—comes from the same place, the city, to reflect on its common concerns, both real and imagined" (Tyrrell and Bennett, *Recapturing Sophocles' "Antigone,"* 29).
80. From the final strophe of the second Choral ode: "When he honors the laws of the land and the gods' sworn right / high indeed is his city [*hupsipolis*]; but stateless [*apolis*] the man / who dares to dwell with dishonor. Not by my fire [*parestios*], / never to share my thoughts, who does these things" (369–72).
81. On this point, Jonathan Goldberg writes, "Plays performed at court were always drawn from the public repertory, and there is no example of a play written for court" ("Social Texts, Royal Measures," in *Critical Essays on Shakespeare's Measure for Measure,* ed. Richard P. Wheeler, 32 [New York: G. K. Hall, 1999]).

CHAPTER 6 ✸ Creature Caliban

1. See Auerbach on *figura:* "[T]his peculiar formation expresses something living and dynamic, incomplete and playful . . . the notion of the new manifestation, the changing aspect, of the permanent runs through the whole history of the word" (Auerbach, "Figura," 12).
2. *Creatura* does not appear in the *Oxford Latin Dictionary.* In Charlton Lewis and Charles Short, the following entry traces the first uses of the word to the Patristic period: "*creatura, ae,* f. [creo], only concr., a creature, thing created (late Lat.); Tertullian, Apologeticum 30; Prudentius, Ham. [?] 508: omnes creaturae tuae, Vulg. Tob. 8,7.—II. The creation: Deus caelorum et Dominus totius creaturae, Vulg. Jud. 9,17: Dei, id. Apoc. 3,14 al." (Charlton T. Lewis and Charles Short, *Latin Dictionary* [Oxford: Clarendon Press, 1962]).
3. See *The Oxford English Dictionary,* 5th ed., s.v. "creature" (1b); cf. Rom 1:25.
4. Ibid., (2).
5. Ibid., (4). In *The Tempest,* Prospero activates this sense when he tells Miranda that Antonio "new created / The creatures that were mine" (1.2.81–82).
6. Stephen Greenblatt, *Learning to Curse: Essays in Early Modern Culture* (New York: Routledge, 1990), 26.
7. See Agamben, *Homo Sacer:* "*The originary relation of law to life is not application but Abandonment.* The matchless potential of the *nomos, its originary 'force of law,'* is that it holds life in its ban by abandoning it" (29).
8. For a sensitive and eloquent rendering of the universalist approach, see Harry Berger Jr.'s assessment of Caliban: "[H]e *stands for* the world; a handy and compact symbol of human nature, not as we know it, but as we might have found it at the beginning of time" ("Miraculous Harp: A Reading of Shakespeare's *Tempest,*" in *William Shakespeare's "The Tempest,"* ed. Harold Bloom, 18 [New York: Chelsea House, 1988]). Psychoanalysis comprises the most vital current strain of the universalist approach; see Meredith Skura's psychoanalytic

critique of culturalist readings, "Discourse and the Individual: The Case of Colonialism in *The Tempest*," *Shakespeare Quarterly* 40, no. 1 (1989): 42–74. Her essay explicitly thematizes the polarization between universalizing and particularizing interpretations. The culturalist view is perhaps best represented by the work of Stephen Greenblatt, *(Learning to Curse);* Paul Brown ("'This Thing of Darkness I Acknowledge Mine': *The Tempest* and the Discourse of Colonialism," in *William Shakespeare's "The Tempest,"* ed. Harold Bloom, 131–51 [New York: Chelsea House, 1988]), and Peter Hulme (*Colonial Encounters: Europe and the Native Caribbean, 1492–1797* [London: Methuen, 1986]), an itinerary recently revisited by Jonathan Goldberg (*Tempest in the Caribbean* [Minneapolis: University of Minnesota Press, 2004]). In a brief footnote, Goldberg takes an early version of this chapter to task for its "universalizing," normative, and theological biases. Although I have tried to stake out a position between the universal and the particular, Goldberg is certainly right that this means moving the discussion back toward the universal in response to the hegemony of the culturalist position in recent years. I hope that the current form of the chapter places additional emphasis on the political (as well as theological) traditions of universalism, and that my discussion of norms throughout the book indicates their creative rather than coercive character.

9. Franz Rosenzweig, *Der Stern der Erlösung* (Frankfurt am Main: Suhrkamp, 1993); trans. as *The Star of Redemption*, by William W. Hallo (Notre Dame: University of Notre Dame Press, 1970).
10. Benjamin, *German Tragic Drama*, 146.
11. Carl Schmitt, *Political Theology: Four Chapters on the Concept of Sovereignty*, trans. George Schwab (Cambridge, MA: MIT Press, 1985), 31–32, 46–47.
12. Benjamin, *German Tragic Drama*, 85.
13. Although New World readings of Caliban have become commonplace in current criticism, the Old World markers are the more insistent and self-evident in the play, and indeed have yielded some of the most promising strains in recent interpretation (e.g., Kim Hall, *Things of Darkness: Economies of Race and Gender in Early Modern England* [Ithaca, NY: Cornell University Press, 1995]). Ralph Hexter's analysis of the "Sidonian Dido" would also usefully illumine the Semitic (Punic and Arab) shadings of the play's Mediterranean world (in *Innovations of Antiquity*, ed. Ralph Hexter and Daniel Selden, 332–84 [New York: Routledge, 1992]). For a summary of the possible geographical coordinates of Caliban, see Alden and Virginia Vaughan, *Shakespeare's Caliban: A Cultural History* (Cambridge: Cambridge University Press, 1991), 23–55. I suggest a Sicilian locale because of the literary kinship between Caliban and Polyphemos, that island's Homeric inhabitant, as well as the later history of contestation and communication between Muslim and Christian forces in that region. Sicily was conquered by the Arabs between 827 and 902, but was reclaimed by Christian invaders later in the tenth century. Sicily's Norman rulers exercised some tolerance toward its Muslim population. A major geographical work, *The Book of Roger*, was written by a Muslim geographer in Sicily under the patronage of the Norman king Roger II in 1154 (see Bernard Lewis, *Muslim Discovery of Europe* [New York: W. W. Norton, 1982], 18, 20, 22, 147).
14. On the history of anti- and postcolonial readings of *The Tempest*, see Trevor Griffith, "'This Island's Mine': Caliban and Colonialism," *Yearbook of English Studies* 13 (1983): 159–80; and Goldberg, *Tempest in the Caribbean*
15. Stephen Orgel, ed., *The Tempest*, by William Shakespeare (Oxford: Oxford University Press, 1987).

16. *Adam,* "man" and "Adam," is linked to *adamah,* "country, earth, ground, husband [~man], [~ry], land." See the Hebrew dictionary in James Strong, ed., *Strong's New Exhaustive Concordance of the Bible* (Iowa Falls, IA: World Bible Publishers, 1980), 119–28.
17. For the play's systematic association of Caliban with muddy "bogs, fens, [and] flats" (2.2.60–61), see John Gillies, "Shakespeare's Virginian Masque," *English Literary History* (winter 1986): 684–85.
18. Rashi, *Chumash,* 1: 16. For a narrative amplification of Rashi, see Louis Ginzberg, *The Legends of the Jews,* vol. 1, *From the Creation to Jacob,* trans. Henrietta Szold (1909; reprint, Baltimore, MD: Johns Hopkins University Press, 1998), 23–24. For a contemporary analysis of Rashi's parable, see Avivah Gottlieb Zornberg, *Genesis: The Beginning of Desire* (Philadelphia, PA: Jewish Publication Society, 1995), 13–14.
19. Friedrich Nietzsche, *On the Genealogy of Morals and Ecce Homo,* trans. Walter Kaufmann (New York: Random House, 1967), 70.
20. Critics have often commented on Caliban's privileged relation to the beauty of the island. See Berger, "Miraculous Harp," 17, and Gillies, "Shakespeare's Virginian Masque," 702.
21. It is worth noting that, if "hurricane" is indeed the unspoken New World coinage behind the play's opening storm, as Peter Hulme has suggested, its transcription of "Huracan," Mayan god of storms, opens onto a world in which rain took both creative and destructive forms, and played a major role in the successive creation and destruction of the orders of the world. See the Mayan epic, *Popol Vuh: The Mayan Book of the Dawn of Life,* trans. and ed. Dennis Tedlock, rev. ed. (New York: Simon and Schuster, 1996). It would be a fascinating project to compare conceptions of creation in *The Tempest* and the *Popol Vuh.*
22. This is the emphasis given the story of the Flood in the Renaissance's greatest treatment of it, Michelangelo's Sistine Chapel fresco, in which salvation on the ark unfolds far in the background, and the state of emergency brought about by natural disaster dominates the foreground. As Howard Hibbard remarks, "We see brother attacking brother in order to survive, and elsewhere we see examples of what Michelangelo thought of primitive life and instincts " an interest that was common in Florence around 1500. Mothers and children, fathers and sons, husbands and wives are shown *in extremis,* saving and clutching, fighting and pushing. Yet one woman calmly saves her belongings amidst the rout. Noah, the chosen man, is seated up in his ark in the far distance: what we witness is the effect of God's wrath" (*Michelangelo,* 2nd ed. [New York: Harper and Row, 1974], 132). See also Don Cameron Allen on the history of Noah iconography, including Michelangelo's humanist treatment (*The Legend of Noah: Renaissance Rationalism in Art, Science, and Letters* [Urbana: University of Illinois Press, 1949]).
23. See Northrop Frye: "The masque has about it the freshness of Noah's new world, after the tempest had receded and the rainbow promised that seedtime and harvest should not cease" (*Spiritus Mundi: Essays on Literature, Myth, and Society* [1976; reprint, Bloomington: University of Indiana Press, 1983], 63). The rabbis imagined the world before the Flood as an Eden spoiled by its own plenty: "The wantonness of this generation was in a measure due to the ideal conditions under which mankind lived before the flood. They knew neither toil nor care, and as a consequence of their extraordinary prosperity they grew insolent" (Ginzberg, *Legends of the Jews,* 1: 152).
24. For example, the *Requerimiento,* the document used by the Spaniards before battling the Indians, begins with a statement of common humanity: "[T]he Lord our God, living and eternal, created the heaven and the earth, and one man and one woman, of whom you and we, and all the men of the world, were and are descendants, as well as those who come after

us" (in *The Spanish Tradition in America,* trans. and ed. Charles Gibson, 58 [Columbia: University of South Carolina Press, 1968]).

25. Suzanne Last Stone, "The Jewish Tradition and Civil Society," in *Alternative Conceptions of Civil Society,* ed. Simone Chambers and Will Kymlicka, 161 (Princeton, NJ: Princeton University Press, 2002).
26. The Hebrew *goyim* is translated as *ethne* in Greek and *gentes* in Latin. The original Hebrew word does not have pejorative connotations (unlike its modern Yiddish equivalent), but in the plural, it does tend to be used of "other nations," that is, nations other than Israel. In the Christian tradition (e.g., Paul), *ethne* generally refers to the nations of the world united in Christ. The Table of Nations introduces the word *goyim* into the discourse of the Bible; as the JPS commentary notes, "Hitherto, all such accounts in Genesis have related to individuals. Now we are given a genealogy of nations" (*JPS Torah Commentary,* 1: 67). This newly divided world is "of one language and one speech" (Gen 11:1), but Babel will be built and destroyed shortly after (Gen 11). On the relation between the Table of Nations and the story of Babel that follows it (with reference to the passages' conflicted legacy of universalism), see Robert Alter's commentary on Genesis, *Genesis: Translation and Commentary* (New York: W. W. Norton, 1996), 42–45.
27. On the role of Ham's curse in the justification of African slavery in Judaism, Christianity, and Islam, see Robin Blackburn, *The Making of New World Slavery: From the Baroque to the Modern, 1492–1800* (London: Verso, 1997), 64–76. In Louis Ginzberg's synthetic redaction of the midrashic tradition, the curse of blackness is tied to Ham's intercourse on the ark, while the enslavement of his progeny occurs as a consequence of viewing his father naked (*Legends of the Jews,* 1: 166–67).
28. On *The Tempest*'s extensive borrowing from the *Aeneid,* see for example Donna B. Hamilton, *Virgil and "The Tempest": The Politics of Imitation* (Columbus: Ohio State University Press, 1990).
29. On the swarming quality of mere creatures, see Zornberg, *Genesis,* 7–14.
30. Rashi, *Chumash,* 1: 5.
31. So too, in Genesis, only humanity is specifically created as "male and female"; sexual difference appears to be a dimension of specifically *human* being that separates man and woman from other creatures. The JPS commentary notes: "No such sexual differentiation is noted in regard to animals. Human sexuality is of a wholly different order from that of the beast" (*The JPS Torah Commentary,* vol. 1, *Genesis* 13).
32. Citing Vico, Greenblatt writes, "Each language reflects and substantiates the specific character of the culture out of which it springs" (*Learning to Curse,* 32).
33. On the genealogy of the phrase "the pursuit of happiness" in Locke, George Mason, Francis Hutcheson, and others, see Garry Wills, *Inventing America: Jefferson's Declaration of Independence* (Garden City, NY: Doubleday, 1978), 244–55.

CHAPTER 7 ✷ Samson Dagonistes

1. Schmitt, *Political Theology,* 5.
2. Ibid., 31–32.
3. Benjamin, *German Tragic Drama,* 65, 238n.
4. Ibid., 85.
5. Ibid., 121.

6. Victoria Kahn, "Political Theology and Reason of State in *Samson Agonistes," South Atlantic Quarterly* 99, no. 4 (fall 1996): 1066.
7. Sharon Achinstein, "*Samson Agonistes* and the Politics of Memory," in *Altering Eyes: New Perspectives on Samson Agonistes,* ed. Mark R. Kelley and Joseph Wittreich, 182 (Newark: University of Delaware Press, 2002).
8. See Achinstein, "Politics of Memory," for a fuller account of Milton's *Samson* as an elaboration of historical trauma.
9. Northrop Frye, among others, has argued for Samson as a type of Christ (*Spiritus Mundi,* 217). F. Michael Krouse provides a monograph in support of the typological reading. Joseph Wittreich has offered a controversial counter-reading of Milton's Samson as a type of Satan (*Interpreting Samson Agonistes* [Princeton, NJ: Princeton University Press, 1986]). Wood develops Wittreich's argument in a different direction by insisting on Samson as "an emblematic or iconic embodiment of [Milton's] vision of Old Testament consciousness: the state of religion under the Law, rigorous, incomplete, enslaved, literalistic, and uncomprehending" (*"Exiled from Light": Divine Law, Morality, and Violence in Milton's Samson Agonistes* [Toronto: University of Toronto Press, 2000], xx).
10. See the essay entitled "Critique of Violence" in Walter Benjamin's *Reflections,* ed. Peter Demetz, trans. Edmund Jephcott, 278 (New York: Harvest, 1978).
11. John Milton, *Paradise Lost,* bk. 7, ll. 505–10, in *Complete Poems and Major Prose,* 173–469. Hereafter cited parenthetically in the text by book and line numbers, with the abbreviation *PL.*
12. Satan first spies Adam and Eve in an encyclopedic landscape that contains them as its ennobling exemplars: "the Fiend / Saw undelighted all delight, all kind / Of living Creatures new to sight and strange: / Two of far nobler shape erect and tall" (*PL* 4: 285–88).
13. John Milton, *Samson Agonistes,* ll. 22–23, in *Complete Poems and Major Prose,* 549–93. Hereafter cited parenthetically by line number in the text.
14. In a forthcoming essay on *Samson,* Brendan Quigley has powerfully explored the phenomenology of Samson's decision to forgive Dalila, a decision that involves first rejecting forgiveness as a principle or criterion of judgment: "Sacrificing the ethical principle that forces one to forgive at least opens up the possibility of his making an authentic decision about forgiveness" ("Milton's Conception of Heroism in *Samson Agonistes," English Literary History* [forthcoming]). When Samson does forgive her, it is, crucially for Quigley, *at a distance:* "Forgiveness at a distance is forgiveness at the limit of forgiveness"—another way of stating the solitariness of the creature deprived of helpmeet.
15. Benjamin, *German Tragic Drama,* 146–47.
16. John Milton, *Prose Writings,* ed. K. M. Burton (London: Dent, 1958), 279.
17. In his "strong reading" of Paul's dictate that it is better to marry than to burn, Milton identifies this fire not with physical lust, but with the yearning for marital conversation: "What is it then but that desire which God put into Adam in Paradise, before he knew the sin of incontinence; that desire which God saw it was not good that man should be left alone to burn in; the desire and longing to put off an unkindly solitariness by uniting another body, but not without a fit soul to his, in the cheerful society of wedlock? Which if it were so needful before the fall, when man was much more perfect in himself, how much more is it needful now against all the sorrows and casualties of this life, to have an intimate and speaking help, a ready and reviving associate in marriage?" (*Prose Writings,* 264).
18. Bablyonlian Talmud, cited in Jeffrey Shoulson, *Milton and the Rabbis: Hebraism, Hellenism, and Christianity* (New York: Columbia University Press, 2001), 254.

19. Milton, *Prose Writings*, 268.
20. Editor Merritt Y. Hughes cites "J. C. Ransom's view in *God without Thunder* (1931), pp. 133–34, that the forbidden fruit symbolizes applied science, which makes Eve's plea foreshadow the sophistries of modern efficiency experts" (Milton, *Complete Poems and Major Prose*, 383n).
21. For a different, more historicist reading of labor in *Samson*, see Blair Hoxby, "At the Public Mill of the Philistines: *Samson Agonistes* and the Problem of Work after the Restoration," in Kelley and Wittreich, *Altering Eyes*, 281–306.
22. Zornberg, *Genesis*, 7–14.
23. Lacan, *Four Fundamental Concepts*, 165.
24. On echoes of *Paradise Lost* in the figure of the prostrate Samson, see for example Wood, *"Exiled from Light,"* xxi–xxii.
25. Agamben, *Homo Sacer*, 29.
26. French *ban* means a "proclamation, publication, summons, proscription, outlawry, banishment, assemblage of military vassals (*The Oxford English Dictionary*, 5th ed., s.v. "ban."), crossing from the positive sense of a public summons or proclamation to the negative sense of an interdiction, excommunication, or curse. To abandon is both to subjugate absolutely (to one's own control or authority) and to give up absolutely (to the jurisdiction of another); see *The Oxford English Dictionary*, 5th ed., s.v. "abandon," I and II.
27. Emmanuel Levinas, *Otherwise Than Being or Beyond Essence*, trans. Alphonso Lingis (Dordrecht: Kluwer Academic Publishers, 1991), 113–14.
28. Wood, *"Exiled from Light,"* xx, xxii.
29. James Harrington, *Prerogative of Popular Government* (London: T. Brewster, 1658), 474. I am indebted to Graham Hammill for pointing out this passage to me.
30. J. Albert Soggin, *Judges: A Commentary*, trans. John Bowden (London: SCM Press, 1981), 2, 3. Leslie Hoppe provides an excursus on charismatic leadership in Judges (*Joshua, Judges, with an Excursus on Charismatic Leadership in Israel* [Wilmington, DE: Michael Glazier, 1982], 213–16). More recently, Raphael Falco, in *Charismatic Authority in Early Modern English Tragedy* (Baltimore, MD: Johns Hopkins University Press, 2000) has examined the relevance of charismatic rule to Milton's *Samson*. Other biblical scholars suggest a more traditional role for the judges; for example, "[T]he 'judges' of the pre-monarchic period in Israel were local leaders and rulers functioning against the changing social and political background of the times" (James Martin, *The Book of Judges* [Cambridge: Cambridge University Press, 1975], 13).
31. Soggin, *Judges: A Commentary*, 3. See Michael Walzer, Menachem Lorberbaum, and Noam J. Zohar, eds., *The Jewish Political Tradition*, vol. 1, *Authority* (New Haven, CT: Yale University Press, 2000), 110. Samuel, the last of the judges and Israel's first "kingmaker," describes to the people the systematic stripping of privileges that kingship will necessarily institute, but they nonetheless choose to "have a king over us, that we also may be like other nations" (RSE, 1 Samuel 8:10–20). Israel will cease to be a political exception among the nations that surround it, and its institution of the exception—the rule of judges—will cede to that of the kings. See the excellent commentary on 1 Samuel 8 provided by Allan Silver in Walzer et al., *Jewish Political Tradition*, 1: 122–26.
32. Hoppe, *Joshua, Judges*, 110–11.
33. Harrington, *Prerogative of Popular Government*, 474.
34. Hoppe, *Joshua, Judges*, 215.
35. Locke, *Two Treatises*, 340.

36. Martin, *Book of Judges,* 1; A. Cohen, *Joshua and Judges: Hebrew Text and English Commentary* (London: Soncino Press, 1967), 154.
37. Wood, *"Exiled from Light."*
38. In this, he resembles Benjamin's baroque melancholic, "secured by immersion in the life of creaturely things, and . . . hear[ing] nothing of the voice of revelation" (*German Tragic Drama,* 152).
39. Milton, "Argument" to *Samson Agonistes,* in *Complete Poems,* 551.
40. Graham Hammill, "'The ruine of a multitude': Marlowe and Radical Political Thought" (paper presented at the annual meeting of the Modern Language Association, 2003), 1.
41. Soggin writes that the Hebrew words translated as judge, judges, and judging *(shofet, shoftim, shapat)* "are used in the book for two types of persons: the so-called 'major judges' . . . and the so-called 'minor' judges. However, these are people who are never associated with any function of judgment or arbitration: in fact the 'major' judges have a specifically military role, and sometimes also act as civil leaders." Soggin goes on to establish the etymological background to the priority of military leadership over judicial judgment in the text (*Judges: A Commentary,* 2–3).
42. Stanley Fish, "Spectacle and Evidence in *Samson Agonistes,*" *Critical Inquiry* (spring 1989): 579; Kahn, "Political Theology," 1086.
43. Kahn notes Schmitt's interest in Benjamin in the context of her reading of Samson ("Political Theology," 1066, 1091n).
44. Benjamin, *Reflections,* 298.
45. See Benjamin's essay entitled "Critique of Violence," in *Reflections,* where he associates foundational or law-making violence with the natural law tradition (which places itself beyond or above mere positive law, which forbids such violence), and law-enforcing violence with positive law, concerned with maintaining a particular legal order.
46. Benjamin, *Reflections,* 300.
47. On judge as deliverer, see Soggin, *Judges: A Commentary,* 3. For a theological reading of deliverance (as an alternative to the economy implied by "redemption") in *Samson,* see John Rogers, "Delivering Redemption in *Samson Agonistes,*" in Kelley and Wittreich, *Altering Eyes,* 72–97.
48. Benjamin, *German Tragic Drama,* 86.
49. Kahn, "Political Theology," 1643.
50. See Fish, "Spectacle and Evidence," 579.
51. Falco, *Charismatic Authority,* 153.
52. Lacan, *Ethics of Psychoanalysis,* 270–87.
53. Arendt writes, "By pressing men against each other, total terror destroys the space between them; compared to the condition within its iron band, even the desert of tyranny, insofar as it is still some kind of space, appears like a guarantee of freedom. . . . [Totalitarianism] destroys the one essential prerequisite of all freedom, which is simply the capacity of motion which cannot exist without space" (*Origins of Totalitarianism,* 466).
54. Dennis Kezar, "Samson's Death by Theatre and Milton's Art of Dying," *English Literary History* 66, no. 2 (1999): 295–336.
55. Benjamin, *German Tragic Drama,* 74–76.
56. Hammill, "Ruine of a multitude," 4, 5.
57. Wood, *"Exiled from Light,"* 33.
58. Kahn, "Political Theology," 1082.
59. See Lupton, *Afterlives,* 43–44.

60. Kahn, "Political Theology," 1088.
61. Again, I am relying here on Hammill's powerful account of the multitude in Marlowe ("'The ruine of a multitude'").
62. Ibid., 4.
63. Benjamin, *Reflections,* 312. The triad "redeems, completes, creates" may recall Rosenzweig's star of redemption, constellated by the movements of Creation, Revelation, and Redemption (see his *Star of Redemption*). The lines from Benjamin cited above appear, appropriately, in an essay in his *Reflections* called "Theological-Political Fragment."
64. Hammill, "'The ruine of a multitude,'" 13.
65. On Shakespeare and normativity, I am indebted to new work by Lars Engle, who proposes "to look at how particular moments in particular plays treat norms. This amounts to an attempt to articulate the complexity of Shakespeare's handling of normativity" ("Shakespearean Normativity," forthcoming).

EPILOGUE

1. Lacan, *Ethics of Psychoanalysis,* 101–14
2. Lisa Freinkel has coined the term *addressivity,* on the model of *aggressivity,* to capture the dynamics of address (of a sacred text's forceful address to its reader) in Augustinian hermeneutics (*Shakespeare's Will: The Theology of Figure from Augustine to the Sonnets* [New York: Columbia University Press, 2001], 60–68).
3. Philip Lorenz has written suggestively on Shakespeare, Almodóvar, and sovereignty ("The Tears of Sovereignty," PhD diss., New York University). Other cinematic instantiations of the citizen-saint include the complex meditations on national identity, social organization, and private desire conducted in the films of Krystof Keiślowski. See both his late-Communist Manifesto, the brilliant ten-part television series *Dekalog* (1988), and his requiem for the new Europe, the trilogy *Trois Colours* (1994). Sifting subjective positions out of the chance crossings of religious and political iconographies, Keiślowski's films represent the late flowering of some of the same typological impulses that animate the public space of Shakespeare's plays. On the films of Keiślowski, see especially Slavoj Žižek, *The Fright of Real Tears: Krysztof Keiślowski between Theory and Post-Theory* (London: British Film Institute, 2001).
4. This epilogue draws on my work with public schools, especially Humanities Out There, an educational partnership between the School of Humanities and the Santa Ana Unified School District, but also my participation in a number of kindred projects, including UCI's California History–Social Science Project; the Teachers as Scholars program sponsored by the Woodrow Wilson National Fellowship Foundation; UCI's Summer Masters program for high school teachers; the Yale–New Haven Teachers Institute; and Imagining America: Artists and Scholars in Public Life.
5. Jean-Luc Nancy, "Myth Interrupted," in *The Inoperative Community,* ed. Peter Connor, trans Peter Connor et al. (Minneapolis: University of Minnesota Press, 1991). Myth, Nancy writes further, is "the poeticity of the political and the politicality of the poetic" ("Myth Interrupted," 56).
6. On literature as the break from myth, see again Nancy: "But the share of myth and the share of literature are not two separable and opposable parts at the heart of the work. Rather, they are shares in the sense that community divides up or shares out work in differ-

ent ways: now by way of myth, now by way of literature. The second is the interruption of the first" ("Myth Interrupted," 63).

7. Richard Seaford, *Reciprocity and Ritual: Homer and Tragedy in the Developing City-State* (Oxford: Oxford University Press, 1994), 342.
8. See William Blake Tyrrell and Frieda S. Brown, *Athenian Myths and Institutions: Words in Action* (New York: Oxford University Press, 1991), 134–35; Seaford, *Reciprocity and Ritual*, 113. For a public application of this zoning experiment, see Ralph Rosen, "Classical Studies and the Search for Community," 177.
9. Tyrrell and Bennett, *Athenian Myths*, 134.
10. J. G. A. Pocock, "The Ideal of Citizenship since Classical Times," in *The Citizenship Debates*, ed. Gershon Shafir, 34 (Minneapolis: University of Minnesota Press, 1998).
11. Ibid., 37. For a helpful summary of the civic humanism debate in relation to current classroom practice in the humanities, see Rebecca Bushnell, *A Culture of Teaching: Early Modern Humanism in Theory and Practice* (Ithaca, NY: Cornell University Press, 1996), 196.
12. Jürgen Habermas, "Three Normative Models of Democracy," in *Democracy and Difference: Contesting the Boundaries of the Political*, ed. Seyla Benhabib, 25 (Princeton, NJ: Princeton University Press, 1996).
13. For the critique of Habermas, see especially Oskar Negt and Alexander Kluge, *The Public Sphere and Experience* (Minneapolis: University of Minnesota Press, 1993). For interpretations of Habermas in response to this critique, see, for example, Bruce Robbins, ed., *The Phantom Public Sphere* (Minneapolis: University of Minnesota Press, 1993); and Michael Warner, *Publics and Counterpublics* (New York: Zone Books, 2002). On Habermas and theology, see Don Browning and Francis Schüssler Fiorenza, eds., *Habermas, Modernity, and Public Theology* (New York: Crossroads, 1992).
14. In both Habermas's writings and in ordinary speech, "deliberation" means public reasoning, but it also orients reasoning toward the moment of decision that brings the process of deliberation to a close. Thus Habermas will use "deliberation" in parallel with "decision-making": for example, "Discourse theory takes elements from both sides (liberalism and civic republicanism) and integrates these in the concept of an ideal procedure for *deliberation and decision-making*" ("Three Normative Models" 26; emphasis added). I am interested in isolating the decisionist moment in Habermas's model of deliberation.
15. Seyla Benhabib, *Democracy and Difference: Contesting the Boundaries of the Political* (Princeton, NJ: Princeton University Press, 1996), 9. Habermas states his position on citizenship and culture as follows: "Democratic citizenship need not be rooted in the national identity of a people. However, regardless of the diversity of different cultural forms of life, it does require that every citizen be socialized into a common political culture" (*Between Facts and Norms: Contributions to a Discourse Theory of Law and Democracy*, trans. William Rehg [Cambridge, MA: MIT Press, 1999], 500).
16. Will Kymlicka, "Territorial Borders: A Liberal Egalitarian Perspective," in *Boundaries and Justice: Diverse Ethical Perspectives*, ed. David Miller and Sohail H. Hashmi, 259 (Princeton, NJ: Princeton University Press, 2001).
17. On Shakespeare and civic culture after the Renaissance, see for example Thomas Cartelli, *Repositioning Shakespeare: National Formations, Postcolonial Appropriations* (London and New York: Routledge, 1999); John Joughin, ed., *Shakespeare and National Culture* (Manchester, UK: Manchester University Press, 1997); and Harish Trivedi, *Colonial Transactions: English Literature and India* (Manchester, UK: Manchester University Press, 1996).

18. On Shakespeare's "multicultural plays," see for example Daniel Vitkus, *Turning Turk: English Theater and the Multicultural Mediterranean, 1570–1630* (New York: Palgrave Macmillan, 2003); and Imtiaz Habib, *Shakespeare and Race: Postcolonial Praxis in the Early Modern Period* (Lanham, MD: University Press of America, 2000).
19. Étienne Balibar, "Propositions on Citizenship," *Ethics* 98 (July 1988): 728.
20. Habermas, *Between Facts and Norms,* 495.
21. Aristotle defends, for example, the reform of Kleisthenes, which included enrolling in tribes "many metics, both strangers and slaves." Since a citizen is "defined by the fact of his holding some kind of rule or office" (and not, Aristotle insists throughout the treatise, by a natural tie to the land or to a family or culture), these newly created citizens must indeed be recognized as legitimate participants in the polis since they meet this minimal formal definition (*Politics* 1275b–1276a).
22. See Fredrick Miller, *Nature, Justice, and Rights in Aristotle's "Politics"* (Oxford: Oxford University Press, 1995): "Historically the term *politeia* (constitution) derived from *polites* (citizen) and originally had the meaning of 'citizenship' (see Herodotus IX.34.1), a connotation it also has in Aristotle (Pol. VII.9.1329a14)" (149).
23. On Aristotle as critic of democracy, and on the productive relation between Athenian democracy and the literature of its critique, see Josiah Ober, *The Athenian Revolution: Essays on Ancient Greek Democracy and Political Theory* (Princeton, NJ: Princeton University Press, 1996), 140–60.
24. See for example Michael Ryan: "To accept academic freedom as a rallying cry is tantamount to accepting a definition of the academy as a separable realm from the social world. . . . Instead of emphasizing the fact that the social world is constructed and that therefore it could be constructed in a different form, the liberal philosophy of academic freedom would make that world appear natural" ("Deconstruction and Pedagogy" 58; cited in Bushnell, *A Culture of Teaching,* 192).
25. See, for example, *Reading/Language Arts Framework for California Public Schools* (Sacramento: California Department of Education, 1999), which spells out the content standards mandated for language arts classrooms throughout California. A major strand is reading comprehension of "informational materials," which includes at various points in the educational pipeline "technical documents," "historically significant speeches," and "public documents."
26. The African Theatre, an African-American institution of antebellum New York, began its first season with a performance of *Richard III.* See William Over, "New York's African Theatre: Shakespeare Reinterpreted" (in *Shakespeare without Class,* ed. Donald Hedrick and Bryan Reynolds, 65–84 (New York: Palgrave, 2000); and Michael Warner's chapter on the African Theatre in *Publics and Counterpublics,* 225–68. Vaclav Havel published his short political writings, many of them occasional in nature, under the provocatively Pauline title, *Open Letters.* On Shakespeare and the new media, including film and the Internet, see especially the work of Richard Burt.
27. See Toby Miller and George Yúdice on literary education as a form of cultural policy: "Literature has been a central strut of public education, as a training in both language and norms. It embodies the public sphere by offering public discussion of the private life of the *bourgeoisie*" (*Cultural Policy* [London: Sage, 2002], 8–9). For a perspective on civic education that addresses the challenge of pluralism without reneging on the universal impulse of citizenship, see Will Kymlicka's chapter entitled "Education for Citizenship" in his book *Politics in the Vernacular* (Oxford: Oxford University Press, 2001).

BIBLIOGRAPHY

SCRIPTURAL WORKS

Jewish and Christian scriptures and traditional commentaries are cited from the following versions.

Genesis Rabbah. 2 vols. Trans. H. Freedman. London: Soncino Press, 1983.

Geneva Bible: The Annotated 1602 New Testament Edition. Ed. Gerald T. Sheppard. New York: Pilgrim Press, 1989.

The JPS Torah Commentary: The Traditional Hebrew Text with the New JPS Translation. General editor, Nahum M. Sarna. 5 vols. *Genesis*. Ed. Nahum M. Sarna. 1989. *Exodus*. Ed. Nahum M. Sarna. 1991. *Leviticus*. Ed. Baruch A. Levine. 1989. *Numbers*. Ed. Jacob Milgrom. 1990. *Deuteronomy*. Ed. Jeffrey H. Tigay. 1996. Philadelphia: Jewish Publication Society.

Meeks, Wayne A., ed. *The Writings of St. Paul*. New York: W. W. Norton, 1972.

The New Jerusalem Bible. Ed. Henry Wansbrough. New York: Doubleday, 1985.

The Oxford Annotated Bible. Revised Standard Edition. Ed. Herbert G. May and Bruce M. Metzger. New York: Oxford University Press, 1962.

Ramban (Nachmanides). *Commentary on the Torah*. 5 vols. Trans. and annotated Charles B. Chavel. New York: Shilo Publishing House, 1973.

Rashi. *Chumash with Targum Onkelos, Haphtaroth and Rashi's Commentary*. 5 vols. Ed. A. M. Silberman. Jerusalem: Feldheim, 1934.

Soncino Chumash: The Five Books of Moses with Haphtaroth. Ed. A. Cohen. London: Soncino Press, 1983.

Tractate Shubbath. Trans. Rabbi H. Freedman. Ed. Rabbi I. Epstein. London: Soncino Press, 1973.

GENERAL WORKS

Achinstein, Sharon. "*Samson Agonistes* and the Politics of Memory." In Kelley and Wittreich, *Altering Eyes*, 168–91.

Adelman, Janet. "Iago's Alter Ego: Race as Projection in *Othello*." *Representations* 48, no. 2 (1997): 125–44.

———. *Suffocating Mothers: Fantasies of Maternal Origin in Shakespeare's Plays*. New York: Routledge, 1992.

Aeschylus. *Aeschylus II: Suppliant Maidens, The Persians, Seven Against Thebes, Prometheus Bound*. Ed. David Grene and Richmond Lattimore. Chicago: University of Chicago Press, 1956.

Agamben, Giorgio. *Homo Sacer: Sovereign Power and Mere Life*. Trans. Daniel Heller-Roazen. Stanford, CA: Stanford University Press, 1998.

———. *Means without End*. Trans. Vincenzo Binetti and Cesare Casarino. Minneapolis: University of Minnesota Press, 2000.

———. *Le temps qui reste*. Trans. Judith Revel. Paris: Bibliothèque Rivages, 2000. Originally published as *Il tempo qui resta. Un commento alla "Lettera ai Romani."* (English translation forthcoming, Stanford University Press.)

Allen, Don Cameron. *The Legend of Noah: Renaissance Rationalism in Art, Science, and Letters.* Urbana: University of Illinois Press, 1949.

Alter, Robert. *Genesis: Translation and Commentary.* New York: W. W. Norton, 1996.

Anderson, Douglas. "The Old Testament Presence in *The Merchant of Venice.*" *English Literary History* 52 (spring 1985): 119–32.

Arendt, Hannah. *The Origins of Totalitarianism.* San Diego: Harcourt Brace, 1973. Orig. pub. 1948.

Aristotle. *Complete Works.* Revised Oxford Translation. 2 vols. Ed. Jonathan Barnes. Princeton, NJ: Princeton University Press, 1984.

Auerbach, Erich. "Figura." In *Scenes from the Drama of European Literature,* 11–76. Minneapolis: University of Minnesota Press, 1984. Orig. pub. in 1959.

Augustine. *Of Christian Doctrine.* Trans. D. W. Robertson. Indianapolis, IN: Bobbs-Merrill, 1958.

———. *The City of God.* Ed. David Knowles. Harmondsworth, UK: Penguin, 1972.

Badiou, Alain. *Saint Paul: La fondation de l'universalisme.* Paris: Presses Universitaires de France, 1997. Translated as *Saint Paul: The Foundation of Universalism,* by Ray Brassier. Stanford, CA: Stanford University Press, 2003.

Baldson, J. P. V. D. *Romans and Aliens.* London: Duckworth Press, 1979.

Balibar, Étienne. "Is There a Neo-Racism?" In *Race, Nation, Class: Ambiguous Identities,* ed. Étienne Balibar and Immanuel Wallerstein, 17–28. Trans. Chris Turner. London: Verso, 1991.

———. "Propositions on Citizenship." *Ethics* 98 (July 1988): 723–30.

———. *We the People of Europe: Reflections on Transnational Citizenship.* Trans. James Swenson. Princeton, NJ: Princeton University Press, 2004.

Banks, Robert. *Jesus and the Law in the Synoptic Tradition.* Cambridge: Cambridge University Press, 1975.

Barber, C. L. "The Merchants and the Jew of Venice: Wealth's Communion and an Intruder." In Barnet, *Twentieth-Century Interpretations of "The Merchant of Venice,"* 11–32.

Barnet, Sylvan. *Twentieth-Century Interpretations of "The Merchant of Venice."* Englewood Cliffs, NJ: Prentice Hall, 1970.

Bartels, Emily C. "Making More of the Moor: Aaron, Othello, and Renaissance Refashionings of Race." *Shakespeare Quarterly* 41 (winter 1990): 433–54.

———. *Spectacles of Strangeness: Imperialism, Alienation, and Marlowe.* Philadelphia: University of Pennsylvania Press, 1993.

Barthelemy, Anthony. *Black Face, Maligned Race: The Representation of Blacks in English Drama from Shakespeare to Southerne.* Baton Rouge: Louisiana State University Press, 1987.

Barton, Stephen C. "'All Things to All People': Paul and the Law in the Light of 1 Corinthians 9.19–23." In Dunn, *Paul and the Mosaic Law,* 271–85.

Benhabib, Seyla, ed. *Democracy and Difference: Contesting the Boundaries of the Political.* Princeton, NJ: Princeton University Press, 1996.

———. "The Democratic Moment and the Problem of Difference." In Benhabib, *Democracy and Difference,* 3–18.

Benjamin, Walter. *Origin of the German Tragic Drama.* Trans. John Osborne. London: New Left Books, 1963. Originally published in German as *Ursprung des deutschen Trauerspiels* (1925).

———. *Reflections.* Ed. Peter Demetz. Trans. Edmund Jephcott. New York: Harvest, 1978.

Bennett, Josephine Waters. *Measure for Measure as Royal Entertainment.* New York: Columbia University Press, 1966.

Berger, Harry, Jr. "Miraculous Harp: A Reading of Shakespeare's *Tempest*." In Bloom, *William Shakespeare's "The Tempest,"* 9–41.

Bernstein, Michael. *Ezra Pound and the Modern Verse Epic: The Tale of the Tribe*. Princeton, NJ: Princeton University Press, 1980.

Bertelli, Sergio. *The King's Body: Sacred Rituals of Power in Medieval and Early Modern Europe*. Trans. R. Burr Litchfield. University Park: Pennsylvania State University Press, 2001.

Bevington, David, ed. *Complete Works of William Shakespeare*. New York: Longman, 1997.

———. *From Mankinde to Marlow: Growth of Structure in the Popular Drama of Tudor England*. Cambridge, MA: Harvard University Press, 1962.

———. "Introduction." In *Othello,* by William Shakespeare, ed. David Bevington, ixx–xxxi. New York: Bantam Books, 1980.

Biberman, Matthew. *From Jew-Devil to Jew-Sissy*. Aldershot, Hampshire: Ashgate, 2005.

The Bible. See "Scriptural Works" at the beginning of the bibliography.

Biddick, Kathleen. *The Typological Imaginary: Circumcision, Technology, History*. Philadelphia: University of Pennsylvania Press, 2003.

Blackburn, Robin. *The Making of New World Slavery: From the Baroque to the Modern, 1492–1800*. London: Verso, 1997.

Bloom, Harold. *The Western Canon: The Books and the School of the Ages*. New York: Harcourt Brace, 1994.

———, ed. *William Shakespeare's "Measure for Measure."* New York: Chelsea House, 1987.

———, ed. *William Shakespeare's "The Tempest."* New York: Chelsea House, 1988. Orig. pub. in 1969.

———, ed. *Shylock*. New York: Chelsea House, 1991.

Bodin, Jean. *On Sovereignty*. Ed. Julian M. Franklin. Cambridge: Cambridge University Press, 1992.

Boose, Lynda. "'The Getting of a Lawful Race': Racial Discourse in Early Modern England and the Unrepresentable Black Woman." In Hendricks and Parker, *Women, "Race," and Writing*, 35–54.

———, and Richard Burt, eds. *Shakespeare, the Movie: Popularizing the Plays on Film, TV, and Video*. London: Routledge, 1997.

Boyarin, Daniel. *A Radical Jew: Paul and the Politics of Identity*. Berkeley and Los Angeles: University of California Press, 1994.

Bradbrook, M. C. "Authority, Truth and Justice in *Measure for Measure*." In Bloom, *William Shakespeare's "Measure for Measure,"* 7–21.

———. "Shakespeare's Recollections of Marlowe." In *Shakespeare's Styles,* ed. Philip Edwards, Inga-Stina Ewbank, and G. K. Hunter, 191–204. Cambridge: Cambridge University Press, 1980.

Braden, Gordon. *Renaissance Tragedy and the Senecan Tradition: Anger's Privilege*. New Haven, CT: Yale University Press, 1985.

Brown, Gillian. *The Consent of the Governed: The Lockean Legacy in Early American Culture*. Cambridge, MA: Harvard University Press, 2001.

Brown, Paul. "'This Thing of Darkness I Acknowledge Mine': *The Tempest* and the Discourse of Colonialism." In Bloom, *William Shakespeare's "The Tempest,"* 131–51.

Browning, Don S., and Francis Schüssler Fiorenza, eds. *Habermas, Modernity, and Public Theology*. New York: Crossroads, 1992.

Bruce, F. F. "Paul in Acts and Letters." In Hawthorne et al., *Dictionary of Paul,* 679–92.

Burt, Richard, ed. *Shakespeare after Mass Media*. New York: Palgrave, 2002.

———. *Unspeakable ShaXXXspeares: Queer Theory and American Kiddie Culture*. New York: St. Martin's Press, 1998.

———, and Lynda E. Boose, eds. *Shakespeare, the Movie II: Popularizing the Plays on Film, TV, Video, and DVD*. New York: Routledge, 2003.

Bushnell, Rebecca W. *A Culture of Teaching: Early Modern Humanism in Theory and Practice*. Ithaca, NY: Cornell University Press, 1996.

Butler, Judith. *Antigone's Claim: Kinship between Life and Death*. New York: Columbia University Press, 2000.

Calimani, Riccardo. *The Ghetto of Venice*. Trans. Katherine Silberblatt Wolfthal. New York: M. Evans, 1987.

Callaghan, Dympna. "Re-reading Elizabeth Cary's *The Tragedie of Mariam, Faire Queene of Jewry*." In Hendricks and Parker, *Women, "Race," and Writing*, 163–77.

Carmichael, Calum. *The Origins of Biblical Law: The Decalogues and the Book of the Covenant*. Ithaca, NY: Cornell University Press, 1992.

Cartelli, Thomas. *Marlowe, Shakespeare, and the Economy of Theatrical Experience*. Philadelphia: University of Pennsylvania Press, 1991.

———. *Repositioning Shakespeare: National Formations, Postcolonial Appropriations*. London and New York: Routledge, 1999.

———. "Shakespeare's *Merchant*, Marlowe's *Jew:* The Problem of Cultural Difference." *Shakespeare Studies* 20 (1988): 255–60.

Cavanaugh, William T. *Theopolitical Imagination*. London: T. and T. Clark, 2002.

Censer, Jack R., and Lynn Hunt. *Liberty, Equality, Fraternity: Exploring the French Revolution*. University Park: Pennsylvania State University Press, 2001.

Chambers, Simone, and Will Kymlicka, eds. *Alternative Conceptions of Civil Society*. Princeton, NJ: Princeton University Press, 2002.

Chaney, Joseph. "Othello's Jealousy and the Triangle of Desire." Unpublished lecture delivered at Indiana University, South Bend, March 1994.

———. *"Sport by sport o'erthrown": Shakespeare and the End of Comedy*. PhD diss. University of California, Irvine, 1993.

Charney, Maurice. "Jessica's Turquoise Ring and Abigail's Poisoned Porridge: Shakespeare and Marlowe as Rivals and Imitators." *Renaissance Drama* 10 (1979): 33–44.

Cheney, Patrick. *Marlowe's Counterfeit Profession: Ovid, Spenser, Counter-Nationhood*. Toronto: University of Toronto Press, 1997.

Chew, Samuel. *The Crescent and the Rose: Islam and England during the Renaissance*. 1937. Reprint, New York: Octagon Books, 1965.

Coghill, Neville. "The Theme of *The Merchant of Venice*." In Barnet, *Twentieth-Century Interpretations of "The Merchant of Venice,"* 108–13.

Cohen, A. *Joshua and Judges: Hebrew Text and English Commentary*. London: Soncino Press, 1967.

Cohen, Boaz. *Jewish and Roman Law: A Comparative Study*. 2 vols. New York: Jewish Theological Seminary, 1966.

Cohen, Hermann. *Religion of Reason Out of the Sources of Judaism*. Trans. Simon Kaplan. Atlanta: Scholars Press, 1995.

Cohen, Stephen. "From Mistress to Master: Political Transition and Formal Conflict in *Measure for Measure*." *Criticism* 41 (fall 1999): 431–64.

———. "'The Quality of Mercy': Law, Equity, and Ideology in *The Merchant of Venice*." *Mosaic* 27 (winter 1994): 35–54.

Colley, John Scott. "Launcelot, Jacob, and Esau: Old and New Law in *The Merchant of Venice.*" *Yearbook of English Studies* 10 (1980): 181–89.

Copjec, Joan. *Imagine There's No Woman: Ethics and Sublimation.* Cambridge, MA: MIT Press, 2002.

Crewe, Jonathan. "Out of the Matrix: Shakespeare and Race-Writing," *Yale Journal of Criticism* 8 (fall 1995): 13–29.

Crook, John. *Law and Life of Rome.* Ithaca, NY: Cornell University Press, 1967.

Cunningham, John, and Stephen Slimp. "The Less into the Greater: Emblem, Analogue, and Deification in *The Merchant of Venice.*" In Mahon and Mahon, *The Merchant of Venice,* 225–82.

Daniel, Norman. *Islam and the West: The Making of an Image.* Edinburgh: Edinburgh University Press, 1960.

Daube, David. *Ancient Jewish Law: Three Inaugural Lectures.* Leiden: E. J. Brill, 1981.

Davies, Alan, ed. *Antisemitism and the Foundations of Christianity.* New York: Paulist Press, 1979.

Davies, W. D. *Paul and Rabbinic Judaism: Some Rabbinic Elements in Pauline Theology.* 1948. Reprint, New York: Harper, 1967.

Davis, Robert C., and Benjamin Ravid, eds. *The Jews of Early Modern Venice.* Baltimore, MD: Johns Hopkins University Press, 2001.

Derrida, Jacques. *The Other Heading: Reflections on Today's Europe.* Trans. Pascale-Anne Brault and Michael B. Naas. Bloomington: Indiana University Press, 1992.

Dunn, James D. G. *Jesus, Paul, and the Law: Studies in Mark and Galatians.* Louisville, KY: Westminster / John Knox Press, 1990.

———, ed. *Paul and the Mosaic Law.* Grand Rapids, MI: William B. Eerdmans, 1996.

———. *Romans 1–8.* Dallas, TX: Word Books, 1988.

Dutton, Richard, ed. *Jacobean Civic Pageants.* Staffordshire, UK: Keele University Press, 1995.

Eberly, Don, and Ryan Streeter, eds. *The Essential Civil Society Reader.* Lanham, MD: Lexington Books, 2002.

The Eerdmans Bible Dictionary, Allen C. Myers, revision editor. Grand Rapids, MI: William B. Eerdmans, 1987.

Elazar, Daniel J. *Covenant and Commonwealth.* 2 vols. New Brunswick, NJ: Transaction, 1996.

Ellickson, Robert C. *Order without Law: How Neighbors Settle Disputes.* Cambridge, MA: Harvard University Press, 1991.

Elrod, John W. *Kierkegaard and Christendom.* Princeton, NJ: Princeton University Press, 1981.

Engle, Lars. "Shakespearean Normativity in *All's Well That Ends Well.*" Forthcoming in *Shakespeare Yearbook,* vol. 14, 2004.

———. "'Thrift Is Blessing': Exchange and Explanation in *The Merchant of Venice.*" *Shakespeare Quarterly* 37 (spring, 1986): 20–37.

Erikson, Peter. "Representations of Blacks and Blackness in the Renaissance." *Criticism* 34 (fall 1993): 499–527.

Euben, J. Peter. *Corrupting Youth: Political Education, Democratic Culture, and Political Theory.* Princeton, NJ: Princeton University Press, 1997.

———, ed. *Greek Tragedy and Political Theory.* Berkeley and Los Angeles: University of California Press, 1986.

Falco, Raphael. *Charismatic Authority in Early Modern English Tragedy.* Baltimore, MD: Johns Hopkins University Press, 2000.

Fiedler, Leslie. *The Stranger in Shakespeare.* New York: Stein and Day, 1972.

———. "'These Be Christian Husbands.'" In Bloom, *Shylock,* 63–90.

Filmer, Robert. *Patriarcha and Other Political Works*. Ed. Peter Laslett. NY: Garland, 1984.
Finley, M. I. *The World of Odysseus*. NY: Viking Press, 1954.
Fish, Stanley. "Spectacle and Evidence in *Samson Agonistes*." *Critical Inquiry* (spring 1989): 556–86.
Fletcher, Angus. *The Prophetic Moment: An Essay on Spenser*. Chicago: University of Chicago Press, 1971.
Fraser, Russell A., and Norman Rabkin, eds. *Drama of the English Renaissance: The Tudor Period*. New York: Macmillan, 1976.
Freinkel, Lisa. *Shakespeare's Will: The Theology of Figure from Augustine to the Sonnets*. New York: Columbia University Press, 2001.
Freud, Sigmund. *Standard Edition of the Complete Psychological Works of Sigmund Freud*. 24 vols. Trans. James Strachey. London: Hogarth Press, 1974.
Frye, Northrop. *Anatomy of Criticism: Four Essays*. Princeton, NJ: Princeton University Press, 1957.
———. *Spiritus Mundi: Essays on Literature, Myth, and Society*. 1976. Reprint, Bloomington: University of Indiana Press, 1983.
Gadamer, Hans-Georg. *Truth and Method*. New York: Crossroad, 1989.
Gager, John G. *Reinventing Paul*. Oxford: Oxford University Press, 2000.
Galinksy, Karl. *The Herakles Theme*. Oxford: Oxford University Press, 1972.
Gardner, Jane. *Being a Roman Citizen*. London: Routledge, 1993.
Gibbons, Brian, ed. *Measure for Measure*, by William Shakespeare. Cambridge: Cambridge University Press, 1991.
Gillies, John. "Shakespeare's Virginian Masque." *English Literary History* (winter 1986): 673–707.
Ginzberg, Louis. *The Legends of the Jews*. Vol. 1 *From the Creation to Jacob*. Trans. Henrietta Szold. 1909. Reprint, Baltimore, MD: Johns Hopkins University Press, 1998.
Girard, René. "'To Entrap the Wisest.'" In Bloom, *Shylock*, 291–301.
Gless, Darryl J. *Measure for Measure, the Law, and the Convent*. Princeton, NJ: Princeton University Press, 1979.
Gnuse, Robert. *Thou Shall Not Steal: Community and Property in the Biblical Tradition*. Maryknoll: Orbis Books, 1985.
Goddard, Harold C. "Portia's Failure." In Bloom, ed., *Shylock*, 27–36. Orig. pub. in 1951.
Godshalk, William Leigh. *The Marlovian World Picture*. The Hague: Mouton, 1974.
Goldberg, Jonathan. "Social Texts, Royal Measures." In Wheeler, *Critical Essays on Shakespeare's Measure for Measure*, 31–40.
———. *Tempest in the Caribbean*. Minneapolis: University of Minnesota Press, 2004.
Goodman, Martin, ed. *Jews in a Graeco-Roman World*. Oxford: Clarendon Press, 1998.
Gramsci, Antonio. *Selections from Cultural Writings*. Ed. David Forgacs and Geoffrey Nowell-Smith. Trans. William Boelhower. Cambridge, MA: Harvard University Press, 1985.
Greenblatt, Stephen J. *Learning to Curse: Essays in Early Modern Culture*. New York: Routledge, 1990.
———. "Marlowe, Marx, and Anti-Semitism." *Critical Inquiry* 5 (1978): 291–307.
———. *Renaissance Self-Fashioning from More to Shakespeare*. Chicago: University of Chicago Press, 1980.
Griffin, Eric. "Un-Sainting James: Or, Othello and the 'Spanish Spirits' of Shakespeare's Globe." *Representations* 62 (spring, 1998): 58–99.
Griffith, Trevor. "'This Island's Mine': Caliban and Colonialism." *Yearbook of English Studies* 13 (1983): 159–80.
Gross, John. *Shylock: A Legend and Its Legacy*. New York: Touchstone, 1992.

Habermas, Jürgen. "Three Normative Models of Democracy." In Benhabib, *Democracy and Difference*, 21–30.

———. *Between Facts and Norms: Contributions to a Discourse Theory of Law and Democracy.* Trans. William Rehg. Cambridge, MA: MIT Press, 1999.

Habib, Imtiaz. *Shakespeare and Race: Postcolonial Praxis in the Early Modern Period.* Lanham, MD: University Press of America, 2000.

Hakluyt, Richard. *Principle Navigations, Voyages, Traffiques, and Discoveries of the English Nation.* 12 vols. Glasgow: MacLehose and Sons, 1904. Orig. pub. in 1600.

Halio, Jay L. *The Merchant of Venice: A Student Casebook to Issues, Sources, and Historical Documents.* Westport, CT: Greenwood Press, 2000.

Hall, Kim F. *Things of Darkness: Economies of Race and Gender in Early Modern England.* Ithaca, NY: Cornell University Press, 1995.

Halper, Louise. "*Measure for Measure:* Law, Prerogative, Subversion." *Cardozo Studies in Law and Literature* 13 (fall 2001): 221–64.

Halpern, Richard. *Shakespeare among the Moderns.* Ithaca, NY: Cornell University Press, 1997.

Hamilton, A. C., ed. *The Faerie Queene.* By Edmund Spenser. New York: Longman, 2001.

Hamilton, Donna B. *Virgil and "The Tempest": The Politics of Imitation.* Columbus: Ohio State University Press, 1990.

Hammill, Graham. "'The ruine of a multitude': Marlowe and Radical Political Thought." Paper presented at the annual meeting of the Modern Language Association, 2003.

———. "Time for Marlowe." Paper presented at the annual meeting of the Shakespeare Association of America, Vancouver, BC, April 2003.

Hanafi, Hasan. "Alternative Conceptions of Civil Society: A Reflective Islamic Approach." In Chambers and Kymlicka, eds. *Alternative Conceptions of Civil Society.* 171–89.

Harrington, James. *Prerogative of Popular Government.* London: T. Brewster, 1658.

Hardt, Michael, and Antonio Negri. *Labor of Dionysus: A Critique of the State-Form.* Minneapolis: University of Minnesota Press, 1994.

Havel, Vaclav. *Open Letters: Selected Writings, 1965–1990.* Ed. Paul Wilson. New York: Vintage/Random House, 1992.

Hawthorne, Gerald F., et al., eds. *Dictionary of Paul and His Letters.* Downers Grove, IL: InterVarsity Press, 1993.

Hays, Richard B. "Three Dramatic Roles: The Law in Romans 3–4." In Dunn, *Paul and the Mosaic Law*, 151–64.

Hegel, G. W. F. *Philosophy of Right.* Trans. T. M. Knox. Oxford: Oxford University Press, 1942.

Heidegger, Martin. *The Question Concerning Technology, and Other Essays.* Trans. William Lovitt. New York: Harper & Row, 1977.

Hendricks, Margot, and Patricia Parker, eds. *Women, "Race," and Writing in the Early Modern Period.* London: Routledge, 1994.

Hexter, Ralph. "Sidonian Dido." In *Innovations of Antiquity*, ed. Ralph Hexter and Daniel Selden, 332–84. New York: Routledge, 1992.

Hibbard, Howard. *Michelangelo.* 2nd ed. New York: Harper & Row, 1974.

Hodgkinson, Virginia A., and Michael W. Foley, eds. *The Civil Society Reader.* Hanover, NH: University Press of New England, 2003.

Hoppe, Leslie, O.F.M. *joshua, Judges, with an Excursus on Charismatic Leadership in Israel.* Wilmington, DE: Michael Glazier, 1982.

Horkheimer, Max, and Theodor W. Adorno. *Dialectic of Enlightenment.* Trans. John Cumming. New York: Continuum, 1986. Orig. pub. in 1944.

Hoxby, Blair. "At the Public Mill of the Philistines: *Samson Agonistes* and the Problem of Work after the Restoration." In Kelley and Wittreich, *Altering Eyes*, 281–306.

Hübner, Hans. *Law in Paul's Thought*. Trans. James C. G. Greig. Ed. John Richies. Edinburgh: T. and T. Clark, 1984.

Hulme, Peter. *Colonial Encounters: Europe and the Native Caribbean, 1492–1797*. London: Methuen, 1986.

Hunt, Lynn. *The French Revolution and Human Rights: A Brief Documentary History*. New York: Bedford/St. Martins, 1996.

Hunter, G. K. *Dramatic Identities and Cultural Tradition: Studies in Shakespeare and His Contemporaries*. Liverpool, UK: Liverpool University Press, 1978.

Janowsky, Oscar L. *The Jews and Minority Rights, 1898–1919*. New York: Columbia University Press, 1933.

Jones, Eldred. *Othello's Countrymen: The African in English Renaissance Drama*. London: Oxford University Press, 1965.

Jordan, Constance. "The Household and the State: Transformations of the Representation of an Analogy from Aristotle to James I." *Modern Language Quarterly* 54, no. 3 (September 1993): 307–26.

Joughin, John J., ed. *Shakespeare and National Culture*. Manchester, UK: Manchester University Press, 1997.

Kahn, Victoria. "Margaret Cavendish and the Romance of Contract." *Renaissance Quarterly* 50, no. 2 (1997): 526–66.

———. "Political Theology and Reason of State in *Samson Agonistes*." *South Atlantic Quarterly* 99 (fall 1996): 1065–97.

Kallendorf, Craig. *Virgil and the Myth of Venice: Books and Readers in the Italian Renaissance*. Oxford: Clarendon Press, 1999.

Kantorowicz, Ernst. *The King's Two Bodies: A Study in Medieval Political Theology*. Princeton, NJ: Princeton University Press, 1997.

Kaplan, Mordecai. *Judaism as a Civilization: Toward a Reconstruction of American-Jewish Life*. Philadelphia, PA: Jewish Publication Society, 1994.

Kaske, Carol V. "Spenser's Pluralistic Universe: The View from the Mountain of Contemplation." In *Contemporary Thought on Edmund Spenser*, ed. Richard C. Frushell and Bernard J. Vondersmith, 121–49. Carbondale: Southern Illinois University Press, 1975.

Kieslowśki, Krystof. *Dekalog*. 1988. Chicago: Facets Video, 2003. Ten-part television series.

———. *Trois couleurs*. 1994. Burbank, CA: Buena Vista Home Entertainment, 2003. Film trilogy.

Kelley, Mark R., and Joseph Wittreich, eds. *Altering Eyes: New Perspectives on "Samson Agonistes."* Newark: University of Delaware Press, 2002.

Kezar, Dennis. "Samson's Death by Theatre and Milton's Art of Dying." *English Literary History* 66, no. 2 (1999): 295–336.

Kierkegaard, Soren. *Attack Upon "Christendom."* Trans. and ed. Walter Lowrie. Princeton, NJ: Princeton University Press, 1944.

Kipling, Gordon. *Enter the King: Theatre, Liturgy, and Ritual in the Medieval Civic Triumph*. Oxford: Clarendon Press, 1998.

Kirsch, Arthur. "The Integrity of *Measure for Measure*." *Shakespeare Survey* 28 (1975): 89–105.

Krouse, J. Michael. *Milton's Samson and the Christian Tradition*. Princeton, NJ: Princeton University Press, for the University of Cincinnati, 1949.

Kruse, Colin G. *Paul, the Law, and Justification*. Leicester, UK: Apollos, 1996.

Kymlicka, Will. *Liberalism, Community, and Culture*. Oxford: Oxford University Press, 1989.

———. *Multicultural Citizenship: A Liberal Theory of Minority Rights*. Oxford: Clarendon Press, 1995.
———. *Politics in the Vernacular*. Oxford: Oxford University Press, 2001.
———, ed. *The Rights of Minority Cultures*. Oxford: Oxford University Press, 1995.
———. *States, Nations, and Cultures*. Amsterdam: Van Gorcum, 1997.
———. "Territorial Borders: A Liberal Egalitarian Perspective." In Miller and Hashmi, *Boundaries and Justice*, 249–75.
Lacan, Jacques. *Seminar VII: The Ethics of Psychoanalysis, 1959–60*. Ed. Jacques-Alain Miller (1982). Trans. Dennis Porter. New York: W. W. Norton, 1992.
———. *Seminar XI: Four Fundamental Concepts of Psychoanalysis*. Ed. Jacques-Alain Miller. Trans. Alan Sheridan. New York: Norton, 1981. Published in French as *Le Séminaire, Livre XI: Les quatre concepts fondamentaux de la psychanalyse*. Ed. Jacques-Alain Miller. Paris: Éditions du Seuil, 1973.
———. *Television*. Trans. Denis Hollier et al. New York: W. W. Norton, 1990.
Laclau, Ernesto. *Emancipations*. London: Verso, 1996.
Lambert, Gregg. "Redemption: Lacan avec Marx." *Journal for Religious and Cultural Theory* 2, no. 1 (December 2000). www.jcrt.org/archives.
Lampert, Lisa. *Gender and Jewish Difference from Paul to Shakespeare*. Philadelphia: University of Pennsylvania Press, 2004.
Lane, Warren J., and Ann M. Lane. "The Politics of *Antigone*." In Euben, *Greek Tragedy and Political Theory*, 162–82.
Leibowitz, Yeshayahu. *Judaism, Human Values, and the Jewish State*. Ed. Eliezer Goldman. Trans. Eliezer Goldman, Yoram Navon et al. Cambridge, MA: Harvard University Press, 1992.
Leo Africanus (Al-Hassan Ibn-Mohammed Al-Wezaz Al-Fasi.) *The History and Description of Africa*. 3 vols. London: Hakluyt Society, 1896. Orig. trans. in 1600 by John Pory.
Lever, J. W., ed. *Measure for Measure*. By William Shakespeare. London: Methuen, 1967.
Levinas, Emmanuel. *Difficult Freedom: Essays on Judaism*. Trans. Seán Hand. Baltimore, MD: Johns Hopkins University Press, 1990.
———. *Otherwise Than Being or Beyond Essence*. Trans. Alphonso Lingis. Dordrecht: Kluwer Academic Publishers, 1991.
Lewalski, Barbara. "Biblical Allusion and Allegory in *The Merchant of Venice*." In Barnet, *Twentieth-Century Interpretations of "The Merchant of Venice,"* 33–54. Also reprinted in Bloom, *Shylock*, 236–51.
Lewis, Bernard. *The Muslim Discovery of Europe*. New York: W. W. Norton, 1982.
———. *Race and Color in Islam*. New York: Harper & Row, 1971.
Lewis, Charlton, and Charles Short. *Latin Dictionary*. Oxford: Clarendon Press, 1962.
Lezra, Jacques. *Unspeakable Subjects: The Genealogy of the Event in Early Modern Europe*. Stanford, CA: Stanford University Press, 1997
Little, Arthur. "'An essence that's not seen': The Primal Scene of Racism in *Othello*." *Shakespeare Quarterly* 44 (fall, 1993): 304–24.
Locke, John. *Two Treatises of Government*. Ed. Peter Laslett. Cambridge: Cambridge University Press, 1970.
Logan, Oliver. *Culture and Society in Venice, 1470–1790: The Renaissance and Its Heritage*. New York: Charles Scribner's Sons, 1972.
Loomba, Ania. "The Color of Patriarchy: Critical Difference, Cultural Difference, and Renaissance Drama." In Hendricks and Parker, *Women, "Race," and Writing*, 17–34.

———. "'Delicious Traffick': Racial and Religious Difference on Early Modern Stages." In *Shakespeare and Race,* ed. Catherine M. S. Alexander and Stanley Wells, 203–24. Cambridge: Cambridge University Press, 2000.

———. *Gender, Race, Renaissance Drama.* Manchester, UK: Manchester University Press, 1989.

Loraux, Nicole. *The Invention of Athens: The Funeral Oration in the Classical City.* Trans. Alan Sheridan. Cambridge, MA: Harvard University Press, 1986.

Lorenz, Philip. "The Tears of Sovereignty." PhD diss. New York University, 2004.

Löwith, Karl. *Meaning in History.* Chicago: University of Chicago Press, 1949.

Lunney, Ruth. *Marlowe and the Popular Tradition: Innovation in the English Drama before 1595.* Manchester, UK: Manchester University Press, 2002.

Lupton, Julia Reinhard. *Afterlives of the Saints: Hagiography, Typology, and Renaissance Literature.* Stanford, CA: Stanford University Press, 1996.

———. "*Othello* Circumcised: Shakespeare and the Pauline Discourse of Nations." *Representations* 57 (1997): 73–89.

Luther, Martin. *Works.* 55 vols. Ed. Jaroslav Pelikan. St. Louis, MO: Concordia, 1955–76.

Machiavelli, Niccolò. *Il Principe e Discorsi sopra la prima deca di Tito Livio.* Ed. Sergio Bertelli. Milan: Feltrinelli Economica, 1960.

Mahon, John W., and Ellen MacLeod Mahon. *The Merchant of Venice: New Critical Essays.* New York: Routledge, 2002.

Malkiel, David J. "The Ghetto Republic." In Davis and Ravid, *The Jews of Early Modern Venice,* 117–42.

———. *A Separate Republic: The Mechanics and Dynamics of Venetian Jewish Self-Government, 1607–1624.* Jerusalem: Magnes Press, Hebrew University, 1991.

Malmo, Jane Beverly. "Beheading the Dead: Rites of Habeas Corpus in Shakespeare's *Measure for Measure.*" *New Formations* 35 (fall 1998): 135–44.

Manley, Lawrence, ed. *London in the Age of Shakespeare: An Anthology.* University Park: Pennsylvania State University Press, 1986.

Manville, Philip Brook. *The Origins of Citizenship in Ancient Athens.* Princeton, NJ: Princeton University Press, 1997.

Marlowe, Christopher. *The Complete Plays.* Ed. Mark Thornton Burnett. London: J. M. Dent, 1999.

Martin, James D. *The Book of Judges.* Cambridge: Cambridge University Press, 1975.

Marx, Karl. "On the Jewish Question." In *The Marx-Engels Reader,* ed. Robert C. Tucker, 26–52. 2nd ed. New York: W. W. Norton, 1978.

Mauss, Marcel. *The Gift.* Trans. I. Cunnison. 1925. Reprint, New York: W. W. Norton, 1967.

McDonald, Russ, ed. *The Bedford Companion to Shakespeare: An Introduction with Documents.* Boston: Bedford/ St. Martin's, 2001.

McPherson, David C. *Shakespeare, Jonson, and the Myth of Venice.* Newark: University of Delaware Press, 1990.

Middleton, Thomas. *The Triumphs of Truth.* In Dutton, *Jacobean Civic Pageants,* 137–68.

Midrash Rabbah. 10 vols. Ed. H. Freedman. London: Soncino Press, 1983.

Miller, David, and Sohail H. Hashmi, eds. *Boundaries and Justice: Diverse Ethical Perspectives.* Princeton, NJ: Princeton University Press, 2001.

Miller, Frederick. *Nature, Justice, and Rights in Aristotle's Politics.* Oxford: Oxford University Press, 1995.

Miller, Steven. *The Fulfillment of the Law: Contestation in Postwar Thought and Fiction.* PhD diss. University of California, Irvine, 2002.

Miller, Toby, and George Yúdice. *Cultural Policy.* London: Sage, 2002.

Milton, John. *Complete Poems and Major Prose*. Ed. Merritt Y. Hughes. Indianapolis, IN: Bobbs-Merrill, 1957.

———. *Prose Writings*. Ed. K. M. Burton. London: Dent, 1958.

Miola, Robert S. "Othello *Furens*." *Shakespeare Quarterly* 41 (spring 1990): 49–64.

Moody, A. C. "An Ironic Comedy." In Barnet, *Twentieth-Century Interpretations of "The Merchant of Venice,"* 100–107.

Muir, Edward. *Civic Ritual in Renaissance Venice*. Princeton, NJ: Princeton University Press, 1981.

Mullaney, Stephen. "The Place of Shakespeare's Stage in Elizabethan Culture." Encyclopedia Britannica Online: eb.com.

———. *The Place of the Stage: License, Play, and Power in Renaissance England*. Chicago: University of Chicago Press, 1988.

Nägele, Rainer. *Theater, Theory, Speculation: Walter Benjamin and the Scenes of Modernity*. Baltimore, MD: Johns Hopkins University Press, 1991.

Nancy, Jean-Luc. "Myth Interrupted." In *The Inoperative Community*, ed. Peter Connor. Trans. Peter Connor et al. Minneapolis: University of Minnesota Press, 1991.

Negt, Oskar, and Alexander Kluge. *The Public Sphere and Experience*. Minneapolis: University of Minnesota Press, 1993.

Neill, Michael. "'Mulattos,' 'Blacks,' and 'Indian Moors': *Othello* and Early Modern Constructions of Human Difference." *Shakespeare Quarterly* 49 (winter, 1998): 361–74.

———. "Unproper Beds: Race, Adultery, and the Hideous in *Othello*." *Shakespeare Quarterly* 40 (winter 1989): 383–412.

Neusner, Jacob. *Introduction to Rabbinic Literature*. New York: Doubleday, 1994.

———. *A Midrash Reader*. Minneapolis, MN: Fortress Press, 1990.

Newman, Karen. "'And wash the Ethiop white': Femininity and the Monstrous in *Othello*." In *Shakespeare Reproduced: The Text in History and Ideology*, ed. Jean E. Howard and Marion F. O'Connor, 143–59. New York: Methuen, 1987.

Nicolet, Claude. *The World of the Citizen in Republican Rome*. Trans. P. S. Falla. Berkeley and Los Angeles: University of California Press, 1980.

Nietzsche, Friedrich. *On the Genealogy of Morals and Ecce Homo*. Trans. Walter Kaufmann. New York: Random House, 1967.

Novak, David. "Land and People: One Jewish Tradition." In Miller and Hashmi, *Boundaries and Justice*, 213–36.

Noy, David. *Foreigners at Rome: Citizens and Strangers*. London: Duckworth, with the Classical Press of Wales, 2000.

Ober, Josiah. *The Athenian Revolution: Essays on Ancient Greek Democracy and Political Theory*. Princeton, NJ: Princeton University Press, 1996.

Oppenheimer, Aharon. "Jewish Penal Authority in Roman Judea." In Goodman, *Jews in a Graeco-Roman World*, 181–91.

Orgel, Stephen, ed. *The Tempest*. By William Shakespeare. Oxford: Oxford University Press, 1987.

Ormand, Kirk. *Exchange and the Maiden: Marriage in Sophoclean Tragedy*. Austin: University of Texas Press, 1999.

Over, William. "New York's African Theatre: Shakespeare Reinterpreted." In *Shakespeare without Class*, ed. Donald Hedrick and Bryan Reynolds, 65–84. New York: Palgrave, 2000.

Panofsky, Erwin. *Early Netherlandish Painting*. 2 vols. 1953. Reprint, New York: Harper & Row, 1971.

Parker, Patricia. "Fantasies of 'Race' and 'Gender': Africa, Othello, and Bringing to Light." In Hendricks and Parker, *Women, "Race," and Writing*, 84–100.

Pateman, Carole. *The Sexual Contract.* Stanford, CA: Stanford University Press, 1988.
Patrick, John J. *The Bill of Rights: A History in Documents.* New York: Oxford University Press, 2003.
Pocock, J. G. A. "The Ideal of Citizenship Since Classical Times." In Shafir, *Citizenship Debates,* 31–41.
The Policy of the Turkish Empire. London, 1597.
Pory, John. "A summarie discourse of the manifold Religions professed in Africa." Addendum to Leo Africanus, *History and Description of Africa,* 3: 1001–71. London: George Bishop, 1600.
Pullan, Brian. *The Jews of Europe and the Inquisition of Venice, 1550–1670.* London: I. B. Tauris, 1997.
———. *Rich and Poor in Renaissance Venice: The Social Institutions of a Catholic State, to 1620.* Oxford: Basil Blackwell, 1971.
———. "Social Hierarchies in the Republic of Venice." In *Orders and Hierarchies in Late Medieval and Renaissance Europe,* 155–72. Toronto: University of Toronto Press, 1999.
Quigley, Brendan. "Milton's Conception of Heroism in *Samson Agonistes.*" *English Literary History.* Forthcoming.
Ranald, Margaret Loftus. "'As Marriage Binds, and Blood Breaks': English Marriage and Shakespeare." *Shakespeare Quarterly* 1 (1979): 68–81.
Reading/Language Arts Framework for California Public Schools, Kindergarten through Grade Twelve. Sacramento: California Department of Education, 1999.
Rawls, John. "Justice as Fairness in the Liberal Polity." In Shafir, *Citizenship Debates,* 53–72.
Reasoner, Mark. "Citizenship, Roman and Heavenly." In Hawthorne et al., *Dictionary of Paul,* 139–41.
"Requerimiento." In *The Spanish Tradition in America,* trans. and ed. Charles Gibson, 58–60. Columbia: University of South Carolina Press, 1968.
Rehm, Rush. *Marriage to Death: The Conflation of Wedding and Funeral Rituals in Greek Tragedy.* Princeton, NJ: Princeton University Press, 1994.
Reinhard, Kenneth. "Freud, My Neighbor." *American Imago* 54 (summer 1997): 165–95.
———, and Julia Reinhard Lupton. "The Subject of Religion: Lacan and the Ten Commandments." *Diacritics.* Forthcoming. Short version published as "Revelation: Lacan and the Ten Commandments." *Journal of Religious and Cultural Theory* 2, no. 1 (December 2000): http://www.jcrt.org/archives/02.1/.
Reinhold, Meyer. *Diaspora: The Jews among the Greeks and Romans.* Sarasota, FL: Samuel Stevens, 1983.
Riesenberg, Peter. *Citizenship in the Western Tradition: Plato to Rousseau.* Chapel Hill: University of North Carolina Press, 1992.
Robbins, Bruce, ed. *The Phantom Public Sphere.* Minneapolis: University of Minnesota Press, 1993.
Rogers, John. "Delivering Redemption in *Samson Agonistes.*" In Kelley and Wittreich, *Altering Eyes,* 72–97.
Romano, Dennis. *Patricians and Popolani: The Social Foundations of the Venetian Renaissance State.* Baltimore, MD: Johns Hopkins University Press, 1987.
Rose, Jacqueline. "Sexuality in the Reading of Shakespeare: *Hamlet* and *Measure for Measure.*" In *Alternative Shakespeares,* ed. John Drakakis, 95–118. London: Methuen, 1985.
Rosen, Ralph M. "Classical Studies and the Search for Community." In *Connecting Past and Present: Concepts and Models for Service-Learning in History,* ed. Ira Harkavy and Bill M. Donovan. Washington, DC: American Association for Higher Education, 2000.

Rosenzweig, Franz. *Der Stern der Erlösung*. Frankfurt am Main: Suhrkamp, 1993. Translated as *The Star of Redemption,* by William W. Hallo. Notre Dame, IN: University of Notre Dame Press, 1970.

Roth, Cecil. *Venice*. Jewish Communities Series. Philadelphia, PA: Jewish Publication Society of America, 1930.

Rupprecht, Arthur A. "Roman Legal System." In Hawthorne et al., *Dictionary of Paul,* 546–50.

Sachedina, Abdulaziz. *The Islamic Roots of Democratic Pluralism*. Oxford: Oxford University Press, 2001.

Sanders, E. P. *Paul, the Law, and the Jewish People*. Philadelphia, PA: Fortress Press, 1983.

———. *Paul and Palestinian Judaism: A Comparison of Patterns of Religion*. Philadelphia: Fortress Press, 1977.

Schmitt, Carl. *Hamlet oder Hekuba; der Einbruch der Zeit in das Spiel*. Düsseldorf: E. Diederichs, 1956.

———. *Political Theology: Four Chapters on the Concept of Sovereignty*. Trans. George Schwab. Cambridge, MA: MIT Press, 1985.

Schochet, Gordon. *Patriarchalism in Political Thought: The Authoritarian Family and Political Speculation and Attitudes Especially in Seventeenth-Century England*. Oxford: Basil Blackwell, 1975.

Scott, Margaret. "'Our Cities' Institutions': Some Further Reflections on the Marriage Contracts in Measure for Measure." *English Literary History* 4 (1982): 790–804.

Seaford, Richard. *Reciprocity and Ritual: Homer and Tragedy in the Developing City-State*. Oxford: Oxford University Press, 1994.

Segal, Alan F. *Paul the Convert: The Apostolate and Apostacy of Saul the Pharisee*. New Haven, CT: Yale University Press, 1990.

Shafir, Gershon, ed. *The Citizenship Debates: A Reader*. Minneapolis: University of Minnesota Press, 1998.

Shakespeare, William. *The Merchant of Venice*. Ed. John Russell Brown. London: Methuen, 1955.

———. *Shakespeare's Sonnets*. Ed. Stephen Booth. New Haven, CT: Yale University Press, 1977.

Shannon, Laurie. *Sovereign Amity: Figures of Friendship in Shakespearean Contexts*. Chicago: University of Chicago Press, 2002.

Shapiro, James. *Shakespeare and the Jews*. New York: Columbia University Press, 1996.

———. "'Which is *The Merchant* here, and which *The Jew*?' Shakespeare and the Economics of Influence." *Shakespeare Studies* 20 (1988): 269–79.

Shell, Marc. *The End of Kinship: "Measure for Measure," Incest, and the Ideal of Universal Siblinghood*. Stanford, CA: Stanford University Press, 1988.

———. *Money, Language, and Thought*. Baltimore, MD: Johns Hopkins University Press, 1982.

Shoulson, Jeffrey S. *Milton and the Rabbis: Hebraism, Hellenism, and Christianity*. New York: Columbia University Press, 2001.

Short, Hugo. "Shylock Is Content: A Study in Salvation." In Mahon and Mahon, *The Merchant of Venice,* 199–212.

Shuger, Debora. *Political Theologies in Shakespeare's England: The Sacred and the State in "Measure for Measure."* Hounsmills, Hampshire, UK: Palgrave, 2001.

Silver, Allan. "Kingship and Political Authority: Commentary on 1 Samuel 8." In Walzer, Lorberbaum, and Zohar, *Jewish Political Tradition,* 1: 122–26.

Simon, Ernst. "The Neighbor (*Re'a*) Whom We Shall Love." In *Modern Jewish Ethics: Theory and Practice,* ed. Marvin Fox, 29–56. Columbus: Ohio State University Press, 1975.

Sims, James H. *Dramatic Uses of Biblical Allusions in Marlowe and Shakespeare*. Gainesville: University of Florida Press, 1966.

Skura, Meredith. "Discourse and the Individual: The Case of Colonialism in *The Tempest*." *Shakespeare Quarterly* 40, no. 1 (1989): 42–74.

Snow, Edward. "Sexual Anxiety and the Male Order of Things in *Othello*." *English Literary Renaissance* 10 (autumn 1980): 384–412.

Soggin, J. Alberto. *Judges: A Commentary*. Trans. John Bowden. London: SCM Press, 1981.

Sophocles. *Antigone*. Ed. Richard Braun. New York: Oxford University Press, 1973.

Spenser, Edmund. *The Faerie Queene*. Ed. A. C. Hamilton. Text ed. Hiroshi Yamashita and Toshiyuki Suzuki. Harlow, England: Longman, 2001.

Stegner, William R. "Paul the Jew." In Hawthorne et al., *Dictionary of Paul*, 503–11.

Stone, Suzanne Last. "The Jewish Tradition and Civil Society." In Chambers and Kymlicka, *Alternative Conceptions of Civil Society*, 151–70.

Strong, James, ed. *Strong's New Exhaustive Concordance of the Bible*. Iowa Falls, IA: World Bible Publishers, 1980.

Sullivan, Garrett A., Jr. "Geography and Identity in Marlowe." In *The Cambridge Companion to Marlowe*, ed. Patrick Cheney, 231–44. Cambridge: Cambridge University Press, 2004.

Tedlock, Dennis, trans. and ed. *Popol Vuh: The Mayan Book of the Dawn of Life*. Rev. ed. New York: Simon and Schuster, 1996.

Tellbe, Mikael. *Paul between Synagogue and State: Christians, Jews, and Civic Authorities in 1 Thessalonians, Romans, and Philippians*. Stockholm: Almquist and Wiksell International, 2001.

Tenenti, Alberto. "The Sense of Time and Space in the Venetian World of the Fifteenth and Sixteenth Centuries." In *Renaissance Venice*, ed. J. R. Hale, 17–46. London: Faber and Faber, 1974.

Thomas, Brook. *American Literary Realism and the Failed Promise of Contract*. Berkeley and Los Angeles: University of California Press, 1997.

Thomson, Ken. *From Neighborhood to Nation: The Democratic Foundations of Civil Society*. Hanover and London: Tufts University and University Press of New England, 2001.

Thucydides. *The Peloponnesian War*. Trans. Steven Lattimore. Indianapolis: Hackett, 1998.

Tomson, Peter J. *Paul and the Jewish Law: Halakha in the Letters of the Apostle to the Gentiles*. Van Gorcum, Assen/Maastricht: Fortress Press, 1990.

Trachtenberg, Joshua. *The Devil and the Jews: The Medieval Conception of the Jew and Its Relation to Modern Antisemitism*. New Haven, CT: Yale University Press, 1943.

Trivedi, Harish. *Colonial Transactions: English Literature and India*. Manchester, UK: Manchester University Press, 1996.

Tyrrell, William Blake, and Larry J. Bennett, trans. *Antigone*. By Sophocles. Available on-line at www.stoa.org/diotima/anthology/ant/antigstruct.htm.

Recapturing Sophocles' "Antigone." Lanham, MD: Rowman and Littlefield, 1998.

———, and Frieda S. Brown. *Athenian Myths and Institutions: Words in Action*. New York: Oxford University Press, 1991.

Vaughan, Alden T., and Virginia Mason Vaughan. *Shakespeare's Caliban: A Cultural History*. Cambridge: Cambridge University Press, 1991.

Vaughan, Virginia Mason. *Othello: A Contextual History*. Cambridge: Cambridge University Press, 1994.

Veit, Richard S. "'Like the Base Judean': A Defense of an Oft-Rejected Reading in *Othello*." *Shakespeare Quarterly* 26, no. 4 (1975): 466–69.

Vitkus, Daniel. "Turning Turk in *Othello:* The Conversion and Damnation of the Moor." *Shakespeare Quarterly* 48 (summer, 1997): 145–76.

———. *Turning Turk: English Theater and the Multicultural Mediterranean, 1570–1630*. New York: Palgrave Macmillan, 2003.

Walters, James C. *Ethnic Issues in Paul's Letter to the Romans: Changing Self-Definitions in Earliest Roman Christianity*. Valley Forge, PA: Trinity Press, 1993.

Walzer, Michael. "Equality and Civil Society." In Chambers and Kymlicka, *Alternative Conceptions of Civil Society*, 34–49.

———. *Regicide and Revolution: Speeches at the Trial of Louis XVI*. Cambridge: Cambridge University Press, 1974.

———. *The Revolution of the Saints: A Study in the Origins of Radical Politics*. New York: Atheneum, 1970.

———, Menachem Lorberbaum, and Noam J. Zohar, eds. *The Jewish Political Tradition*. Vol. 1. *Authority*. New Haven, CT: Yale University Press, 2000.

Warner, Michael. *Publics and Counterpublics*. New York: Zone Books, 2002.

Watson, Alan. *Jesus and the Law*. Athens: University of Georgia Press, 1996.

Weber, Max. "Citizenship in Ancient and Medieval Cities." In Shafir, *Citizenship Debates*, 43–52.

Weller, Barry, and Margaret W. Ferguson, eds. *"The Tragedy of Mariam, the Fair Queen of Jewry," by Elizabeth Carey, Lady Falkland*. Berkeley and Los Angeles: University of California Press, 1994.

Wettinger, Godfrey. *The Jews of Malta in the Late Middle Ages*. Malta: Midsea Books, 1985.

Wheeler, Richard P., ed. *Critical Essays on Shakespeare's "Measure for Measure."* New York: G. K. Hall, 1999.

Williams, Margaret. *The Jews among the Greeks and Romans: A Diasporan Sourcebook*. Baltimore, MD: Johns Hopkins University Press, 1998.

Wills, Gary. *Inventing America: Jefferson's Declaration of Independence*. Garden City, NY: Doubleday, 1978.

Wilson, Richard, ed. *Christopher Marlowe*. London: Longman, 1999.

Winger, Michael. *By What Law? The Meaning of* Nomos *in the Letters of Paul*. Atlanta, GA: Scholars Press, 1992.

Winkler, John J. "The Ephebes' Song: *Tragôidia* and *Polis*." *Representations* 11 (summer 1985): 6–43.

Wisdom, Jeffrey R. *Blessing for the Nations and the Curse of the Law: Paul's Citation of Genesis and Deuteronomy in Gal 3:8–10*. Tübingen: J. C. B Mohr (Paul Siebeck), 2001.

Wittreich, Joseph. *Interpreting Samson Agonistes*. Princeton, NJ: Princeton University Press, 1986.

Wood, Derek N. C. *"Exiled from Light": Divine Law, Morality, and Violence in Milton's Samson Agonistes*. Toronto: University of Toronto Press, 2000.

Zeitlin, Froma. "Thebes: Theatre of Self and Society in Athenian Drama." In Euben, *Greek Tragedy and Political Theory*, 101–41.

Žižek, Slavoj. *The Fright of Real Tears: Krysztof Kieślowski between Theory and Post-Theory*. London: British Film Institute, 2001.

———. *The Sublime Object of Ideology*. London: Verso, 1989.

Zornberg, Avivah Gottlieb. *Genesis: The Beginning of Desire*. Philadelphia, PA: Jewish Publication Society, 1995.

INDEX